Under-Rewarded Efforts

Under-Rewarded Efforts
The Elusive Quest for Prosperity in Mexico

Santiago Levy

Inter-American Development Bank

Cataloging-in-Publication data provided by the
Inter-American Development Bank
Felipe Herrera Library

Levy, Santiago.
Under-rewarded efforts: the elusive quest for prosperity in Mexico / Santiago Levy.

    p. cm.
    Includes bibliographic references.
    978-1-59782-304-3 (Paperback)
    978-1-59782-305-0 (PDF)

1. Economic development-Social aspects-Mexico. 2. Labor productivity-Mexico. 3. Labor policy-Mexico. 4. Human capital-Government policy-Mexico. 5. Public investments-Mexico. 6. Education-Economic aspects-Mexico. 7. Social security-Mexico. 8. Business enterprises-Mexico. 9. Mexico-Economic policy. 10. Mexico-Social policy. I. Inter-American Development Bank. Vice Presidency for Sectors and Knowledge. II. Title.

HC135. L48 2018
IDB-BK-177

Copyright © 2018 Inter-American Development Bank. This work is licensed under a Creative Commons IGO 3.0 Attribution-NonCommercial-NoDerivatives (CC-IGO BY-NC-ND 3.0 IGO) license (http://creativecommons.org/licenses/by-nc-nd/3.0/igo/legalcode) and may be reproduced with attribution to the IDB and for any non-commercial purpose. No derivative work is allowed.

Any dispute related to the use of the works of the IDB that cannot be settled amicably shall be submitted to arbitration pursuant to the UNCITRAL rules. The use of the IDB's name for any purpose other than for attribution, and the use of the IDB's logo shall be subject to a separate written license agreement between the IDB and the user and is not authorized as part of this CC-IGO license.

Note that the link provided above includes additional terms and conditions of the license.

The opinions expressed in this publication are those of the authors and do not necessarily reflect the views of the Inter-American Development Bank, its Board of Directors, or the countries they represent.

Inter-American Development Bank
1300 New York Avenue, N.W.
Washington, D.C. 20577
www.iadb.org

Table of Contents

Preface by Dani Rodrik ix

Acknowledgements xiii

Foreword xv

Chapter 1: **Introduction and Summary** 1
    The Puzzle 3
    The Central Hypothesis: Large and Persistent Misallocation 6
    Objectives and Organization of the Book 10
    Key Concepts and Basic Facts 13
    Misallocation: Magnitude, Patterns, and Persistence 21
    Understanding the Role Played by Human Capital 33
    From the What to the Why 35
    Refocusing the Policy Discussion on Productivity and Growth 47
    Where to Next? 52

Chapter 2: **Conceptual Framework** 55
    Resources and Environment 55
    Salaried and Non-Salaried Labor 58
    Observed and Potential Productivity 59
    Misallocation and Low Productivity 64
    Formality and Informality 66
    Informality, Illegality, and Types of Firms 68
    Formality, Informality, and Productivity 71
    Technology, Entrepreneur-Worker Contracts, and Firm Size 73
    Causation 74

Chapter 3: **Data and Descriptive Statistics** 77
    Scope of the Economic Census 78
    Establishment Sample and Measurement of Capital and Labor 80
    Firms versus Establishments 81
    Size and Type Distribution of Firms, 1998–2013 83
    Resource Allocation 86
    Firm Incorporation 89
    Firms and Employment beyond the Census 90
    Presence of Informal Firms across Localities of Different Sizes 92
    Firms and Resource Allocation across Sectors 95

Chapter 4: **Measuring and Characterizing Misallocation** 99
    The Hsieh-Klenow Model 100
    Dispersion of Total Revenue Productivity 108
    Productivity Gains from Eliminating Misallocation 111
    Correlations between Firm Size, Type, and Productivity 111
    Misallocation within and across Manufacturing, Commerce,
        and Services 119
    Formal-Informal and Salaried-Non-salaried Productivity
        Distributions 121
    Resource Allocation and Productivity Distributions 123
    Productivity beyond the Census Data 125

Chapter 5: **Misallocation and Firm Dynamics** 127
    Definitions and Stylized Facts 128
    Patterns of Survival by Size and Type 130
    Patterns of Entry and Exit by Size and Type 133
    Productivity Distributions and Resource Allocation of Exiting,
        Entering, and Surviving Firms 134
    Net Effects of Exit, Entry, and Survival on Resource Allocation
        and Productivity 147
    Extrapolation of Firm Dynamics between 1998 and 2013 150
    Firm Dynamics and Job Changes 154
    Firm Dynamics beyond the Census Data 156
    Firm Dynamics and the Allocation of Individuals across
        Occupations 157

Chapter 6: The Misallocation of Human Capital 159
    A Few Stylized Facts 160
    Human Capital, Misallocation, and Productivity 164
    Misallocation and the Level of Returns to Education 167
    Misallocation and the Trends in the Returns to Education 174
    Misallocation and the Opportunities to Acquire Human Capital 179
    Misallocation and the Incentives to Invest in Human Capital 188

Chapter 7: Policies, Institutions, and Misallocation 191
    Core Stylized Facts 191
    Misallocation and the World of Entrepreneur-Worker Relations 193
    Misallocation and the World of Taxation 206
    Misallocation and the World of Market Conditions 226
    The Joint Effects of $E(L,T,M)$ on Misallocation 238

Chapter 8: Why Did Misallocation Increase between 1998 and 2013? 245
    Changes in the World of Entrepreneur-Worker Relations 246
    Changes in the World of Taxation 251
    Changes in the World of Market Conditions 255
    The Joint Effects of Changes in $E(L,T,M)$ on Misallocation 256

Chapter 9: Conclusions 261
    Why Has Prosperity Eluded Mexico? 261
    Recent Policy Reforms 270
    Rethinking Policy Priorities 273
    A Program for Prosperity 280

Appendix 285

References 291

Index 299

Preface

A few years ago as I was finishing up my *book Economics Rules: The Rights and Wrongs of the Dismal Science* (Norton 2015), I realized that the manuscript contained a serious omission. I had written at length about how and why economists misuse the powerful tools of their discipline, but had said little about the successes. So I decided I would open the book with three vignettes of economics at its best. Each vignette would have its hero: an economist who combined economic models with real-world judgement to make life better for lots of people.

Santiago Levy was one of the three heroes I chose. (The names of the other two heroes will let the reader gauge how demanding the standard was that I applied: John Maynard Keynes and William Vickrey.) Santiago was the principal force behind the anti-poverty program Progresa in Mexico that quickly became a model for many other countries. This was an innovative, incentive-based program that was novel at the time, in 1997. It replaced inefficient price subsidies with direct cash grants to poor families as long as their children were kept in school and received periodic health checks. So successful was the program that subsequent Mexican political administrations would seek credit for it by renaming it; hence Progresa would turn into Oportunidades, which eventually became Prospera.

When sound economics is combined with a practical, pragmatic bent it can be a potent force for good. There are very few people who are as good a living embodiment of this as Santiago Levy. I learned this a very long time ago, during the late 1980s, when I found myself on a visit with him to Bolivia. We were both young and inexperienced. But what stood out in him, even back then, was an imaginativeness and creativity in policy that were sorely missing from the academic literature I was steeped in. I don't remember much about our assignment, but I have vivid memories of Santiago bursting with out-of-the-box ideas.

Santiago has been puzzling for a very long time about the paradoxes of Mexico's economic performance. And what a major puzzle the country poses to received wisdom about development policy!

The country has made major strides in social progress—thanks not least to Santiago's own efforts as policymaker and advisor. School attendance has increased greatly, while educational quality has improved. Fiscal and monetary policies have ensured a stable macroeconomy and have kept financial crises at bay. No country has tried harder to integrate into the world economy. And yet in overall productivity, the gains have been meager. Since 1996, Mexico's economy has expanded at barely over 1 percent per year in per capita terms, and labor productivity has grown at less than 0.5 percent.

Santiago points his finger to the persistent (and worsening) misallocation of resources as the culprit for Mexico's poor productivity performance. Simply put, labor and capital do not go to the most productive firms. The best-performing firms in Mexico are doing very well indeed—in all respects except for increased employment. The underperformance of the less-productive parts of the economy undoes whatever progress the better-performing parts generate.

Santiago's conclusions are based on a rich, firm-level analysis using census and employment data and covering millions of firms from the late 1990s to 2013. He documents that productive heterogeneity actually increased over this time: there is more informality, larger productive differences, and greater gaps in firm size. But this is not a simple and oft-told story of formal versus informal sectors. Santiago shows that the constitutionally mandated difference between "salaried" and "non-salaried" workers does more of the work in accounting for misallocation than the traditional formal/informal divide. For example, small or informal firms need not be less productive than large firms if they are employing salaried workers (albeit illegally).

Santiago Levy's meticulous diagnostic work leads him to conclude that the policy failures behind these patterns are highly specific to Mexico. He draws attention in particular to three different facets of the Mexican policy environment: social insurance mechanisms, tax policies, and poor contract enforcement. Together, these elements conspire to produce a disproportionate burden on formal, large, salaried firms while effectively subsidizing non-salaried workers. He shows that these policies have had larger adverse effects over time in recent decades.

Santiago emphasizes that this is not a book on policy, but readers will find a rich policy menu here, targeted at real problems of productivity.

The thesis of the book is as challenging as it is fascinating. It is not only a rebuke to the standard view that open trade, stable macroeconomics, or investment in human capital are enough to generate rapid growth. Santiago also argues that the attempt to provide broad social insurance to the Mexican people has backfired by taxing the more organized and productive segments of the economy.

This is applied development economics at its best. We would not expect less from Santiago Levy.

Dani Rodrik
Harvard University

Acknowledgements

During the last decade, as a member of the staff of the Inter-American Development Bank, I had the privilege of learning from many talented colleagues. In writing this book I benefited from discussions and interactions with Matteo Bobba, Mariano Bosch, Matias Busso, Victoria Fazzio, Luca Flabbi, David Kaplan, Carmen Pagés, David Razu, Gerardo Reyes, José Juan Ruiz, Norbert Schady, and Cesar Tamayo. I am grateful to all of them. I also want to thank Magda Massaro and Yulissa Arrivillaga, who helped me in a different but equally valuable way. Beyond the IDB, I have also learned much from many friends with whom, in different contexts, I have had the good fortune to engage. I first want to thank Chang-Tai Hsieh, who was kind enough to read this entire manuscript and make many useful and valuable suggestions. Dani Rodrik was equally kind to write a preface for the book. I am also grateful to Arturo Antón, Angel Calderón, Fausto Hernández, Ravi Kanbur, Luis Felipe López-Calva, William Maloney, Andrés Neumeyer, Manuel Ramos Francia, and Miguel Székely for enriching discussions and exchanges. Separate recognition is due to Mexico's Instituto Nacional de Estadística, Geografía e Informática (INEGI) for its support. Natalia Volkow was extremely helpful facilitating access to INEGI's Center for Micro-Data. Triana Yentzen provided valuable research assistance. David Einhorn did a splendid job editing the manuscript, and Stephen Kennedy did the same proof-reading it. Rita Funaro was extremely helpful coordinating the production of the book. Special gratitude and recognition, however, is due to Oscar Fentanes, who spent many hours at the Center for Micro-Data performing the computations and did a splendid job with all tasks associated with this book. Needless to say, all errors are mine.

Washington, D.C.
May, 2018.

Para ti, Julieta

Foreword

My hope is that this book will appeal to all those interested in Mexico's development. With that purpose in mind, I tried to write a book with a minimum of specialized language and technical terms, so it could be read by many. I hope academic economists find that the central elements of the narrative are sufficiently supported by empirical evidence, even if not all of them are treated with the technical rigor that they would like to see. For them, the value of the book resides in putting together various pieces of research into what I believe is a consistent and coherent story that answers a key development question:

Why has a country that has done so many things right failed to grow fast?

In parallel, I hope that more policy-oriented readers will not be deterred by my use of some algebraic expressions. A few appear in Chapters 2, 4, and 7, but these expressions are just convenient abbreviations, and I try to explain them in the text. There is no calculus and no statistics beyond simple regressions and distributions. Many thanks for your patience!

Ideally, the book will also appeal to those interested in development beyond Mexico. While there is some necessary institutional detail that is specific to this country, the core issues discussed here—growth, productivity, informality, misallocation, and human capital—are also center stage in other Latin American countries (and beyond). There are intense debates on these issues among economists and policymakers. This book's value-added in this debate is, on one hand, the use of what by Latin American standards is an extremely rich and detailed database of firms, and, on the other, a methodological approach that tries to bring clarity by separating the "what is going on" from "why what is going on is occurring." Of course, it is the reader who will judge the extent to which the effort has been successful.

Santiago Levy

CHAPTER 1

Introduction and Summary

Workers, entrepreneurs, and policymakers have labored hard over the last two decades to bring growth and prosperity to Mexico, but their efforts have been under-rewarded. From 1996 to 2015, the country's per capita GDP growth averaged only 1.2 percent per year.[1] Moreover, this unimpressive figure arguably overestimates Mexico's performance, as it reflects the fact that because of the country's demographic transition, its labor force grew more rapidly than its population during these years (2.2 versus. 1.4 percent). In fact, GDP per worker grew on average by only 0.4 percent on an annual basis, far from what is required to create a prosperous country. Regional comparisons confirm Mexico's underperformance. Over the same two decades, accumulated per capita GDP growth in Mexico was 25.7 percent, less than every country in Latin America except Venezuela.[2]

This book tries to explain why prosperity has eluded Mexico and argues that a policy shift is necessary to achieve it. Two premises have underlined the design of public policy in the country in the last two decades. One is that, in a context of macroeconomic stability and an open trade regime, Mexico

---

[1] The analysis begins after Mexico's 1994–1995 financial crisis and ends before any effects could be felt in Mexico from the uncertainty surrounding the future of the North American Free Trade Agreement that followed the 2016 presidential election in the United States.

[2] According to the World Bank's World Development Indicators, accumulated per capita GDP growth was 122 percent in Panama, 105 percent in the Dominican Republic, 86.9 percent in Peru, 65.3 percent in Costa Rica and Uruguay, 61.4 percent in Chile, 58 percent in Nicaragua, 55.4 percent in Bolivia, 53.2 percent in Colombia, 41 percent in Honduras, 40 percent in Ecuador, 39.8 percent in El Salvador, 31.8 percent in Argentina, 31 percent in Paraguay, 30 percent in Brazil and Belize, and 28.3 percent in Guatemala.

needs to increase investments in physical capital and improve the education of its workforce in order to accelerate growth, with the expectation that these steps, together with sector-specific reforms to increase efficiency, will create better-paid jobs with social insurance benefits and labor protection. The second premise is that while more of these jobs are created, the country needs to enhance social inclusion through programs to provide social insurance to workers who cannot obtain it through their job, programs to transfer income in cash or in kind, exemptions to consumption taxes, and special tax regimes and other measures to help entrepreneurs running small firms.

A central objective of this book is to argue that these two premises are inconsistent. The policies and institutions deployed to enhance social inclusion tax the high-productivity sector of the economy and subsidize the low-productivity sector, stifling productivity and dampening growth. It is not a question of waiting for the benefits of educational investments and sector-specific reforms to come to full fruition. The real issue is that, despite those reforms, and despite macroeconomic stability and openness, current institutions and policies will impede fast growth *and* social inclusion from happening at the same time—or, more precisely, will continue to impede them from happening. As a result, the book attempts to shift the debate on growth in Mexico from a discussion of the policies that affect human and physical capital accumulation to a discussion of the institutions and policies that impede the efficient use of the country's human and physical capital (and which in turn reduce the incentives to accumulate physical and human capital).

This is a critical shift. The book points out that the main policies and institutions impeding growth are those related to taxation, labor and social insurance regulations, and enforcement of contracts. By documenting the central relevance of these issues to growth in Mexico, the book is an implicit criticism of the view that good macro, trade, and competition policies, accompanied by investments in education, are by themselves sufficient to bring prosperity to the country. It is also an implicit criticism of the view that *any* combination of policies to enhance social inclusion is welcome, so long as it is mindful of the government's budget constraint. Finally, it is an implicit criticism of the view that increasing transfers through multiple social programs, or by raising minimum wages, should compensate for the low earnings associated with stagnant productivity.

The call for a shift in the debate should not at all be construed as an argument for lower taxation and reduced social spending. On the contrary, Mexico needs to increase its tax burden and expand the scope, coverage, and quality of programs to increase workers' welfare and help those in need. But it must do so through policies that help productivity, not hurt it. Rhetoric aside, growth with social inclusion will only result if the incentives implicit in public policies are aligned to deliver both of these objectives *simultaneously*. A shift in the debate in Mexico is vital because it is doubtful that low growth with increasing redistribution is a sustainable equilibrium.

Nor should the position presented in this book be construed as a statement that macroeconomic stability and an open trade regime have not served Mexico well and should be abandoned. On the contrary, these are first-order achievements that need to be preserved. The shift called for here centers on reverting the productivity-stifling incentives associated with current tax, social insurance, and labor protection policies, and with the under-performance of judicial institutions. The book shows that these incentives have been powerful enough to depress growth and under-reward Mexico's reform efforts over the last two decades. But the book should begin at the beginning.

The Puzzle

Mexico's low growth is clearly disappointing. But it is also puzzling. In fact, one would have expected the opposite result, for many of the reasons discussed below.

Macroeconomic Management Has Been Effective

The painful lesson of the lost decade of the 1980s for Mexico was that high inflation and large fiscal and current account deficits are anathema to growth. But since 1996 the country has experienced macroeconomic stability. Inflation rates fell rapidly after the 1994–1995 financial crisis. In the last 15 years inflation has averaged around 4 percent, while fiscal and current account deficits averaged around 1.5 percent of GDP. Investors' perceptions of risks in Mexico, as measured by spreads on Emerging Market Bond Indices, are among the lowest in Latin America. Since 2002, Mexico's sovereign bonds have been rated as investor grade by rating agencies. And while Mexico's public debt as a share of GDP has increased since 2009, it was still below 50 percent in 2015.

Like most countries, Mexico benefited during these years from positive external shocks and suffered from negative ones as well. The price of oil—critical for public finances—was volatile but displayed an upward trend overall. The country enjoyed a large windfall as real oil prices increased from an index of 1.0 in 1996 to 4.5 in 2008, although some of that windfall diminished afterwards, as the index fell to 2.2 by 2015. But through the purchase of insurance and other measures aptly applied by policymakers, the economy was by and large insulated from these fluctuations.

Mexico benefited from fast growth in the world economy, particularly the United States, during the second half of the 1990s, but it also suffered as a result of the global financial crisis of 2008–2009. Once again, however, the strengthening of the economy's shock absorbers—in this case with the timely support of the International Monetary Fund—along with appropriate fiscal and monetary measures ensured that the effects of the shock were transitory.

This is not to say that in the last two decades macroeconomic management was flawless. But it is to say that, overall, it was sound and effective, and while there may be many reasons why Mexico's growth has disappointed, deficient macroeconomic management is not one of them.

The Foreign Trade Regime Has Been Appropriate

Twelve free trade agreements signed with various countries, most notably Canada and the United States, have opened new opportunities for Mexican firms since the mid-1990s. There have been some negative shocks as well, like China's entry into the World Trade Organization (WTO) in 2000, which affected Mexican manufacturing. But the effects of this event were not large enough to significantly dent Mexico's growth rate (Chapter 8).

All in all, Mexico has benefited from an open trade regime, as evidenced by rapid export growth. As a share of GDP, exports increased from 25 percent in 1996 to 35 percent in 2015, and in value terms, from US$100 billion to US$350 billion. In parallel, the share of manufactured exports in GDP increased from 19 to 27 percent. A telling indicator is that in 2015 the value of Mexico's manufactured exports exceeded the rest of Latin America's combined.

There Is More and Better Human Capital

Mexicans work very hard: the country ranks second out of the 35 countries that are members of the Organization for Economic Cooperation and Development in terms of hours worked per week (OECD 2017). In addition, the labor participation rate—that is, the share of individuals aged 18 to 65 who are either working or looking for work—increased from 60 percent in 1996 to 62 percent in 2015.

More importantly, Mexicans have invested heavily in education. Average years of schooling of persons aged 18 to 65 years increased from 7.7 years in 1996, when only 19 percent completed high school, to 9.6 years in 2015, when that figure rose to 33 percent. Mexico's educational effort in the last two decades exceeds that of the average for Latin American countries (Levy and Székely 2016). And while internationally comparable indicators show that the quality of basic education in Mexico is low relative to other OECD countries, it is also the case that over time those indicators have gradually improved, and that all national indicators of educational quality also show steady improvements, both for basic and higher education. Moreover, as noted, these educational improvements occurred while the population aged 18 to 65 was growing more rapidly than the overall population, and while the participation rate was increasing. In other words, during the two decades under study, the quantity and quality of human capital unambiguously increased.

The Investment Rate Is Higher

Mexico's investment rate gradually increased from an average of 19 percent of GDP in the first five years of the period under consideration to 21.6 percent in the last five. These rates are low relative to East Asian countries but compare favorably with other Latin American countries that have grown more rapidly than Mexico.[3] In the context of various free trade agreements, including the North American Free Trade Agreement (NAFTA) with Canada and the United States, Mexico experienced a significant increase in foreign direct investment between 1996 and 2015, from an average of US$13.4 billion per year in the first five years of the period to US$30.7 billion in the last five.

There Have Been Many Efforts to Increase Efficiency

Finally, Mexican policymakers have made significant efforts to increase efficiency as a means of accelerating growth, while preserving macroeconomic stability. As with any long-term undertaking, there have been periods when these efforts have slowed and periods when they have accelerated. Starting in the early 1990s, many state-owned enterprises were privatized. Competition increased through trade liberalization, regulatory measures, and new legislation. Pensions were reformed to increase long-term savings. Laws and regulations were modified to improve the functioning of financial markets. More recently, reforms have been put in place to raise the quality of education, strengthen competition across the economy, including enhancing competition in the telecommunications sector and introducing it in the energy sector. Most of these reforms have tackled important shortcomings, but though some are still works in progress, the evidence indicates that so far they have failed to accelerate growth.

---

[3] According to the World Bank's World Development Indicators, the average investment rate for the entire period in Mexico was 20.8 percent, the eighth highest of the 17 countries in Latin America (except Venezuela), and higher than Colombia (20.6 percent), Costa Rica (20.4 percent), Belize (20 percent), Brazil (18.7 percent), Uruguay (17.2 percent), Argentina (16.8 percent), Guatemala (16.5 percent), Paraguay (15.9 percent), and El Salvador (15.4 percent). All of those countries grew more than Mexico.

Superficially, the Problem Is Productivity

So why has growth been so slow? Why have all these efforts been under-rewarded? From a purely accounting perspective, and without implying any causality, the answer is that productivity stagnated.

Over the medium term, growth occurs because the labor force increases (in quantity and quality), because there is more investment in physical capital, and because the productivity of labor and capital (total factor productivity – TFP) increases. Decomposing Mexico's growth over this period into these three components, one finds that TFP growth averaged only 0.14 percent annually, without any corrections for the quality of the labor force. Considering increases in schooling (that is, taking into account that workers with more years of schooling can potentially contribute more to output than those with fewer years), yields a negative TFP growth rate of 0.53 percent.[4] In other words, regardless of how labor input is measured, the result is that Mexico's GDP growth has resulted only from the accumulation of physical capital and growth of the labor force. There have been no improvements in efficiency. Thus, by and large the question of why Mexico grows so slowly is equivalent to the question of why productivity has stagnated.

Why, then, when human and physical capital is being accumulated in a context of "free trade and sound money," has productivity growth stagnated? Why is it that ever-more educated Mexican entrepreneurs and workers cannot improve productivity over time even though they face little macroeconomic uncertainty and enjoy the benefits of access to global trade and financial markets and technology? Why have policymakers' efforts, so fruitful on the macroeconomic front, yielded such poor results in terms of their impact on productivity? Have reforms failed to focus on the real obstacles to productivity? Or have other policies and programs inadvertently nullified the effects of productivity-enhancing reforms?

The Central Hypothesis: Large and Persistent Misallocation

This book argues that persistent misallocation of resources is the main reason why productivity growth in Mexico has stagnated and, in turn, why growth has been disappointingly low.

---

[4] These results are obtained using output, capital, and labor force data from the Penn World Tables Version 9.0 and educational data from Barro and Lee (2013). The raw series are filtered using the Hodrick-Prescott technique with a smoothing parameter of 7; see Fernández-Arias (2017a, 2017b) for details. The series in the Penn World Tables are corrected for purchasing power parity to make them comparable across countries. The same calculations were repeated here

Misallocation is interpreted here as a situation where the distribution of individuals across occupations, the distribution of firms across sectors or sizes, and the match between firms and workers of different abilities is far from optimal. In an economy with misallocation, some individuals who, given their talents and abilities, should participate in economic activity as workers, do so as entrepreneurs instead, and vice versa.

Similarly, under misallocation some low-productivity firms attract more capital and labor than they should, while more productive ones fail to receive sufficient resources. Furthermore, the Schumpeterian process of "creative destruction" is dislocated: unproductive firms stay in the market while productive ones exit or fail to grow; entering firms have lower productivity than existing firms; many firms enter and then rapidly exit; and a large share of firm churning is basically useless.

In parallel, when large misallocation is present, workers are not matched with firms where their abilities can be fully used. Individuals end up in tasks that do not require their level of education (like the paradigmatic engineer driving a taxi). In addition, the contracts offered by firms to workers are not the right ones: some get short-term contracts leading to too much rotation and insufficient training and on-the-job learning, while others stay too long given their contribution to the firm's output.

Furthermore, under misallocation firms behave in ways that are privately profitable but socially inefficient. To elude or evade various regulations, they modify their size, failing to achieve economies of scale or scope. For the same reasons, they change their contractual structure even though this lowers their productivity. They also may restrict their sources of intermediate inputs, or the customers with whom they engage. Or they may have high entry and low survival rates, generating short-lived jobs.

In short, in an economy with large misallocation, capital is not invested in the best projects, workers are not matched with firms that require their abilities, and the dynamics of firm entry, exit, and growth are not congruent with firms' underlying productivity. Without misallocation, the same individuals with the same education and abilities, working the same number of hours, investing the same amounts of money, and with access to the same technologies would produce more. Over time, better firms would grow, bad firms would die, workers would acquire more skills during their life cycle, and productivity would increase.

---

without such corrections. In that case, TFP growth over the period was −0.78 percent considering the improved years of schooling of the labor force, or −0.32 percent without doing so. Other analyses of TFP growth in Mexico show equivalent results (Kehoe and Meza 2012; ECLAC 2016).

Misallocation Is the Manifestation of a Deeper Social and Political Phenomenon

Misallocation is viewed here as the outcome of policies and institutions that, through various channels, affect the behavior of entrepreneurs and workers in ways that hurt productivity. Policies reflect the ideas, theories, and understandings of policymakers, and are reflected in laws and regulations with regards to, say, international trade, innovation, domestic competition, or financial regulation. More importantly, policies also reflect core aspects of the country's social fabric such as taxation, the regulation of relations between entrepreneurs and workers, the scope and financing of social insurance, and the mechanisms used to reduce income disparities.

But institutions also matter. The modus operandi of those in charge of collecting taxes, contributions, and fees is relevant because tacit understandings determine the forcefulness with which regulations are enforced. The modus operandi of those responsible for delivering social services is important because it affects the benefits that entrepreneurs and workers get from participating in them. The modus operandi of those tasked with adjudicating commercial, credit, tax, and labor disputes is relevant because when the de facto and the de jure rules of the game differ, entrepreneurs and workers learn that the law is not always the law, at least not for all, and they adjust their behavior accordingly. And the modus operandi of those in charge of keeping markets competitive matters because when they fail to reach their objectives, firms prevail not because they are more productive but by exercising monopoly power.

Therefore, misallocation should not be seen only as the outcome of the government's failure to set the right tax or subsidy here, or to correct a market failure or externality there. These policy failures certainly matter. But misallocation also results from the functioning—or, rather, malfunctioning—of core institutions that affect the daily lives of workers and entrepreneurs. Altogether, deficient institutions fail to create the conditions necessary for reasonably efficient markets, or fail to deliver services of reasonable quality and thus induce behaviors that are privately profitable but socially inefficient.

In this context, the persistence of misallocation results from the fact that some policies and institutions detrimental to productivity—particularly those associated with relations between entrepreneurs and workers and taxation—are deeply ingrained in Mexico's political discourse or reflect underlying political equilibriums that are very hard to change (see the collection of essays in Levy and Walton 2009). Inefficient policies and malfunctioning institutions persist partly as a result of long-held views, and partly as a result of a specific political equilibrium. In short, persistent misallocation is just the technical term—short-hand, one might say—for a deep and complex social and political phenomenon.

Misallocation and Policy Reforms

Critically for economic growth in Mexico, large and persistent misallocation is compatible with macroeconomic stability. Some taxes and subsidies may reduce productivity, but they can be made compatible with the government's budget constraint by adjusting other taxes or expenditures. Critically as well, free trade agreements can make some product markets more contestable, although they cannot substitute for malfunctioning institutions tasked with collecting taxes and contributions, providing social services, or enforcing contracts.[5] Nor can they correct for inadequacies in the country's labor regulations and social insurance architecture. Neither, for that matter, can investments in human and physical capital correct for such inadequacies. While clearly welcome, these investments do not reduce misallocation, and in fact the returns made on them are lower because of it.

Some of the policies and institutions that generate misallocation in Mexico have been part and parcel of the country's landscape for decades, and have not been the subject of systematic reform efforts. Others have experienced deep reforms, like those associated with promoting domestic competition and ending public sector monopolies in energy, though they have yet to yield their full results. On the other hand, since the 1994–1995 crisis, other policies have inadvertently increased misallocation. The empirical evidence presented in this book shows that their combined effect has offset the positive impact on aggregate productivity derived from the efficiency-oriented reforms of the two past decades. As in Homer's Odyssey, there is a Penelope undoing at night the knitting of the day.

The policies and institutions at the root of misallocation in Mexico touch individuals in all areas of economic activity. They impact the attitudes, expectations, and behavior of millions of workers and entrepreneurs, affecting the allocation of labor, capital, and other resources throughout the economy. In this context, measures to enhance competition and open or broaden investment opportunities in specific sectors (for example, telecommunications or energy), while undoubtedly positive, cannot by themselves offset the broader forces of misallocation. These sectors are too small in

---

[5] Investment protection and dispute settlement mechanisms in these agreements can aide the subset of firms directly engaged in international trade or cross-border investments, but in Mexico this subset is very small.

terms of the labor and capital that they absorb to make a large dent in aggregate productivity.[6]

These observations shed light on the puzzle set out at the start of this introduction. They should not, obviously, be read as a case against macroeconomic stability, open trade regimes, investments in human and physical capital, or measures to increase competition. On the contrary, Mexico's efforts on these fronts are extremely valuable, and need to be forcefully pursued. But the observations explain why these efforts have been under-rewarded. Looking forward, to avoid the perpetuation of this unfortunate outcome, it will be essential to tackle the policies and institutions that result in persistent misallocation.

Objectives and Organization of the Book

This book brings to the debate on Mexico's growth underperformance issues that have not received the attention they deserve. As a result, the book does not focus on the traditional explanations of long-run growth—innovation and human and physical capital accumulation—and even less on issues associated with short-run macroeconomic management. Rather, the book focuses on the microeconomic incentives embedded in Mexico's policies, institutions, and rules of the game. At the most general level, the monograph argues two points:

- Misallocation is the central part of the explanation of why productivity and growth in Mexico have stagnated.
- Misallocation results from policies and institutions that affect the decisions of entrepreneurs and workers along dimensions that are detrimental to productivity, and not from underlying shortcomings in their characteristics or abilities (in terms of risk-taking, saving effort, inventiveness, education, or disposition to work, learn or innovate).

Focus on Firms

Firms are the arena where the efforts of entrepreneurs and workers coalesce to generate economic value; the space where managerial talent, workers' toils, and capital investments jointly produce goods and services. Firms are Mexico's main wealth-creating engines, and their performance largely determines the performance of the economy.

---

[6] That said, enhanced competition is very welcome even if its impact on aggregate productivity is second-order. Final consumers benefit from lower prices, better quality, and increased options. In parallel, reduced monopoly rents improve the distribution of income and diminish the political power of those capturing rents (Guerrero, López-Calva, and Walton 2009).

A simple relation captures this key point. Assume that there are only two firms in the economy (Firms A and B), that their productivity is, respectively, TFP_A and TFP_B, and that the share of resources (capital and labor) captured by each is S_A and S_B. It is the case then that:

$$\text{Aggregate Productivity} = TFP = S_A \cdot TFP_A + S_B \cdot TFP_B; \; S_A + S_B = 1.$$

If $TFP_A = TFP_B$, it does not matter whether Firm A captures more resources than Firm B, or vice versa. It is as if there were only one firm, and the productivity of the economy would equal the productivity of that firm. But if the firms' productivity differs, aggregate productivity will depend on the differences in productivity between them, and on the share of resources allocated to each.

As simple as this example is, it captures a deep truth: Mexico's aggregate productivity is nothing more than the weighted average of the productivity of its firms, where the weights are the share of resources allocated to each. If many firms underperform, aggregate productivity suffers even if there is a small subset of firms that perform very well.

For these reasons, it matters greatly how many firms there are, who manages them, and which ones grow, exit or enter the market. One might think that tiny low-productivity firms can hardly make a difference to aggregate productivity, but if there a lot of them, their sum will indeed make a difference. This book shows that in Mexico this is the case. One might also presume that as long as large high-productivity firms do well, the economy will do well too. However, if these firms fail to attract sufficient resources, this presumption will be flawed. This book documents that in Mexico this is also the case.

The number of firms in Mexico is surprisingly large. What is perhaps most striking is that the differences in productivity between them are very big, even if we compare firms that are producing almost the same good. Mexican firms are very heterogeneous, to say the least. On one extreme, some are world competitors, using the most advanced technologies and management practices, with thousands of workers distributed over many establishments across the country and sometimes the globe. At the other extreme are firms in a single establishment with two or three workers, using simple technologies and primitive management practices, and at times carrying out their activities on the streets and avenues of the country's cities. The latter set of firms is more numerous and, contrary to what one would expect, has attracted more resources than the former over the last two decades.

Firms are very important for workers. There are no good jobs in bad firms. Some firms hire workers illegally, hurting their social rights. Some offer stable jobs and invest in workers' training more than others. Firm behavior is critical for the schooling composition of the demand for labor. Firms that innovate or adopt complex technologies need engineers and computer programmers, while firms with simple processes require workers with only basic numeracy and literacy. The country can produce many university graduates, but if firms do not need them, they will be in excess supply and their wages will fall. Unfortunately for Mexico, this has been the case.

Methodological Approach

This book devotes considerable attention to establishing key stylized facts about the characteristics of firms in Mexico: size, legal status, contractual agreements with workers, location, sector of activity, and access to credit. In parallel, the book develops firm-level measures of productivity. It then asks whether there are any systematic patterns between firm characteristics and firm productivity, and whether these patterns are constant over time. In parallel, the book studies how capital and labor are allocated across firms, and how these allocations change as firms enter the market, exit, grow, or contract. Are changes in resource allocation in line with changes in firms' productivity?

Identifying patterns between firm characteristics, productivity, and dynamics is a very useful preliminary step toward the more complex causal analysis linking policies and institutions with productivity outcomes. In other words, better understanding what is going on provides clarity and direction to the more challenging task of explaining why what is going on is occurring.

The methodological approach followed in this book separates the analysis of outcomes from the analysis of the causes behind those outcomes. The first task is relatively straightforward and in principle not subject to much controversy. The second task is more complex, considering, on the one hand, that there is no single policy that is "*the*" cause of misallocation, and, on the other, that the tools required to identify and quantify the relative contribution of each policy to the observed productivity outcomes are still works in progress.

For the first task we need good data, measures of firm productivity, and reasonable measures of misallocation. For the second we need more complex models that can establish causality. We also need an effort at interpretation, to the extent that there is no single causal force.

Separating these two tasks is critical. By extensively documenting the presence and persistence of large misallocation, the book aims to center the debate on its causes, not on its presence or relevance to Mexico. Put differently, ideally the debate is about why what is going on is occurring, and not about whether what is going on is in fact occurring.

Because misallocation results from the interaction of many policies and institutions, there is understandable debate as to which policies and institutions are the most relevant ones. That said, this book narrows the analysis of all possible policies that might conceivably cause misallocation to the subset that is consistent with the systematic patterns documented in the first task. This identifies priorities for policy and institutional reforms that could bring prosperity to Mexico. There are many obstacles to productivity growth in Mexico, but they are not all equally important.

Key Concepts and Basic Facts

The first task is to introduce key concepts and relations, and to provide structure to the discussion throughout the book. With this purpose in mind, Chapter 2 presents a simple analytical framework. In line with the methodological approach mentioned, the chapter initially skews a discussion of the causal links between policies and misallocation. At this stage, the critical issue is to pin down two ideas: first, that resource misallocation leads to productivity losses; and second, that misallocation results from flawed policies and malfunctioning institutions—without identifying which or how. In consequence, the framework is purposely cast at a very general level.

Institutions, Policies, and the Environment

Behind the large number of very small firms in Mexico lies the decision of an equal number of individuals to manage their own firm rather than be employed in somebody else's firm. And behind the large number of self-employed individuals lies a decision to work for themselves rather than, again, for somebody else. Similarly, behind an illegally hired worker lies the decision of an entrepreneur to break the law, and behind a skilled and well-trained worker who moves up the job ladder lies the decision of another entrepreneur to give the worker a long-term contract and invest in that worker's training. Because these decisions are critical determinants of productivity, this book focuses attention on the social and economic context faced by individuals making them. This context—labeled as the "environment" throughout the book—is summarized in three "worlds:"

- **The "world of entrepreneur-workers relations":** This covers the laws and institutions that regulate how entrepreneurs and workers can associate to form firms and create wealth. Special emphasis is placed on the implications that different contractual arrangements have on the scope and financing of social insurance, and on the rules regulating how contracts can be terminated.
- **The "world of taxation":** This covers the laws and institutions that determine how workers, firms, and consumers are taxed. Special emphasis is placed on the implications of taxing workers differently depending

on their labor contract, taxing firms differently depending on their size, and taxing consumption differently depending on the good or service.
- **The "world of market conditions":** This covers all other laws and institutions that impact the functioning of markets, with an emphasis on those that determine the trust that agents (banks, firms, workers) place in the institutions enforcing contracts, and the degree of competition in product markets.

The policies and associated institutions in these three "worlds" capture the context in which the central players in this book—entrepreneurs and workers—make their decisions. Since these policies appear again and again, it is convenient to refer to them using three symbols: L for entrepreneur-workers relations, T for taxation, and M for market conditions. Together, they make up Mexico's social and economic environment, in turn symbolized by $\boldsymbol{E}(L,T,M)$.

This is a book about how Mexico's $\boldsymbol{E}(L,T,M)$ stands in the way of its prosperity.

Formality and Informality

Discussions of productivity in Mexico inevitably touch on the issue of informality. To some, informality is a transitory nuisance that will fade away as soon as other obstacles retarding growth are removed (for example, monopolies in energy and telecommunications, scarcity of skilled workers, macroeconomic uncertainty, insufficient investment, or inadequate international competition). To others, informality is the reason why productivity is low, while yet others argue that the opposite is true, that informality is the result of low productivity.

Indeed, the word "informality" evokes different images to different readers. To avoid generating more heat than light by its use, it is essential to define it with precision. The definition used here is derived from Mexico's legal framework. Following Mexico's constitution, this book distinguishes between salaried and non-salaried contracts between workers and entrepreneurs. *This is a critical distinction that looms large throughout the book and without which it is not possible to understand Mexico's productivity problem.*

Salaried workers are hired by entrepreneurs/firms in a relation of subordination and receive wages in return for their efforts (fixed payments per unit of time), a topic more closely examined in Chapter 2. Non-salaried workers can be self-employed or associated with firms but not in a subordinated relation, receiving remuneration in various forms (per unit produced or sold, per task accomplished, profit-sharing, and the like), but not wages.

In other countries, the distinction between salaried and non-salaried contracts is probably innocuous. But in Mexico it is central because, following constitutional mandates, since the middle of the past century many of Mexico's policies and institutions have been designed specifically for salaried workers, with obligations imposed on firms only when they hire salaried workers. Among these are the obligations to pay for workers' social insurance, to comply with dismissal regulations, and to withhold workers' income taxes. In parallel, other policies have been designed for non-salaried workers, with different obligations on firms. Among these are the provision of free social insurance benefits, and the exemption of firms from dismissal regulations and withholding obligations. As a result, laws with respect to labor taxes, pensions, health, day care, housing, and separation from employment differ depending on the nature of the contract between firms and workers. In parallel, the institutions in charge of enforcing obligations or providing benefits to salaried and non-salaried workers also differ.

If the laws governing relations between firms and workers were always observed, that would be the end of the story. There would be two types of firms, with salaried or non-salaried workers, and in parallel two types of workers, salaried and non-salaried (including the self-employed). Salaried workers would be formal, non-salaried workers would be informal and, correspondingly, firms with salaried workers would be formal and firms with non-salaried workers informal. Unfortunately, the issue is more complex because firms sometimes mix salaried and non-salaried workers, and sometimes also break the law. As a result, it is necessary to distinguish between legally and illegally hired salaried workers.

Figure 1.1 captures this complexity and clarifies the relation between formality and legality. Salaried workers who have a contract with a firm that complies with the obligation to enroll them in social insurance programs and observes dismissal and other labor regulations are formal. Salaried workers hired by firms that do not comply with these obligations are informal. On the other hand, non-salaried workers are informal, either because they are self-employed, or because given their contract, the firms that they work for are not obligated to comply with the regulations that apply only to salaried workers. Both types of informal workers are highlighted in the upper rectangle in Figure 1.1. The critical point about these workers is that they are neither covered by dismissal regulations nor enjoy the social insurance benefits that formal workers receive, regardless of whether or not this results from an illegal act.

Firms can be of four types. If they hire only salaried workers and comply with the associated obligations, they are fully formal. If they offer their workers a combination of salaried and non-salaried contracts, they are mixed. In

Figure 1.1: Firm-Worker Contracts, Formality and Legality

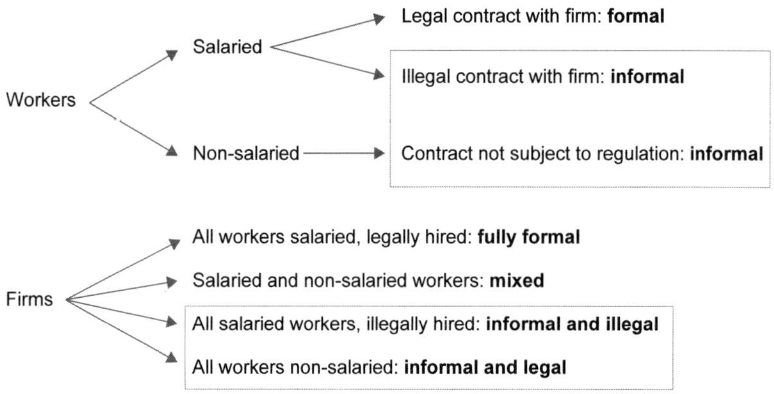

Workers
- Salaried
  - Legal contract with firm: **formal**
  - Illegal contract with firm: **informal**
- Non-salaried → Contract not subject to regulation: **informal**

Firms
- All workers salaried, legally hired: **fully formal**
- Salaried and non-salaried workers: **mixed**
- All salaried workers, illegally hired: **informal and illegal**
- All workers non-salaried: **informal and legal**

Source: Prepared by the author.

this book, these two firm types are sometimes grouped together and simply referred to as formal firms. However, firms can also offer workers salaried contracts, but evade the law completely, in which case they are informal and illegal, based on the understanding that the illegal act is committed by the firm, not the worker. Finally, firms can offer their workers non-salaried contracts, in which case they are informal but legal, since they are not obligated to observe dismissal regulations, pay for their worker's social insurance, or withhold their income taxes. In this book, legal and illegal informal firms are sometimes grouped together and referred to simply as informal firms. They are highlighted in the lower rectangle in Figure 1.1.

So much for definitions. How is this related to productivity and misallocation? The analytical framework developed in Chapter 2 serves to answer this question. The key point is that the decisions of entrepreneurs and workers in Mexico are not taken in a vacuum; they are taken in the context symbolized by $E(L,T,M)$. This social and economic environment determines the number of self-employed individuals, and the number of firms and their investment, employment, and production levels. In parallel, this context also determines whether firms offer their workers salaried or non-salaried contracts, and the extent to which they comply with applicable laws.

Put differently, the allocation of resources across firms of varying productivity levels, and the formal or informal status of each firm (that is, the combination of salaried/non-salaried, and legal/illegal contracts with its workers), are simultaneously determined by the incentives that workers and entrepreneurs face given current policies and institutions, symbolized by $E(L,T,M)$. As a result, the level of aggregate productivity—which, as noted, is nothing but the weighted average of the productivity of existing firms—and the formal-informal composition of the economy are joint outcomes of more primitive characteristics of the country, including its laws and policies, and the functioning of the institutions behind them. If policies differed, or if the associated institutions functioned differently, the number of firms, their size, contractual composition, and the extent to which they comply with the law, would differ and, in turn, so would the level of aggregate productivity and the formal-informal composition of the economy.

In other words, informality is not the cause of anything, nor is low productivity. Both are outcomes of the interactions between millions of individuals in Mexico who, given ***E**(L,T,M)*, end up working for themselves or for entrepreneurs, who in turn decide whether they hire few or many workers, whether they offer them salaried or non-salaried contracts, and whether they comply with the law. In this context, discussions as to whether low productivity is the cause of informality, or informality the cause of low productivity, are misplaced. Neither is the chicken or the egg.

The coexistence of formal and informal firms is not a transient phenomenon or a minor feature of Mexico's economy. It is the normal way in which business is carried out, and it is a direct result of the country's constitution and its laws, policies, and institutions—in a nutshell, its ***E**(LT,M)*. Combining formal and informal contractual relations is the response of savvy and increasingly educated individuals—entrepreneurs and workers—to the current rules of the game. It is a response that will continue until these rules change. The view that informal firms are remnants of still-surviving but dwindling "traditional production," or that they are confined to a few areas of activity, is at odds with the empirical evidence. The number of informal firms in Mexico has increased in the last two decades, they have attracted more resources, and they have spread to a larger set of activities in manufacturing, services, and commerce. Some of these firms are small and short-lived, giving rise to the only-partly-correct association between informality and precariousness. Some break the law, giving rise to the also only-partly-correct association between informality and illegality. Some are large and more permanent, some comply with the law; and, in fact, some are as productive as their formal counterparts.

Establishing Basic Facts

Many useful insights can be gained by systematically analyzing the available data. How many firms are there in Mexico, how many resources are absorbed by each, and what type of contractual relations between entrepreneurs and workers are found among them? Before trying to explain firm behavior, it is essential to first document it. As a result, Chapters 3 to 6 omit any discussion of the connection between individual policies in the environment, $E(L,T,M)$, and observed outcomes. They only describe different dimensions of those outcomes—in other words, they focus only on documenting "what is going on."

Chapter 3 describes the data and presents basic facts. It draws on Mexico's Economic Census for 1998, 2003, 2008 and 2013, which contains detailed information on firms of all sizes. The chapter analyzes 2.7 million firms in 1998, 2.9 million firms in 2003, 3.6 million firms in 2008, and 4.1 million firms in 2013 in manufacturing, commerce, and nonfinancial services.[7] This is, at least by Latin American standards, an unusually rich database, opening a broad window to investigate Mexican firms. The census allows to group them by the type of good produced, which is done at a very narrow level (the six-digit sector classification). Altogether, the chapter groups all firms in manufacturing, commerce, and services into 691 sectors. To give a sense of the level of detail, in 2013 there are 742 firms producing shirts, and 441 firms producing pasta for soups. This means that firms within each sector are producing very similar goods.

While this is indeed a very large dataset, it still does not cover the universe of all firms in Mexico because the census leaves out all economic activity carried out in localities with fewer than 2,500 inhabitants and in firms without fixed premises (street stands and the like), even if the latter are in localities of more than 2,500 inhabitants.

This is a substantial omission. Indeed, and surprisingly, despite the broad coverage of the census, firms captured in it account for only 44 percent of total employment in Mexico. In other words, firms and workers excluded from the census are very important, and it is essential to consider them in a study of productivity, even if data limitations preclude a complete analysis. To do so, the Economic Census is complemented with data from Mexico's Employment Survey. Although by design focused on households, the survey allows to make some inferences about the number of firms excluded from the census.

Five Findings from the Census Data

The first finding from the census data is that most firms in manufacturing, commerce, and services are informal. In 2013 informal firms:

- Represented 90 percent of all firms
- Absorbed more than 40 percent of the capital stock and 55 percent of employment

---

[7] For reasons described in Chapter 3, firms in energy and mining, transport, construction, and financial services are excluded from the analysis, even though they are captured in the census.

- On a sector-by-sector basis, constituted the majority in 51 percent of all six-digit sectors in manufacturing, 81 percent in commerce, and 88 percent in services.

In other words, informal firms absorb a significant amount of capital and labor and are found throughout the economy. They are not confined to "traditional" or "less modern" activities. The view of the informal sector as made up only of street vendors and tiny firms, altogether absorbing few resources, is mistaken. Informal economic activity is large and widespread and is certainly not confined to the streets—indeed, the numbers above exclude firms that are in the streets.

Second, the association between informality and illegality is flawed. As it turns out, 81 percent of all informal firms in the 2013 census had non-salaried relations with their workers. In other words, most informal firms are legal, at least from the perspective of complying with labor, social insurance, and tax-withholding regulations. This implies that informality in Mexico is primarily not the result of imperfect enforcement of the laws that apply to salaried labor. Rather, it is the result of a deeper phenomenon rooted in the constitutional distinction between salaried and non-salaried relations. Firms with non-salaried contracts absorbed 71 percent of all labor in informal firms and 78 percent of all capital. There certainly is a relevant overlap between informal firms and illegal firms, but that overlap is not large.

The third finding is that the association between firm informality and small size is partly right. Most informal firms, legal or illegal, are very small, with up to five workers.[8] It is true that each one individually absorbs a miniscule amount of resources and, on this basis, one might conclude that from the point of view of productivity these firms are basically irrelevant. But the census data point out that that would be a big mistake. Taken together, in 2013 very small and small informal firms accounted for 17 percent of the capital stock and 40 percent of employment captured in the census (and more if firms excluded from the census are considered, as noted below). That said, the association between firm informality and small size is not wholly correct, because there are some medium-size and large informal firms as well.

The fourth finding is that formal and informal firms are present in all localities in Mexico. Focusing on firms captured in the census, there are no significant differences in firm informality across localities of differing sizes or with different access to physical infrastructure, financial services, or

---

[8] Throughout the book, "very small firms" are those with one to five workers, "small firms" those with six to 10 workers, "medium-size firms" those with 11 to 50 workers, and "large firms" those with 51 workers or more.

courts for settling disputes. In other words, firm informality is not a regional phenomenon—it is equally present in larger urban conglomerates and smaller localities. To be exact, in 2013, 88.9 percent of all firms in Mexico City were informal, compared to 90.2 percent in the rest of the country.

But isn't this result contrary to the well-established fact that informality is more pronounced in the south of the country? No, because that fact refers to labor informality, which indeed is higher in the south, since the share of urban self-employment and rural employment, which is practically all informal, is higher there. Firms captured in the census, on the other hand, mix salaried and non-salaried and illegal and legal contracts in similar proportions throughout the country, a not-so-surprising result when one considers that the environment that they face, $E(L,T,M)$, is pretty much the same across the territory.

The fifth and last finding focuses on trends between 1998 and 2013. The comparison of the four censuses shows that, contrary to what one would expect, the composition of economic activity shifted over time towards the informal sector, measured by the number of firms, the number of six-digit sectors where these firms are a majority, and the share of capital and labor absorbed by them. In parallel, the average size of formal firms increased, and they became more capital-intensive, but the average size of informal firms fell. The net result of all these trends was a fall in average firm size, and larger differences in capital intensity between formal and informal firms, within informal firms, and across firm sizes. In other words, heterogeneity increased across firm sizes and types.

Importantly, these trends—and particularly increased firm informality and smaller firm size—are not due to the changing composition of the economy in terms of manufacturing, services, and commerce. It is true that on average firm formality and size is higher in manufacturing, and that in relative terms commerce and services expanded while manufacturing shrank. But it is also true that firm formality and average size also fell in manufacturing. Increasing informality and smaller firm size thus reflect deeper forces in the economy beyond changes in its composition.

What about Firms Excluded from the Census?

While it is impossible to offer precise numbers regarding the numbers of firms excluded from the census, the Employment Survey suggests that in 2013 there were 2.6 million such firms in manufacturing, commerce, and services. When added to the 4.1 million firms in the same activities captured in the census, the result is that in 2013 there were approximately 6.7 million firms in those three broadly defined activities. Although it is not possible to obtain data on capital, firms excluded from the census are very relevant from the point of view of labor:

Table 1.1: Firms and Workers in Manufacturing, Commerce and Services, 2013
(millions)

	1–5 Workers	6–10 Workers	11–50 Workers	51+ Workers	Total
Firms	6.30	0.27	0.13	0.03	6.73
Workers	13.4	2.1	3.0	6.4	24.9

Source: Author's calculations based on data from the Economic Census and the Employment Survey.

they employed 7.6 million workers, which contrasts with the 17.4 million workers employed by firms in the census in those same activities. In other words, for every worker in a firm included in the census there were 0.4 workers in firms excluded from it (not counting the one-person firms of the self-employed). Firms excluded from the census were practically all informal and very small.

So, all in all, considering firms excluded and included in the census, how are workers and firms distributed by firm size? While for reasons described in Chapter 3 it is not possible to give an exact answer, Table 1.1 provides a good approximation. More than half of all workers are in very small firms, doubling the number of workers in large firms. In turn, practically all firms are very small. Indeed, there were only 31,000 firms with more than 50 workers, compared to 6.3 million with fewer than five.

These numbers imply that production is very dispersed. Indeed, if one were to choose a single word to describe economic activity in Mexico, it would probably be "scattered." Altogether, considering firms included and excluded from the census, in 2013 the average firm in manufacturing, commerce, and services had 3.7 workers. Another illustrative statistic takes into account the self-employed and all privately employed workers in urban areas. In this case, in 2013, 59 percent of workers were self-employed or worked for a firm with at most five employees, which is 1 percent higher than in 2000.

Misallocation: Magnitude, Patterns, and Persistence

So, what if workers work on their own? Or if firms are small or large? Or if they are formal or informal? At the end of the day, we care about the productivity of Mexico's workers and the capital invested by the entrepreneurs who employ them, regardless of size, sector, or contractual arrangements.

Chapter 4 turns to measuring productivity and misallocation. This requires imposing more structure on the analytical framework presented in Chapter 2. A key concept is the revenue productivity of resources in each firm, which measures how much value a firm produces with a given amount of capital and labor. This measure provides an index of firm productivity used throughout the book.

Ideally, one peso of capital and labor should produce the same value regardless of the firm to which it is allocated.[9] In other words, ideally the revenue productivity of resources should be the same across all firms. In practice this is not the case, and differences in revenue productivity across firms provide measures of misallocation: the larger the difference, the larger the degree of misallocation. In turn, the association between misallocation and low productivity is straightforward: if resources could be shifted from firms where their revenue productivity is low to firms where it is high, the same resources would produce more output, aggregate productivity would increase, and GDP would be higher.

In all countries there is some degree of misallocation, but Chapter 4 finds that by international standards misallocation is Mexico is substantially larger than in the United States, and larger than in Latin American countries for which comparable data are available. For example, in manufacturing in the United States, the difference in revenue productivity between a firm in the 90th and the 10th percentile of the revenue productivity distribution is 92 percent, while in Mexico it is 173 percent.

Misallocation in Mexico is large in commerce and services and, to a lesser extent, in manufacturing, a result associated with manufacturing's greater exposure to international competition. More worrisome, misallocation increased in the last two decades, and it did do similarly in manufacturing, commerce, and services. In 1998, the difference in revenue productivity between a firm in the 25th and the 75th percentile of the productivity distribution was 23 percent; by 2013 it had increased to 39 percent. This last finding provides empirical support to the assertion made earlier in this chapter: that while some policies in Mexico's *E(L,T,M)* changed to increase efficiency, others did so in the opposite direction and, at the end of the day, dominated.

Characterizing the Patterns of Misallocation

Misallocation manifests itself in many ways, all relevant to Mexico. These include the distribution of individuals across occupations, the size of sectors,

---

[9] Of course, firms differ in their capital intensity, so the division of one peso of resources between capital and labor varies across firms. In capital-intensive firms, that intensity may be, say, 80 cents of capital and 20 cents of labor, while in labor-intensive firms it may be the opposite. What matters is to have a metric of resource use comparable across firms, as well as a metric of the value that those resources produce.

the number, size and contractual structure of firms within each sector, and the matches between firms and workers of varying educational levels and abilities.

To sharpen the analysis, Chapter 4 compares the productivity of firms that are producing similar goods (that is, within the same six-digit sector). An important finding is that in the same sector some firms are very productive and others extremely unproductive, but somehow both survive in the market. For instance, in 2013 the most productive firm was 64 times more productive than the average firm, while the least productive firm was 1/64 times less productive than the average firm. If the resources channeled to the least productive firms could be channeled to the more productive ones, Mexico's GDP would be higher without anybody having to invest or work more.

Why do firms producing similar goods with very different productivity levels coexist in the market? This question is answered in Chapter 7, but to pave the way towards the answer, Chapter 4 first devotes considerable attention to identifying patterns between firms' productivity levels and characteristics—sector of activity, age, size, location, formality, and legality status.

The key finding is that misallocation is far from random. There are systematic patterns between firm characteristics and productivity that hold across manufacturing, commerce, and services, across firms of any size, across firms of various ages, across firms located in small cities and in large urban areas, and across time.

What are these patterns? There is a clear ranking of firms' productivity levels depending on firms' contractual structure:

- Firms that hire salaried workers legally are on average the most productive, followed by those that mix salaried and non-salaried workers (that is, fully formal and mixed firms).
- Next in line are firms that hire salaried workers illegally (that is, informal and illegal firms).
- Finally, the least productive firms are those that have only non-salaried workers (informal and legal).

These rankings hold controlling for firm size, location, and age, as well as across time—in other words, they are very robust.

While formal firms are on average more productive than informal ones, it is critical to point out that productivity differences within informal firms are very large. In fact, the productivity of informal firms hiring salaried workers illegally is not that much lower than the productivity of formal firms, but is substantially higher than the productivity of informal firms with non-salaried contracts. In other words, the more significant differences in productivity are between firms that have salaried workers (whether hired legally or illegally) and those with only non-salaried workers. Firms with salaried workers (legal or illegal) are on average 40 to 80 percent more productive than those with non-salaried contracts. This implies that, from the point of view of productivity, *the distinction between firms with salaried and non-salaried contracts is more relevant than the distinction between formal and informal firms*. This finding is central for Mexico: its environment $E(L,T,M)$ makes it difficult for firms with salaried contracts, particularly legal ones, to attract more resources even though they are more productive.

Another angle on this finding is that there is substantial heterogeneity within informal firms, or, put differently, that the composition of the informal sector matters considerably for productivity. As a result, one cannot establish an association between the level of aggregate productivity and the size of the informal sector (as measured, say, by the number of informal firms and informal workers). If, magically, resources in firms with non-salaried workers could be reallocated to firms with illegally hired salaried workers, the size of the informal sector would not change, but productivity would increase. Chapter 4 thus helps to refine the questions that Chapter 7 needs to answer. Why are resources continuously misallocated to informal firms? And, more importantly, why are those resources misallocated towards firms with non-salaried contracts?

Firm Type versus Firm Size

The productivity rankings described above focused only on firm type, but extending these rankings to consider firm size provides additional insights. Figure 1.2 does this for all firms included in the 2013 census. The vertical axis lists firms by size and type, and the horizontal axis measures the percentage difference in revenue productivity of firms of a given size and type relative to that of informal and legal firms with one to five workers (normalized at zero). In principle, of course, if there were no misallocation the revenue productivity of resources would be the same in all firms regardless of size or type, so all the rectangles should have the same height. Mexico's reality is far from this ideal situation, as the previous discussion already pointed out. From this perspective, Figure 1.2 just provides additional visual evidence of misallocation. But it also provides information about firm size that was not discussed before.

The results are very clear: firms with legal salaried contracts and more than 50 workers are by far the most productive of all; one peso of capital and labor produces 80 percent more value in those firms than in very small informal and legal firms. The second most productive firms also have more than 50 workers and salaried contracts, although illegal in this case. In turn, the third most productive firms are medium-size ones with legal salaried contracts. At

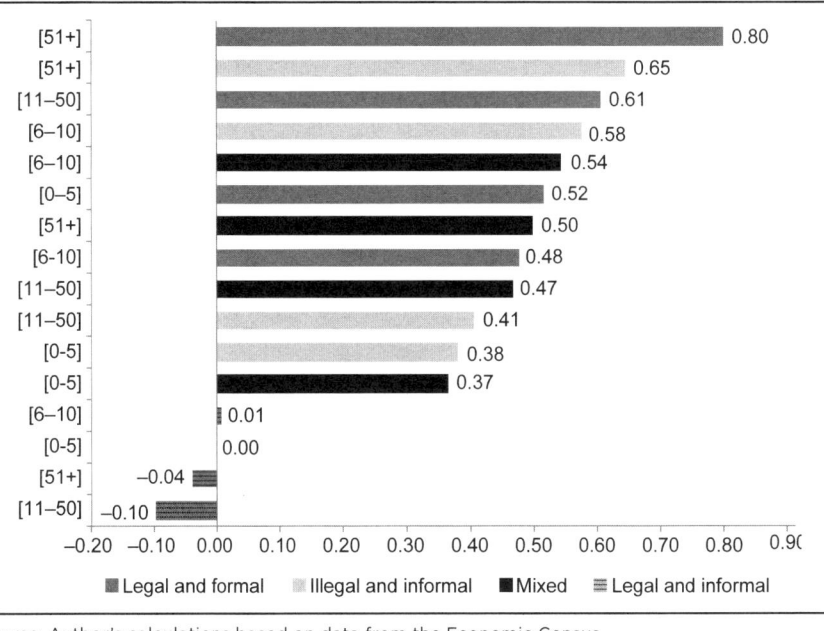

Figure 1.2: Revenue Productivity by Firm Size and Type, 2013

Size	Value
[51+]	0.80
[51+]	0.65
[11–50]	0.61
[6–10]	0.58
[6–10]	0.54
[0–5]	0.52
[51+]	0.50
[6–10]	0.48
[11–50]	0.47
[11–50]	0.41
[0-5]	0.38
[0-5]	0.37
[6–10]	0.01
[0-5]	0.00
[51+]	–0.04
[11–50]	–0.10

Legend: ■ Legal and formal ▨ Illegal and informal ■ Mixed ≡ Legal and informal

Source: Author's calculations based on data from the Economic Census.

the other extreme, informal and legal firms of any size are the least productive of all. In between these extremes, rankings are more mixed across sizes, but quantitatively not that different between them. All in all, Figure 1.2 yields an important message: within the set of firms with salaried contracts, larger ones are more productive.

Figure 1.2 is a cause of concern because firms with non-salaried contracts are the most numerous. And since they attract a significant share of capital and labor, they are the ones most responsible for pulling down Mexico's aggregate productivity. Some numbers illustrate the relevance of this. In 2013, there were only 10,998 firms with legal salaried contracts and more than 50 workers, absorbing 13.6 percent and 20.6 percent of all labor and capital captured in the census, respectively. At the same time, there were 2,983,612 firms with non-salaried contracts, absorbing 39.6 percent and 33.5 percent of labor and capital (and more if firms excluded from the census were considered).

These results provide empirical support to an earlier assertion: that the constitutional distinction between salaried and non-salaried contracts between entrepreneurs and workers, reflected in the policies and institutions summarized in $E(L,T,M)$, is central to understanding Mexico's productivity problem.

Another implication of these results that is important to highlight is that it is usual to associate firm size with firm productivity: large firms are large because they are more productive. And while this association is correct in many countries, in Mexico it is somewhat misleading. As Figure 1.2 shows, some small firms are as productive as some medium-size ones, so long as they have salaried workers; and some large firms (with non-salaried contracts) are less productive than small or medium-size firms (with salaried contracts). Of course, since most small firms in Mexico have non-salaried workers, and since these firms are very unproductive, the result is the natural association made between small size and low productivity.

These distinctions are not academic; they matter for policy. Chapter 7 documents that some public policies in Mexico are designed specifically to help small firms, without distinguishing whether they have salaried or non-salaried contracts, while other policies are specifically designed to help small firms with non-salaried contracts. The results of Chapter 4 raise questions about the pertinence of these policies. Yes, some small productive firms have difficulties growing and need help. But these are the minority. Most small firms are very unproductive, and helping them attract more resources is the opposite of what is needed to increase productivity.

Productivity Distributions

Not every single formal firm is more productive than every single informal firm. The results above are averages, and there are some informal firms, including ones with non-salaried contracts, that are very productive. In other words, the results described above refer to patterns, not absolute rules. Identifying these patterns is very valuable for the discussion in Chapter 7, which tries to link productivity outcomes with policies. But our understanding of Mexico's productivity problem is enhanced if we consider the complete range of firms' productivity, not only mean values. This book does so by ranking all firms by their revenue productivity, and then constructing a frequency distribution, which is then referred to as the revenue productivity distribution.

Chapter 4 plots these distributions for 1998, 2003, 2008, and 2013 and finds that they are very wide, reflecting large differences in firm productivity inside each six-digit sector. More importantly, it finds that these distributions *widened* over this 15-year period. There were more high-productivity firms in 2013 than in 1998. This is welcome news: a subset of Mexican firms over the last two decades have performed very well, which supports the image of a productive Mexico successfully competing in the international arena.

But this is not the whole story. There were also more low-productivity firms in 2013 than in 1998. And the unwelcome news is that those firms attracted even more resources than the high-productivity ones. This result serves to make a key point: simply noting that over time there are more high-productivity firms, and that these firms are growing, is not enough to claim that things are moving in the right direction. One must also consider the left-tail of the productivity distribution, and when this is done, one finds the image of an unproductive Mexico, lagging other regions of the world.

Because the left tail attracted more resources than the right one, productivity stagnated during this period. This outcome is troubling, and Chapter 5 is devoted to analyzing the process of firm entry and exit that produced it. But before turning to that issue, it is necessary to complete the static productivity picture by considering economic activity outside the census.

What can be said about the productivity of the 2.6 million firms excluded from the census? The available data, unfortunately, do not allow for computing their revenue productivity. But to the extent that these firms are mostly very small and have non-salaried contracts, one can speculate that their productivity is like that of very small informal and legal firms captured in the census, which were found to be among the least productive. After all, the differences between small legal and informal firms included and excluded from the census derive more from the data-gathering methods of Mexico's statistical institute than from underlying differences in their behavior (aside from the fact that some carry out their activities on fixed premises and some in the streets or in localities with less than 2,500 inhabitants). It thus stands to reason that if firms excluded from the census are considered, as they should be, the productivity losses derived from misallocation are larger than the ones measured with the census data. This observation is doubly relevant because the share of total employment allocated to firms excluded from the census grew from 30 percent in 2000 to 31.7 percent in 2013—yet another indicator that resources shifted in the wrong direction.

Firm Dynamics and the Persistence of Misallocation

Markets are supposed to eliminate unproductive firms and foster productive ones. Indeed, static misallocation would eventually be irrelevant if through the process of exit low-productivity firms left the market, allowing surviving high-productivity firms to gain market share and more resources, and if through the process of entry, new, higher-productivity firms joined the market. But if firm dynamics fail to do this, static misallocation will persist from one year to the next. How does the Schumpeterian process of creative destruction work in Mexico?

It is useful to extend the simple example introduced before to consider two years. In year 1 there are again only two firms in the economy, Firms A and B. As before, the share of resources attracted by each are S_{A1} and S_{B1}, and aggregate productivity is:

Year 1 Aggregate Productivity = $TFP_1 = S_{A1} \cdot TFP_{A1} + S_{B1} \cdot TFP_{B1}$;
$S_{A1} + S_{B1} = 1$.

One year later (year 2), Firm A exits the market while Firm B survives and a new firm, C, enters the market, so that:

Year 2 Aggregate Productivity = $TFP_2 = 0 + S_{B2} \cdot TFP_{B2} + S_{C2} \cdot TFP_{C2}$;
$S_{B2} + S_{C2} = 1$.

If $TFP_{A1} < TFP_{B1} < TFP_{C2}$, firm dynamics would increase aggregate productivity (so that $TFP_2 > TFP_1$), because the low-productivity firm died, the high-productivity firm survived, and the entering firm was more productive than the surviving one. In addition, if $TFP_{B2} > TFP_{B1}$, aggregate productivity would also increase because the surviving firm became more productive.

But if instead the high-productivity firm died and the low-productivity one survived, the result would be ambiguous—that is, it would depend on the productivity of the entering firm, and the share of resources attracted by it. Things would worsen if in addition the entering firm had lower productivity than the surviving one. Even if the surviving firm became more productive, the result would depend on the differences in productivity between the two firms, and on the share of resources attracted by each given their investment and hiring decisions. The key point, of course, is that the change in aggregate productivity between years one and two depends on which firm dies, which one survives, and which one enters, and on the resources released by dying firms and attracted by surviving and entering firms.

Chapter 5 extends this example to the census data, taking advantage of an extremely valuable feature of the 2008 and 2013 censuses, which is that the same firm can be identified in both years and thus compared over time (that is, that these censuses have a panel structure). A first finding is that there is large entry and exit or, in other words, large "firm churning." Of the 3.6 million firms found in the 2008 census, only 2 million survived to the 2013 census, and 2 million out of the 4.1 million firms found in the 2013 census did not exist five years before.

But the main finding, very worrisome to Mexico, is that this large firm churning failed to increase productivity. There are three inter-related problems:

- The exit process does not distinguish sufficiently between high- and low-productivity firms, so many low-productivity firms survive, and many high-productivity ones die.
- There is little sorting of entering firms by productivity levels, so many low-productivity firms enter.

- There is a bias in favor of the entry of new firms and against the growth of existing firms, even if the latter have higher productivity.

To document these problems, Chapter 5 classifies firms by their position in the productivity distribution of the six-digit sector to which they pertain. Low-productivity firms are in the bottom 25th percentile; high-productivity ones in the top 25th percentile; and medium-productivity ones in between. The chapter then finds that:

- Forty-seven percent of all low-productivity firms in 2008 survived to 2013, while 43 percent of all high-productivity firms died, confirming that the exit process is flawed.
- The probability that an entering firm was a high-productivity one was 23 percent, smaller than the probability that it was a low-productivity one (27 percent), confirming in turn that the entry process is also flawed.

In addition, the chapter considers the jobs and capital destroyed by exit, or created by entry, in each segment of the productivity distribution. The critical result here is that, all in all, the processes of entry and exit did not shift the allocation of capital and labor in the direction of increased productivity.

What about firms that survived? Many changed size and type between 2008 and 2013. Surprisingly, changes from informal to formal status were almost equally offset by changes in the opposite direction. In parallel, more firms became smaller than larger. This suggests that, in the case of Mexico, the view that informal firms that survive in the market grow and formalize is mostly flawed. That said, the process of change within surviving firms was productivity-enhancing: consistently high-productivity firms (in the top 25th percentile in both years) attracted more resources than consistently low-productivity ones.

The fact that resource allocation within surviving firms moved in the direction of higher productivity is good news. Unfortunately, this news was offset by two other findings. First, surviving firms did not create any additional jobs—in fact, their employment fell. Instead, these firms grew by capital deepening. Second, surviving firms attracted only about half of all new capital investments during the period, with the other half going to entering firms, which were also responsible for all job creation.

Unfortunately, as noted above, some of the capital invested in entering firms was channeled to low-productivity ones. It would have been much better if fewer low-productivity firms had entered, and instead the same capital investments had been channeled to higher-productivity surviving firms. In other words, high-productivity surviving firms did not increase their market share as much as they should have, partly because new low-productivity firms entered and took market share from them, and partly because other low-productivity firms survived and took market share as well.

There are two implications of these results. First, Mexico's environment ***E****(L,T,M)* makes it difficult for productive firms to grow, something that is very costly to productivity. A comparison illustrates this point. Given a firm's size at birth, over a 40-year time span the average manufacturing firm in Mexico grows by a factor of two versus seven in the United States, which over time generates a 25 percent difference in productivity (Hsieh and Klenow 2014).

The second implication is that by channeling a significant share of capital investments to low-productivity firms, Mexico's environment ***E****(L,T,M)* weakens the association between more investment and higher productivity. We will return to this second implication later in this chapter, but it is worth highlighting because it provides empirical evidence to counter the view that all the country needs to do to raise productivity is to invest more. Unfortunately, it is not as simple as that.

In sum, Chapter 5 finds that the positive effects on productivity from resource reallocation within surviving firms were more than offset by the negative effects of entry and survival of low-productivity firms, and by the exit of high-productivity ones. At the end of the day, in 2013 the share of capital and labor in low-productivity firms was higher than in 2008, and the share in high-productivity firms smaller.

It is as if in Mexico the Schumpeterian process of creative destruction was countered by a parallel process of destructive creation. A vicious circle is present: misallocation induces dysfunctional firm dynamics, and dysfunctional firm dynamics serve to reproduce misallocation from one year to the next. As a result, on balance, the allocation of capital resulting from new investments, and the allocation of labor resulting from growth in the labor force, fail to increase aggregate productivity. *In the absence of misallocation, and under different firm dynamics, the same capital investments and the same labor force growth would have produced more output and a higher rate of GDP growth.*

Relation between Growth and the Level and Composition of Informality

The findings in Chapters 4 and 5 shed light on the causal relation between growth and informality. Suppose that between 2008 and 2013 Mexico's environment ***E****(L,T,M)* had evolved differently, allowing more low-productivity firms to die, reducing the obstacles to the growth of more productive surviving firms, and making the process of entry more selective. All in all, capital investments would have been channeled to more productive firms and better jobs would have been created. Under different firm dynamics, GDP would have been higher and firm informality lower at the end of the period. Looking at these hypothetical facts ex post, some would claim that growth accelerated because informality fell, while others would claim that informality fell because growth was faster. But both claims would be flawed. Growth accelerated, and informality fell, because the environment *E(L,T,M)* changed. This is just the dynamic counterpart of an earlier point: informality does not cause low productivity, and low productivity does not cause informality. Similarly, in our hypothetical counterfactual, falling informality did not cause faster growth, nor did faster growth cause falling informality. The two phenomena were the joint outcomes of a changing environment *E(L,T,M)*.

That said, suppose now that between 2008 and 2013 the environment *E(L,T,M)* had changed such that illegal and informal firms expanded while legal and informal ones contracted and formal firms stayed constant. Given the results of Chapter 4, such a change in the allocation of resources *within* the informal sector would increase productivity, and so growth would have been higher. However, in this case aggregate firm informality would be the same. Looking again ex-post at these hypothetical facts, some would claim that growth and informality are unrelated. And that argument would appear to be correct, but only superficially so, as it would miss the fact that growth increased because the composition of the informal sector changed.

The point of all this is to highlight that it is perilous to make simple associations between growth and informality in a context like Mexico's. Ignoring factor accumulation, growth increases when productivity increases, and the connection between that and informality is not direct given the large heterogeneity within the informal sector, and the fact that the formal and informal productivity distributions overlap. Moreover, the measures of informality used to make those connections are too crude. In the end, what matters is that the environment *E(L,T,M)* changes in the direction of channeling more resources to productive firms, regardless of their labels. And in this context, it is probably for the better if the search for a causal relation between growth and informality is recognized as futile. Similar remarks could be made about labor informality.

Dysfunctional Firm Dynamics and Low Human Capital Acquisition

What are the implications for workers of Mexico's dysfunctional firm dynamics? The other side of the coin of large firm churning is large firm-induced job changes—as firms exit and enter, workers transit from job to job. Chapter 5 documents that the exit of high-productivity firms caused the loss of high-productivity jobs, and the entry of low-productivity firms implied the creation of low-productivity jobs. As noted, no net jobs were created in surviving firms because these firms grew mostly by capital deepening. All in all, the census data reveal that between 2008 and 2013 job changes associated with firm churning were almost equally balanced between productivity-reducing and productivity-enhancing ones. Useless firm churning translated into useless job changes.

But this is not all. The census data underestimate the extent of firm churning in Mexico. This is because some firms entered and exited in the inter-census period, and were thus never recorded in the census, and because some firms fall outside the scope of the census (lacking fixed premises or being in localities with less than 2,500 inhabitants). While not documented here, it is difficult to think that firm churning among excluded firms contributed to increasing productivity. On the contrary, to the extent that most excluded firms are informal and legal, it is likely that such churning among them was as useless as that of their peers included in the census.

At the same time, firm churning among census-excluded firms also implies that firm-induced job changes over the period were larger than the changes that can be documented with the census data. Many workers in Mexico lose their job because the firm that employs them dies, only to find a job in another firm that will also die soon after that.

Dysfunctional Firm Dynamics and Unproductive Entrepreneurship

There is another facet of misallocation revealed by these results. The entry, at times survival with no growth, and at times exit of numerous very small low-productivity firms suggests that the individuals managing them have little entrepreneurial ability, and that their productivity could be higher if they deployed their efforts as workers in a firm. In Mexico there are many bad matches between individuals' innate abilities and their occupation. Put differently, many individuals are in the wrong occupation, devoting their time to activities for which they have little, if any, comparative advantage.

Certainly, some individuals want to try their luck as entrepreneurs and manage their own firm. Ex ante, individuals may not know, or may overestimate, their abilities as managers, and ex-post there will always be some "productivity-reducing" entry. But in Mexico this phenomenon is exacerbated because the environment $E(L,T,M)$ facilitates entry, and allows low-productivity entrants to survive, particularly under the condition of informality. It also allows high-productivity firms to die, and makes it difficult for surviving firms to grow, limiting the number of high-productivity jobs. The result could be called "unproductive entrepreneurship": the scarcity of high-productivity jobs given the scarcity of high-productivity firms, induces some individuals to be entrepreneurs, even if they do not have the talent or resources to do so. They would rather manage their own low-productivity firm than work for somebody else's low-productivity firm.

Under a different environment $E(L,T,M)$, there would be more jobs in high-productivity firms, entry would be costlier and more selective, survival would be more difficult, and individuals with relatively less entrepreneurial talent would be deterred from investing their savings and devoting their time and effort to managing their own low-productivity firms. But because the policies in Mexico that misallocate resources persist, the phenomenon just described is repeated year after year. It features limited growth of, and therefore limited jobs in, high-productivity firms; individuals opting to be self-employed or entrepreneurs managing their own very small firms rather than working as employees of larger firms; entry of and more capital and labor into new low-productivity firms rather than into the growth of existing and more productive firms; subsequent exit or survival of those low-productivity firms; and, along the way, large firm-induced job changes, but on average not better jobs. The cycle goes on and on; in the end *much movement but, really, no improvement.*

Understanding the Role Played by Human Capital

Chapter 6 challenges the view that productivity growth in Mexico has suffered because of the shortage of skilled workers. It documents substantial accumulation of human capital over the period considered, as evidenced by increases in the schooling of the labor force. It also documents that, contrary to what is at times asserted, the quality of education has improved. This is not to say that Mexico does not lag other countries, particularly other members of the OECD, or that further efforts to increase quality are unnecessary. They surely are necessary. But it is to say that the evidence clearly indicates that there has been an unambiguous increase in the country's human capital.

This finding contrasts sharply with another finding noted already: productivity growth in Mexico between 1996 and 2015 was either close to zero or negative, depending on the measure used. Taken together, these two findings highlight a key point: accumulating human capital will not automatically translate into higher productivity. It may, but there is no guarantee. Whether it does or not depends critically on the policies and institutions that determine how the improved human capital is used—that is, it depends on $E(L,T,M)$. And in Mexico's case, the sobering fact is that in the last two decades more human capital did not translate into higher productivity. Human capital was accumulated in a context of large and growing misallocation, and this impeded converting the additional human capital into higher productivity.

Indeed, if insufficient high-quality human capital were a systemic deterrent to productivity growth in Mexico, one would expect the market would signal this problem. Wages of individuals with high school or university education should rise, at least for those at the top of the wage distribution, since these are the top-notch workers, probably graduates from the best schools, and supposedly the ones most demanded. But Chapter 6 documents that wages of university graduates in the top 20 percent of the wage distribution were, in real terms, the same in 2015 as in 1996. The same is true for the wages of those in the top 10, 5, or even the top 1 percent of the distribution, and there has been a similar stagnation for high school graduates as well. There is precious little evidence that firms desperate for skilled workers have been systematically bidding up their wages.

But that is not the end of it. Rather than being a constraint to more efficient allocation of resources, Mexico's human capital suffers from misallocation. This occurs for three reasons. The first is the underutilization of the education that workers acquire prior to their entry into the labor force. Chapter 6 documents that informal firms are less intensive in educated workers than formal ones, even controlling for size. This is not because they produce very different goods—as shown, they coexist with formal firms in many narrowly defined sectors. It is because given their smaller scale, contractual arrangements, and sometimes illegal status, they use simpler techniques and processes, and because it is more difficult for them to innovate and adopt more complex technologies. As a result, they need fewer engineers, lawyers, computer programmers, and accountants. Concomitantly, the earnings of workers with these qualifications are depressed.

The second reason that Mexico's human capital suffers from misallocation is because the dysfunctional firm dynamics associated with misallocation reduce workers' opportunities to accumulate human capital once they have completed whatever schooling they invested in and are in the labor force. High firm entry and exit rates imply large firm-induced labor turnover. As seen, however, a lot of firm churning is useless from the point of view of productivity. As a result, workers transit from job to job without improvements in the quality of the jobs, as measured by the productivity of the firm that employs them. Many workers have short job spells, with few opportunities to receive training or to learn on the job.

The third reason, finally, is that to the extent that the incentives to invest in education depend on the returns that are obtained from doing so, and given that misallocation lowers these returns, Mexican workers invest less in education prior to entering the labor force. This has long-term implications for the stock of human capital available to the country.

To buttress these assertions, Chapter 6 provides empirical evidence showing that in the last two decades the returns to education in Mexico fell. This is exactly the opposite of what one would expect if human capital were constraining growth, and it is the opposite as well of what happened in the United States and other high-income countries, where the returns to education increased. Moreover, the chapter argues that the fall in the returns to education is at least in part caused by misallocation and is substantial: a simple counterfactual exercise suggests that, controlling for individual characteristics, earnings of informally employed university workers would be 29 percent higher if instead they were employed by formal firms. Misallocation is bad news for all workers, but particularly for those with more years of schooling.

Chapter 6 also documents that the returns to experience in Mexico are not only lower than in other countries of the OECD, but also lower than in Chile and Brazil, the other two Latin American countries with comparable data. In addition, the chapter documents that the returns to experience fell between 2005 and 2015. The implication of this trend is powerful: given whatever education workers acquired while young, their earnings paths once they entered the labor market were basically flat over that decade. Put differently, the returns to their experience were nil.

The combination of falling returns to education and falling returns to experience is very disconcerting. New cohorts of workers in Mexico start their careers with lower wages than their elder peers with the same education, but then fail to progress through time as their elder peers did, that is, if they progress at all. It is difficult to find a stronger indicator of the lack of opportunities for advancement caused by misallocation.

Finally, Chapter 6 reports numerical simulations showing that the impact of misallocation on workers' decisions to invest in education is substantial, and that if there were no misallocation or less of it, workers would acquire more education. As things stand, however, why stay longer in school if the market does not reward these additional efforts?

None of this is to say that education or skills are unimportant, even less that policies to improve their quality are irrelevant. Clearly, more and better education is welcome, providing benefits to society beyond the performance of the economy. But it is to say that from the point of view of productivity, over the last two decades the main problem has not been with the quality of Mexico's workers, but with the quality of the firms that employ them.

From the What to the Why

Summarizing the Main Findings

The main findings of Chapters 3 to 5 can be summarized in four "core" stylized facts that describe the manifestation of Mexico's productivity problem:

- **Stylized Fact 1**: Mexico's *E(L,T,M)* allocates too many resources to firms with non-salaried contracts relative to firms with salaried contracts, and, within the latter, to those that violate applicable labor, tax, and social insurance regulations.
- **Stylized Fact 2**: Mexico's *E(L,T,M)* induces the dispersion of production in smaller firms. One corollary of this dispersion is that too many individuals participate in economic activity as entrepreneurs, rather than as workers in firms. Another corollary is that there is too much self-employment.
- **Stylized Fact 3**: Mexico's *E(L,T,M)* favors the entry of new firms rather than the growth of existing ones, even if incumbents have higher productivity. In parallel, it allows the survival of low-productivity firms, and the exit of high-productivity ones.
- **Stylized Fact 4**: Despite important reforms to various elements of Mexico's *E(L,T,M)* over the last two decades, misallocation increased. Dysfunctional firm dynamics deepened stylized facts one and two.

In parallel, there is a critical implication of the discussion of Chapter 6: these core stylized facts do not result from human capital considerations. In other words, there are many reasons why productivity has stagnated in Mexico, but lack of educated workers is not one of them.

All of this suggests that the debate on economic growth in Mexico should focus on explaining these core stylized facts. Chapters 7 and 8 present an explanation that readers hopefully will find convincing. But even if that is not the case, it is important to separate disagreements regarding the explanation of the causes of these core stylized facts from disagreements that these facts are indeed the ones that need to be explained. In other words, even if the analysis of Chapters 7 and 8 is found lacking, this would not imply that the stylized facts found in Chapters 3 to 6 are flawed. Rather, it would imply that an alternative explanation consistent with those stylized facts needs to be proposed.

Policies and Institutions behind Misallocation

What is it in Mexico's E(L,T,M) that produces stylized facts one to four? For reasons elaborated on below, it is not feasible to provide a simple answer to this question. Many policies and institutions affect misallocation in Mexico through different transmission channels. Because complex phenomena are rarely the outcome of a single cause, one cannot identify *"the"* cause of misallocation. That said, not all policies are equally important. The ones that matter most must be those that are consistent with the four stylized facts listed above, as they are the policies and institutions at the root of Mexico's productivity problem.

Chapter 7 focuses on the subset of policies in *E(L,T,M)* that have the largest impact on the first three stylized facts, while Chapter 8 considers *changes* in those policies that can account for the fourth fact. Importantly, the discussion centers on the impact of policies on misallocation, without considering their underlying objectives or motivations (social, fiscal, and so on). While the chapters are not exhaustive, and the policies and institutions analyzed are not the only ones that matter, they are the most relevant to the core facts that need to be explained.

Misallocation and the "World of Entrepreneur-Worker Relations"

Many policies regulate how entrepreneurs and workers in Mexico associate and produce wealth. But two are central: those governing social insurance, and those governing how contracts between workers and firms can be terminated. These policies are implemented by some of Mexico's most important institutions, and their functioning is also central because they determine how in practice these policies affect workers and entrepreneurs.[10] In a nutshell, the main findings in Chapter 7 are:

- **Salaried relations between workers and entrepreneurs are implicitly taxed by the policies and institutions associated with contributory social insurance**. Despite government subsidies of approximately 0.50 percent of GDP, workers do not fully value the contributions that they, and the firms that hire them, are obligated to make. This occurs for two reasons. The first is the bundling of health insurance, retirement pensions, housing loans, disability and life insurance, child care services, and access to sport and cultural facilities in a fixed-proportion package costing approximately 30 percent of the wage. The second is because of rules that limit access to these benefits, and the underperformance of the institutions charged with delivering them. Thus, for instance, most workers saving for a pension will not qualify for one because they will not accumulate the required contribution times. For the same reason,

---

[10] The main institutions in charge of providing formal workers with social insurance and protections against the loss of employment are the Social Security Institute (Instituto Mexicano del Seguro Social – IMSS); the Housing Institute (Instituto del Fondo Nacional para la Vivienda de los Trabajadores – Infonavit); the courts adjudicating entrepreneur-worker disputes (Juntas de Conciliación y Arbitraje – JCA); and the firms administering workers' savings for retirement (Administradoras de Fondos para el Retiro – Afores). In turn, the main institutions providing social insurance benefits to informal workers are the federal and state ministries of health and social development, as well as federal and state agencies in charge of housing and day care programs.

they will not qualify for health benefits when they retire. In addition, while working they receive health services of insufficient quality, and their access to child care and other benefits is rationed. The result is that the value of a legal salaried contract to a worker is less than what the firm pays for it. The difference is equivalent to an implicit tax on salaried contracts of around 12 percent. This tax induces behavior consistent with stylized fact one.

- **Larger firms with salaried contracts are de facto taxed more than smaller ones.** This is because enforcement of social insurance contributions by IMSS and Infonavit is concentrated in larger firms. Firms with two or three or perhaps even up to six or seven workers are very unlikely to be fined if they break the law. That said, these firms will have difficulty growing, since the probability of being fined increases with size. Imperfect enforcement induces behavior consistent with stylized facts two and three.
- **Salaried relations between workers and entrepreneurs are subject to large uncertainty.** Because the law does not recognize lower demand or labor-saving technical change as "just" causes for dismissal, firms are reluctant to expand their salaried workforce when there is a positive shock, unless they consider it to be permanent. And because firms know that if they experience a negative shock they will not be able to reduce their workforce, they are reluctant to hire salaried workers to begin with in order to grow. In addition, given deficiencies in the operation of the courts adjudicating entrepreneur-worker disputes (the JCAs), firms and workers face large uncertainty and high legal costs. On the one hand, controlling for workers' tenure, settlements for dismissals can vary up to 5.5 times in granted amounts. On the other, workers are granted only approximately 30 percent of established claims, and only about 40 percent of plaintiffs granted compensation can eventually collect from the firm. These regulations induce behavior consistent with stylized facts one and three.
- **Relations between non-salaried workers and entrepreneurs are subsidized by non-contributory social insurance programs.** While the health, pension, day care, and other benefits provided by these programs have smaller scope than those provided by contributory programs, two features make them very attractive to firms and workers. First, from their perspective, they are free, since they are fully financed by government revenues. Second, there are no prerequisites for workers to access benefits other than not being formal, and firms have no obligations or responsibilities to enroll workers with IMSS or Infonavit. Nor do they face any transaction costs or risks of inspections. As a result, the value of a non-salaried

contract to a worker is higher than what the firm pays for it. In 2013, resources for these programs equaled 1.7 percent of GDP, generating an implicit subsidy of 16 percent of average earnings to non-salaried relations. This implicit subsidy induces behavior consistent with stylized fact one.

- **Relations between non-salaried workers and entrepreneurs involve no uncertainty regarding separation**. This is because non-salaried workers are not considered by law to be subordinated employees of the firm with which they are engaged. Since firms cannot be sued for "unfair" dismissal in the JCAs, they face no contingent costs from hiring, can take advantage of positive transitory shocks, and can adjust to negative shocks by changing the number of workers, or their remunerations. This regulation induces behavior consistent with stylized fact one.

- **Relations between illegally salaried workers and entrepreneurs are implicitly subsidized by non-contributory programs**. This is because the benefits of these programs extend to all workers excluded from contributory programs, regardless of whether this is because they are non-salaried, or because they are salaried but the firm that hired them is breaking the law. De facto, salaried workers get free benefits, but only if the firm hiring them does so illegally. Since only smaller firms will do this, this subsidy mostly benefits them, so long as they stay small. This situation induces behavior consistent with stylized facts two and three.

Misallocation and the "World of Taxation"

Tax policy affects many dimensions of firm and worker behavior, but the focus in Chapter 7 is only on those dimensions that impact the core facts under analysis. Of course, the effects of tax policy also depend on the institutions in charge of enforcement, as workers and entrepreneurs partly react to what the law stipulates, and partly to how they perceive it is being applied.[11] In a nutshell, the main findings are:

- **Relations between firms and salaried workers are more heavily taxed than relations between firms and non-salaried workers**. Firms' obligations with respect to the income taxes of their workers depend on the type of contract. Only when firms hire salaried workers are they obligated to withhold these taxes (commonly called payroll taxes); non-salaried workers

---

[11] The principal institution is the federal agency in charge of tax collection, the Servicio de Administración Tributaria, SAT, but state agencies also matter, since they collect the state tax on salaried employment and up until 2014 they also collected taxes on small firms benefiting from the special corporate regime (see below).

must file on their own. Because the Tax Administration Service (Servicio de Administración Tributaria – SAT) faces more obstacles collecting taxes from non-salaried workers, the result is a substantial imbalance in the distribution of the tax burden. In 2013, despite subsidies for low-wage salaried workers, the net burden from federal payroll taxes was 2.1 percent of GDP, a burden that must be absorbed by workers and entrepreneurs when they agree on a salaried contract, with no direct benefit to either party. This widens the wedge between what the firm pays and what the salaried worker gets beyond that created by workers' undervaluation of contributory social insurance benefits. In contrast, in 2013 the burden on non-salaried workers was only 0.1 percent of GDP, rather than 0.5 percent if the law were perfectly enforced. This asymmetry induces behavior consistent with stylized fact one.

- **Taxation by states increases the burden on salaried relations between firms and workers.** State governments impose taxes on salaried employment of between 2 and 3 percent of firms' wage bill, but do not tax non-salaried employment. In 2013, this payroll tax generated a burden on salaried contracts of 0.39 percent of GDP, which adds to the burden of 2.1 percent of GDP stemming from the federal payroll tax, for a total burden of 2.5 percent of GDP—and this excludes the implicit burden associated with workers' undervaluation of contributory benefits. This tax induces behavior consistent with stylized fact one.
- **Smaller firms de facto face lower labor taxes than larger firms.** Imperfect enforcement by the SAT allows smaller firms to avoid payroll taxes more than larger ones, although doing so makes it difficult for them to grow. This situation induces behavior consistent with stylized facts two and three.
- **Smaller firms face lower statutory corporate tax rates than larger ones.** This is because the corporate tax has one regime for firms whose annual revenues are below 2 million pesos (Régimen de Pequeños Contribuyentes – Repeco), and a second one, known as the general regime, for firms with revenues above that threshold. Firms are taxed at 2 percent of revenues in the Repeco but at 30 percent of profits in the general regime, a very large difference. In 2013, up to 93 percent of firms captured in the census could qualify for the Repeco, absorbing 52 percent of all labor and 25 percent of all capital of firms recorded in the census. Because its tax burden is minimal, the Repeco allows many small firms to survive even if they have low productivity, and it makes it unprofitable for high-productivity firms in the Repeco to grow. In fact, a simple numerical simulation shows that if firms under the Repeco were taxed at the general rate, their after-tax profit margins would fall

substantially, and many would not survive. A second simulation shows that for most firms close to but below the threshold, after-tax profits would fall if they expanded, since they would now be taxed under the general regime. This is very unfortunate, since these firms are substantially more productive than the average. The Repeco-general regime dichotomy induces behavior consistent with stylized facts two and three.

- **Imperfect enforcement of the Repeco implies that most firms pay less than the already low statutory burden, and some pay nothing at all**. It is estimated that in 2013, when the Repeco regime was enforced by state governments, firms paid only 3.8 percent of what they should have paid (which in any event is very little). The resulting implicit subsidy to small firms equals approximately 0.5 percent of GDP, measured relative to the already very low statutory rate. This situation induces behavior consistent with stylized facts two and three.
- **Special regimes in the value-added tax (VAT)—a zero-rate regime and an exempt regime—contribute to misallocation**. These regimes, which cover 42 percent of the base of the tax, cost 1.5 percent of GDP in foregone revenues and affect 25 percent of GDP, facilitate the survival of informal firms, and distort their sourcing decisions, inducing them to purchase intermediate inputs from other informal firms. Special regimes induce behaviors consistent with stylized facts one and two.

Misallocation and the "World of Market Conditions"

Many policies influence the functioning of markets in Mexico, but two are central to the stylized facts under discussion because they directly affect the ability of firms to grow by diversifying their ownership structure or by accessing credit: those determining how contracts are enforced, and those regulating competition. And, as before, the functioning of the institutions behind these policies is central, as entrepreneurs adjust their behavior when they perceive that the de jure and de facto rules differ.[12] The key findings in this case are:

- **Imperfect contract enforcement reduces firm size.** Firms transact at arm's length with many agents (suppliers, clients) when the institutions

---

[12] The main institutions in charge of enforcing contracts are federal and state courts, but state governments also matter because they execute courts' orders to seize assets or apply sanctions when contracts are breached. With regard to competition in product markets, including the banking sector, the key institution is the Federal Competition Commission. But the agencies in the Ministry of Finance in charge of regulating banks also matter because they determine regulatory barriers to entry.

charged with enforcing commercial contracts work well. But when they do not, firms restrict their client base or supply networks to agents that can be trusted, limiting their growth potential. Contract enforcement also impacts the ownership structure of firms. Individuals who own all the assets of a firm may be unwilling to risk more of their wealth augmenting their investments in it. At the same time, they may be unwilling to diversify ownership and bring in new shareholders to expand the size of the firm if property rights are enforced imperfectly and courts allow opportunistic behavior. For their part, minority shareholders may be deterred from investing if they think their wealth is not protected by courts. The evidence shows two facts: large variation in the quality of contract enforcement across states in Mexico, and smaller firm size when the quality of contract enforcement is low. Estimates show that if the judicial quality of all states equaled that of the best state, firm size would increase by two-thirds. In parallel, imperfect contract enforcement reduces commercial banks' incentives to lend to firms, given the costs and uncertainty associated with seizing collateral. Imperfect contract enforcement induces behavior consistent with stylized facts two and three.

- **Market concentration and imperfect contract enforcement result in too little credit to firms**. As a share of GDP, firms in other countries of the OECD get five times more credit than firms in Mexico, and firms in Chile (the only other Latin American country in that organization) get four times more. In fact, Mexico's credit-to-GDP ratio is the same as the average country in sub-Saharan Africa (López 2017). Regardless of size, most firms get no credit from commercial banks, and need to finance themselves through a mix of their own cash flow, suppliers' credit, nonbank financial intermediaries, and relatives. Credit constraints result partly from high concentration in the banking sector, and partly from an environment where contracts are imperfectly enforced given deficiencies in the operation of the registries of property, credit bureaus, and procedures for seizure and repossession of assets pledged as collateral. This situation induces behavior consistent with stylized fact three.
- **Smaller firms face greater difficulties accessing credit from commercial banks**. Insufficient competition in product markets leads to credit concentration in a few large firms in oligopolistic sectors, misallocating the scarce credit from commercial banks towards larger but not necessarily more productive firms. Most small and even medium-size firms have little or no access to commercial bank credit, even if they are very productive. Credit concentration in larger firms induces behavior consistent with stylized fact two.

Other policies and institutions also cause misallocation in Mexico, but the ones listed above are the ones that matter most because they are consistent with stylized facts one to three. And it is not surprising that they are the most important ones given their centrality to the lives of all workers and entrepreneurs. Some determine workers' after-tax earnings, access to health, pensions, housing, child care, and protections against the loss of employment. Some determine entrepreneurs' after-tax profits, or their ability to respond to transitory shocks by adjusting their workforce or accessing credit. Others determine the ability of firms to enforce contracts with suppliers, clients, and banks, or to grow by bringing in new shareholders. They also affect firms' risk of being sued in a labor court or the risk of losing market share when they comply with the law but their competitors do not.

The Joint Effects of E(L,T,M)

All these policies are present at the same time and reinforce one another. Firms may not grow because, in a context of imperfect contract enforcement, they have little access to credit and distrust bringing in new shareholders; because they are risk-averse and do not want to increase the contingent liabilities associated with hiring more salaried workers; because they are evading IMSS or SAT and do not want to increase their exposure; or because their after-tax profits would fall when growth implies changing from the Repeco to the general corporate tax regime. Similarly, there are many reasons why firms prefer non-salaried relations: because they see no point in paying the implicit tax associated with contributory social insurance programs, rather than enjoying the subsidy from non-contributory programs; because they cannot bear the federal and state payroll taxes; because they face uncertain demand and need flexibility to adjust their workforce without risks from being sued for "unfair" dismissal; and so on. Misallocation in Mexico is overdetermined, and the search for the single cause is futile.

Policy Design versus Institutional Functioning

Critically, misallocation in Mexico is inherent to the design of some policies, regardless of the functioning of the institutions behind them. Some policies discriminate by the salaried/non-salaried composition of the firm (social insurance, dismissal regulations, state payroll taxes), others by firm size (the corporate tax), and still others by the firm's sector of activity (the VAT). These policies induce misallocation even if the institutions responsible for applying them function perfectly.

This observation matters greatly for the distinction between informality and illegality, and for the often-expressed view that informality is mostly a result of imperfect enforcement. So long as its workers are non-salaried, a firm in Mexico has no obligation to engage with the IMSS or Infonavit, or to expose itself to the risk of being sued for "unfair" dismissal in a JCA. For the same reason, the firm is not subject to the state payroll tax on employment. And for the same reason again, it does not have to withhold federal payroll taxes. If the firm produces a good subject to the zero-tax regime of the VAT, it also does not have to pay any VAT on its inputs or charge VAT on its sales. In fact, the firm's sole obligation is to pay corporate income taxes, and if its revenues are below 2 million pesos, it can comply with this obligation by paying a tax of 2 percent on them, an almost negligible burden. This informal firm may be very unproductive, but it is in complete compliance with the law; moreover, its workers get free social insurance benefits. However, this unproductive firm will take away resources and market share from more productive firms with salaried workers that must comply with a very different set of policies, including paying for the social insurance of their workers, withholding their federal and state payroll taxes, and facing the risks of being sued in a labor court. Mutatis mutandis, similar observations apply to self-employed individuals running their own one-person firm.

That said, the effects of some policies on misallocation are magnified by the underperformance of the institutions in charge of applying them, whether that involves delivering social benefits, adjudicating labor disputes, collecting taxes or contributions, or enforcing contracts. In other words, the problem is partly with policy design, partly with the quality of service provision, and partly with imperfect enforcement.

Mexico's productivity problem is very complex because it has many causes; because some causes are associated with the design of policies and others with the functioning of the institutions in charge of them; because some causes span deeply sensitive aspects of the social fabric like social insurance, taxation, and protections against dismissal; because other causes are associated with concentrated market structures rooted in the country's political economy; because malfunctioning institutions, including those in charge of enforcing contracts, are sometimes under the purview of the federal government and sometimes under the purview of the states; and because in the absence of models that can provide quantitative assessments of the relative importance of each cause, there is understandably room for subjective elements of interpretation as to what elements of $E(L,T,M)$ are most important.

Why Did Misallocation Increase between 1998 and 2013?

Chapter 8 identifies changes in $E(L,T,M)$ consistent with the fourth stylized fact. Although the evidence is not systematic, and data are not always available for all years, the following changes stand out as inducing behavior consistent with this fact:

- Increasing resources for non-contributory programs from 0.4 percent of GDP in 1996 to 1.7 percent in 2015, implying in turn increasing subsidies to non-salaried and illegal salaried contracts from 3 to 16.5 percent of average earnings in the same period.
- A more-than-doubling of federal payroll taxes on salaried workers, net of subsidies, from 1.5 percent of GDP in 1996 to 3.2 percent in 2015—this while the burden of labor taxes on non-salaried workers stayed constant at 0.1 percent of GDP. In parallel, state payroll taxes on salaried employment increased from 0.17 percent of GDP in 2000 to 0.41 percent in 2015.
- Increasing evasion by firms in the Repeco, as revenues from this tax fell from 0.036 percent of GDP in 2000 to 0.022 in 2013. In parallel, the tax burden on firms in the general regime increased from 2.1 percent of GDP in 1996 to 3.1 percent in 2015.
- Deteriorating contract enforceability between 2001 and 2011 in two-thirds of the states.

These are all substantial changes indeed. To put some of them in perspective, the additional resources for non-contributory programs implied that by 2015 they absorbed four times the budget allocated to Mexico's main targeted poverty program (Progresa-Oportunidades-Prospera). Equally, the increase in payroll taxes (2 additional percentage points of GDP, summing up federal and state taxes) implied that by 2015 the federal-plus-state burden from this tax was 3.6 percent of GDP, the largest of any country in Latin America.[13] In fact, considered jointly, taxes on salaried employment and subsidies to non-salaried employment changed from 2.1 percent of GDP in 1996 to 5.3 percent in 2015, a whopping increase of 3.2 percentage points. This is a powerful force inducing workers and firms into more non-salaried or illegal salaried contracts—that is, into increased firm informality.

Other elements in Mexico's $E(L,T,M)$ also changed during this period, and although their effects cannot be quantified, their impact is also consistent with increasing misallocation. One highlighted in Chapter 8 is the 1996 legal reform modifying the scope and financing of contributory social insurance programs that, for two reasons, may have increased the implicit tax associated with these programs. This is because, first, from the point of view of workers, retirement pensions are less valuable than under the previous law, under

---

[13] In parallel, because of the extensive exemptions to the VAT, its burden measured as a share of GDP was the lowest.

which approximately 75 percent of the pension was subsidized. Second, many workers who entered the labor force after the new law came into effect will not qualify for a retirement pension, and thus will not have access to contributory health benefits when they retire, despite contributing to the health benefits of workers retired under the old law. This would be yet another force inducing workers and firms into non-salaried or illegal salaried contracts.

What about China?

The entry of China into the WTO in 2000 constituted a major shock to Mexican firms, as it represented more competition in Mexico and in the United States, the country's main export market. Chapter 8 summarizes the results of studies tracing the effects of this event in Mexico. There are two central findings. First, what could be called the "China shock" reduced formal employment in manufacturing by about 5 to 7 percent, with a similar increase in informal employment. Second, this shock was transitory, with its effects pretty much dissipating by the end of 2008.

These two findings need to be placed in the context of the broader trends towards more misallocation documented in Chapter 4. As shown there, these trends started before China entered the WTO, were also present in services and commerce, which are activities not directly affected by that event, and continued after the effect of China had receded. It can thus be concluded that while the China shock did contribute to increasing misallocation, its effect was secondary, only transitorily adding to the more powerful trends in the environment $E(L,T,M)$ identified above that permanently affected all areas of economic activity.

All in all, however, considering not only the effect of China but the broader context created by NAFTA and other trade agreements, productivity in Mexico benefited from the country's active participation in international markets, as evidenced by the lower level of misallocation in manufacturing compared to commerce and services. But that participation did not offset the negative effects of the changes in the environment $E(L,T,M)$ described above, as evidenced by the fact that misallocation in manufacturing increased in parallel to services and commerce. Put differently, misallocation in Mexico is very much a domestic phenomenon. International trade may hurt sometimes and help other times, but is not the driving force.

In Sum

The fact that misallocation increased between 1996 and 2015 is not surprising given the changes in $E(L,T,M)$ documented above. But it is nonetheless disappointing because during these two decades many reforms were carried out to improve resource allocation and increase efficiency. While these efforts are not discussed in Chapter 8, the stylized facts documented in this book—which capture the effects of all policy changes for and against efficiency—point out that the balance during these two decades was towards more misallocation. At the end of the day, when all is said and done, *total factor productivity stagnated over the period considered*.

Refocusing the Policy Discussion on Productivity and Growth

Many measures are proposed to accelerate growth in Mexico: better infrastructure, improved education, entrepreneurship programs to foster technology adoption, resources for research and development, public-private partnerships to solve coordination failures or exploit complementarities between firms, institutions to protect intellectual property rights, venture funds to facilitate firms' access to capital, new trade agreements to open more markets, government-sponsored training programs for workers, sector-specific interventions to remove bottlenecks, expanded firm credit from development banks, more direct foreign investment in technologically advanced areas, and so on.

These measures probably tackle key constraints to productivity and growth in other countries, but, at present, not in Mexico. It is not that they are flawed and should not be pursued. It is that so long as the policies and institutions that stand behind misallocation persist, the efforts invested in them will be under-rewarded. In the end, productivity is the outcome of the decisions of millions of firms responding to a complex set of incentives and constraints. The measures listed remove constraints to some firms and tilt incentives in the direction of better resource allocation. *But they combat a powerful undertow of other incentives that are continuously pushing in the opposite direction*, and that affect all firms in all sectors. Judging by the empirical evidence presented in Chapters 3 to 6, this latter set of incentives has so far had the upper hand.

Chapter 9 makes the case to refocus priorities. Without suggesting that other efforts to raise productivity and accelerate growth in Mexico be abandoned, the chapter holds that the most effective route to reach those objectives is to reform the main policies and institutions that stand behind misallocation.

This is not a book on policy reform, and Chapter 9 provides only a rough sketch of the suggested reforms to tax, labor, and social insurance policies to accelerate growth and bring prosperity to Mexico. Broadly, social insurance should not discriminate between salaried and non-salaried workers. Protection against risks that are common to all workers should be funded from the same source of revenues, and the scope and quality of services should be equal for all. Protection against risks that are specific to salaried workers should be funded from a source of revenue specific to salaried contracts. Dismissal regulations should be replaced by proper unemployment insurance, and unemployed workers should at all times have access to the common benefits of social insurance. Firms should be able to flexibly adjust their labor force to changes in output or technology. Corporate taxes should not discriminate between firms of different sizes, special tax regimes should be reconsidered, and exemptions to the VAT should be phased out, while low-income households should be compensated for the real income loss. Finally, the balance between payroll and other taxes needs to shift towards the latter.

There are, of course, many details that need elaboration, both with respect to the scope of the changes and the speed and sequence with which they should be pursued. There is certainly ample room to discuss alternatives. No option will be perfect, and trade-offs will be inevitable. But these are not the most relevant issues at this point. What at present is more relevant, and indeed critical, is to arrive at a collective understanding that Mexico's tax-cum-social insurance-cum-labor protection system is the main obstacle to faster growth, and that it is urgent to look for a better alternative.

Developing such an understanding would induce a much-needed discussion on issues that need to be at the core of efforts to accelerate growth in Mexico, including:

- The scope of social insurance, including unemployment insurance
- The appropriate role of key institutions such as the IMSS and Infonavit
- The objectives of programs to provide special support to small firms and exemptions to consumption taxes
- The balance between income, consumption, and other sources of tax revenues.

What about the Investment Rate?

Mexico's investment rate is currently around the mean of Latin American countries but below that of the fast-growing East Asian ones. Raising it would increase the country's growth rate. But its impact on productivity is less certain. The usual presumption is that more investments will raise productivity, as new capital goods embody more recent technologies. When there is little misallocation and firm dynamics are Schumpeterian, this presumption is broadly correct. As low-productivity firms die, higher-productivity surviving firms grow by investing in new equipment. In addition, because entry is more selective, entrants need to invest in the latest technologies to compete with incumbents.

As noted earlier, over the two decades considered here the investment rate in Mexico increased by about 2½ percentage points of GDP, yet productivity stagnated. As with education, the efforts made to invest more were under-rewarded. This book documents that many investment projects in Mexico were carried out because the environment $E(L,T,M)$ made them privately profitable, not because they were productive. Looking forward, Mexico does not need more investments in unproductive firms with short lives that create jobs where workers have no opportunities to learn, and where their education is under-utilized. Nor does it need more investment in longer-lived firms that are equally unproductive but stay in the market because the policy environment props them up. And finally, as things stand, it does not make much sense to invest in firms that are productive, but that will soon be expelled from the market or face obstacles to growth because the environment discriminates against them.

Moreover, one cannot separate the factors determining the volume of aggregate investment from those determining its composition. Aggregate investment is the sum of firms' investments. Some productive investment projects that could make a positive contribution to productivity are not occurring because other unproductive projects are taking market share from them. With less misallocation, more productive firms would have bigger market shares and be more profitable, and their natural response would be to increase their investments. Reducing misallocation produces a double dividend—more and better allocation of capital.

The recent reforms to allow private participation in energy and to increase competition in telecommunications will likely increase the investment rate and thus contribute to raise the growth rate. But these reforms affect only the marginal increase in investment, the additional 1 or 2 points of GDP, say, that will be invested because of them. Reducing misallocation, on the other hand, affects all investment, including the inframarginal investment occurring even in the absence of the recent reforms. Reducing misallocation is thus complementary to these reforms but operates in all sectors and on a much larger share of total resources. The gains from it are therefore bound to be larger.

First Things First

To sum up, from the point of view of growth, Mexico's most pressing challenge is not to invest more in physical capital, although doing so would surely help.

Nor is it, as Chapter 6 documents, to invest more in human capital, although of course these investments are welcome and will benefit the country. Nor is it to invest more in research, innovation, and technology adoption, even though those investments would also help growth. Mexico's main challenge is to remove the obstacles that currently under-reward these investments, and in parallel dampen the incentives to undertake them.

Reducing misallocation is not a panacea that will fix all of Mexico's problems. Nor is it a permanent source of long-term growth. But it would remove what is *at present* the main drag on the country's development. Of course, after misallocation is reduced, many challenges will remain. But these challenges would correspond to an economy that functions much better because incentives are well aligned in the direction of productivity, and because it has a social contract that better protects workers. At that point, the country's challenges would be similar to those of countries where large misallocation is not a substantive issue. Those challenges include fostering research, innovation, and technology adoption; developing public-private partnerships for worker training and vocational education; adapting education to changing technological needs; solving market failures and coordination problems between firms; and tackling the implications of advances in robotics and artificial intelligence (which will likely blur the lines between salaried and non-salaried labor and make current labor and social insurance regulations even more obsolete). All of these are critical challenges, and the temptation is to focus on them, as they are discussed intensely in many domestic and international fora. But this book argues that as critical as these challenges are, Mexico first needs to fix $E(L,T,M)$ *and* strengthen the foundations of a productive economy.

Relation to Social Policy

Some policies central to misallocation in Mexico are motivated by key social objectives, whether through taxation, social insurance, or labor regulations. In this book, however, these objectives are in the shadow. The focus all along is on the impact of policies on the behavior of workers or entrepreneurs along dimensions that impact productivity.

That said, the book indirectly suggests that some of these policies are ineffective judging from the perspective of their *own* objectives. Because workers transit from formal to informal jobs, many will not qualify for a contributory pension, even if they save for one. In fact, most workers entering the labor market after 1997, when the law was reformed, will not get a pension, will not qualify for contributory health benefits when they retire, are not always covered by disability and life insurance, and will get lower quality healthcare.[14] And because dismissal regulations cover less than half of the labor force, most workers are poorly protected from the loss of employment. Similarly, given the country's large income inequality, less than 15 cents of every peso foregone from exemptions to the VAT benefit households in the lowest three deciles of the distribution. And while the special tax regime for small firms allows these firms to survive, in many cases they also trap the individuals working in them in low-paid occupations with few prospects of improvement; and make it more difficult for higher-productivity firms to grow and eventually offer those same individuals better earning opportunities.

Thus, Mexican workers are losing doubly. They are not well protected by current policies, and at the same time these policies stand in the way of their getting more productive and better-paid jobs. As a result, *there is a large overlap in the policy reforms needed to increase productivity and the policy reforms needed to improve Mexico's welfare system*. The discussions to accelerate growth alluded to above are also, by and large, necessary to improve the mechanisms to protect all workers, and to more effectively redistribute in favor of those in need.

If these discussions take place, four points should be kept in mind:

- Taxes, social programs, and labor regulations need to be conceptualized as parts of a single incentive structure that has large implications for productivity. Ignoring those implications ends up hurting everyone.
- What matters from the point of view of social welfare is the net effect of all taxes, subsidies, labor regulations, and social programs together, not the effect of any one of them on its own.
- Any proposals to reform or create new taxes, reform or create new social programs or programs to transfer income (targeted or universal), or create or change earnings mechanisms such as raising minimum wages, need to be judged in terms of how they contribute to solving, or potentially aggravating, the country's main social and economic problem, which is widespread misallocation.
- It is indispensable that reform efforts better address the functioning of the institutions in charge of implementing policies, delivering benefits,

---

[14] Formal-informal transits imply that workers sometimes have the right to be treated at IMSS clinics and sometimes not. Doubova et al. (2018) provide a relevant example. They study the implications of these transits for patients with type 2 diabetes and find that during a three-year period, 31.7 percent of patients lost their right to healthcare. In turn, the lack of continuity in treatment is associated with a 43.2 percent decline in the quality of care and a 19.2 percent reduction in clinical outcomes.

and enforcing contracts in order to substantially narrow the gap between the de facto and de jure rules of the game.

What is needed in Mexico is recognition that good intentions are not enough, and that when labor regulations and social insurance programs induce large misallocation, what they give with one hand they take away with the other. In other words, social policy should not be an agglomeration of programs, the more the merrier. Similarly, what is needed is recognition that when tax policy induces misallocation, it reduces the size of the tax base and punishes productivity—as is the case with special tax regimes for firms or for certain consumption goods. Finally, there needs to be recognition that even the best tax and social policy design will not be good enough if the institutions supporting them malfunction.

None of the above means that Mexico should give up on its aspirations to increase social welfare and redistribute to those in need. As discussed in Chapter 9, these aspirations are embedded in the constitution, and are one of the country's great strengths. But it does mean that Mexico needs to give up on the deeply held beliefs and widespread political discourse that stand behind the policies causing misallocation and recognize that those policies have not fully delivered on those aspirations. This book by no means advocates giving up on those aspirations. But it does argue that a policy shift is indispensable to achieve them. It is all about the means, not the ends.

Where to Next?

After the lost decade of the 1980s, Mexico embarked on a program to restore growth focused on macroeconomic stability, an open trade regime, investments in human capital, promotion of domestic competition, and sector-specific reforms to increase efficiency. This program was accompanied by a substantive expansion of social spending, and provided a narrative for the country's growth strategy—that is, a where to and a why.

Chapter 9 provides a brief listing of the main achievements under this program, most of them very welcome, and some very impressive. On the other hand, on the basis of the findings in this book, the chapter also argues that this program was unable to deliver growth with social inclusion. The combination of tax, social insurance, and labor regulations deployed to increase social welfare taxed the high-productivity segment of the economy and subsidized the low-productivity segment, impeding productivity growth and thwarting rapid GDP growth. It also failed to provide workers with satisfactory levels of protection and efficient coverage against risks, while limiting their opportunities to get better paid jobs congruent with their increased schooling. Thus, over a quarter of a century later, it is not possible to assert that this program delivered the prosperity expected from it.

This does not mean that this program should be abandoned. In fact, most of its components were right on the mark, and need to be consistently pursued. But it does mean that, with the benefit of hindsight, this program had an Achilles' heel: it did not address the main reasons for large and persistent misallocation, and in fact exacerbated some of them. And, looking forward, it implies that continuing to pursue only this program will not address this shortcoming, and that prosperity will continue to elude Mexico. In other words, more of the same will not do.

A new perspective is essential, one which recognizes that entrepreneurs and workers interact in a social context, and that the quality of their interactions—the firms that they create, destroy, cultivate, or punish—depends on the quality of that context. Economic activity in the country cannot be divorced from the broader social context in which this activity takes place. Economic policy that ignores social institutions is poor economic policy, and social policy that ignores economic incentives results in a poor economy. It is difficult for inclusive growth to occur under exclusive and malfunctioning institutions.

Where to next? Mexico is far from reaching a consensus that misallocation is the reason why everybody's efforts have been under-rewarded, and that the policies and institutions here identified as standing behind it need to be reformed as the core component of a program to accelerate growth and create a prosperous country. This book tries to contribute to that consensus and provide the evidence to support it.

CHAPTER 2

Conceptual Framework

No country in the world produces with complete efficiency, and everywhere there are losses of output because resources are misallocated. Mexico is no exception. As documented in Chapter 4, Mexico suffers from a large gap between what it could produce with its existing resources and what it in fact produces—in other words, its productivity is low. More worrisome, the gap has been widening. Mexico also has many informal firms and, equally worrisome, their number has been increasing. Are there too many informal firms because productivity is low, or is productivity low because there are too many informal firms? Or are informality and low productivity manifestations of more primitive characteristics of the economy? This chapter develops a framework to discuss the relationship between misallocation, productivity, and informality in Mexico. The discussion is purposely cast at a general level. The chapters that follow provide more structure on some relations needed to make empirical estimates, but at this stage the objective is to introduce key concepts that can guide the analysis throughout.

Resources and Environment

Assume Mexico's economy is populated by a fixed number of individuals who can participate in economic activity working on their own as self-employed, working with firms as salaried or non-salaried workers (see below), or working as entrepreneurs (managing a firm with at least one worker other than the individual him or herself). Each individual I_i has a level of ability or human capital H_i, which is given by his or her years of schooling, experience, managerial talent, and so on. As a result, $I.H$ are the available human resources.[1] The economy also has capital goods resulting from previous investment efforts denoted by K, so that:

$$F = [I.H, K], \quad (2.1)$$

which reflects the available factors of production. In any year F is given, but it changes over time because of population growth, improvements in the education and abilities of individuals, or investments in physical capital.

A critical aspect for our purposes is the environment where economic activity takes place, labeled E. This environment should be thought of very broadly as summarizing the social and economic context that individuals in Mexico face when making decisions to start a business, produce, invest, work for themselves or for somebody else, take risks, and so on. Although all encompassing, it is useful to think of E as made up of three broad areas.

The first area pertains to the modalities under which entrepreneurs and workers can associate, their respective rights and obligations, and the institutions in charge of enforcing those modalities, rights, and obligations. This is labeled as the "world of entrepreneur-worker relations," and represented by L. The second area refers to the ways individuals are taxed as workers, entrepreneurs, or consumers and, correspondingly, the functioning of the institutions in charge of collecting taxes. This is the "world of taxation," symbolized by T.

The third area concerns all other policies and institutions that impact the behavior of workers and entrepreneurs and is therefore very broad. For lack of a better name, this is labeled the "world of market conditions," symbolized by M. It includes, saliently, regulations governing domestic and foreign competition and the functioning of the institutions enforcing contracts. But it also includes public sector monopolies (such as energy), mechanisms to promote public-private cooperation, subsidies to research and development (R&D), and so on.

At a very general level, the environment is symbolized by:

$$E = (L, T, M). \quad (2.2)$$

Although the policies, programs, rules, and regulations in each of the three areas are numerous, to fix ideas it is useful to list the most relevant ones in Mexico:

---

[1] $H_i \geq 1$, so $I_i.H_i$ is "effective labor" of the ith individual. (A dot is used to denote multiplication and the asterisk is kept to refer to optimal values.) At any point in time, differences in H_i across individuals reflect differences in abilities. Over time, H_i can increase as individuals acquire more education, training, and so on.

- Area $L = \{L_1, L_2, ...\}$ = {policies on social insurance for salaried and non-salaried labor; policies on salaried labor regarding duration of contracts, conditions for dismissal, minimum wages, unionization and the like; enforcement of policies; trust in courts adjudicating labor disputes}.
- Area $T = \{T_1, T_2, ...\}$ = {income taxes on firms and workers; value-added taxes; special tax regimes (by firm size, sector, or region); costs of firm registration and compliance with tax authorities; enforcement of regulations; trust in tax administration courts}.
- Area $M = \{M_1, M_2, ...\}$ = {international trade regime (including free trade agreements); domestic competition laws; conditions of access to credit from private sources, from public development banks and from government-sponsored micro-credit programs; presence of public enterprises in some sectors; policies to promote specific activities (like subsidies to output or R&D); trust in courts adjudicating competition, commercial or trade disputes}.

Two observations are relevant. First, $E(L,T,M)$ captures the regulations bearing on labor, credit, and output markets, which are critical determinants of the efficiency with which these markets operate. But, equally important, $E(L,T,M)$ captures the functioning of institutions in charge of enforcing those regulations, or providing benefits. Put differently, $E(L,T,M)$ reflects what individuals consider to be the de facto rules of the game, which can differ from the de jure rules depending on how individuals perceive the fairness and efficiency of the courts in charge of enforcing contracts and resolving disputes, or the quality of the benefits provided by the institutions charged with service delivery. Thus, $E(L,T,M)$ captures individual beliefs and valuations of benefits, trust in institutions, trust in counterparts with whom there is exchange, perceptions of risks of violating laws, perceptions of potentially corrupt behavior by public employees, and so on.[2]

Second, $E(L,T,M)$ also reflects government programs and policies to correct market failures or provide public goods, i.e., it incorporates not only the government's tax and regulatory activity, but also the degree to which it directly participates in some sector of the economy (like energy), or implements programs to promote activities considered to have positive externalities or to correct for coordination or other market failures (IDB 2015).

---

[2] Fukuyama (1995) emphasizes the critical role played by trust and social capital in the development of successful economies and the birth of the large modern firm. The relationship between trust and the size and type of firms is underemphasized in Mexico, particularly as it pertains to the presence and persistence of small firms where all the participants are relatives (family firms). As documented below, this type of firm is the most common in Mexico.

Salaried and Non-Salaried Labor

A fundamental feature of Mexico's $E(L,T,M)$ pertains to the "world of entrepreneur-worker relations." This is so because, based on longstanding constitutional mandates, labor, social insurance, and other laws make a sharp distinction between salaried and non-salaried contracts among entrepreneurs and workers (Levy 2008). *This distinction plays a vital role in this book.* Indeed, it is not possible to understand misallocation in Mexico without it. For this reason, this chapter delves into this distinction in some detail.

A salaried worker is a subordinated employee performing the tasks set by the boss/entrepreneur in the location and at the time of the boss's choosing. That worker receives a payment per unit of time (wage) regardless of the output produced. The worker must be paid at least a minimum wage and has the right to form a union and strike. Moreover, the worker can be fired by the firm only if there is a "just" cause as determined by law and interpreted by a labor tribunal. The worker can be reinstated in his or her job if fired for an "unjust" cause, with the firm paying all salaries foregone during the adjudication period. In addition, the worker is entitled to a bundled package of social insurance benefits. Firms have the obligation to enroll workers in the institutions providing these benefits and pay for them through a contribution proportional to workers' wages (contributory social insurance).[3] Firms also have the obligation to withhold workers' personal income taxes.

Non-salaried workers, on the other hand, can be associated with a firm but are not subordinated employees. Legally, they are not hired by the firm, and there is no boss/entrepreneur giving them orders. There is no minimum remuneration set by law, and remuneration takes the form of commissions, profit-sharing, or payments per unit produced or sold, and does not represent a wage per se. Workers cannot form a union, and the duration of their relationship with the firm is not regulated by law. Firms can disassociate from workers at will and face no contingent costs from separation or uncertainty from litigation. Non-salaried workers also receive social insurance benefits, but these are different in three respects from those received by salaried workers: first, their scope and quality differ; second, they are paid directly from general government revenues; and third, firms are not obligated to

---

[3] Contributory social insurance in Mexico includes health, life, work risk and disability, housing loans, day care services, sports and cultural facilities, and retirement pensions. Thus, its scope is much broader than social security in the United States or in Western Europe. There is no unemployment insurance in Mexico. However, as noted in the text, salaried workers are protected against the loss of employment by regulations on dismissal (see Chapter 7; and Levy 2008).

enroll workers in the institutions providing these benefits (non-contributory social insurance).[4]

Firms of varying sizes and in diverse activities can associate with workers under non-salaried contracts. One example is insurance companies, which can be very large, and whose sales agents get remunerated based on the value and number of policies sold. But a particularly relevant example in Mexico is firms where all the workers are relatives of each other, and where remunerations are set by profit-sharing or by implicit cultural norms. By their very nature, these firms have few people working in them, perhaps three or four, but rarely more than, say, 10. These firms, which can be labeled as "family firms," are quantitatively very important—indeed, they are by far the most common type in Mexico.

The law in Mexico treats self-employed workers as non-salaried workers, an important consideration because the border between some firms with non-salaried workers (particularly family firms) and self-employment is fuzzy. In Mexico, most firms with non-salaried contracts have roughly two workers, including the entrepreneur running the firm. Thus, the difference between those firms and a self-employed worker running a one-person firm is tenuous. The point here is that from a legal and institutional perspective, the critical difference in Mexico is not between self-employed workers and workers associated with firms, but between salaried and non-salaried workers, regardless of whether the latter are associated with a firm or work on their own.

In sum, workers' rights vary significantly depending on their contractual modality, and so do firms' responsibilities. The asymmetry between salaried and non-salaried status highlights the deep social dimension of the relation between workers and entrepreneurs. Indeed, apart from the family, it is difficult to think of a social relation in Mexico that is more important than the one between workers and entrepreneurs. And from the point of view of productivity, it is almost impossible to think of a social relation that is more important.

Observed and Potential Productivity

Determinants of Occupational Outcomes

An important determinant of the productivity of any economy is the division of individuals between those who manage firms as entrepreneurs, those who

---

[4] Non-contributory social insurance benefits in Mexico include health and life insurance, retirement pensions, day care services, and housing subsidies. As opposed to contributory social insurance, these benefits bear no relationship to workers' earnings, as they are distributed on a per capita basis. There are no benefits when the worker ends the relationship with a firm, and no contingent costs to firms from severance pay or disputes in labor courts when disassociating with non-salaried workers (see Chapter 7; and Levy 2008).

work for firms, and those who work on their own. This issue is particularly relevant for Mexico. Chapters 4 and 5 present evidence that many individuals who participate in economic activity as entrepreneurs managing very small firms do so with extremely low levels of productivity, and that aggregate productivity would be higher if some of those individuals participated instead as workers in firms.

What determines who does what? Given individuals' abilities and talents as captured by *H*, their division between entrepreneurs, workers in firms, and the self-employed depends partly on the available technology, which is the blueprint describing how goods and services are produced and is denoted by *T*, partly on the available physical capital *K*, and partly on the environment *E(L,T,M)*. Individuals' motivations are to maximize after-tax profits (if they are entrepreneurs) or, if they are workers or self-employed, maximize utility (after-tax earnings plus the value of benefits from contributory and non-contributory social insurance programs and labor protection regulations).

At a very general level, the process of deciding "who does what" can be represented by a relation:

$$\{ \boldsymbol{E}(L, T, M), \boldsymbol{T}, \boldsymbol{F}[I_i H, K] \} \longrightarrow \boldsymbol{R}, \qquad (2.3)$$

where *R* denotes the set of realizations or equilibrium outcomes. In principle, *R* provides a complete picture of how resources are allocated. Among many outcomes, it describes the following:

- Division of individuals between entrepreneurs managing firms, the self-employed, and workers in firms (and therefore how many firms exist)
- Distribution of the capital stock *K* across firms
- Size of firms (by number of workers) and their salaried/non-salaried contractual structure
- The degree of compliance with regulations in *L, T,* and *M* in *E(L,T,M)*.

In other words, relation (2.3) is an abstract representation of the very complex process by which individuals end up in this or that occupation, and firms are formed and organized. One way or another, this process occurs in all economies. What is of interest here is how this process works in Mexico, given its laws, institutions, and rules of the game—that is, given its environment *E(L,T,M)*.

Figure 2.1 provides a stylized view of the distribution of individuals across occupations in Mexico. The upper line is a list of all individuals participating in economic activity (50 million people in 2013). Each individual I_i has his or her own level of human capital H_i. The lower line depicts how individuals are

Figure 2.1: Hypothetical Distribution of Individuals across Occupations

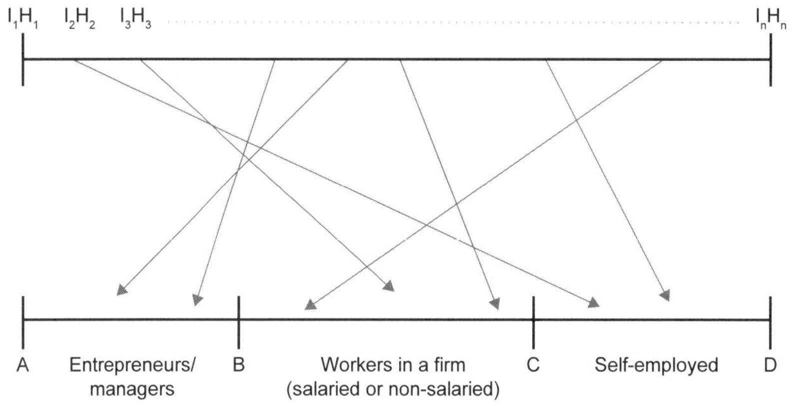

I_1H_1 I_2H_2 I_3H_3 .... I_nH_n

| A | Entrepreneurs/ managers | B | Workers in a firm (salaried or non-salaried) | C | Self-employed | D |

Source: Prepared by the author.

distributed between those who are entrepreneurs (from point A to B), those who work with a firm (from B to C), and those who work on their own (from C to D).

The location of point B matters, as it determines how many entrepreneurs there are, and thus how many firms. It matters as well where point C is, as it determines how many individuals work on their own. But given points B and C, it also matters which specific individuals are in each category. Depending on the environment $E(L,T,M)$, there may be too many entrepreneurs or too many self-employed workers (or vice versa). And even if the total numbers in each occupation are optimal, they may not be the right individuals: somebody with little entrepreneurial talent may be a manager when it would be more efficient if he or she were a worker, while a very creative individual who should be a manager is a worker. Further, maybe a self-employed individual would produce more if instead he or she worked in a firm, and maybe a worker is matched with a firm where his or her education is under-used. This discussion may seem very abstract. But Chapters 3 to 6 provide evidence to show that the process depicted in Figure 2.1 works badly in Mexico, and that the productivity costs of this phenomenon are very high.

There is another aspect of relation (2.3) that is relevant for Mexico. Consistent with the empirical evidence presented below, entrepreneurs and workers sometimes decide that it is in their best interests to break the law. Some firms fail to register with the tax authorities, others underpay their corporate taxes, and yet others do not enroll their salaried workers with the institutions providing contributory social insurance benefits. For their part, some non-salaried workers may avoid paying their income taxes. The list goes on.

Observed Productivity

The next chapter uses the available data in Mexico to describe the outcomes of relation (2.3), that is, to describe the realization set **R**. At this point we just highlight that this information, although very interesting in its own right, says very little about productivity. To examine productivity, it is necessary to associate resource allocation with how much is produced, that is, with aggregate output, denoted here by **Q**. Again, at a very general level, this is symbolized by the following relation:

$$\{ \mathbf{E}(L,T,M),\ \mathbf{T},\ \mathbf{F}[I.H, K] \} \longrightarrow \mathbf{Q}. \tag{2.4}$$

Importantly, this relation should not be interpreted as the traditional aggregate production function. On the contrary, the emphasis is on the fact that the environment **E**(L,T,M) significantly affects the level of production obtained from a fixed set of factors **F**[I.H,K] given a technology **T**.

Since we are interested in productivity, relation (2.4) is just an intermediate step. But given **Q**, it is easy to obtain an index of the efficiency with which resources are used, which naturally takes the form of a ratio of output to inputs. Because all factors of production are considered here jointly, this index measures total factor productivity, **TFP**:[5]

$$\mathbf{TFP} = \mathbf{Q}/\mathbf{F}[I.H, K]. \tag{2.5}$$

Combining relations (2.4) and (2.5), we can establish a very general relation between resources, the environment, and productivity:

$$\{ \mathbf{E}(L,T,M),\ \mathbf{T},\ \mathbf{F}[I.H, K] \} \longrightarrow \mathbf{TFP}. \tag{2.6}$$

In other words, given a technology **T**, the productivity with which Mexico's resources are used—that is, the talents and abilities of its individuals and the capital goods obtained from previous investment efforts—depends on the policies, institutions, programs, and rules of the game, symbolized by **E**(L,T,M).

The two most important relations for this book are (2.3) and (2.6). Indeed, Chapter 3 is a description of set **R**, while Chapters 4, 5, and 6 characterize

---

[5] Note that **TFP** is measured with respect to the input of "effective" labor, *I.H*. One could alternatively measure it as **TFP'** = **Q**/**F**[*I, K*], measuring labor as the number of individuals, ignoring differences in abilities. These distinctions matter. Chapter 1 pointed out that average annual total factor productivity growth between 1996 and 2015 was −0.53 percent if measured by **TFP** and 0.14 percent if measured by **TFP'**.

the relations between the size and type of firms and productivity. In turn, Chapter 7 analyzes how *E(L,T,M)* determines **TFP**, and Chapter 8 looks at how changes in *E(L,T,M)* affect changes in **TFP**. At this stage both relations are very abstract, but hopefully they will soon come alive, so to speak.

That said, there are two important observations about relations (2.3) and (2.6). First, they occur simultaneously; that is, the process that determines how individuals are divided across occupations, how many firms there are, and the size and contractual structure of those firms (i.e., relation 2.3) is the same process that determines how efficiently resources are being used (i.e., relation 2.6). They are two sides of the same coin: one cannot change without the other. If, for example, a self-employed individual decided to work for a firm, average firm size would increase and productivity would change. The economy would lose the output produced by the individual as self-employed and would gain the output produced by that individual as an employee.

The second point is that economists' understanding of these relations is incomplete. Having detailed knowledge of how these two relations operate would be the equivalent of having a complete understanding of the functioning of the human genetic code! No such knowledge exists, and the shortcomings in our knowledge appear in Chapters 7 and 8. That said, all that is needed at this stage is to see that, at a conceptual level, the process by which individuals maximize profits or utility given their human capital, the available capital goods, the environment in which they interact, and the available technology, determines the complete pattern of resource allocation in the economy and, simultaneously, its level of productivity.

Potential Productivity

In principle, there is a maximum level of output that can be obtained when all policies and regulations in the environment are set optimally, the institutions in charge of those policies and regulations work perfectly, and individuals trust those institutions. This is evidently an idealized situation that is far from the reality in Mexico (or any other country), but it is nonetheless a useful reference point.

Naturally, the maximum level of output is associated with the maximum level of total factor productivity, **TFP***. Put differently, in the optimal environment **E***(L*, T*, M*):

$$\{ \boldsymbol{E}^* (L^*, T^*, M^*),\ \boldsymbol{T},\ \boldsymbol{F}[I.H,\ K]) \} \longrightarrow \boldsymbol{TFP}^*, \tag{2.7}$$

where the asterisk refers to the optimal level of a variable.

The emphasis here is that the maximum or potential **TFP*** is defined with respect to the environment **E***(L*,T*,M*), taking as given whatever the economy's available human and capital resources are. Thus, relation (2.7) is simply a statement declaring that when the environment is optimal the economy is producing somewhere along its "production possibility frontier," but not within it. Of course, as shown in Chapters 4, 5, and 6, the relevant case for Mexico is given by relation (2.6) because its environment is far from optimal. Note that the difference between **TFP*** and **TFP** reflects the hypothetical productivity gains that could be achieved if the environment were optimal. For future reference it is useful to measure these productivity gains, PG, as:

$$PG = (\textbf{TFP*} - \textbf{TFP})/\textbf{TFP*}. \qquad (2.8)$$

Misallocation and Low Productivity

In the framework developed here, the concept of low productivity can only be interpreted as a gap between **TFP** and **TFP***. In turn, that gap can only result from misallocation. The interpretation is straightforward: the same individuals who populate the economy, with the same education and abilities, and with the same physical capital, could produce more output if the environment were different. Alternatively, because the environment is not optimal, resources are misallocated and there are productivity losses. It should be reiterated that in any economy, not only Mexico's, there will always be misallocation and productivity losses. For Mexico, the issue is whether these losses are larger or smaller than in other countries and, perhaps more importantly, whether they are diminishing or increasing over time.

In this framework, it is not possible to say that low productivity (= misallocation) is caused by low schooling or low abilities of individuals. Nor can it be argued that low productivity results from too little physical capital. Productivity refers to the efficiency with which the existing human and physical capital are used, whatever these may be. Logically one cannot use the factors of production whose productivity is being measured as the explanation for the productivity of those factors.[6]

---

[6] This does not imply that, relative to some other standard (perhaps another country, for example), human capital is "low" because the education or skills of its workers are low, or that physical capital is "low" because, again compared to another country, the amount of capital per worker is low. If human and physical capital are low, even if the environment is optimal, the total output obtained by the country will be low relative to the output obtained by individuals in another country who have the same environment and technology but more human and

A property of the equilibrium yielding the maximum level of productivity is critical for the empirical analysis in the next chapters: the marginal revenue products of capital *(MRPK)* and labor *(MRPL)* across all firms in a sector, as well as across sectors, are the same. Put differently, in the optimal environment there are no possibilities to increase the value of output by changing individuals from one occupation to another (i.e., from entrepreneur to worker, or from worker to self-employed), or capital goods or workers from one firm to another.

This property is exploited extensively in Chapters 4 and 5, and so it is useful to make it explicit. In the optimal environment:

$$MRPK^*_i = MRPK^* \text{ and } MRPL^*_i = MRPL^* \text{ for all } i, \qquad (2.9)$$

where *i* refers to the number of firms in the economy.

There is an important implication of relation (2.9): if there are differences in the marginal revenue product of capital and labor across firms, it must be because ***E**(L,T,M)* differs from ***E***(L*,T*,M*)*. This is a very useful result given that the environment ***E**(L,T,M)* is an abstract concept, not an object that can be measured. One cannot develop empirical tests to see whether ***E**(L,T,M)* differs from ***E***(L*,T*,M*)* because neither is directly observed. However, the marginal revenue product of capital and labor in each firm can be measured and compared across firms. To the extent that they are not the same, this provides indirect but very valuable evidence that indeed the environment is not optimal. Moreover, the magnitude of the differences—sometimes called wedges—in the marginal revenue products across firms can serve as a metric of the extent of misallocation that is present.

Four types of misallocation may occur:

- Across individuals, between those who are workers, those who are self-employed, and those who are entrepreneurs (so that in Figure 2.1 there are either too few or too many entrepreneurs, or too few or too many self-employed individuals)
- Across firm sizes in a sector (so that some firms attract more, or less, capital or workers than they should compared to other firms in the same sector given their underlying productivity)
- Across sectors, as some are larger or smaller than others where the value of the same resources would be lower (or higher)
- Across abilities (so individuals are not matched with firms where their abilities are fully used).

---

physical capital. But this is a different concept from the notion of low productivity associated with misallocation, which is measured for a given level of human and physical capital.

The next chapters will provide evidence on misallocation in Mexico. But before delving into numerical results, the next section discusses the role played by formality and informality.

Formality and Informality

From the point of view of productivity and misallocation, the concepts of formality and informality are unnecessary. What is essential is to have in mind that the observed occupational choices of individuals, and the observed allocations of capital and labor across firms, are the result of relation (2.3). In turn, it is important to keep in mind relation (2.6) associating the observed occupational choices and resource allocations with a level of total factor productivity. Chapter 2 could end here, and we could go on to Chapters 3, 4, 5, and 6 to see what the data say about relations (2.3) and (2.6). However, because the concepts of formality and informality are frequently present in discussions of productivity in Mexico (and elsewhere), it is necessary to discuss their relationships.

The words "formal" and "informal" are used in many settings and at times refer to different phenomena. As Guha-Khasnobis, Kanbur, and Ostrom (2006, 3) write, these words "are better thought of as a metaphor that conjures up a mental picture of whatever the user has in mind at a particular time." Different people, however, have different mental pictures, and so the metaphors formal and informal usually generate more heat than light—people are using the same words to refer to different things.

Kanbur (2009) brings much needed clarity to this context, emphasizing that formality needs to be defined with reference to the observance of a single specific policy or regulation. This is the approach followed here, selecting a specific regulation from Mexico's environment $E(L,T,M)$ as the reference point. If the regulation is observed by the worker or the firm, formality is present; if it is not, informality is present.

Inspection of Areas L, T, and M (as defined in page 57) shows that there are many policies or regulations to which reference could be made to define formality in Mexico. Consider, for instance, a specific regulation from the "world of taxation" in Area T: registration of firms with the tax authorities. In this case, firms or self-employed individuals registered with the tax authorities are formal, and those that are not are informal. This provides a clear-cut definition that can be extended to individuals who work for firms: formal workers are those employed in firms that are registered with the tax authorities.

Of course, one could choose another policy or regulation from the "world of taxation," say, formal firms are those that comply with regulations on value-added taxes. This again provides a clear-cut definition that can be extended to workers: formal workers are those employed by firms that pay their value-added taxes. Note that because there are many potential reference regulations, firms and workers can be formal or informal depending on the reference regulation chosen. In the examples above, if the firm is registered with the tax authorities but fails to pay value-added taxes, it is formal per one regulation but informal per the other. There are clearly many possibilities, and in the literature various reference regulations are used without always being clear as to which one is being alluded to, which is at times a source of confusion.[7]

We argue here that in the case of Mexico the relevant regulation is one from the "world of entrepreneur-worker relations" in relation (2.1) and, specifically, the regulation on social insurance and dismissal separating salaried from non-salaried workers. The following definition make matters precise:

Definition 1

Formal workers receive contributory social insurance benefits and are protected from dismissal; informal workers receive non-contributory social insurance benefits.

This definition is rooted in one of the most important provisions of Mexico's Constitution (Article 123), and is relevant for four reasons. The first one is social: it calls attention to the fact that workers' protection against various risks (illness, disability, death, longevity, dismissal, and so on) depends on their formal or informal status, given differences in the scope of contributory and non-contributory social insurance programs, and given that workers are protected against dismissal only when they are formally employed. The second reason is fiscal: it calls attention to the fact that the fiscal costs of social insurance programs depend on the formal-informal composition of the labor force given that, as pointed out in Chapter 7, government subsidies to contributory and non-contributory social insurance programs differ. The third reason is related to aggregate savings: since only formal workers are obligated to save for their retirement, the formal-informal composition of the labor force matters for the volume and composition of savings.

The fourth reason is the critical one from the point of view of productivity. The fact that a worker is formally employed indicates that the hiring firm both offered that worker a salaried contract and is complying with all the regulations

---

[7] An example from social life may be useful. Suppose that the reference regulation to describe "a formal man" is punctuality: formal men are those who arrive on time. Alternatively, however, the reference regulation could be wearing a tie. In this case, formal men are those who wear one, and informal ones those who do not. Now, a man who wears a tie but arrives late to his appointments is formal with respect to one regulation, but informal with respect to the other.

that apply to salaried labor. On the other hand, the fact that a worker is informally employed indicates that the worker was offered a non-salaried contract by the firm, or was offered a salaried contract but the firm is evading the regulations on salaried labor, or the worker is self-employed. These distinctions matter greatly for firm performance. Whether the firm is complying with the regulations on salaried labor may affect its access to credit from commercial banks, to training programs sponsored by the government, or to protection of its intellectual property. Whether the firm offers its workers non-salaried contracts may affect its possibilities of adopting more complex technologies or becoming larger.

Furthermore, the formal-informal distinction matters for firms' expected labor costs. When a worker is formal, in addition to the worker's wage and social insurance contributions, firms' labor costs include severance pay if the worker is fired and, potentially, the costs of litigation and settlement if the worker sues the firm for doing so. In addition, the firm must withhold the worker's federal personal income taxes and pay state payroll taxes. When the worker is informal, firms' labor costs include remunerations only if the worker is non-salaried or, if salaried, wages plus any expected penalty from breaking the law. But in both cases, the costs of non-contributory social insurance benefits are excluded, since these are paid from general revenues, and they exclude any dismissal or litigation costs.[8] Moreover, when workers are non-salaried, firms have no obligations with respect to their personal income taxes. Nor do firms pay any state payroll taxes for employing them.

Finally, the formal-informal distinction matters for how firms adjust to shocks. If there is a fall in demand, the formal firm cannot lower wages, and may not be able to reduce its workforce because the law does not recognize output adjustment as a "just" cause for dismissal. The same is true if there is labor-saving technical change. The informal firm, on the other hand, can freely adjust remunerations and the size of its workforce.

Informality, Illegality, and Types of Firms

Under the definition used here, informality and illegality are not the same. As noted, the law in Mexico exempts firms offering their workers non-salaried contracts from the requirement of enrolling them in contributory social insurance programs and from regulations on dismissal and withholding. The same is true of self-employed workers (a special case of a non-salaried relation). Thus, non-salaried workers are informal, but legally so. This contrasts with informal salaried

---

[8] Wages and remunerations will of course reflect the existence of contributory and non-contributory social insurance benefits and adjust depending on the value that workers attach to each; see Levy (2008), Antón, Hernández, and Levy (2012), and the discussion in Chapter 7.

employment, which is illegal. As shown in Chapter 3, these distinctions are empirically relevant in Mexico, and as shown in Chapters 4 and 5, they matter greatly for productivity.

While under Definition 1 workers can be unambiguously classified as formal or informal, the same is not true of firms, since they can have various combinations of salaried and non-salaried contracts (given the firm's technology), and since firms may violate contributory social insurance regulations with respect to some or all the salaried workers they hire. Thus, there are four relevant firm types, as outlined in the following definition:

Definition 2

Fully formal: *Only salaried workers, fully complying with contributory social insurance regulations*
Mixed: *Salaried and non-salaried workers, but may partly evade contributory social insurance regulations*
Informal and legal: *Only non-salaried workers*
Informal and illegal: *Only salaried workers but completely evading contributory social insurance regulations.*

Since firms in Mexico are the ones responsible for enrolling salaried workers in contributory social insurance programs, when this fails to happen the illegal act is committed by the firm, not the worker. Further, note that legality is measured with respect to contributory social insurance regulations, and not tax regulations. Thus, a firm can be fully formal under the definition used here, but still evade corporate or value-added taxes. In fact, if the reference regulation to define formality had been "compliance with value added taxes," the firm in this case would have been informal and illegal. Therefore, firms may be formal under one reference regulation and informal under another. This will be important in Chapter 7, which discusses issues of tax evasion and illustrates the need for precision in the reference regulation.[9]

Given the definition of formality used here, workers can be aggregated into formal and informal, but firms cannot be aggregated because mixed firms

---

[9] An additional issue is that contributory social insurance regulations differ across countries, so even with the same definition of informality, the classification of firms and workers into formal and informal, and legal and illegal, will differ. In particular, not all countries' laws make the distinction made in Mexico between salaried and non-salaried contracts for the purposes of social insurance obligations. Moreover, in some countries self-employed workers are obligated to participate in contributory social insurance programs. These institutional differences make intra-country comparisons of informality very difficult.

can have salaried and non-salaried workers simultaneously. Nor can the share of the capital stock that is formal and informal be accurately measured, since capital can be used in mixed firms. In consequence, the "formal sector" and the "informal sector" are not measured with precision, and neither is the share of resources (capital and labor) allocated to each.

The next definition arbitrarily defines the informal sector as consisting of those firms that are completely informal (legal or illegal) and the workers associated with them, as well as self-employed workers. The formal sector is defined as those firms that are either fully formal or mixed, and the workers associated with them. Thus, this definition of the informal sector is narrow (since there are informal workers in mixed firms). It is useful to highlight these definitions for future reference:

Definition 3

Formal sector: Fully formal + mixed firms, and the capital and workers in those firms
Informal sector: Legal + illegal informal firms, and the capital and workers in those firms + self-employed workers and the capital used by them

Note that the use of the word "sector" in Definition 3 can be confusing. The issue is that the same word is also used to refer to groupings of firms and workers producing distinct goods or services, as in the manufacturing sector or the services sector. But this is not the connotation of "sector" in Definition 3. In Mexico the formal and informal sectors are not producing different goods. On the contrary, as documented in Chapter 3, formal and informal firms overlap in very narrowly defined sectors, and the degree of overlap has increased in the last two decades.

In other words, it is of the essence to clarify that the informal sector should not be equated with the "traditional" sector, that the formal sector should not be equated with the "modern" sector, and that informal firms are not producing things that are very different from formal ones. The essential difference between them resides in the contractual and at times legal status of their workers, not in the goods or services that they produce. From this perspective, it would probably be more accurate if Definition 3 were to use the word "segment," rather than "sector," and refer to the formal and informal "segments" of Mexico's economy. But somewhat reluctantly, we defer to the traditional usage of the terms, with the critical clarification offered above.

Definitions 1, 2, and 3 give precision to the formal and informal expressions. That said, they are just that, definitions. There is no implication that some types of firms are more productive than others—this depends critically on the environment $E(L,T,M)$. In fact, for the purposes of this book we could do without these definitions and refer throughout to firms with legal salaried contracts, firms with illegal salaried contracts, and so on. And, indeed, from the point of view of productivity these expressions are better suited because they are informative of a very relevant behavioral dimension of the firm. On the other hand, the words formal and informal are extensively used in the academic literature and in policy discussions, so using them also has some advantages. This book will refer to firms using both expressions interchangeably, always with the understanding that what matters is what firms do, not how they are labeled.

Formality, Informality, and Productivity

The realization set *R* in relation (2.3) provides a list of the division of individuals across occupations, how many firms are in each sector, how much capital and how many workers are in each firm, and the contractual modalities between firms and workers (salaried/non-salaried and legal/illegal). These realizations are the data captured in the Economic Census and Employment surveys used in the next chapters. With these data, one can compute the marginal revenue product of capital and labor in each firm and sector, identify the extent to which they are equalized, measure the extent of misallocation, and compute an index of total factor productivity following relation (2.6). For all this, the concepts of formality and informality are unnecessary.

Of course, given our reference regulation to define formality, and given the data captured in the Economic Census, the formal and informal labels can be applied to firms in accordance with Definition 2 and identify how much physical capital and labor is allocated to each. In addition, the formal and informal sectors can be identified using the convention described in Definition 3. But note two points about these classifications: first, they can only be carried out once the realization set *R* is observed; and second, they provide no further information about the extent of misallocation in the economy and the underlying determinants of relations (2.3) and (2.6).

The crucial point here is that the resources allocated to the formal and informal sectors and the level of *TFP* jointly result from the maximizing behavior of individuals given an environment $E(L,T,M)$. They are two facets of the same process: one refers to relation (2.3) and one to relation (2.6). Following the discussion above, the formal and informal classifications are just useful short-hand. Instead of referring to "salaried workers legally hired by firms," we simply refer to "formal workers." Similarly, instead of referring to "firms that only have non-salaried workers," we refer to "informal and legal firms."

The point being made here can be stated differently: if Mexico's environment $E(L,T,M)$ were different, with the same technology T and the same resource endowment $F[I.H,K]$, the data observed in the Economic Censuses and the Employment Surveys would be different. That is because in a different environment, the number and size of firms, their contractual structure, the degree of illegal behavior, and so on, would differ. As a result, the number of workers and firms classified as formal or informal would differ as well. In turn, under a different $E(L,T,M)$ the wedges between the marginal revenue product of K and L across firms would also differ, as would the degree of misallocation.

Put differently, misallocation and the size of the informal sector are simultaneous outcomes of a specific environment $E(L,T,M)$; logically, neither is the cause of the other, and there is no meaningful sense in which one can say that misallocation (= low productivity) is a result of informality or, conversely, that informality results from misallocation (= low productivity). They are both the result of the same process.

There is a longstanding association between informality and low productivity. But from a strictly conceptual level, in Mexico this association is flawed. To see this, imagine that the observed environment coincides with the optimal one, so that there is no misallocation and productivity is at its maximum. It would be extremely unlikely if in this equilibrium there were no self-employed workers and no firms with non-salaried workers. This is so because there are efficiency reasons for firms to offer non-salaried contracts to workers, or for some individuals to work on their own.[10] This implies that in the productivity-maximizing equilibrium there would be, under the definitions given above, an informal sector (that is, some firms with non-salaried workers and some self-employed individuals) and, moreover, that that informal sector would be optimal from the perspective of efficient resource allocation.

The implication is clear: the simple observation that in the economy there are some firms and workers that are informal—that is, some firms that offer their workers non-salaried contracts and some workers that work on their own—cannot be taken by itself as evidence that in that economy there is misallocation. Under the definitions used here, some informality is efficient. In fact, from the point of view of productivity one could think of situations where the informal sector is too small, that is, situations where for whatever

---

[10] Psychiatrists, lawyers, artists, and doctors are individuals who often participate in economic activity as self-employed workers, as are farmers who cultivate their small plot of land, and electricians and plumbers who offer their services door to door. Insurance companies usually offer their agents non-salaried contracts, paying them commissions because these agents are working at times of their choosing and companies cannot observe their efforts. And sharecropping agreements in agriculture are sometimes optimal to share risks between landlords and tenants.

reason there are not enough firms with non-salaried contracts, and not enough individuals working on their own (perhaps, for example, the ex-Soviet Union). Thus, whether the informal sector is too large or too small from the point of view of productivity is an empirical matter.

Technology, Entrepreneur-Worker Contracts, and Firm Size

The technology of the economy, *T*, has so far been passive. But it matters for our discussion because it provides the blueprint for how goods and services are produced, and in doing so indicates the type of labor contract that is most efficient for the task at hand. When production requires a boss to coordinate the effort of many workers and dictate the time and location in which labor input is required, salaried contracts are called for (as in the assembly line of a factory). Salaried contracts are also usually more appropriate when the scale of operation is large, because the subordination of workers in a hierarchy is essential to coordinate activities, determine the division of labor inside the firm, manage inventories, and control quality.

On the other hand, non-salaried contracts are called for when the location of work is variable, effort cannot be directly observed by the firm and needs to be elicited, some risks need to be shared, or there is no need to coordinate efforts between workers. Non-salaried contracts may also be appropriate when the scale of operation is small, because the effort of everybody participating in production can be observed and remunerations assigned based on each individual's contribution to output. This contractual arrangement is particularly appropriate when workers are relatives and form a small family firm. In this case the hierarchy needed to determine the division of labor inside the firm is established by cultural norms, not written labor contracts. And, of course, this contractual arrangement is the one that applies to self-employed workers, as they are their own bosses.

These considerations suggest that even in the optimal environment $E^*(L^*,T^*,M^*)$, larger firms will have proportionately more salaried workers then smaller ones. Put differently, informal firms will be, on average, smaller than formal ones. And because this occurs in the optimal environment, there is no misallocation and no loss of productivity. Regardless of size, all firms are equally productive.

But when the environment differs from the optimal one, there is a second reason why informal firms are smaller, associated with the functioning of the institutions in charge of enforcing the laws that apply to salaried labor. If, for whatever reason, firms hiring salaried workers have incentives to break those laws, but perceive that the probabilities of detection and sanction by the authorities for doing so increase with firm size, illegal behavior will be more prevalent among smaller firms (a presumption corroborated in Chapter 4).

There are thus two separate reasons why informal firms in Mexico are smaller than formal ones.[11] The distinction between them is critical because it brings to light the fact that informality is not only a result of imperfect enforcement of the laws that apply to salaried labor, but is also a result (and in the case of Mexico, more saliently) of policies that expressly discriminate between the rights and obligations of firms and workers depending on their contractual structure. As shown in Chapter 7, even if there were perfect enforcement, the size distribution of firms would still be biased towards smallness, given that Mexico's $E(L,T,M)$ discriminates in favor of firms with non-salaried contracts.

Causation

Finally, it is important not to confuse a definition of informality derived from a regulation of the "world of entrepreneur-worker relations" in $E(L,T,M)$, on the one hand, with an assertion that this regulation is the only determinant of the size of the informal sector, on the other. By construction, the asymmetry in the regulation of salaried and non-salaried labor is the basis of the formal-informal distinction. But there is a difference between a statement about how the informal sector is defined given a specific reference regulation, and a statement that the only determinant of the observed size of that sector is that specific regulation.

Many policies can make the size of the informal sector deviate from its optimal level. For instance, the asymmetry in the scope, financing, and workers' valuation of contributory and non-contributory social insurance benefits may imply a tax on legal salaried contracts and a subsidy to non-salaried and illegal salaried contracts, inducing "too much" informality. At the same time, other regulations from the "world of entrepreneur-worker relations" can also cause too much informality. For example, the costs and uncertainties associated with dismissal regulations that apply only to salaried workers can tilt firms' decisions in favor of non-salaried contracts.

Regulations from the "world of taxation" can do the same. State payroll taxes that apply only to salaried workers create incentives in favor of

---

[11] The notion that informal firms are small to evade the tax authorities is widespread (La Porta and Schleifer 2008). In the case of Mexico, however, this notion is mostly flawed. Chapter 3 documents that even though some small informal firms are illegal, most are legal from the point of view of complying with labor and social insurance laws. And Chapter 7 documents that some small informal firms comply with their tax obligations. The small size of most informal firms in Mexico derives more from organizational and technological considerations than from reasons of tax evasion.

non-salaried relations between firms and workers. Special tax regimes for firms with sales below a certain threshold may also cause too much informality since they induce the proliferation of smaller firms, which tend to be more intensive in non-salaried contracts. Regulations from the "world of market conditions" are also relevant. Subsidized credit programs provided by development banks or microcredit programs provided by government ministries may favor small firms that typically have non-salaried contracts.

Mexico is a country where all these policies, as well as others discussed in Chapter 7, are present at the same time. Together, they result in a suboptimal distribution of individuals across occupations and in wedges in the marginal revenue products of capital and labor across firms that jointly cause misallocation and change the salaried/non-salaried and legal/illegal composition of firm-worker contracts. There is no single cause of misallocation (for example, the VAT, the corporate income tax, this or that contributory or non-contributory health, housing, or pension program, this or that credit subsidy), and for the same reason no single cause either of the observed size of the informal sector.

Analyzing the causes of misallocation is central for policy design. This analysis is complex because the list of policies that can cause it is potentially very large. To focus the analysis on the main ones, it is indispensable first to identify key stylized facts. Many useful insights can be gained by systematically analyzing the available data, and these insights help to narrow the scope of the analysis of the causes of misallocation.

Therefore, the next four chapters do not discuss causation. Rather, they center attention on providing basic stylized facts on firms and workers (Chapter 3); measuring misallocation and the characteristics of firms such as size, sector, formality status, location, and age that are associated with their productivity (Chapter 4); describing patterns of firm entry, exit, and survival, and analyzing how these patterns correlate with firms' productivity levels, size, and formality status (Chapter 5); and considering the implications of firm behavior for the allocation (or, rather, misallocation) of workers of different educational levels (Chapter 6).

Better understanding what is going on can provide clarity and direction to the more complex task of explaining why what is going so is occurring. This latter task is undertaken in Chapters 7 and 8, which discuss the available evidence linking specific components of Mexico's *E(L,T,M)* with misallocation and the salaried/non-salaried and formal/informal composition of the economy. As a result, during the next four chapters the reader is encouraged *not* to think about the specific policies or institutions in *E(L,T,M)* that are causing misallocation. Rather, the reader is encouraged to focus on what is going on, and not on why what is going on is occurring.

CHAPTER 3

Data and Descriptive Statistics

The main source of data for this book is Mexico's Economic Census, which compiles information on establishments of any size producing goods and services for the market in localities with 2,500 or more inhabitants. The census gathers data only on establishments with fixed premises, with walls and a roof. Activities carried out by street vendors or in mobile street markets or the like are excluded, which is an important omission in the case of Mexico. The census excludes governmental activities like the provision of health and social services, although it does include public enterprises in the energy sector. It also excludes activity by private organizations not engaged in production for the market (such as religious institutions, embassies, and so on). Finally, it excludes agriculture, livestock, forestry, and related activities, as well as establishments in localities with fewer than 2,500 inhabitants, even if these establishments have fixed premises and produce goods and services for the market like those produced by establishments captured in the census.

The census is gathered every five years, and this book has used those for 1998, 2003, 2008, and 2013. Establishments are classified following the North American Industrial Classification System (NAICS), and are aggregated into sectors up to the six-digit level, a very narrow aggregation that implies that establishments within a sector produce very similar goods.[1] Henceforth, when reference is made to sectors, it means the six-digit NAICS classification. When it helps the presentation, data are shown for all establishments in

---

[1] For example, sector 311820 refers to the manufacture of pasta for soups (where there were 441 establishments in 2013) and sector 315222 refers to the manufacture of shirts (742 establishments in 2013).

manufacturing together, and this is referred to as the manufacturing sector. The same is done for commerce and services. However, all computations are done at the six-digit level. For each establishment, the census gathers data on its location, value, and composition of its capital stock (equipment, buildings), value added, output, number of workers, remuneration of workers and the composition of that remuneration in terms of wages and other labor income, and payments for contributory social insurance benefits, among other variables.

The secondary source of data for this book is Mexico's Employment Survey, a household-based data set that provides a complete picture of the composition of employment including localities and activities excluded from the census. It also gathers data not contained in the census such as workers' age, gender, and schooling.

Scope of the Economic Census

Table 3.1 uses the Employment Survey to approximate the composition of total employment between 2000 and 2013.[2] For each year, the table shows the number of workers (in thousands) and the share of them that are informal by size of locality and the fixed or mobile nature of the premises where they are employed. Values in the first line refer to workers in establishments with fixed premises in localities of 2,500 or more inhabitants engaged in the same activities included in the census. They are estimated from the Employment Survey taking advantage of the fact that it records the size of the locality where workers live, and the activity performed. These values should correspond to the number of workers captured in the census. However, the match between the Economic Census and the Employment Survey is not perfect. The data from the survey refer to individuals aged 16 to 65 years of age. This filter cannot be applied to the census because it does not capture this variable. There may be other sources of differences, since the description of activities in the survey is not as detailed as in the census. That said, the differences are small: for example, in 2013 the census recorded 21.5 million workers, while the estimate here using the Employment Survey is 21.9 million.

Table 3.1 serves to make three points. First, employment captured in the census accounts for between 42 and 44 percent of total employment. In 2013, for instance, there were 21.9 million workers captured in the activities included in the census, but 15.7 million were not captured even though they

---

[2] Mexico's Employment Survey has changed in name, scope, and methodology over the last two decades, and it is not possible to compile a consistent series starting in 1998. Table 3.1 refers to all employed individuals between 16 and 65 years old.

Table 3.1: Employment by Size of Locality and Formality Status, 2000-2013
(Thousands of workers; and percent share that are informal)

	2000 Number	2000 Share Informal	2003 Number	2003 Share Informal	2008 Number	2008 Share Informal	2013 Number	2013 Share Informal
Locality > 2,500								
In census[a]	17,060	64.0	18,099	61.3	19,348	57.8	21,949	57.0
Not in census[b]	8,490	75.2	9,399	76.9	9,989	83.2	11,048	82.4
Locality < 2,500								
Activities in census[c]	3,589	71.7	3,782	72.3	4,110	77.6	4,734	76.9
Agriculture	6,522	85.1	6,036	87.5	5,945	91.5	6,615	89.8
Public sector workers	4,367	19.4	4,520	20.1	4,926	12.2	5,197	14.2
Total	40,030	54.7	41,838	56.7	44,319	58.0	49,544	58.2
Census/Total[d]	42.6		43.2		43.6		44.3	

Source: Author's calculations based on data from Mexico's Employment Survey.
[a] In establishments with fixed premises that work in activities included in the census.
[b] In activities excluded from the census or included in it but carried out in establishments with mobile premises.
[c] In fixed or mobile premises.
[d] Share of total employment captured in the census.

were engaged in the same activities. This is for two reasons: because even though they were in a locality with 2,500 or more inhabitants, they worked in an establishment without fixed premises (11 million); or because they were in a locality with less than 2,500 inhabitants, regardless of whether they worked for an establishment with fixed or mobile premises (4.7 million). Thus, despite its broad coverage, the census provides an incomplete picture of economic activity in Mexico.

The second point from Table 3.1 is that in all years, over half of all employment captured in the census is informal. The third and final point is that employment in establishments excluded from the census is substantially more informal. This, together with the fact that employment in agriculture is also mostly informal, implies that *the extent of informal economic activity captured in the census underestimates the phenomenon at the national level.*

Establishment Sample and Measurement of Capital and Labor

Table 3.2 provides descriptive statistics from the four censuses. For 2013, the census contains information on 4.2 million establishments, classified into 884 six-digit sectors. The analysis here focuses on manufacturing, nonfinancial services, and commerce.[3] In 2013, these activities represented 97 percent of all establishments in the census, 691 out of the 884 six-digit sectors, and 80 percent of employment.

The census captures firms' total outlays for labor, which are the sum of payments to workers from wages or other forms of remuneration reflecting their education and ability. To incorporate differences in human capital intensity across firms in the productivity measures, this value is used as the measure of labor input, although the total number of workers regardless of

Table 3.2: Establishments, Six-Digit Sectors, and Employment in the Economic Census

	1998	2003	2008	2013
Establishments				
Total census	2,804,984	3,005,157	3,724,019	4,230,745
Sample[a]	2,693,568	2,885,484	3,603,518	4,099,100
Sample/Census[b]	96.0	96.0	96.7	96.8
Six-digit sectors				
Total census	840	868	883	884
Total in sample (of which)	672	679	687	691
Manufacturing	278	282	283	279
Commerce	142	142	153	154
Services	252	255	251	258
Employment				
Sample/Census[b]	79.0	81.0	80.0	80.0

Source: Author's calculations based on data from Mexico's Economic Census.
[a] Manufacturing, commerce, and nonfinancial services.
[b] Percent share.

---

[3] Efforts were made to include transportation, but consistency checks found problems with the employment numbers that could not be reconciled. Mining and energy are excluded given the large presence of public enterprises, and financial services are excluded because of difficulties in the definition and measurement of value added.

their education or ability is used as a measure of the size of the establishment. In terms of the discussion of Chapter 2, labor input is measured as $H.l$, where H is given by relative wages for each schooling or ability level. (Chapter 6 discusses differences in workers' educational levels.)

An important issue with the census, mostly concentrated in smaller establishments, is that some workers appear as non-remunerated, in the sense that there is no monetary payment made by the establishment. This does not imply that these workers have no opportunity cost, of course. To account for this cost, we calculate the average pay of workers in establishments with 10 or fewer workers in the same state and six-digit sector and impute this average to non-remunerated workers in the corresponding state and sector. By concentrating on the same state, opportunity costs are calculated taking as a reference the local labor market. By concentrating on establishments of the same size and in the same six-digit sector, workers with similar abilities are considered.[4]

The census contains the value of all land, buildings, and machinery purchased by the establishment, which is referred to here as own-capital. The census also records the payments made for renting machinery and buildings, which is referred to here as rented capital. To measure more accurately the capital used by the establishment, the value of rented capital is capitalized (at a 10 percent rate) and added to the value of own-capital. In parallel, the measurement of value added is corrected, adding to it the payments made for rented capital goods. The procedure is equivalent to one where all capital goods used by the establishment are owned by it.[5]

Firms versus Establishments

The census collects information at the establishment level. The 2008 and 2013 censuses identify how many establishments belong to the same firm. Table 3.3 shows that more than 99 percent of all firms in manufacturing, commerce, and services have one establishment, and only 0.01 of a percent have more than 50 establishments. Thus, the computations performed at the establishment level essentially reflect what happens at the firm level. To

---

[4] This procedure worked in 95 percent of all cases. For the remainder, establishments aggregated into five-digit sectors were considered.

[5] As a check on the procedure, we take advantage of the fact that price deflators for capital goods for 1998–2013 are available (separately for buildings and machinery and equipment). Using these price deflators, 41.6 percent real growth can be calculated in the total capital stock of establishments in the census, which is very similar to the 43 percent growth reported in the national accounts for the same period.

Table 3.3: Firms and Establishments, 2008 and 2013
(Number of firms and establishments; percent share of firms)

	2008			2013		
	Firms	Establishments	Percent Share of Firms	Firms	Establishments	Percent Share of Firms
Firms with:						
1 establishment	3,499,327	3,499,327	99.66	3,968,711	3,968,711	99.71
2–5 establishments	9,143	25,188	0.26	8,252	22,966	0.21
6–10 establishments	1,480	11,069	0.04	1,512	11,367	0.04
11–50 establishments	1,173	24,160	0.03	1,339	28,325	0.03
51+ establishments	239	43,774	0.01	313	67,731	0.01
Total	**3,511,362**	**3,603,518**	**100.0**	**3,980,127**	**4,099,100**	**100.0**

Source: Author's calculations based on data from Mexico's Economic Census.

make results for 2008 and 2013 comparable with those for 1998 and 2003, all calculations are performed at the establishment level. However, the Appendix to this book presents the relevant calculations at the firm level for 2008 and 2013. As can be verified there, results with firm-level data are very similar to those obtained with establishment level-data. Thus, for practical purposes, the discussion here uses the terms firm and establishment interchangeably.

Size and Type Distribution of Firms, 1998–2013

The interest here is in the size distribution of establishments, given by the number of workers, and in the type distribution, given by their formality status according to Definition 2 in Chapter 2. For the size distribution, all establishments are grouped into four categories: 1–5 workers, which are labeled as very small firms; 6–10 workers, small firms; 11–50 workers, medium-size firms; and 51+ workers, large firms.

To obtain the distribution by type, an index of formality and an index of legality for each establishment are first constructed as follows:

Formality index = Establishment's contributory social insurance payments/ (wages of salaried workers + payments to non-salaried workers).
Legality index = Establishment's contributory social insurance payments/ wages of salaried workers.

The formality index considers all the firm's labor payments in the denominator, and is positive when the establishment pay for contributory social insurance, which occurs only if it hires salaried workers and enrolls at least some of them in contributory social insurance programs. If the index is zero, it is because the establishment offered only non-salaried contracts to its workers, or because it hired salaried workers but did not enroll any in contributory social insurance programs. In either case, the establishment is informal. On the other hand, the legality index considers only wage payments, and is zero only if the establishment hired all its workers without contributory social insurance coverage. If the establishment has only non-salaried workers, it is undefined.

Noting that in Mexican legislation firms' contributory social insurance payments are on average 18 percent of salaried workers' wages, these two indices are used together to classify establishments per the ranges given by Table 3.4.

With four sizes and four type categories, all establishments in each census are mapped into a four-by-four matrix, depicting the complete size/ type distribution. Table 3.5 allows for several observations on the evolution of that distribution between 1998 and 2013.[6] First, in all years, more than 90

Table 3.4: Establishment Classification by Type

Establishment Type	Index of Legality	Index of Formality
Fully formal	>= 18%	>= 18%
Informal and illegal	0%	0%
Informal and legal	Not defined	0%
Mixed	0 to 18%	0 to 18%

Source: Prepared by the author.

percent of establishments had at most five workers, and over 95 percent at most 10. At the other end, less than 1 percent had 50 or more workers. Second, the size distribution was relatively constant, although average establishment size fell from 4.4 to 4.2 workers.

Turning now to the type distribution, the first observation is that it is quite skewed in the direction of informal firms: depending on the year, between 83 and 90 percent of all establishments were informal. Next, very importantly, notice that most informal establishments were legal, a result that highlights the critical distinction between informality and illegality and, more importantly, that most firms in Mexico offer their workers non-salaried contracts.

Notice as well that as opposed to the size distribution, the type distribution changed significantly. In 1998, 16.4 percent of establishments were formal (legal and mixed), but by 2013, this share had fallen to 9.9 percent. The flip side is a growing share of informal establishments, legal and illegal. This growth has been mostly at the expense of mixed establishments, reflecting the fact that firms that were mixing salaried with non-salaried workers have shifted their contract mix in the direction of non-salaried ones (and, to a lesser extent, illegal salaried ones).

The next observation relates to differences in average size across firm types. In accordance with the discussion of Chapter 2, formal firms (legal and mixed) are substantially larger than informal ones. But note the differences within informal firms: those with non-salaried contracts (i.e., legal ones) are significantly smaller than those with salaried contracts (i.e., illegal ones). Lastly, the fact that legal informal establishments have about two workers each underlines the short distance that separates them from the one-person firm of the self-employed.

---

[6] Table A.1 in the Appendix to this volume compares the size and type distribution of firms in 2008 and 2013 and shows that they are very similar to the ones presented here at the establishment level for those years.

Table 3.5: Establishment Distribution by Type and Size, 1998–2013
(Percent shares and average size)

		1998 Share	1998 Average Size[a]	2003 Share	2003 Average Size[a]	2008 Share	2008 Average Size[a]	2013 Share	2013 Average Size[a]
Size	1–5	91.3	1.7	90.8	1.9	90.0	2.0	91.6	1.8
	6–10	4.4	7.4	4.9	7.3	5.7	7.3	4.5	7.4
	11–50	3.4	20.6	3.4	20.9	3.4	20.1	3.1	20.8
	51+	0.8	206.9	0.8	210.2	0.8	200.6	0.7	210.6
	All establishments	100.0	4.4	100.0	4.5	100.0	4.5	100.0	4.2
Type	Fully formal	4.6	19.6	4.0	33.1	3.0	27.8	4.2	22.1
	Mixed	11.8	15.2	8.4	13.7	6.7	16.2	5.7	16.5
	Informal Legal	68.1	1.6	68.7	2.0	67.7	2.4	72.8	2.3
	Informal Illegal	15.4	3.4	18.9	3.7	22.6	4.0	17.2	3.9
	All establishments	100.0	4.4	100.0	4.5	100.0	4.5	100.0	4.2

Source: Author's calculations based on data from Mexico's Economic Census.
[a] Workers per establishment.

Resource Allocation

Table 3.6 presents basic stylized facts on the allocation of capital and labor in the establishments captured in the 2013 census.[7] The upper block reports the distribution of all establishments by size, measured by the number of workers and by type. The middle block reports the distribution of all workers by the size and the type of the establishment in which they work. The lower block reports the same for capital. Starting with the distribution of employment, note that informal establishments, legal and illegal, account for over 55 percent of total employment. Note also that the largest share of informal

Table 3.6: Resource Allocation by Establishment Size and Type, 2013
(Percent shares)

	Fully Formal	Mixed	Informal and Legal	Informal and Illegal	Total
Establishments[a]					
1–5	1.98	3.46	71.16	14.99	91.58
6–10	0.92	1.14	0.94	1.54	4.55
11–50	1.02	0.94	0.48	0.68	3.12
51+	0.27	0.24	0.20	0.04	0.75
Total	4.19	5.77	72.79	17.26	100.0
Workers[b]					
1–5	1.39	2.50	26.84	8.96	39.69
6–10	1.65	2.02	1.57	2.66	7.90
11–50	5.19	4.64	2.46	3.03	15.31
51+	13.64	13.31	8.82	1.33	37.10
Total	21.86	22.47	39.69	15.98	100.0
Capital[c]					
1–5	1.95	2.32	9.86	4.60	18.73
6–10	2.14	1.65	1.49	1.43	6.71
11–50	5.38	3.84	4.18	1.86	15.26
51+	20.62	19.41	17.90	1.37	59.29
Total	30.10	27.22	33.44	9.25	100.0

Source: Author's calculations based on data from Mexico's Economic Census.
[a] Total = 4.1 million establishments.
[b] Total = 17.4 million workers.
[c] Total = 5,998 million 2013 pesos.

---

[7] Table A.2 in the Appendix to this volume shows almost equivalent results at the firm level.

employment is non-salaried (i.e., it occurs in informal and legal firms). This confirms, from the side of workers, that the non-salaried contract is the most common contractual arrangement between firms and workers in Mexico, on the one hand, and that most informal employment is legal, on the other.

Next, note that the share of employment in very small informal and legal establishments is, by far, the largest. In fact, employment in these establishments, by itself, exceeds employment in fully formal establishments of all sizes. Put differently, even though these establishments have on average only 2.3 workers each, such that at the individual level they would hardly matter for productivity, their very large number ends up absorbing over a quarter of the labor force in manufacturing, commerce, and services captured in the census, a magnitude that clearly matters for productivity.

The importance of very small establishments for resource allocation is confirmed by noting that all of them together (formal and informal) account for a larger share of employment than large establishments of all types (39.7 versus 37.1 percent). This difference is in fact much larger when account is taken of firms excluded from the census, where, as discussed below, employment occurs mostly in very small firms.

Consider now the allocation of capital. Formal establishments of all sizes (both fully formal and mixed) account for 57 percent of the capital stock. This share is higher than their share of employment (44 percent), indicating that they are more capital-intensive than informal establishments. On the other hand, the fact that informal establishments (legal and illegal) of all sizes account for almost 43 percent of the capital stock indicates that, contrary to what is commonly thought, the informal sector attracts a very relevant share of Mexico's capital investments.

Very small informal establishments (legal and illegal) are the least capital-intensive. Each absorbs very little capital, but, again, because there are so many of them, when added up they end up attracting a non-negligible share of the capital stock, 15 percent. Focusing on size, very small establishments of all types (formal and informal) account for almost 19 percent of the capital stock, lower than their share of employment (39 percent). This indicates that they are less capital-intensive than large establishments. Finally, note that there are significant differences in capital intensity within large establishments. Formal ones are more capital-intensive than informal ones, and within informal establishments, illegal ones are more capital-intensive than legal ones.

How did resource allocation change between 1998 and 2013? Table 3.7 helps to answer this question. As in Table 3.6, establishments are classified by size by the number of workers, and workers and capital are in turn classified by the size of the establishment where they are employed or used. Focusing initially on the aggregates, one notes that the number of establishments

Table 3.7: Changes in Resource Allocation, 1998-2013
(Accumulated real growth, percent)

	Fully Formal	Mixed	Informal and Legal	Informal and Illegal	Total
Establishments					
1–5	9.05	−26.17	60.66	62.06	**52.55**
6–10	75.95	−21.04	190.62	154.28	**57.00**
11–50	100.22	−30.00	259.34	184.92	**40.40**
51+	54.68	−29.09	642.29	82.12	**34.00**
Total	**38.68**	**−26.00**	**62.55**	**70.53**	**52.18**
Workers					
1–5	21.46	−24.09	75.99	76.13	**60.17**
6–10	75.95	−20.97	181.25	156.88	**55.29**
11–50	104.19	−29.95	300.32	193.55	**41.71**
51+	46.00	−14.06	604.00	19.06	**36.40**
Total	**56.59**	**−19.64**	**124.55**	**93.14**	**47.34**
Capital					
1–5	55.86	−28.78	31.78	71.20	**27.60**
6–10	175.04	−31.34	274.00	184.24	**64.17**
11–50	203.71	−33.61	462.38	163.67	**68.54**
51+	39.11	−12.84	573.01	−54.99	**38.57**
Total	**61.10**	**−19.26**	**196.27**	**33.44**	**41.61**

Source: Author's calculations based on data from Mexico's Economic Census.

increased more than employment, reflecting the already-mentioned reduction in average establishment size. There is a notable increase in the number of informal establishments, and an equally noticeable fall in the number of mixed establishments. All in all, there is a clear and significant trend towards more firm informality.

Changes in the allocation of labor provide further insights. Employment in fully formal establishments and in both types of informal establishments grew more than overall employment, a reflection of the drastic decline in employment in mixed firms. Put differently, the composition of employment became more polarized, although on average there was a shift towards more informality. This shift is also reflected in the fact that employment in smaller establishments grew substantially more than in larger ones. Note that employment in informal and illegal establishments also grew more than the average, indicating an increase in firms' illegal behavior.

The allocation of capital also became more polarized. In fully formal establishments it grew more than employment, indicating that these establishments became more capital-intensive. Note the differences in the evolution of capital between very small informal establishments: in illegal ones it grew substantially more than in legal ones. Since employment and the number of establishments grew at similar rates in both cases, the differences in capital intensity widened.

Firm Incorporation

The census records whether firms are incorporated as self-standing legal entities, implying that the assets of the firm are separated from the assets of its owners. Table 3.8 captures the share of firms in each size and type category incorporated under any of the legal categories available in Mexican law.[8] Unsurprisingly, more than 95 percent of large establishments are incorporated, regardless of whether they are formal or informal. Rates of incorporation fall with firm size, but it is still the case that more than half of all medium-size formal or informal firms are incorporated. This highlights the perils of making a one-to-one association between firm informality with lack of firm registration or incorporation. The picture is more nuanced, and many informal firms are incorporated.

That said, there are sharp differences in incorporation rates between very small formal and informal firms. While more than a third of fully formal firms are incorporated, less than 2 percent of informal and legal firms are.

Table 3.8: Share of Firms Incorporated as a Legal Entity
(Percent shares)

	Fully Formal	Mixed	Informal and Legal	Informal and Illegal
Firms with 1–5 workers	35.7	20.7	1.8	5.9
Firms with 6–10 workers	58.6	42.5	53.7	25.4
Firms with 11–50 workers	78.7	71.2	90.1	58.5
Firms with 51+ workers	97.7	96.7	99.8	94.6

Source: Author's calculations based on data from Mexico's Economic Census.

---

[8] Mexico's corporate law contemplates various alternatives, from firms that issue stocks to those organized as cooperatives. The numbers in Table 3.8 refer to any of these alternatives, all of which have in common the fact that the firm is registered and has a separate legal standing from its owners.

Although this cannot be verified directly from the census data, the presumption is that these latter firms are family firms (in the sense mentioned in Chapter 2, where workers and owners are relatives). The presumption that these firms are family firms is strengthened by the fact that they account for most workers captured in the census without monetary remuneration. In some cases, production may be taking place in the same premises where the household members live. But regardless of the location of production, the assets of the family and the firm are merged. The shareholders of these unincorporated firms—one may call them proprietorships—are also the firm workers.

Firms and Employment beyond the Census

The census leaves out significant private economic activity relevant to the study of misallocation in Mexico. As was shown in Table 3.1, in 2013 firms captured in the census accounted for 21.9 million workers. But in the same year, excluding the public sector and agriculture and other rural activities, there were an additional 15.7 million workers producing goods and services for the market: 11 million in localities of more than 2,500 inhabitants, and 4.7 million in localities below that threshold. Some of these workers were involved in activities outside the scope of the census, including delivery of health, education, and social services, representations of foreign governments, religious services, and the like. However, the majority were employed by firms producing goods and services competing with firms captured in the census. The firms employing these workers were excluded from the census because their activities were carried out in mobile premises, or in localities of less than 2,500 inhabitants, even if they produced in fixed premises.

This section tries to give a sense of the magnitude of nonagricultural economic activity excluded from the census. This activity is very heterogeneous. It includes self-employed street vendors selling goods (newspapers, candy, umbrellas) and services (parking and cleaning cars, shining shoes) as well as self-employed individuals working home-to-home as domestic servants or gardeners, or performing small house repairs (plumbing, and so on). But it also includes firms that carry out activity on semi-fixed premises on stands that are literally on the sidewalks of the main avenues and streets of Mexico's cities, selling clothing, medicines, furniture, electronic goods, and custom jewelry, among many other items; delivering services like car repairs, haircuts; preparing a myriad of foodstuffs; or even producing simple manufactures like apparel and furniture. And it includes firms selling produce, foodstuffs, home cleaning materials, shoes, clothing, electronics, medicines, and other products in markets that move daily within a given city area with a fixed schedule (so-called *tianguis*, the Nahuatl word for market). These undertakings usually employ two to three workers each, but some can be larger, as evidenced by the data (and by casual inspection).

Because the source of data is the Employment Survey, and because in the survey the unit of observation is the worker and not the firm, the number, size, and types of firms excluded from the census cannot be identified. However, the survey contains two valuable pieces of information to make a reasonable approximation: the formal and informal status of workers, and the size of the establishment that employs them. Table 3.9 classifies workers excluded from the 2013 census using these two criteria.

Table 3.9: Workers Excluded from the Economic Census, 2013
(Millions)

	Self-employed	1–5 Workers	6–10 Workers	11–50 Workers	51+ Workers	Total
Formal	0.1	0.2	0.2	0.8	1.4	2.7
Informal	5.4	6.5	0.7	0.4	0.0	13.0
Total	5.5	6.7	0.9	1.2	1.4	15.7

Source: Author's calculations based on data from Mexico's Employment Survey.

Two assumptions are now made: first, that all formal workers, regardless of the size of the establishment where they work, are allocated to the activities outside the scope of the census mentioned above (health and educational services, religious services, embassies, and so on); and second, that all informal workers associated with a firm produce goods and services in manufacturing, commerce, and services.[9] Under these assumptions, 7.6 million workers, excluding the self-employed, were employed in these three broadly defined sectors both in establishments with mobile premises excluded from the census in localities of more than 2,500 inhabitants, and in establishments on fixed or mobile premises in localities with less than 2,500 inhabitants. This is a considerable number given that 17.4 million workers were employed in the establishments captured in the census in these same broadly defined sectors. For every worker in a firm captured in the census in manufacturing, commerce, and services, there were approximately 0.4 workers in firms excluded from the census in those same sectors.

For the reasons previously described, it is not possible to determine the number of firms excluded from the census. However, to give a sense of the orders of magnitude, the midpoint size is assumed in each cell in Table 3.9; that is, the assumption is that the 6.5 million informal workers in establishments

---

[9] The other activity where informal workers participate is transportation. However, most of these workers would be self-employed, so our assumptions seem reasonable.

with up to five workers were employed in firms with 2.5 workers each; that the 700,000 informal workers in firms with six to 10 workers were employed in firms with 7.5 workers each; and that the 400,000 workers in firms with 11 to 50 workers were employed in firms with 30 workers each.[10] Under these assumptions, in 2013 there were 2.6 million firms with up to five workers, 900,000 firms with six to 10 workers, and 100,000 firms with 11 to 50 workers, for a total of 2.61 million firms excluded from the census. This compares with 4.1 million firms captured in the census in the same activities.

While these figures are approximations, they nevertheless suffice to call attention to the fact that the size and type distribution of firms associated with Mexico's *E(L,T,M)* is significantly more tilted in the direction of small and informal firms than was indicated by Tables 3.5 and 3.6. In 2013, the average size of a firm, in terms of workers, in manufacturing, services, and commerce in Mexico, considering firms excluded from the census, was 3.7 (rather than 4.2 in Table 3.5). Moreover, 44 percent of all workers associated with firms in manufacturing, commerce, and services were employed in establishments of up to five workers (as opposed to 39 percent in Table 3.6). Thus, the picture that emerges from the combined Economic Census and Employment Survey data is that of an economy where *close to half of all workers in manufacturing, services, and commerce are employed in firms with at most five workers*.

It is illustrative to provide a few statistics to describe changes in the composition of the nonagricultural labor force between 2000 and 2013 (excluding, as before, public sector workers). As was shown in Table 3.1, out of 29.1 million workers in 2000, 52 percent were employed in informal firms, while in 2013, out of 37.7 million workers, 58 percent were employed in informal firms. In 2000, 49 percent of all workers were self-employed or worked in establishments (of any type and in any activity) of up to five workers, while in 2013, 55 percent of workers fell into this category.

Presence of Informal Firms across Localities of Different Sizes

Are informal firms concentrated mostly in smaller urban areas, but not present in Mexico's larger cities? Or are the patterns of firm informality similar between Mexico's larger and more modern cities and its smaller and more traditional cities? These

---

[10] This compares with an average size of 1.8 workers for firms captured in the census with 1–5 workers, 7.4 for firms with 6–10 workers, and 20.8 for firms with 11–50 workers (Table 3.5). Put differently, the assumption here is conservative in the sense that the average size of firms excluded from the census exceeds that of those included in the census. If one were to assume the same census size, the number of firms excluded from the census would be larger.

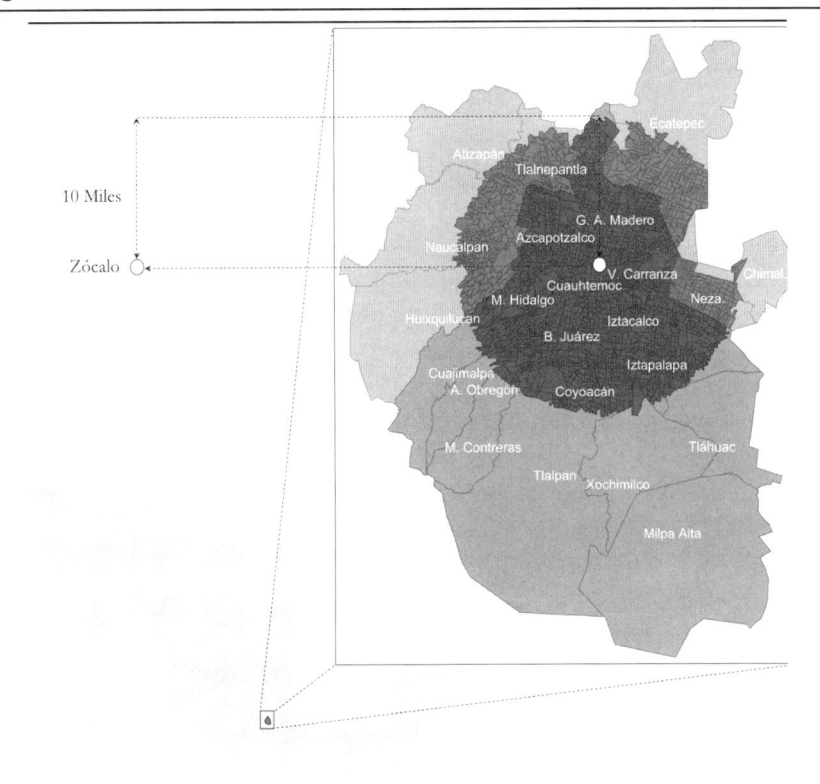

Figure 3.1: "The Circle" Around the Zócalo Central Square

Source: Prepared by the author based on data from Mexico's Economic Census.

questions are relevant because one could argue that there may be a dimension of firm informality associated with the size of localities hidden in the aggregate numbers.

Answering these questions again involves focusing on the census data and comparing the size and type distribution of firms between the most urbanized and densely populated area of Mexico, Mexico City, and all other localities captured in the census. To perform this comparison, we take advantage of the fact that the census provides very detailed information on the location of each establishment.[11] Figure 3.1 shows a circle with a radius of 10

---

[11] Mexico's statistical institute divides all localities with 2,500 or more inhabitants in Mexico into 56,193 Basic Geo-Statistical Areas (Areas Geo-Estadísticas Básicas – AGEBs). These areas are substantially smaller than the 32 states and the 2,438 municipalities into which Mexico is divided for political and administrative purposes. AGEBs are constructed based on population density and are the basic unit of analysis for data-gathering purposes in urban areas. The Economic Census registers the AGEB where each establishment is located.

Table 3.10: Establishments and Resources in Mexico and the Mexico City "Circle," 2013
(Number of establishments and percent shares)

	Mexico City "Circle"	Rest of Mexico	All of Mexico
Establishments	443,771	3,655,329	4,099,100
Share of capital	14.7	85.3	100
Share of labor	19.9	80.1	100
Type distribution			
Fully formal	4.8	4.1	4.2
Informal and legal	68.3	73.3	72.8
Mixed	6.3	5.7	5.8
Informal and illegal	20.6	16.9	17.3
Total	**100.0**	**100.0**	**100.0**
Size distribution			
1–5 workers	88.2	92.0	91.6
6–10 workers	5.8	4.4	4.5
11–50 workers	4.8	2.9	3.1
51+ workers	1.3	0.7	0.7
Total	**100.0**	**100.0**	**100.0**

Source: Author's calculations based on data from Mexico's Economic Census.

miles centered in Mexico City's central square, the Zócalo, where the National Cathedral and the National Palace are located. This area, which for short is labeled here as "the circle," encompasses parts of Mexico City (in darker grey) and parts of the bordering State of Mexico (in lighter grey). The area to the right missing from the circle corresponds to Mexico's City new airport (under construction). This circle is the largest and most densely populated urban conglomerate in the country. The most recent population census available, for 2010, indicates that 86.9 million people lived in localities of 2,500 inhabitants or more, of which 9.7 million (11.1 percent) were in the circle. Although not documented here, the circle has among the best, if not the best, transport and telecommunications infrastructure in Mexico, and the broadest access to banking and financial services and to courts and tribunals for the settlement of commercial, credit, and labor disputes. It is the heart of economic activity in the country and, of course, its political center.

Table 3.10 compares the size and type distribution of firms and resource allocation between the circle and all other localities included in the census. Of the nearly 4.1 million establishments captured in the 2013 census, 443,771 were in the circle (10.8 percent). These establishments, in turn, account for 19.9 percent of employment captured in the census, and 14.7 percent of the capital stock. As expected, average firm size in the circle is larger than in the rest of the country: 7.8 versus 3.8 workers per establishment. In the circle, 6.1 percent of all establishments have 11 or more workers; in the rest of the country only 3.6 percent do. That said, it is still the case that the vast majority of establishments inside and outside the circle are small or very small (94 and 96.4 percent, respectively).

The most revealing feature of Table 3.10, however, is that the type distribution of firms in the circle is almost the same as in the rest of the country. Of all establishments in the circle, 88.9 percent are informal, in contrast to 90.2 for all localities outside of the circle. Interestingly, while the share of firm informality is almost the same, the composition differs. There are proportionately fewer informal and legal firms in the circle (probably fewer family firms) and, correspondingly, more informal and illegal firms.

It is important to note that the fact that *firm* informality is the same across localities of diverse sizes does not imply that *labor* informality is also similar. Table 3.10 refers only to establishments captured in the census, and localities probably differ in the share of firms excluded and included in the census. Furthermore, Table 3.10 refers only to manufacturing, commerce, and services, and localities differ in the share of the labor force dedicated to agriculture and other rural activities. As a result, labor informality differs across regions and, broadly, is higher in the southern states of Mexico. That said, the critical result for purposes here is that, at least with respect to firms captured in the census, firm informality is not associated with the size of a locality, with remoteness from larger urban conglomerates, or with differences in access to physical infrastructure or courts and administrative tribunals. Put differently, Mexico's environment **$E(L,T,M)$** has a systemic effect on firms' and workers' contractual agreements regardless of the size of the locality where these agreements take place.

Firms and Resource Allocation across Sectors

This section explores the patterns of firm informality across manufacturing, commerce, and services. Are firm size and firm types the same across these broadly defined sectors? Is the increase in aggregate firm informality concentrated in some sectors, or is it a broad-based phenomenon?

Table 3.11 provides information to answer these questions. To facilitate its reading, the table is divided into three blocks, for manufacturing, commerce and services, respectively. In the upper part of each block, the distribution of aggregate resources is measured across the three broadly defined sectors. The

Table 3.11: Resource Allocation and Measures of Firm Informality, 1998-2013
(Percent shares, average firm size, and number of sectors)

	1998	2003	2008	2013
Manufacturing				
Share of total labor	35.9	30.7	27.8	28.3
Share of total capital	45.9	43.5	37.6	40.3
Share of total value added	45.0	42.4	49.0	45.2
Average firm size[a]	12.5	12.4	10.4	10.1
Six-digit sectors	278	282	283	279
Share of sectors with >50% informal firms	34.5	39.0	51.5	51.2
Share of labor in informal firms	15.1	23.2	34.1	34.8
Share of capital in informal firms	16.5	15.2	27.7	32.0
Commerce				
Share of total labor	33.9	37.9	37.8	36.7
Share of total capital	22.7	26.2	27.9	30.5
Share of total value added	30.9	31.3	24.5	27.8
Average firm size[a]	2.8	3.1	3.3	3.1
Six-digit sectors	142	142	153	154
Share of sectors with >50% informal firms	61.9	71.8	90.1	81.1
Share of labor in informal firms	52.7	58.5	70.0	68.5
Share of capital in informal firms	31.4	41.3	57.1	57.5
Services				
Share of total labor	30.1	31.2	34.4	34.9
Share of total capital	31.3	30.2	34.4	29.1
Share of total value added	24.0	26.2	26.4	27.0
Average firm size[a]	3.9	4.2	4.2	3.8
Six-digit sectors	252	255	251	258
Share of sectors with >50% informal firms	66.2	82.6	87.2	87.9
Share of labor in informal firms	45.9	52.3	62.0	56.1
Share of capital in informal firms	35.4	40.0	46.2	41.9

Source: Author's calculations based on data from Mexico's Economic Census.
[a] Workers per firm.

key point to make here is that over time manufacturing has attracted a smaller share of resources: in 1998, it absorbed 35.9 percent of all labor and 45.9 percent of the capital stock, but by 2013 those shares had fallen to 28.3 percent and 40.3 percent, respectively. Resources have shifted towards commerce and services.

The lower part of each block provides three measures of firm informality. Two are very direct: the share of labor and the share of capital in informal firms (legal and illegal). The third focuses on the presence of informal firms over six-digit sectors in order to determine whether firm informality is concentrated in a few six-digit sectors or spread over a wider spectrum. More precisely, the share of informal firms in the total number of firms in each six-digit sector in manufacturing is first measured. The share of all six-digit sectors in manufacturing where informal firms are a majority (50 percent or more of all firms) is then measured. This procedure is repeated separately for commerce and services.

Inspection of Table 3.11 shows two results. First, by any of these three measures, firm informality in manufacturing is substantially lower than in commerce and services. That said, second, by any measure, firm informality has increased in all three broadly defined sectors. For example, in manufacturing, informal firms accounted for 15.1 percent of workers and 16.5 percent of the capital stock in 1998; by 2013 these figures were 34.8 and 32 percent, respectively. Moreover, this increase occurred over a larger number of six-digit sectors. In 1998, informal firms were a majority in 34.5 percent of all six-digit sectors in manufacturing; by 2013 that share increased to 51.2. Mutatis mutandis, comparable results are observed in commerce and services.

Table 3.11 corroborates a point made in Chapter 2: informality in Mexico is not confined to a small number of "traditional" sectors (say, handicrafts or food preparation), or to a small number of activities in services and commerce. Formal and informal firms coexist in a large and growing number of activities.

Finally, note that while average firm size in manufacturing is larger than in commerce and services, it fell between 1998 and 2013. This is important because the fact that manufacturing is less informal and has a higher average firm size than commerce or services could suggest that the aggregate increase in firm informality and the fall in average firm size pointed out in Table 3.5 result from the diminishing importance of manufacturing in resource allocation. But this suggestion is flawed. While there are differences in the *level* of firm informality between manufacturing, on the one hand, and commerce and services, on the other, the *trend* towards increased firm informality is common to all three sectors.

CHAPTER 4

Measuring and Characterizing Misallocation

The stylized facts described in Chapter 3 can be usefully related to the discussion of Chapter 2. Although incomplete because they refer mostly to establishments in manufacturing, commerce, and services captured in the census, these facts are the outcome of relation (2.3) in Chapter 2 linking the environment *E(L,T,M)*, technology *T*, and factors of production *F[I.H,K]* with the set of realizations *R*. Tables 3.4 to 3.11 in Chapter 3 presented the number of firms (and thus implicitly the number of individuals participating in the economy as entrepreneurs); the number of workers in each firm; the salaried and non-salaried composition of firms' labor forces; the degree of firm compliance with the regulations that apply to salaried labor; the allocation of capital across firms; and the allocation of firms, labor, and capital across localities of different sizes, and across manufacturing, commerce, and services. These descriptions of the realization set *R* summarize how entrepreneurs and workers in Mexico react to the environment *E(L,T,M)*. However, by themselves they provide no information about misallocation or productivity.

This chapter develops measures of firm productivity and misallocation, and characterizes patterns between key attributes of firms—size, type, age, sector, and location—and their productivity. The chapter provides content to relation (2.6) in Chapter 2, in much the same way that the previous chapter did for relation (2.3). However, as before, there is no discussion of causation—that is, there is no discussion as to what specific elements in *E(L,T,M)* drive the allocation of resources to firms with different productivity levels. This task is left to Chapter 7. However, the results of this chapter are extremely useful for that discussion because identifying characteristics of firms that are consistently associated with misallocation serves to narrow down considerably the number of policies in $E(L,T,M)$ that need to be analyzed to establish its root causes.

The Hsieh-Klenow Model

To measure firm productivity and misallocation it is necessary to move from the general framework of Chapter 2 to a more specific formulation. In this context, the model developed by Hsieh and Klenow (2009) is very useful because it allows for computing firm-level measures of productivity. Furthermore, the Hsieh-Klenow model allows for aggregating firm-level indices of productivity into an economy-wide index of total factor productivity (**TFP**) and to compare this index in the observed environment $E(L,T,M)$ with the one that would obtain in the optimal environment, $E^*(L^*,T^*,M^*)$.

Figure 4.1 places the Hsieh-Klenow model in the context of the occupational choice discussion depicted in Figure 2.1 in Chapter 2. As before, the first line is the number of individuals in the economy, and the second their division into entrepreneurs, workers associated with firms, and the self-employed. The Hsieh-Klenow model takes as given the location of points B and C in the second line, i.e., it takes as given the total number of individuals who are in each occupation. Since the total number of entrepreneurs is given, so is the number of firms. Moreover, the model also takes as given the

Figure 4.1: Entrepreneurs, Workers, and Firms in the Hsieh and Klenow Model

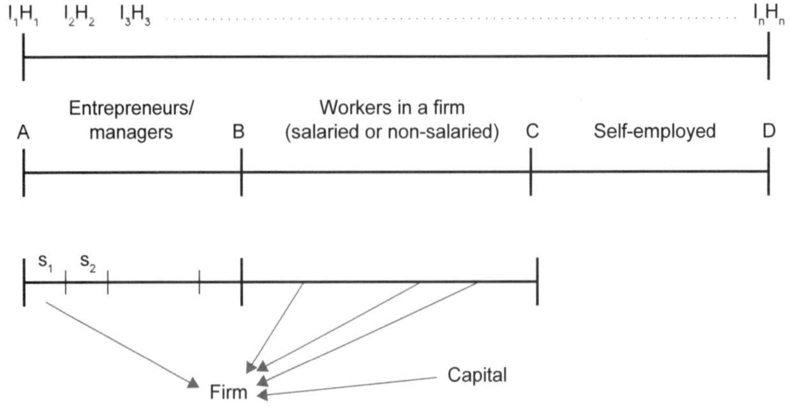

Source: Prepared by the author.

total number of six-digit sectors, and the number of entrepreneurs (firms) that are in each sector. This is depicted in the third line of Figure 4.1, where the vertical lines show s_1 entrepreneurs in sector 1, s_2 in sector 2, and so on. The association of an entrepreneur of a given ability with physical capital and workers of various abilities forms a firm. This is the unit of analysis in the Hsieh-Klenow model, and the unit observed in the data in the Economic Census. The Hsieh-Klenow model then focuses attention on the number of workers and the amount of capital allocated to each firm. Note in the third line of Figure 4.1 that by focusing on firms, the self-employed are not considered in the Hsieh-Klenow model.

To provide empirical content to their model, Hsieh and Klenow assume that the technology *T* is characterized by constant returns to scale for all firms and that firms' production functions are:

$$Q_{is} = A_{is} K_{is}^{\alpha_s} L_{is}^{1-\alpha_s}, \qquad (4.1)$$

where Q_{is} is physical output of the *i*th firm in the *s*th six-digit sector, K_{is} and L_{is} the capital and labor allocated to that firm, α_s the capital coefficient in sector *s* (which is assumed to be the same for all firms in that sector), and A_{is} an exogenously given index of the firm's physical TFP.

Very importantly, the values of A_{is} differ across firms within a sector. These indices summarize a lot of information about the firm: the technology used (patented or copied; complex or simple), the know-how for organizing production, and the talent and ability of the entrepreneur managing the firm. In terms of Figure 4.1, the A_{is} of a firm partly reflects the human capital H_i of the individual I_i that is in segment A-B of line 3 and that, for reasons unexplored in the Hsieh-Klenow model, ends up participating in economic activity as an entrepreneur. In the Hsieh-Klenow model, the A_{is} are all given.

Clearly, the higher the value of A_{is}, the higher the firm's physical productivity, as the same capital and labor produce more physical output. Note that since the capital coefficient is assumed equal for all firms in a sector, firms differ only in the value of their A_{is}. Indeed, if all firms in a sector had the same A_{is}, they would all be equal and, from the point of view of productivity, the division of capital and labor among them would be immaterial; it would be as if there were only one firm. Thus, the within-sector dispersion of firms' A_{is} provides a measure of the dispersion of firms' underlying physical productivity in that sector.

To highlight that A_{is} refers to the *physical* productivity of the firm, Hsieh and Klenow also use the expression total physical factor productivity, $TFPQ_{is}$, in the understanding that $TFPQ_{is} = A_{is}$. This is to be distinguished from total *revenue* factor productivity, discussed below.

Firms in a sector are assumed to produce goods that are imperfect substitutes for one another, and thus each firm faces a downward sloping demand curve for its own product. When the environment faced by firms is the optimal one, so that $E(L,T,M) = E^*(L^*,T^*,M^*)$, more-productive firms (with A_{is} higher than the average) will be larger than less-productive ones (with A_{is} lower than the average). But even though there are constant returns to scale, the most-productive firm will not take over the whole market because as it expands production, the unit price received for its output will fall. In turn, as the output price falls, the value to the firm of an additional unit of capital and an additional worker—that is, the marginal revenue product of capital and labor—will fall as well. Thus, in each sector, a firm's output level (and hence output price) adjust until the marginal revenue product of capital and labor are equalized across all firms in that sector.

The implication of this market adjustment is that despite exogenously given differences in a firm's physical productivity, the revenue total factor productivity of the firm, defined as the value of output that can be produced with one peso of capital and labor in that firm, will be the same across all firms. Hsieh and Klenow denote this measure of revenue total factor productivity as TFPR, and show that:

$$TFPR^*_{is} = TFPR^*_{js} \text{ for all firms } i \text{ and } j \text{ in sector } s, \qquad (4.2)$$

where the asterisk highlights that this holds only when $E(L,T,M) = E^*(L^*,T^*,M^*)$.

Relation (4.2) is an intuitive way of capturing an efficient allocation: the value that can be obtained with one peso of capital and labor is the same regardless of the firm to which that peso is allocated. Put differently, in the optimal environment no shifting of capital or labor across firms would be able to increase the total value of output; at the margin, resources are equally valuable in all firms.

In the Hsieh-Klenow model the difference between the optimal and the observed environment is represented by firm-specific wedges that affect the value of the firm's output, $\tau_{Q_{is}}$, or the cost of its labor inputs, $\tau_{L_{is}}$. More precisely, a firm's profits, π_{is}, are given by:

$$\pi_{is} = \left(1 - \tau_{Q_{is}}\right) P_{is} Q_{is} - RK_{is} - \left(1 + \tau_{L_{is}}\right) wL_{is}, \qquad (4.3)$$

where R is the rental rate of capital, P_{is} the price received by the firm for its output, and w the wage. The firm-specific wedge affecting the value of output, $\tau_{Q_{is}}$, can represent effective tax rates on profits, tariff rates if the good is internationally traded, value-added taxes, specific taxes associated with the firm's size or location given special tax regimes, access to credit, a firm's perceptions of being fined if it evades taxes, or any other factor that affects the value of the firm's output. In parallel, the wedge affecting labor, $\tau_{L_{is}}$, can represent the effects of labor taxes, the costs of social insurance contributions given the salaried/non-salaried composition of the firm's labor force, the expected penalties of violating labor or social insurance laws, the contingent costs of dismissal of legally hiring salaried workers, or any other element that changes the relative costs of labor versus the cost of capital.[1]

More generally, these wedges result from the interaction of many policies in $E(L,T,M)$ relating to taxes, credit, costs of labor, degree of enforcement of regulations, availability of public goods, subsidies, domestic competition and openness to international trade, and proximity to infrastructure, as well as any market failures or government interventions that may affect firms differently depending on their size, contractual structure, location, sector, and other individual characteristics.

Very importantly, the Hsieh-Klenow model does not explain how the various policies in $E(L,T,M)$ translate into the wedges faced by firms; it just measures these wedges. In other words, while the Hsieh-Klenow model serves to measure the extent and costs of misallocation, it does not explain the specific policies or market failures that drive it. This task is left to Chapter 7, which describes the main policies and institutions in Mexico's $E(L,T,M)$ that stand behind these wedges, and shows that there are many reasons indeed why they differ across firms.

It should be emphasized that these wedges are a simplified representation of a complex phenomenon. In Mexico, as elsewhere, firms face a very varied set of circumstances, and it is all but impossible to capture them all in two scalars affecting output and input prices only. Aside from responding to taxes, subsidies, access to credit, and similar variables, firms may adopt certain behaviors because they do not trust the institutions where they must solve their disputes, because of expectations of policy changes, or even due to perceptions of public safety.[2] That said, to be able to provide empirical approximations to the issue at hand, it is unavoidable to simplify these circumstances and condense them in a few parameters that can be recovered from the census data.

---

[1] One could alternatively write the wedge affecting the cost of capital and not labor in relation (4.3). The point is that the interaction of the wedges on outputs and inputs affects both the level of output and the composition of inputs.

[2] Sadly, the later issue appears to be increasingly relevant in Mexico, where firms may choose to become smaller in size or to adopt simpler technologies in order to avoid extortion from organized crime or drug-related gangs. See Rios (2016).

A very useful result of the Hsieh-Klenow model is that firms' $TFPR_{is}$ is proportional to the values of the firm-specific wedges:[3]

$$TFPR_{is} \propto \left(1+\tau_{L_{is}}\right)^{1-\alpha_s} \Big/ \left(1+\tau_{Q_{is}}\right). \tag{4.4}$$

Three properties of relation (4.4) are important for our purposes here. First, note that if the environment were optimal such that there were no wedges and $\tau_{Q_{is}} = \tau_{L_{is}} = 0$ for all i and s, even if firms had different A_{is} the value of $TFPR_{is}$ would be the same for all, as in relation (4.2). The second property is that when the environment differs from the optimal one, firms within a sector have different levels of TFPR because they face different wedges (and not because they have different physical productivity). In this case, shifting capital or labor across firms would increase the value of total output. Thus, differences in levels of TFPR across firms are evidence that resources are misallocated. More pointedly, the dispersion of firms' levels of TFPR within a sector provides a measure of the degree of misallocation: *the greater this dispersion, the greater the degree of misallocation.*

The third property of relation (4.4) is that firms with higher values of TFPR are the ones where resources are more valuable. Put differently, reallocating capital and labor from firms with low levels of TFPR to firms with high levels would increase the value of the output produced, and hence total factor productivity (since more is produced with the same resources). Naturally, the fact that this reallocation does not occur is the result of some elements in the environment **E**(L,T,M) that allow relatively less-productive firms to attract more capital and labor than they should. Or, alternatively, this reallocation does not occur because certain elements in **E**(L,T,M) limit more-productive firms from attracting more capital and labor.

An important implication of an environment **E**(L,T,M) that differs from the optimal one **E***(L*,T*,M*) is that firms with higher physical productivity need not be larger than those with lower physical productivity. This depends on the nature of the wedges implicit in the observed environment. For instance, firms with low A_{is} relative to the average may get subsidized credit, tax exemptions, or more favorable tax regimes, or have lower contingent costs for labor because

---

[3] Hsieh and Klenow (2009) also show that $TFPR_{is} = P_{is}(Q_{is})^*A_{is}$. This alternative relation highlights that the revenue productivity of the capital and labor used by the firm is a function of its underlying physical productivity and of the market valuation of the good produced by it, P_{is}. Relation (4.4) is used here because it makes explicit the role played by wedges in a context where the environment is not the optimal one. Of course, P_{is} is endogenous to the firm's output level, and the fact that selling more output reduces price translates into a lower variation in revenue productivity across firms relative to the variation in physical productivity.

most of their workers have non-salaried contracts. Or they may evade social insurance contributions even if they hire salaried workers because enforcement is imperfect, or they may receive more contracts from the government because of special connections. As a result, even though these firms are relatively unproductive, they are large and attract a significant share of resources. In parallel, firms with high A_{is} may face more onerous tax regimes, pay higher contingent costs for labor because they require more salaried workers, pay higher wages because their workers are unionized, or face higher probabilities of extortion from gangs. As a result, they are smaller than they should be.

Alternatively, some sectors may not attract as much capital and labor as they should because of the government's failure to solve a coordination problem between firms, provide public infrastructure, or ensure intellectual property protection, or because the supply of some key intermediate input produced by a public enterprise is erratic or too costly (e.g., energy). Finally, some firms may be favored by some policies (say, exemptions from value-added taxes) and hurt by others (say, credit restrictions), with an ambiguous effect on their level of TFPR. Clearly, many possibilities are present.

Whatever the possibilities, the important implication is that the distribution of firms by size and contractual structure will differ from what would be observed if $\boldsymbol{E}(L,T,M) = \boldsymbol{E}^*(L^*,T^*,M^*)$. It is critical to have this observation in mind when interpreting the data from the four censuses. Indeed, larger firms need not always be the more productive ones. Some smaller firms may be more productive than larger ones, and some firms may exist that otherwise would not, implying in turn that some individuals are participating in economic activity as entrepreneurs rather than as workers. The actual outcome depends greatly on the magnitude and the distribution of the firm-specific wedges, and on how firms—given their underlying A_{is}—respond to these wedges by adjusting their size, capital, mix of labor contracts, and degree of compliance with tax and contributory social insurance and labor regulations.

Aside from providing measures of misallocation at the sector level, the Hsieh-Klenow model also generates an economy-wide measure of TFPR, labeled here **TFPR** (differentiated by the boldface), as in relation (2.6) in Chapter 2. The basic idea is that **TFPR** is a weighted average of the TFPRs of all sectors, which in turn is the weighted average of the $TFPR_{is}$ of firms in each sector. Thus, the aggregate weighted average reflects firms' underlying physical productivity as captured in their A_{is}, together with the share of total resources absorbed by each firm given the wedges that it faces.

Clearly, when and $\boldsymbol{E}(L,T,M) = \boldsymbol{E}^*(L^*,T^*,M^*)$ there are no wedges, and each firm absorbs the optimal amount of capital and labor given its physical productivity and the demand for its output. In this scenario, the economy is producing with maximum productivity and the economy-wide index of TFPR is at its maximum value, **TFPR***, as in relation (2.7) in Chapter 2. In the Hsieh-Klenow model the value of **TFPR*** is obtained by eliminating all the wedges for all firms, thereby assigning the optimal amount of capital and labor to each.

In turn, the difference between **TFPR*** and **TFPR**, as in relation (2.8) in Chapter 2, yields a measure of the productivity gains that could be obtained if, miraculously, all policies, programs, and regulations in ***E**(L,T,M)* were set perfectly, all the institutions in charge of implementing those policies and regulations operated optimally, and everybody trusted those institutions.

Evidently, no economy will ever achieve the maximum level of productivity. **TFPR*** is just a measure of what would obtain in an idealized situation. In all countries there are institutions that work imperfectly, market failures that go uncorrected, and policies or regulations that induce inefficiencies. All countries experience some degree of misallocation, and therefore some productivity losses. Nevertheless, relation (2.8) in Chapter 2 provides a useful aggregate measure of misallocation because the observed **TFPR** can be compared with an objective benchmark. Furthermore, comparisons of **TFPR** and **TFPR*** for various years provide a measure of whether misallocation has been falling or increasing through time.

The Hsieh-Klenow model is useful because it has an intuitive interpretation, is tractable, and allows for empirically measuring the size of the firm-specific wedges and the values of $TFPQ_{is}$ and $TFPR_{is}$. By doing so, it allows for measuring the dispersion of $TFPR_{is}$ and the extent of misallocation. That said, it not without its limitations. As discussed in Chapter 2, four types of misallocation are possible:

- Across individuals, between those who work for a firm, those who are self-employed, and those who are entrepreneurs
- Across workers and capital within firms in a sector, as some firms attract more (or less) capital and workers than they should
- Across sectors, as some are larger (or smaller) than others where the same resources would be more (or less) valuable
- Across abilities (such that some individuals with high abilities are employed in occupations where these abilities are underutilized or not required).

The Hsieh-Klenow model captures only the second type of misallocation, because it takes as given the number of firms in a sector and the total number of firms. Put differently, given the education and abilities of individuals as captured by their H_i, the model does not explain why the number of entrepreneurs is what it is, nor who ends up as an entrepreneur. (In terms of Figure 4.1, the location of point B and, within the segment A-B, the location of the lines separating s_1 from s_2, are exogenously given.) This is a substantive issue for productivity in Mexico because, as will be shown below, some firms have extremely low productivity levels, suggesting that the entrepreneurs managing those firms have little talent to do so, and that most likely under a different environment $E(L,T,M)$ some of those entrepreneurs would be participating in economic activity as workers (so that there would be fewer but larger firms).

The Hsieh-Klenow model is also silent on whether there are too many or too few self-employed workers, again a prominent issue for productivity in Mexico since, as shown in Table 3.1 in Chapter 3, self-employment absorbs a large share of the labor force. (In terms of Figure 3.1 in Chapter 3, the model does not say why point C is located where it is.)

The model is equally silent on whether some sectors are too large or small relative to other sectors. This matters for Mexico, because critical sectors like energy are reserved exclusively for public enterprises, and because over 40 percent of the consumption basket receives some form of exemption from value-added taxes, probably enlarging the size or number of firms producing those goods; because some sectors are more exposed to international competition; and because there is monopoly behavior in some sectors not exposed to such competition. The model is silent as well on whether some individuals who appear in the data as workers should be entrepreneurs running firms (because, say, they have high managerial talent but no access to credit), since those firms are never observed in the census data.

Finally, and again of great relevance to Mexico, the Hsieh-Klenow model has little to say on an under-emphasized manifestation of misallocation—discussed further in Chapter 6—which is that workers with high human capital are not matched with firms where that human capital is fully utilized.

For these reasons, the Hsieh-Klenow model provides an incomplete picture of misallocation in Mexico. That said, it allows for an economically meaningful interpretation of the census data and, as shown immediately below, sheds considerable light on the country's misallocation problem. It is thus very useful. Moreover, because the same model with the same assumptions is applied to the four censuses, results can be compared over time, in the understanding that *differences across censuses are not the result of changing assumptions, measurement methods, or data sources or collection techniques, but rather of changes in the underlying behavior of entrepreneurs and workers.*

Dispersion of Total Revenue Productivity

The standard procedure to depict the dispersion in firms' productivity is to construct a distribution, and this is what is done here. In each six-digit sector, the mean value of total revenue productivity, $TFPR_s$, is calculated, and then the productivity of each firm in that sector is measured relative to the mean, which by construction is unity. The sector distribution of TFPR reflects the dispersion of an individual firm's $TFPR_{is}$ in that sector around the mean. Thus, depending on the year, between 672 and 691 distributions are constructed (see Table 3.2 in Chapter 3). For presentation purposes only, six-digit sectors are aggregated into manufacturing, commerce, and services, and into the whole (census-captured) economy, but all computations are done at the six-digit sector level.

Table 4.1 presents three alternative measures of the dispersion of $TFPR_{is}$ computed in all cases at the establishment level.[4] The first measure is the

Table 4.1: Dispersion of Revenue Total Factor Productivity, 1998–2013

	1998	2003	2008	2013
All sectors				
Standard deviation	0.95	0.98	1.08	1.11
25th–75th percentile	1.23	1.25	1.38	1.39
10th–90th percentile	2.39	2.44	2.72	2.80
Manufacturing				
Standard deviation	0.90	0.86	0.96	1.05
25th–75th percentile	1.15	1.11	1.24	1.23
10th–90th percentile	2.24	2.15	2.41	2.73
Commerce				
Standard deviation	0.97	1.02	1.15	1.14
25th–75th percentile	1.28	1.32	1.50	1.43
10th–90th percentile	2.47	2.59	2.93	2.86
Services				
Standard deviation	0.91	0.93	1.04	1.05
25th–75th percentile	1.20	1.19	1.36	1.38
10th–90th percentile	2.32	2.35	2.66	2.67

Source: Author's calculations based on data from Mexico's Economic Census.

---

[4] Following Hsieh and Klenow (2009), outliers that could bias the results are eliminated, and in each six-digit sector 1 percent of the firms with the lowest and highest productivity are trimmed. Firms with zero value added are also eliminated.

standard deviation of TFPR, and the other two are the difference in the value of TFPR between firms in the 25th and 75th percentile, and the 10th and 90th percentile, of the TFPR distribution.[5]

There are two key results. First, there is significant misallocation. Consider, for instance, the results for 2013 for all sectors combined. The difference between a firm sitting in the 25th and 75th percentile of the revenue productivity distribution implies that the same amount of capital and labor produces 39 percent more value if it is allocated to the latter firm rather than to the former. For firms in the 10th and 90th percentile of the distribution, the difference is substantially larger, 180 percent.

Second, misallocation is persistent and slightly increasing, as the dispersion of TFPR increased between 1998 and 2013. Thus, the significant differences in the productivity of resources across firms are not a transient phenomenon, or the reflection of a firm's adjustment to some transitory shock, but rather a structural feature of Mexico's economy. There are some elements in Mexico's environment **$E(L,T,M)$** that generate significant misallocation. *Despite many policy changes over these 15 years, these elements have not only persisted, but deepened.*

Is misallocation in Mexico larger than in other countries? Comparisons of the dispersion of TFPR across countries are difficult given differences in the coverage and availability of firm-level data. That said, Syverson (2004) finds that in the manufacturing sector of the United States, the difference in TFPR between a firm in the 10th and the 90th percentile of the revenue productivity distribution is 92 percent. This compares with 173 percent for Mexico's manufacturing sector in 2013, as shown in Table 4.1. Moreover, Syverson's computations are carried out at the four-digit level, and one expects smaller differences at the six-digit level (which is the one used in the Mexican data). Clearly, misallocation is much larger in Mexico than in the United States, its closest neighbor and largest trading partner.

Comparisons with other countries of Latin America are complicated because few of them have data that cover establishments of all sizes, as is the case in Mexico. Nevertheless, Busso, Madrigal, and Pagés (2010) compute the gains in TFP that would be observed if the dispersion in TFPR were eliminated in various countries of the region, focusing only on firms with 10 or more workers in manufacturing. These gains would be 95 percent for Mexico, 65 percent for Venezuela, 61 percent for Bolivia and El Salvador, 60 percent for Uruguay and Argentina, 54 percent for Chile, and 51 percent for Colombia.

---

[5] Table A.3 in the Appendix to this volume shows that for 2008 and 2013 the dispersion of TFPR at the firm level is very similar to the dispersion at the establishment level, and that this holds for manufacturing, commerce, and services.

Figure 4.2: Distribution of Physical Total Factor Productivity, Manufacturing Sector, Mexico versus the United States

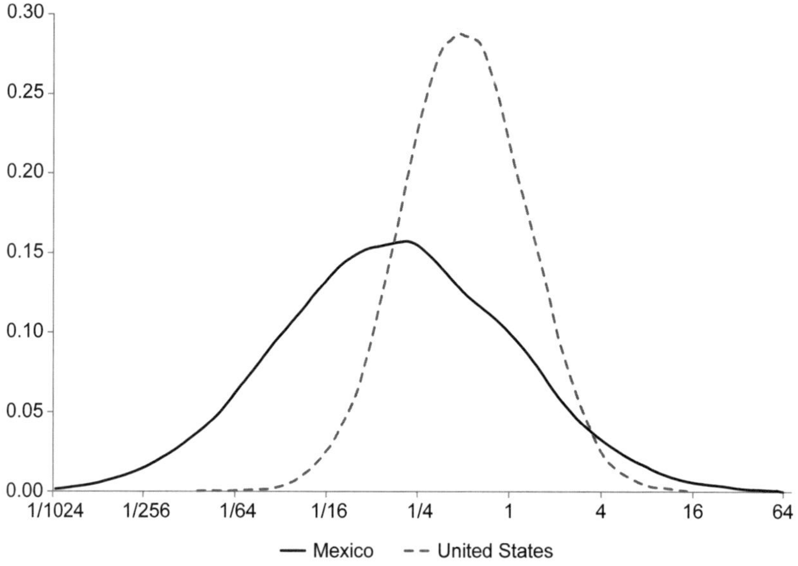

Source: Inter-American Development Bank (2010).

The fact that the gains are highest for Mexico derives from the fact that the underlying dispersion in TFPR there is highest.

Figure 4.2 provides an alternative answer to the same question. It compares the distribution of the physical productivity of all manufacturing establishments in Mexico and the United States, i.e., the distribution of TFPQ.[6] The horizontal axis measures the productivity of firms in each sector relative to mean productivity in that sector; the vertical axis measures the frequency of observations. To facilitate the comparisons, both distributions are normalized to have a mean productivity of one.

The figure is very revealing. In the United States, the most-productive establishments are approximately four times more productive than the average, whereas in Mexico the most productive establishments are 16 times more productive than the average. At the opposite end of the spectrum, in the United States the least-productive establishments are about 1/16th less productive than the average, versus some 1/256th less productive in Mexico. Thus, in Mexico the differences in productivity between manufacturing

---

[6] The computations are carried out at the four-digit level in both cases; see the discussion in IDB (2010).

establishments in the same sectors are substantially larger. The fact that firms with such enormous differences in productivity can coexist in the market in Mexico reflects the fact that policies and institutions there generate significantly more misallocation than policies and institutions in the United States.

Productivity Gains from Eliminating Misallocation

Table 4.2 presents the productivity gains that would be observed in Mexico if the environment $E(L,T,M)$ were optimal. The numbers are the values of relation (2.8) in Chapter 2 calculated in the context of the Hsieh-Klenow model. The first line corresponds to the aggregate of all six-digit sectors in manufacturing, commerce, and services. The next lines correspond to the aggregate of six-digit sectors within each of these three broadly defined sectors.

Gains increase over time, consistent with the increasing misallocation shown in Table 4.1. In 1998, the value of output in manufacturing, services, and commerce combined potentially could have been 63 percent higher in the absence of misallocation, and in 2013 it could have been 148 percent higher. These trends hold separately for each of the three broadly defined sectors.

While measures of potential TFP gains are informative, it needs to be reiterated that the reference point for the values in Table 4.2 is an ideal situation that is not observed anywhere in the world, and that under no realistic set of circumstances would be observed in Mexico. Nevertheless, the magnitude of the potential gains does indicate that Mexico's environment $E(L,T,M)$ is very far from the optimal one indeed, and that in turn this situation is very costly to the country.

Correlations between Firm Size, Type, and Productivity

Table 4.1 documented large and persistent misallocation but provided no information as to its patterns. Are there any systematic differences between firms with high and low levels of TFPR? If so, are they associated with sectors, or with the

Table 4.2: Total Factor Productivity Gains, 1998-2013
(Percent)

	1998	2003	2008	2013
All	1.63	1.58	1.72	2.48
Manufacturing	0.88	0.89	0.95	1.26
Commerce	1.75	1.78	1.99	2.93
Services	1.51	1.62	1.85	2.02

Source: Author's calculations based on data from Mexico's Economic Census.

size or the type of firms? Are these patterns the same between 1998 and 2013? Or is misallocation randomly distributed across sectors and firm types, sizes, and years without any common characteristics?

To identify patterns between firm sizes, types, and productivity, various ordinary least squares regressions are run. In line with the discussion in Chapter 2, these regressions should not be interpreted as implying causation. The regressions are simply the statistical tool used to identify correlations and measure average differences in productivity between firms.

Table 4.3 begins presenting the correlations between establishment type and physical and revenue measures of productivity, obtained from regressing *log TFPR$_{is}$/log TFPR$_s$* on a dummy for firm types, with controls for firms' size, age, and location, where *TFPR$_s$* is the average TFPR of all establishments in the corresponding six-digit sector (and similarly for *TFPQ*). The regression specification is included in the Appendix to this volume. Here it suffices to point out that the excluded category is fully formal, so the coefficients are interpreted as the average percentage difference in productivity of other establishment types compared to fully formal ones.[7]

The central result is that for all four censuses, and regardless of whether physical or revenue productivity is considered, *all firm types are on average less productive than fully formal ones*.[8] Table 4.3 also reveals that the differences in productivity between mixed and fully formal firms are small, and that mixed firms are also, with one exception, always more productive than informal firms, legal or illegal.

Taken together, these two results imply that in the case of Mexico resources are on average more valuable in formal firms (legal and mixed) than in informal firms (legal and illegal). Put differently, these results document that misallocation in Mexico results in too much informality. Something in Mexico's environment ***E**(L,T,M)* impedes formal firms from absorbing more resources; alternatively, something in Mexico's ***E**(L,T,M)* channels too much capital and labor to informal firms.

Following the discussion in Chapter 2, it should be emphasized that this finding derives from the specific patterns of wedges faced by firms in Mexico; it is not a logical necessity. If these patterns differed because Mexico's ***E**(L,T,M)* were different, the signs of the coefficients in these regressions could be the

---

[7] Table A.4 in the Appendix to this volume presents the same regressions with firm-level data for 2013 and shows that results are quite similar to the ones presented here with establishment-level data.

[8] There are two exceptions in the TFPR measures: for mixed establishments in 1998 (where the difference is 1 percent but not statistically significant), and for informal and illegal establishments in 2003 (a 2.3 percent difference).

Table 4.3: Correlation between Productivity and Firm Type, 1998–2013

	1998 TFPQ	1998 TFPR	2003 TFPQ	2003 TFPR	2008 TFPQ	2008 TFPR	2013 TFPQ	2013 TFPR
Mixed	−0.053 (0.0034)	0.001 (0.0020)	−0.058 (0.0031)	−0.029 (0.0019)	−0.040 (0.0036)	−0.032 (0.0022)	−0.186 (0.0033)	−0.177 (0.0020)
Legal-informal	−1.403 (0.0037)	−0.414 (0.0023)	−1.207 (0.0035)	−0.360 (0.0022)	−1.189 (0.0037)	−0.401 (0.0023)	−1.557 (0.0031)	−0.633 (0.0019)
Illegal informal	−0.458 (0.0040)	−0.120 (0.0024)	−0.167 (0.0037)	0.023 (0.0022)	−0.488 (0.0039)	−0.162 (0.0024)	−0.705 (0.0035)	−0.184 (0.0021)
Observations	2,368,471	2,368,471	2,537,348	2,537,348	2,655,551	2,655,551	3,371,272	3,371,272
R-squared	0.430	0.091	0.414	0.056	0.414	0.072	0.388	0.072

Source: Author's calculations based on data from Mexico's Economic Census.
Note: Numbers in parentheses are standard errors; all coefficients are significant at the 99 percent confidence level except for TFPR for mixed firms in 1998.

opposite, in which case misallocation could result in too little informality, or in a different ranking of productivity levels by firm type. Table 4.3 indicates that this is not the case for Mexico.

Yet another result is that, again for all measures and censuses, there are major differences in productivity between informal firms: illegal ones are always more productive than legal ones, and by a substantial margin. This result implies that from the point of view of productivity, the composition of the informal sector matters greatly. In the case of Mexico, shifting resources from legal to illegal informal firms would leave the size of the informal sector unchanged, but would increase productivity. Put differently, and in line with the discussion in Chapter 2, one cannot establish a one-to-one mapping between the size of the informal sector and productivity.

Note that differences in revenue productivity across firms are smaller than differences in physical productivity, consistent with the fact that firms' output prices mitigate differences in their physical productivity. That said, note that differences in revenue productivity—which are the ones that matter for misallocation—are substantial. In 2013, compared to fully formal firms, one peso of capital and labor produced on average 17 percent less value if allocated to a mixed firm, 63 percent less if allocated to an informal and legal firm, and 18 percent less if allocated to an informal and illegal firm.

Table 4.4 presents the same regressions as in Table 4.3 but separately for each firm size. For reasons of space, only values for 2013 are presented, with the understanding that results for other years are similar.

The previous results are confirmed: comparing only firms of the same size, fully formal firms are the ones where resources are most productive. Take firms with up to five workers: compared to fully formal firms, one peso of capital and labor yields 15 percent less value if allocated to a mixed firm, 50 percent less if allocated to an informal and legal one, and 12 percent less to an informal and illegal one. This underlies that there are large productivity differences among very small firms, and that, within these, informal and legal firms are by far the least productive. These results hold up for other firm sizes. In fact, for medium-size firms (with 11 to 50 workers) and large ones (more than 50), the differences in TFPR between fully formal and informal firms are even larger than for firms with up to five workers. Results are also consistent with previous analyses using the same census data for 1998, 2003, and 2008; see Busso, Fazio, and Levy (2012).

Table 4.5 completes the analysis with a regression in which each type and size category is considered separately.[9] Importantly, in this case the

---

[9] See the Appendix to this volume for the exact specification and the complete regression statistics.

Table 4.4: Correlation between Productivity and Firm Type by Firm Size, 2013

	Very Small (1–5 Workers) TFPQ	Very Small (1–5 Workers) TFPR	Small (6–10 Workers) TFPQ	Small (6–10 Workers) TFPR	Medium (11–50 Workers) TFPQ	Medium (11–50 Workers) TFPR	Large (51+ Workers) TFPQ	Large (51+ Workers) TFPR
Mixed	−0.209 (0.0052)	−0.150 (0.0034)	0.115 (0.0127)	0.067 (0.0077)	−0.189 (0.0156)	−0.144 (0.0088)	−0.118 (0.0333)	−0.237 (0.0178)
Informal-Legal	−1.472 (0.0043)	−0.504 (0.0028)	−0.864 (0.0145)	−0.462 (0.0087)	−1.000 (0.0172)	−0.711 (0.0097)	−1.912 (0.0334)	−0.883 (0.013)
Informal Illegal	−0.506 (0.0046)	−0.119 (0.0030)	−0.132 (0.0128)	0.103 (0.0077)	−0.706 (0.0171)	−0.190 (0.0096)	−1.891 (0.0578)	−0.187 (0.031)
Observations	3,092,3181	3,092,318	157,461	157,461	101,696	101,696	19,797	19,797
R-squared	0.115	0.042	0.044	0.037	0.059	0.063	0.324	0.209

Source: Author's calculations based on data from Mexico's Economic Census.
Note: Numbers in parentheses are standard errors; all coefficients are significant at the 99 percent confidence level.

Table 4.5: Resource Allocation and Revenue Total Factor Productivity by Firm Size and Type, 2013

Type and Size of Firm	Revenue Total Factor Productivity	Number of Establishments	Percent Share of Workers	Percent Share of Capital
Fully formal (51+ workers)	0.800	10,998	13.6	20.6
Informal and illegal (51+ workers)	0.646	1,803	1.3	1.5
Fully formal (11–50 workers)	0.606	41,802	5.2	5.4
Informal and illegal (6–10 workers)	0.576	63,238	2.6	1.4
Mixed (6–10 workers)	0.544	46,617	2.0	1.6
Fully formal (1–5 workers)	0.517	81,003	1.4	2.0
Mixed (51+ workers)	0.498	9,686	13.3	19.4
Fully formal (6–10 workers)	0.477	37,882	1.6	2.1
Mixed (11–50 workers)	0.467	38,479	4.6	3.8
Informal and illegal (11–50 workers)	0.405	27,837	3.0	1.9
Informal and illegal (1–5 workers)	0.381	614,512	8.9	4.6
Mixed (1–5 workers)	0.365	141,631	2.5	2.3
Informal and legal (6–10 workers)	0.007	38,734	1.6	1.5
Informal and legal (1–5 workers)	Excluded	2,916,867	26.8	9.9
Informal and legal (51+ workers)	−0.039	8,143	8.8	17.9
Informal and legal (11–50 workers)	−0.096	19,868	2.4	4.2
Total		3,371,272	100.0	100.0

Source: Author's calculations based on data from Mexico's Economic Census.
Note: Numbers in parentheses are standard errors; all coefficients are significant at the 99 percent confidence level except for informal and legal (6–10 workers).

excluded category is informal and legal establishments with up to five workers; as before, controls for location and age are included. For reasons of space, only results for 2013 are presented, and, for convenience, the regression coefficient together with the number of establishments in each category is reported, as are the respective shares of total capital and labor. Categories are listed by declining values of TFPR and, to facilitate reading, the table is divided into four groups.

When all size and type categories are jointly compared, one finds large (51+ workers) and fully formal firms to be the ones in which, on average, resources are most productive: one peso of capital and labor in those firms produces 80 percent more value than in very small (1–5 workers) informal and legal firms. At the other end of the spectrum, resources are least productive, and significantly so, in informal and legal firms of any size. Between these two extremes there are differences in TFPR across size/type categories, but less than between these categories and any informal and legal firms. In this middle range, average differences in TFPR are relatively small, and there is no clear ordering by size or type. For instance, small (6–10 workers) and large (51+ workers) informal and illegal firms are among the most productive, while very small (1–5 workers) fully formal firms are more productive than firms with larger sizes but of other types.

There is a sharp contrast between firms' productivity rankings as shown by the regression coefficients, on the one hand, and the allocations of capital and labor, on the other. Large fully formal firms attract 13.6 percent of labor and 20.6 percent of capital. Very small informal and legal firms, which are 80 percent less productive, absorb almost double the labor and almost half the capital. But the biggest contrast is between firms with non-salaried contracts of any size, and all other firms. The former are, by a significant amount, the least-productive firms in Mexico, yet they absorb 39.6 percent of all labor and 33.5 percent of all capital.

One key message follows from Table 4.5: *the most significant differences in productivity are between firms that have non-salaried contracts and all other firms, not between formal and informal ones.* In other words, Mexico's $E(L,T,M)$ channels too many resources to firms with non-salaried contracts, of any size relative to firms with salaried contracts, of any size or legal status. From the point of view of productivity, the salaried versus non-salaried distinction in entrepreneur-worker relations, deeply embedded in Mexico's constitution, laws, and institutions, is substantially more relevant than the distinctions between firm size or legal status.

Table 4.5 clarifies the relationship between size, legality and formality status, and productivity. Conventional wisdom associates informality, smallness, illegality, and low productivity, on the one hand, and largeness, formality, legality, and high productivity, on the other. The analysis here indicates that in Mexico this characterization is too coarse and somewhat misleading. It is true that a clear majority of low-productivity firms are very small and informal, but most of these firms are legal. Since they are the most numerous, these firms are very visible and validate the conventional wisdom associating smallness with informality and low productivity. But this should not obscure the existence of other very small firms that are significantly more productive, and that can be formal, or informal (but with salaried contracts). On the other hand, it is equally true that formal, legal, and large firms on average have higher productivity. Together with mixed firms, they are the most numerous among large firms. For these reasons, conventional wisdom associates largeness, formality, and legality with high productivity. However, there is a relevant segment of firms that are large and legal (absorbing almost 9 percent of all labor and 17 percent of all capital in the sample), but informal and quite unproductive. And in parallel there are some very small informal and illegal firms that are in the middle range of productivity. Recognition of the significant heterogeneity that exists within Mexico's informal sector is critical.

Table 4.5 also sheds light on two contradictory views as to whether large or small firms are helped or hurt by the environment. In Mexico, some small firms are punished by $E(L,T,M)$, in the sense that their TFPR is higher than other firms that are larger. This lends support to the view that small firms face more difficulties than larger firms in attracting resources, and that policies and programs should thus be directed toward helping these smaller firms. But Table 4.5 also indicates that other small firms clearly benefit from $E(L,T,M)$, since their TFPR is substantially lower than that of other medium-size and larger firms. This lends support to the view that policy should stop allowing small firms to waste so many resources.

The distinction between firms with salaried and non-salaried contracts is key to reconciling these views. In Mexico, some very small firms, particularly with legal salaried contracts, are discriminated against by $E(L,T,M)$. But these are a minority, totaling 81,003 firms according to Table 4.5. The majority—2,916,867 firms according to the same table—are characterized by non-salaried contracts and are clearly subsidized. It would be a mistake to further help these firms attract more resources. Ignoring this distinction can lead to a common but flawed across-the-board policy prescription that small firms need help. Quite the contrary, in Mexico most small firms do not need such help. Equally importantly, Table 4.5 indicates that larger firms with salaried contracts are the ones most punished by $E(L,T,M)$. Despite being more productive, for reasons explored in Chapter 7, they have more difficulties than all other firms in attracting resources.[10] On balance, it is clearly the case that medium-size and large firms should attract more resources.

---

[10] This view that small firms need help is associated with De Soto (1989). See Hsieh and Olken (2014) for a recent discussion of alternative views on small versus large firms in developing countries. These views matter for Mexico, where the belief that small firms should be helped is common in public policy discussion (see Chapter 9 for more on this issue).

Misallocation within and across Manufacturing, Commerce, and Services

This section looks to determine if there are systematic differences in misallocation between manufacturing, commerce, and services. This is relevant because manufacturing is relatively more exposed to international competition than commerce or services, and because as a result of the North American Free Trade Agreement (NAFTA) and other trade agreements, international competition faced by Mexican firms increased in the mid-1990s. This section assesses differences in the levels, patterns, and trends in misallocation between these three broadly defined sectors.

Consider first a striking feature of Table 4.2: the productivity gains from eliminating misallocation are substantially lower in manufacturing than in commerce or services, indicating that misallocation is lower in the first broadly defined sector. While other factors are at play, this result is consistent with the hypothesis that activities that are more exposed to international competition have lower misallocation. A second striking feature of Table 4.2, however, is that while the level of misallocation in manufacturing is lower, it increased between 1998 and 2013 (consistent with the increasing dispersion of TFPR shown in Table 4.1).

These two features taken together suggest that NAFTA and similar liberalization efforts had a substantial effect in lowering misallocation in manufacturing.[11] But they also suggest that other elements in Mexico's $E(L,T,M)$ not associated with its foreign trade regime have increased misallocation in manufacturing since then, in much the same way they did in commerce and services. As shown in Table 3.11 in Chapter 3 and Table 4.1, trends common to all three sectors include increased penetration of informal firms over more six-digit sectors, more resources in informal firms, lower average firm size, and a higher dispersion of TFPR.

Consider next patterns of misallocation. Table 4.6 presents the results of the same regressions in Table 4.3, including the same controls for size, location, and age. However, the regressions are run separately for establishments in manufacturing, commerce, and services. For reasons of space, only the TFPR values for the 1998 and 2013 censuses are reported, although results are very similar for the other two in between.

Patterns found before are repeated here. In all three broadly defined sectors and in both years, resources have the highest productivity in fully formal firms (except for differences of 5 percent or less for mixed firms in 1998

---

[11] To confirm this statement, one would need the 1993 census, which unfortunately is not available.

Table 4.6: Correlation between Firm Type and Revenue Total Factor Productivity by Broadly Defined Sectors, 1998 and 2013

	Manufacturing		Commerce		Services	
	1998	2013	1998	2013	1998	2013
Mixed	0.052	−0.217	0.011	−0.086	−0.074	−0.222
	(0.0043)	(0.0046)	(0.0029)	(0.0032)	(0.0040)	(0.0033)
Informal and legal	−0.542	−0.668	−0.346	−0.481	−0.470	−0.649
	(0.0061)	(0.0055)	(0.0031)	(0.0027)	(0.0042)	(0.0032)
Informal and illegal	−0.097	−0.132	−0.061	−0.051	−0.248	−0.300
	(0.0062)	(0.0063)	(0.0035)	(0.0030)	(0.0043)	(0.0033)
Observations	292,193	372,649	1,280,277	1,673,772	796,620	1,325,107
R-squared	0.161	0.146	0.069	0.045	0.108	0.061

Source: Author's calculations based on data from Mexico's Economic Census.
Note: Numbers in parentheses are standard errors; all coefficients are significant at the 99 percent confidence level.

in manufacturing and commerce). As before, informal and legal firms are the least productive, by a large margin, followed by informal and illegal firms. Thus, the patterns of misallocation across firm types within manufacturing are the same as within commerce and services. Moreover, note that in manufacturing, as in commerce and services, the differences in TFPR between firm types were larger in 2013 than in 1998, consistent with the observation that independent of the foreign trade regime, other elements in Mexico's $E(L,T,M)$ have widened the differences in productivity between formal and informal firms.

Can anything be said about the relation between international competition and aggregate misallocation? Following Chapter 2, one can think of the aggregate productivity gains from reducing misallocation as a weighted average of the gains from reducing it in manufacturing, commerce, and services separately, where the weights are the share of resources absorbed by each. Two facts are relevant in this context: commerce and services absorb about two-thirds of all resources (see Table 3.11 in Chapter 3); and misallocation in those two sectors is higher than in manufacturing (Table 4.1). Given these facts, it is not surprising that Table 4.2 showed that the gains from eliminating misallocation in the three sectors combined are very close to those from eliminating it in commerce or services. This observation is important because it indicates that while reducing misallocation in manufacturing is obviously welcome, its effects on aggregate misallocation by itself are not large enough to offset the greater misallocation in commerce and services. The importance of this observation is reinforced by noting that the share of resources absorbed by manufacturing has been falling (Table 3.11).

This does not mean that foreign competition is irrelevant—far from it, it has contributed to improving resource allocation in manufacturing, as noted earlier. But it does mean that additional measures are needed to reduce misallocation in commerce and services (and to reverse the factors that are increasing misallocation throughout all three sectors). To put things in perspective, in 2013 manufacturing establishments captured in the census employed 4.9 million workers, versus 6.4 million and 6.1 million establishments in commerce and services, respectively. In that year there were 49.5 million workers in the whole economy (see Table 3.1 in Chapter 3).

Formal-Informal and Salaried-Non-salaried Productivity Distributions

This chapter has established that, on average, formal firms (legal and mixed) are substantially more productive than informal firms (legal and illegal). But that is not to say that every formal firm is more productive than every informal one. Some informal firms can be more productive than formal ones. Similarly, firms with non-salaried contracts are on average less productive than firms with salaried contracts, but this is not true for every single firm. This section further examines this phenomenon.

Figure 4.3 plots the revenue productivity distribution of all firms in 2013. The lower panel plots the division of that distribution between formal (legal and mixed) and informal (legal and illegal) firms. The upper panel depicts again the whole distribution, but divided now between firms with non-salaried contracts only, and firms with salaried contracts of any type (legal, illegal, or mixed). As before, the horizontal axis measures the productivity of firms in each sector relative to the mean productivity of the sector, which is normalized at one. The vertical axis measures frequency of observations.

Consider first the lower panel. Consistent with Table 4.5, the formal and informal productivity distributions overlap. Because there are nine times more informal establishments than formal ones, the shape of the overall distribution is close to that of informal establishments. Nevertheless, it is visible that the formal distribution has more mass to the right of the mean, indicating that a larger share of these firms have productivity above the average. Note that the right and left tails of both distributions extend out similarly, indicating that some informal firms are as productive as the most productive formal ones, and that some formal firms are as unproductive as the most unproductive informal firms. That said, this refers to a few extreme cases, as there are proportionately more informal firms in the left tail. More precisely, only 5.3 percent of formal establishments are to the left of the one-fourth mean productivity versus 18.4 percent of informal ones, visually

Figure 4.3: Distribution of Revenue Total Factor Productivity, 2013

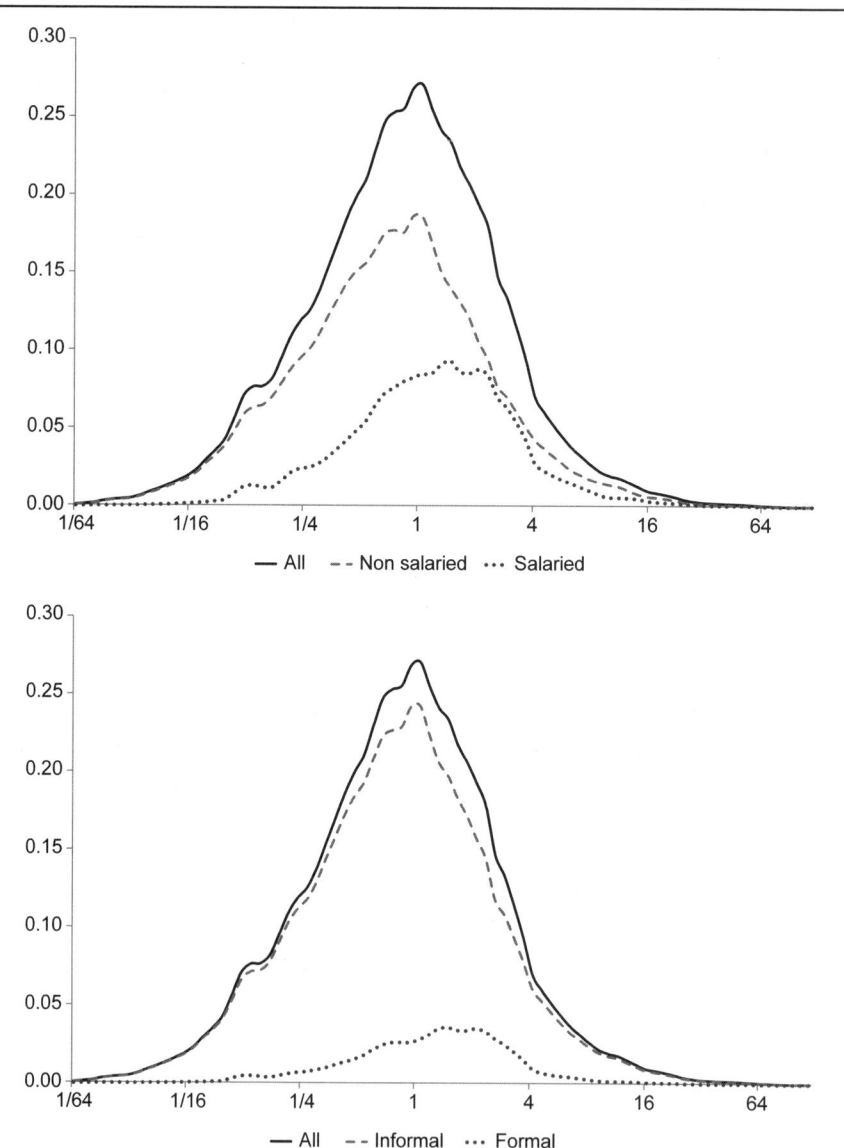

Source: Author's illustration based on data from Mexico's Economic Census.

confirming that informal firms account for the largest share of Mexico's most unproductive firms.

The upper panel zooms in on firms that have only non-salaried contracts, comparing their TFPR distribution with that of firms with salaried contracts of any type. Consistent with Table 3.6 in Chapter 3, this panel provides visual evidence that most firms in Mexico have non-salaried contracts. More importantly, and consistent with Table 4.5, it shows that on average these firms are less productive than the rest, although, of course, a few are as productive as the most-productive firms with salaried contracts. But, clearly, the left tail of the non-salaried distribution has more mass than that of the salaried one: 21.5 percent of all firms versus 6.9 percent have a TFPR below a quarter of the mean. Finally, note that the share of firms with non-salaried contracts whose TFPR is below a quarter of the mean is higher than the share of all informal firms below the same threshold, 21.5 versus 18.4 percent, visually confirming that within the set of informal firms, those with non-salaried contracts account for the largest share of the least productive firms.

Resource Allocation and Productivity Distributions

Figure 4.4, which is constructed in the same manner as Figure 4.3, compares the 1998 and 2013 TFPR distributions. For both, the mean is normalized at one, so they can be directly compared. Although not shown to avoid cluttering the figure, following the previous discussion, formal and informal firms as well as firms with salaried and non-salaried contracts are found throughout the entire distribution in both years, although proportionately more informal firms are found to the left of the mean.

In accordance with the results of Table 4.1, which showed that measures of TFPR dispersion increased, the 2013 distribution is wider than the 1998 one, with fewer firms in the middle (the highest point in 2013 is below that of 1998). Importantly, the 2013 distribution has more mass in both tails than the 1998 one. This illustrates greater heterogeneity: compared to 1998, there were more firms in 2013 with productivity above the mean, a welcome result. However, there were also more firms with productivity below the mean, an unwelcome result.

From the point of view of productivity, depicting the distribution of establishments is only part of the story; the other part is associated with the capital and labor absorbed by establishments of each productivity level. The importance of this point can be highlighted with an extreme example. Consider an economy with 100 firms, and that has substantial dispersion in firms' TFPR values, such that there is large misallocation. Assume, however, that the firm with the largest TFPR value absorbs 99 percent of all the capital and labor in the economy, while the other 99 firms absorb the remaining 1 percent. In this economy, eliminating misallocation would increase aggregate productivity, but not by much because most resources are already efficiently allocated.

Figure 4.4: Distribution of Revenue Total Factor Productivity, 1998 and 2013

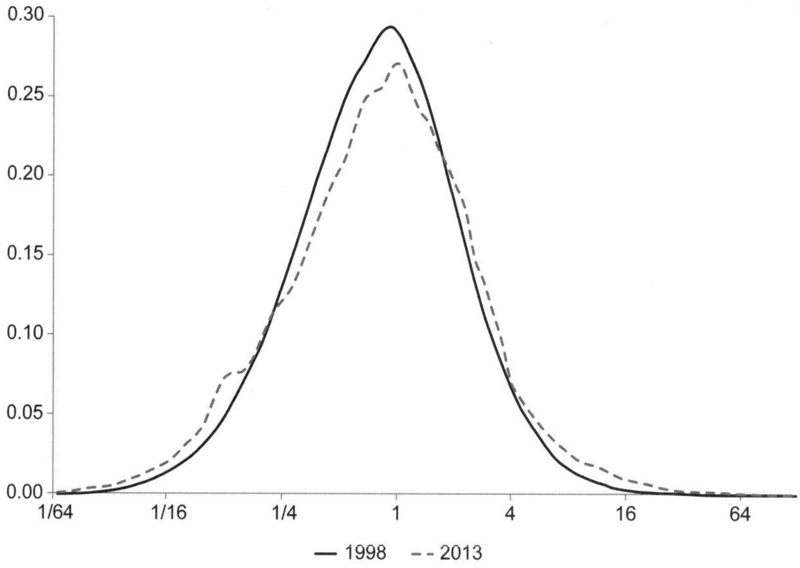

Source: Author's illustration with data from Mexico's Economic Census.

With this observation in mind, Table 4.7 reports the share of establishments and the share of capital and labor allocated to each along three segments of the 1998 and 2013 distributions. On the left tail are those establishments with one-fourth or less of the mean TFPR; on the right tail are those with four times or more the mean TFPR. The reminder are in the middle.

As expected, in both years the share of establishments is larger in the left tail than in the right one, because there are many more informal than formal establishments, and because informal establishments are on average less productive. In parallel, because these establishments are also smaller, their share of capital and labor is lower than their share of establishments. Notice that in 2013 the share of establishments in both tails is higher than in 1998, confirming the visual evidence from Figure 4.4.

The result that deserves more attention, however, is that between 1998 and 2013 the left tail attracted more resources than the right one. The share of capital allocated to the least-productive firms increased by almost 3 percentage points, while the share allocated to the more-productive firms increased by less than one-tenth of a percentage point. Changes in the allocation of labor are qualitatively similar, although the differences are smaller: an increase of 2.5 percentage points to the left tail versus 2.1 points to the right one.

Table 4.7: Share of Capital and Labor in Tails of Revenue Total Factor Productivity Distribution, 1998 and 2013
(Percent shares)

	Less than a Quarter		Between One Quarter and More than Four Times		More than Four Times	
	1998	2013	1998	2013	1998	2013
Establishments	14.05	17.21	82.23	76.76	3.72	6.03
Capital	8.61	11.58	90.26	87.2	1.13	1.22
Labor	9.08	11.57	87.45	82.86	3.47	5.57

Source: Author's calculations based on data from Mexico's Economic Census.

Put differently, given the evolution of Mexico's $E(L,T,M)$ during this 15-year period, entrepreneurs' investment and employment decisions resulted in both more firms with high productivity (> 4 times mean TFPR), and more firms with low productivity (< 1/4th mean TFPR). The net result of those decisions, however, resulted in relatively more capital and labor allocated to the low-productivity segment of the economy. This is an important insight, as it highlights that simply noting that over time there are more high-productivity firms, and that these firms are attracting more resources, is insufficient to ensure that resource allocation is improving. One needs to also pay attention to the other end of the spectrum. The analysis shows that, from the point of view of productivity, firms have responded in conflicting directions to Mexico's $E(L,T,M)$, and that, on balance, *the elements in $E(L,T,M)$ pulling resources in the direction of low-productivity firms have dominated those pulling them in the direction of high-productivity firms.*

Productivity beyond the Census Data

With the help of the Employment Survey, Chapter 3 estimated that in 2013 there were 2.6 million firms in manufacturing, commerce, and services excluded from the census, and that most of them were informal. Can anything be said regarding the productivity of these firms? Unfortunately, the Employment Survey does not capture data on the value of capital, value added, and other areas that would allow for computing these firms' TFPR. That said, some indirect inferences based on firms' size and contractual structure can be made.

Recall from Chapter 2 that firms with non-salaried contracts have neither relations of subordination between entrepreneurs and workers, nor sharply defined rights and obligations between them. These workers are not paid wages, but rather commissions based on effort or output, and for reasons associated with monitoring and shirking, these firms tend to be small. Because of this, and as discussed in Chapter 3, the presumption is that very small firms with non-salaried contracts are mostly family firms. These firms are the smallest of all the firms in Mexico, as can be inferred from Table 3.6 in Chapter 3. On average they have 2.3 workers each, and as can be seen in Table 3.7, almost none are incorporated.

Most informal firms excluded from the census are comparable in size and participate in the same sectors of economic activity as informal firms found in the census. Thus, although no direct information is available from the Employment Surveys, the presumption is that they are also family firms, with non-salaried contractual relations. In other words, these firms are informal but legal.

If this is so, their TFPR should be very similar to the TFPR of the very small informal and legal firms included in the census, which, as shown in Tables 4.4 and 4.5, have among the lowest TFPR of all firms. Indeed, it would be rather surprising if firms excluded from the census, with comparable size and contractual structure to those included in the census, were to have significantly higher TFPR. At the end of the day, the difference between the small informal and legal firms included and excluded from the census is driven more by the techniques used by Mexico's statistical institute to gather data than by considerations about the motivations and abilities of workers and entrepreneurs.

These observations are very relevant for Mexico. Its aggregate productivity is a weighted sum of the productivity of all its firms, with the share of resources captured by each firm as weights. The census data show that even though very small and small firms individually capture a minuscule share of Mexico's resources, the aggregate of those firms captures a significant share. And because these firms are on average less productive than the rest, their punishing effect on aggregate productivity is substantial.

The number, size, and type of firms excluded from the census is determined by Mexico's $E(L,T,M)$ through the same process that determines the number, size, and type of firms included in the census. As noted, the division between them derives only from data-gathering considerations. This division does not imply that excluded firms do not absorb resources. Most excluded firms are small or very small, so their individual effect on aggregate productivity in Mexico is close to irrelevant. But the Employment Survey data illustrate that their sum is very relevant, at least from the point of view of the allocation of labor. The analysis in this section suggests that the productivity losses from misallocation associated with Mexico's $E(L,T,M)$ are in all likelihood *larger* than what was documented in the previous sections with the census data.

CHAPTER 5

Misallocation and Firm Dynamics

How does the Schumpeterian process of "creative destruction" operate in Mexico's context of large misallocation? This chapter studies the patterns of firm entry, exit, and change. Firm dynamics are key to the analysis. Indeed, productivity losses from misallocation would not be so costly if low-productivity firms left the market and released resources, and if those resources, plus additional ones from new investments and labor force growth, were destined for new or surviving firms with higher productivity. If this were so, average productivity would increase over time. But if firm dynamics fail to do this, productivity losses persist. Misallocation is transmitted from one year to the next and translates into stagnant productivity growth.

To study firm dynamics, it would be ideal to track individual establishments over the four censuses. Unfortunately, this can only be done for the last two, which have the same establishment identifier and allow for constructing an exact panel. Thus, this chapter mainly presents evidence for the 2008–2013 period, though some extrapolations are carried out that consider the 1998–2013 period. Data at the establishment level are used, but as before in the text the term establishment is used interchangeably with the term firm.

One way to think about the analysis that follows in the context of the Hsieh and Klenow (2009) model used in Chapter 4, is to consider that in 2008 a firm is characterized by its individual productivity parameter A_{is}, by the wedges that it faces, $\tau_{Q_{is}}$ and $\tau_{L_{is}}$ given how the 2008 environment $E(L,T,M)$ affects it, by the amount of labor and capital that it attracts, and by its salaried/non-salaried and legal/illegal mix of labor contracts. One can then observe that same firm in 2013, in which case one also observes its 2013 productivity parameter (which may be higher if, for example, the firm adopted a new technology, or lower if, for example, the firm lost a good manager); the wedges corresponding to the 2013 environment $E(L,T,M)$; and the firm's capital, labor, and contract mix. If firms survive, one can observe if they changed type or size, and whether they are relatively more or less productive than other firms that also survived. Of course, one may not observe some firms in 2013 that were present in 2008 because of firm exit. Similarly, one may observe some firms in 2013 that were not there in 2008 because of firm entry.

Clearly, differences between 2008 and 2013 can derive from many factors that changed over the five-year period. But as in Chapter 4, we do not inquire here about the modifications in the environment $E(L,T,M)$, or technology T, that stand behind the process of firm exit, entry, and change. Instead, the concern is only with identifying the relevant patterns, measuring how these patterns affected the allocation of resources during these five years, and with determining the corresponding implications for productivity.

Definitions and Stylized Facts

All firms in the 2008 and 2013 censuses are classified into three categories:

- **Exiting firms**: Present in the 2008 census but not in the 2013 census
- **Surviving firms**: Present in both censuses
- **Entering firms**: Present in the 2013 census but not in the 2008 census

By construction, exiting plus surviving firms equals the total number of firms in 2008; and surviving plus entering firms equals the total for 2013.

To analyze the process of exit, exiting and surviving firms by type and size are first identified. Next, the value of firms' revenue total factor productivity (TFPR) in 2008 is computed. Comparing the location of exiting and surviving firms in the same six-digit sector TFPR distribution, an assessment is then made of whether exiting firms are more or less productive than surviving firms. Finally, the capital and labor released by exiting firms of various productivity levels is measured, and the question is posed whether on balance the exit process modified the allocation of resources in the direction of increased productivity.

A similar procedure is followed for the entry process. Patterns by size and type are initially identified. Next, the 2013 TFPR for both entering and surviving firms is computed. The location of each firm in the corresponding six-digit sector TFPR distribution is then used to compare the productivity

Table 5.1: Establishment Entry, Survival and Exit, 2008–2013

	Establishments	Employment	Average Size[a]	Capital[b]	Capital/Labor[c]
2008					
Exiting	1,516,909	5,239,175	3.4	1,675,311	319.7
Surviving	2,086,609	10,983,576	5.2	3,850,343	350.5
Total	**3,603,518**	**16,222,751**	**4.5**	**5,525,654**	**340.6**
2013					
Surviving	2,086,609	10,721,424	5.1	4,074,436	380.0
Entering	2,012,491	6,672,952	3.3	1,923,781	288.3
Total	**4,099,100**	**17,394,376**	**4.2**	**5,998,217**	**344.8**

Source: Author's calculations based on data from Mexico's Economic Census.
[a] Number of workers per firm.
[b] Millions of 2013 pesos.
[c] Thousands of pesos per worker.

of entering versus surviving firms. Finally, the capital and labor absorbed by entering firms of various productivity levels is measured to determine whether the entry process improved the allocation of resources.

The survival process is more complex. In this case, firms' size and type in both 2008 and 2013 are identified and then studied to determine whether they changed type (from formal to informal or vice versa) or size (larger or smaller in 2013 versus 2008). Firms' TFPR in 2008 and 2013 is then computed to consider two issues: first, changes in the relative position of firms in their six-digit sector TFPR distribution between 2008 and 2013;[1] and second, the net effect of firm stagnation, growth, or contraction on the allocation of capital and labor.

Table 5.1 presents basic stylized facts. Over 58 percent of establishments in 2008 survived to 2013. This implies that on average every year approximately 8 percent of establishments exited. On the other hand, 49 percent of all establishments present in 2013 entered after 2008, approximately 10 percent per year. The higher entry rate explains a net growth in the number of establishments of almost 14 percent over the five-year period, or 2.7 percent yearly, a rate that exceeds the growth rate of GDP in the same period

---

[1] Importantly, no comparison is made as to whether surviving firms are more productive in an absolute sense in 2013 than in 2008. Put differently, the productivity growth of surviving firms is not measured. In principle, the Hsieh-Klenow model could be used for these purposes, but it would require price deflators at the establishment level (or, at least, at the six-digit level) to measure value added in constant prices. Unfortunately, these price data are not available.

(1.9 percent). On average, surviving establishments are larger than the rest. But note that their size falls between 2008 and 2013. That, together with a smaller size of entering versus exiting establishments, accounts for a smaller average establishment size in 2013.

Overall employment over the five-year period increased by 7.2 percent, or 1.4 annually. Because employment in surviving establishments contracted, this growth is wholly due to entering ones. Put differently, entering establishments replaced all the employment lost by exiting ones, part of the employment lost in surviving ones, and still accounted for a net increase. For its part, the capital stock in 2013 was 8.5 percent higher than in 2008. Because this exceeded employment growth, there was a marginal increase in average capital intensity. There are significant differences across firms, however. Surviving ones are more capital-intensive than the rest, and they also became more capital-intensive over the period. More interesting is the fact that entering firms have a lower capital/labor ratio than exiting ones. Because of these trends, the difference in capital intensity between exiting and surviving firms, on the one hand, and entering and surviving firms, on the other, widened.

The net increase in the value of the capital stock was 472,563 million pesos, made up of two parts: investments by surviving firms of 224,093 million pesos; and investments by entering firms that, after replacing the capital stock of exiting firms, generated a net increase in the capital stock of 248,470 million pesos.[2] Thus, of the increase in the total capital stock, 47.4 percent resulted from the investment decisions of surviving firms and 52.6 percent from the decisions of entering ones. Performing a similar decomposition for the increase in employment, one finds that (-)22.3 percent was due to the decisions of surviving firms, and 122.3 percent to the decisions of entering firms. Put differently, from the point of view of the allocation of capital investments between 2008 and 2013 entering firms are as important as surviving ones. From the point of view of employment creation, entering firms are substantially more important than surviving ones.

Patterns of Survival by Size and Type

The size and type changes of surviving firms are now considered. Table 5.2 shows transitions across sizes and formality status between 2008 and 2013.

---

[2] The census data do not allow for tracking what happened to the capital stock of exiting firms, but presumably not all is lost. These firms may sell at least part of their capital (say, a truck, a computer, a warehouse) to a surviving or entering firm. The numbers in Table 5.1 reflect the net change.

To reduce the number of possibilities, fully formal and mixed firms are aggregated into the formal category, and legal and illegal informal firms into the informal category. Each row shows how firms of a given size and type in 2008 were distributed by size and type in 2013. By construction, the rows add to 100 percent. The main diagonals of the upper left and lower right panels (in bold) show the share of firms that experienced no change, i.e., firms that had the same type and were in the same size range in both censuses. The last column shows the total number of firms by size and type in 2008. The last row shows the same for 2013, and is the net result of the transits across sizes and types over this five-year period.

Table 5.2 shows that there was remarkable change over the period. Consider the 112,013 firms that were very small (1–5 workers) and formal in 2008. Five years later, only 39 percent stayed in that category. Surprisingly, 48 percent stayed in the same size range, but changed to informal status (or "informalized"). Very few grew: 9.8 percent switched into the small size category (6–10 workers), 2.2 percent into medium size (11–50), and only 0.2 percent into large (51+). Contrast this with the 1,737,334 firms that were also very small but informal in 2008: almost 95 percent remained in that category, only 4 percent changed to formal status (or "formalized"), and only 2 percent grew. Patterns for firms that were small (6–10 workers) in 2008 are similar. Of those that were formal, 40 percent kept the same size, 46 percent shrank, and only 14 percent grew. In parallel, 35.2 percent informalized. For those that started as informal, changes were more dramatic: only 26 percent kept the same size, almost two-thirds got smaller, and only 8.3 percent grew. In parallel, 22.5 percent formalized. In sum, a larger share of very small and small firms informalized than formalized, and most did not change size range (and in the case of small firms that did, more got smaller than larger). The dominant tendency among firms that were very small or small in 2008 and survived to 2013 was towards informalization and smaller size.

Patterns for medium-size firms (11–50 workers) are more mixed. Of the 50,697 that were formal in 2008, 62.1 percent stayed in the same size range, 32.1 percent shrank, and only 5.7 percent grew. Of the 30,827 that were informal, 50 percent stayed in the same size range, 45.7 percent shrank, and only 4 percent grew. Again, the tendency towards smaller size dominated. This contrasts with type changes: 22 percent informalized while 35.8 percent formalized. Finally, with respect to large firms (51+ workers), 31.8 percent of formal ones and 38.3 of informal ones got smaller. In parallel, 14.3 percent of formal firms informalized, while 21.3 percent of informal ones formalized. The dominant tendency of firms that were medium or large in size in 2008 and survived to 2013 was towards formalization but smaller size.

Table 5.2: Transits of Surviving Firms by Size and Type, 2008–2013
(Percent shares and number of firms)

		Formal in 2013				Informal in 2013				Total in 2008	
		(1–5)	(6–10)	(11–50)	(51+)	(1–5)	(6–10)	(11–50)	(51+)	Share	Number
Formal in 2008	(1–5 workers)	**39.3**	7.0	1.7	0.2	48.5	2.8	0.5	0.0	100	112,013
	(6–10 workers)	23.7	**30.0**	10.8	0.3	22.2	10.0	3.0	0.0	100	54,375
	(11–50 workers)	5.8	15.0	**52.2**	5.0	6.0	5.3	9.9	0.7	100	50,697
	(51+ workers)	1.3	1.4	14.8	**68.2**	1.4	0.5	2.8	9.6	100	15,581
Informal in 2008	(1–5 workers)	3.4	0.5	0.1	0.0	**94.6**	1.2	0.2	0.0	100	1,737,334
	(6–10 workers)	9.6	9.1	3.7	0.1	56.1	**16.9**	4.4	0.1	100	79,554
	(11–50 workers)	4.0	8.7	21.3	1.8	20.2	12.8	**29.0**	2.2	100	30,827
	(51+ workers)	0.6	0.7	5.7	14.3	3.4	1.3	12.2	**61.7**	100	6,228
Total number of establishments in 2013		128,445	49,811	48,807	15,284	1,763,540	50,064	23,943	6,715		2,086,609

Source: Author's calculations based on data from Mexico's Economic Census.
Note: Figures in bold show the share of firms that experienced no change, i.e., firms that had the same type and were in the same size range in both censuses.

There are three net results of surviving firms' movements across sizes and types. First, average size fell slightly, from 5.2 to 5.1 workers. Second, there was a very marginal increase in the share of formal firms, from 11.2 to 11.6 percent, wholly due to an increase in the number of very small formal firms (from 112,013 to 128,445). In turn, third, the higher number of very small formal firms resulted mostly from the fact that larger formal firms shrank but kept the same status, and to a much lesser extent from the fact that very small informal firms formalized. These results suggest that the view that informal firms that survive in the market grow and formalize is, by and large, flawed. A clear majority of surviving informal firms remained informal, and very few grew. And some formal firms that survived did so by becoming informal.

Patterns of Entry and Exit by Size and Type

Table 5.3 describes patterns of exit and entry by firm type and size, showing the share of establishments in the corresponding category in each year. By construction, columns add up to 100 percent. Exit and entry rates are higher for informal than formal establishments. These results are partly mimicked when size is considered: entry and exit rates fall as establishment size increases. All in all, Table 5.3 indicates that there is substantially more entry and exit in smaller firm sizes.

Table 5.3: Exit and Entry by Firm Type and Size
(Percent shares)

	Fully Formal	Mixed	Informal and Illegal	Informal and Legal	(1–5)	(6–10)	(11–50)	(51+)
2008								
Exited	32.2	33.8	41.4	43.6	43.0	35.6	34.6	21.7
Survived	67.8	66.2	58.6	56.4	57.0	64.4	65.4	78.3
Total	100.0	100.0	100.0	100.0	100.0	100.0	100.0	100.0
2013								
Entered	39.1	41.7	52.0	49.6	49.6	46.4	43.2	28.2
Survived	60.9	58.3	48.0	50.4	50.4	53.6	56.8	71.8
Total	100.0	100.0	100.0	100.0	100.0	100.0	100.0	100.0

Source: Author's calculations based on data from Mexico's Economic Census.

Productivity Distributions and Resource Allocation of Exiting, Entering, and Surviving Firms

What are the productivity implications of the firm dynamics described above? In an economy without large misallocation, one would observe that regardless of firm type or size, on average surviving firms would be more productive than exiting ones, entering firms more productive than surviving ones, and, within surviving firms, expanding firms more productive than those that contract or maintain the same size. This section considers whether these patterns are observed in Mexico.[3]

The Exit Process

We introduce the concepts of "productivity-enhancing" and "productivity-reducing" exit. The first occurs when low-productivity firms exit the market; that is, when market forces do what they are supposed to do. But when high-productivity firms exit the market, "productivity-reducing" exit occurs—that is, the market is malfunctioning because firms that should survive fail to do so.[4]

These concepts are operationalized dividing each six-digit sector TFPR distribution into three segments: a low-productivity segment, populated by firms with TFPR up to the 25th percentile of the respective distribution; a medium-productivity segment, populated by firms with TFPR between the 25th and 75th percentile; and a high-productivity segment, populated by firms with TFPR above the 75th percentile.[5] These cut-off points imply that for firms at

---

[3] The number of firms in this section is smaller than in previous ones because, as in Chapter 4, to compute the TFPR distributions, the tails are trimmed and only firms with positive value added are considered.

[4] Many elements in Mexico's $E(L,T,M)$ can account for the exit of high-productivity firms: negative shocks that cannot be accommodated by reducing the number of workers or lowering their salaries; unfair competition from other firms that enjoy special tax regimes or get generous contracts from the government; tax audits that result in large liabilities that cannot be paid; large liabilities resulting from adverse rulings by labor courts in cases of unjustified dismissal; and loss of a large customer in a context where there is no credit to help the firm survive a negative transitory shock. Similarly, low-productivity firms may survive because they do not pay taxes or contributory social insurance; get subsidized credit from a development bank; benefit from special tax regimes; or obtain special contracts from the government (see Chapter 7).

[5] Table 4.7 and Figure 4.4 in Chapter 4 had used greater than four times and less than a quarter times mean TFPR as criteria to separate high- from low-productivity firms. These criteria, however, generate a much larger share of low- versus high-productivity firms. In this chapter, we opt for the 25th/75th percentile criteria so that the share of firms of both types is the same (as more firms are classified as high-productivity ones). As discussed later, results are consistent using either criterion.

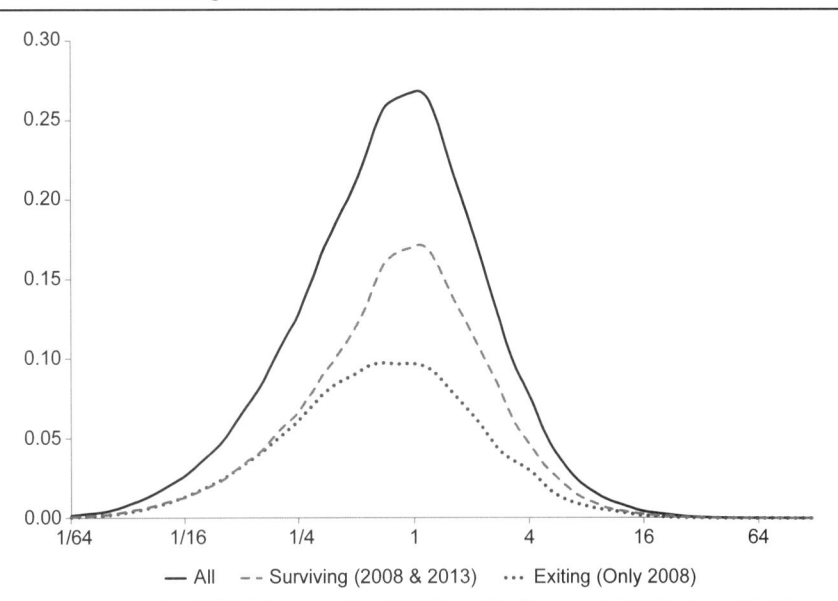

Figure 5.1: Revenue Total Factor Productivity Distribution of Exiting and Surviving Firms, 2008

[Chart showing TFPR distributions with x-axis from 1/64 to 64 and y-axis from 0.00 to 0.30. Three curves: All, Surviving (2008 & 2013), Exiting (Only 2008).]

Source: Author's illustration based on data from Mexico's Economic Census.

the border of the high- and low-productivity segments there is, on average, a 38 percent difference in TFPR, and that this difference increases for firms to the right and left, respectively, of these borders. For instance, for firms in the 90th and 10th percentile, the difference is around 172 percent (see Table 4.1 in Chapter 4). It is then asserted that "productivity-enhancing" exit occurs when firms in the low-productivity segment leave the market, and "productivity-reducing" exit when firms in the high-productivity segment do so.

Figure 5.1 plots three TFPR distributions for 2008: for all firms and separately for those that exited and those that survived. This figure, and subsequent ones, follow the format used in Figures 4.3 and 4.4 in Chapter 4: the horizontal axis measures the revenue productivity of firms in each sector relative to the mean revenue productivity of firms in that sector, and the vertical axis the frequency of observations. As before, each distribution is the sum of the 687 individual six-digit sector distributions. There is more mass in the distribution of surviving firms, in accordance with Table 5.1, which showed that 58 percent of firms in 2008 survived to 2013. More important is the fact that the distribution of exiting firms has more mass to the left of the mean than that of surviving firms, although the differences are small: 67 percent of exiting firms have productivity below the mean versus 61 percent of surviving ones. Moreover, observe that for TFPR values below a quarter of the mean, both distributions are similar (23 percent of exiting firms and 18 percent of surviving ones are at or below that threshold). In parallel, note that for TFPR values larger than four times the mean, the differences in the two distributions are also not large: 4.3 percent of exiting firms and 5.6 percent of surviving ones are on or above that cut-off point. The expectation is that there would be significant differences in the shape of these two distributions. But the fact that this is not the case is evidence that, given Mexico's *E(L,T,M)*, *many low-productivity firms are surviving, and many high-productivity firms are exiting.*

Table 5.4 considers the resource implications of these phenomena. The two upper left columns identify the shares of capital and labor allocated to firms in the high- and low-productivity segment of the TFPR distribution. By construction, 25 percent of all firms are in each segment. Firms in the high-productivity segment absorb 29.1 percent of all labor and 21.5 percent of all capital. Firms in the low-productivity segment absorb 19.7 of all labor and 23.7 percent of all capital.

The two upper right columns show the share of all high- and low-productivity firms that exited. Of all high-productivity firms, 43.5 percent left the market, in contrast to 53.1 percent of all low-productivity firms. While to the best of the author's knowledge there are no international benchmarks with which to compare these numbers, it is noteworthy that a large share of high-productivity firms exited, and that this share is not that different from that of low-productivity firms. The other side of the coin is that almost 47 percent of all low-productivity firms survived, again not that different from 57 percent for the case of high-productivity

Table 5.4: Exiting Firms by Productivity Segment and Type, 2008
(Percent shares)

	High-Productivity Firms	Low-Productivity Firms	High-Productivity Firms that Exit	Low Productivity Firms that Exit
Share of firms	25.0	25.0	43.5	53.1
Share of all labor	29.1	19.7	12.5	9.5
Share of all capital	21.5	23.7	9.4	10.8
Fully formal	41.6	8.8	39.8	44.4
Mixed	33.9	12.7	41.0	42.5
Informal and legal	22.3	30.3	43.9	54.6
Informal and illegal	26.6	17.9	43.3	49.7

Source: Author's calculations based on data from Mexico's Economic Census.

firms. These patterns of exit and survival are contrary to expectations based on a naïve view of market selection, and provide evidence that Mexico's $E(L,T,M)$ sorts very poorly which firms should exit the market and which should stay.

The two upper right columns also show the share of all capital and labor released by high- and low-productivity exiting firms. The share of labor released by high-productivity firms, 12.5 percent, exceeds the share released by low-productivity ones, 9.5 percent. Put differently, the exit process is eliminating more jobs in high-productivity firms than in low ones. For capital, the results are the opposite, but the numbers are similar: 9.4 versus 10.8 percent. Of course, the release of capital and labor by the exit of low-productivity firms is a good thing, but in the case of Mexico it is offset by the release of capital and labor from high-productivity firms, which is clearly undesirable. Because resources released in both directions are similar, on balance, the exit process between 2008 and 2013 did not contribute to improving the allocation of capital and labor in the direction of higher productivity.

The lower rows of Table 5.4 consider patterns by firm type. The two left columns show the share of high- and low-productivity firms. Unsurprisingly given the results of the previous chapter, the share of fully formal firms that is highly productive exceeds by a large margin the share of informal and legal firms: 41.6 versus 22.3 percent. Conversely, a much larger share of informal and legal firms has low productivity compared to fully formal ones: 30.3 versus 8.8 percent. (As usual, mixed and informal and illegal firms are in between.)

More importantly for our purposes here, the two lower left columns show the probabilities of exit for each firm type, conditional on belonging to the high and low segments of the productivity distribution. The probability that a high-productivity fully formal firm exits is lower than that of a high-productivity informal and legal firm, but not by much: 39.8 versus 43.9 percent. For low-productivity firms the differences are somewhat larger, 44.4 versus 54.6 percent. That said, the figures in these columns allow for an important observation: the probability that high-productivity firms of any type exit is quite large.

The exit of high-productivity firms is unfortunate because capital and labor is in such cases essentially wasted: worthwhile investment and employment decisions are nullified because something in Mexico's $E(L,T,M)$ impedes these firms from continuing in the market. In parallel, the survival of low-productivity firms is also a form of waste because the resources tied up in those firms have better uses elsewhere, but again, something in Mexico's $E(L,T,M)$ allows these firms to stay in the market. Table 5.5 provides data to quantify this issue. The first column lists the share of each firm type; the second column lists the share of high-productivity exiting firms and their associated

Table 5.5: Resources in High-Productivity Exiting Firms and Low-Productivity Surviving Firms, 2008
(Percent shares)

	All Firms	High-Productivity Exit			Low-Productivity Survival		
		Firms	Labor	Capital	Firms	Labor	Capital
Fully formal	3.3	0.56	2.79	2.52	0.16	0.73	2.14
Mixed	7.7	1.07	3.59	3.08	0.56	1.41	2.75
Informal and legal	62.5	6.12	3.03	2.18	8.62	5.79	6.47
Informal and illegal	26.4	3.12	3.04	1.67	2.38	2.25	1.54
Total	100.0	10.87	12.45	9.45	11.72	10.18	12.90

Source: Author's calculations based on data from Mexico's Economic Census.

labor and capital; and the third column lists low-productivity surviving firms and associated resources. To make numbers comparable, they are all expressed as shares of the total number of firms, capital, and labor present in 2008.

Consider first high-productivity exit. Although formal firms (fully formal and mixed) are a minority in this category, they are over-represented: they are 11 percent of all firms, but 15 percent (= (0.56 + 1.07)/10.87) of all high-productivity exiting ones. The exit of any high-productivity firm is unwelcome, of course, but the exit of high-productivity formal firms is particularly unwelcome because they are on average larger and more capital-intensive than informal ones. As a result, formal firms account for over half of all labor and capital wasted by high-productivity exit.

The contrast with low-productivity survival is stark. Most of that contrast, and most of the resources wasted, is due to informal firms (legal and illegal). Formal firms are under-represented in this case: despite being 11 percent of all firms, they are 6.1 percent (= (0.16+0.56)/11.72) of all low-productivity survivors. But again, because they are larger and more capital-intensive, they represent a disproportionate amount of capital and labor. That said, it stands out that informal and legal firms—that is, those with non-salaried contracts—account for the bulk of low-productivity survival. And again, even though most are very small, because they are so numerous they account for much of the resources tied up in low-productivity survival.

These results can be summarized as follows: Mexico's *E(L,T,M)* allows too many resources to be wasted through the exit of high-productivity firms, particularly formal firms, and it allows too many resources to be wasted by the survival of low-productivity firms, particularly informal firms and, within these, firms with non-salaried contracts.

The Entry Process

Figure 5.2 plots the TFPR distribution of all firms in 2013 (constructed in this case from the sum of 691 six-digit sector distributions) and, separately, the distributions of surviving and entering firms. The latter two distributions overlap substantially but, contrary to what one would expect, that of entering firms has more mass to the left of the mean: 64 percent of entering firms have productivity levels below the mean versus 57 percent of surviving firms. Further, 19.6 percent of entrants have TFPR values less than one-fourth of the mean, in contrast to 15 percent of survivors; and only 5.1 percent of entrants have TFPR values greater than four times the mean versus 6.8 percent of survivors. This indicates that, as with exit, Mexico's $E(L,T,M)$ does a poor job separating high- from low-productivity entrants.

Following the same reasoning as earlier, "productivity-reducing" entry is defined as that associated with firms that entered the market in the low-productivity segment of their six-digit sector TFPR distribution; and "productivity-enhancing" entry is defined as that associated with firms in the high-productivity segment. Table 5.6 has the relevant information. The upper-left columns show the share of high- and low-productivity firms in 2013. By

Figure 5.2: Revenue Total Factor Productivity Distributions of Entering and Surviving Firms, 2013

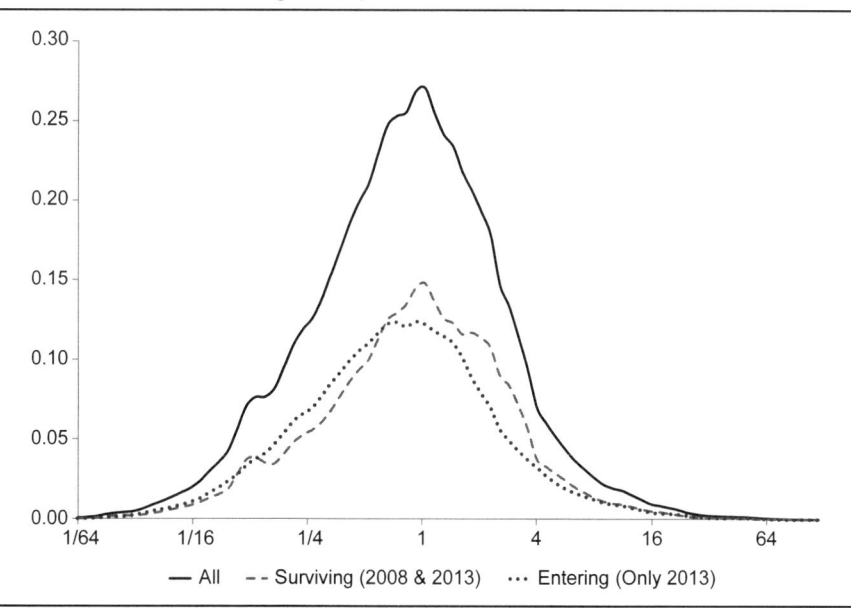

Source: Author's illustration based on data from Mexico's Economic Census.

construction, they are 25 percent in each case. High-productivity firms attract 27.4 percent of all labor and 17.2 percent of all capital, while low-productivity firms attract 20 percent of all labor and 26.4 percent of all capital.

Table 5.6: Entering Firms by Productivity Segment and Type, 2013
 (Percent shares)

	High-Productivity Firms	Low-Productivity Firms	High-Productivity Firms that Entered	Low-Productivity Firms that Entered
Share of firms	25.0	25.0	54.8	64.1
Share of all labor	27.4	20.0	14.1	11.8
Share of all capital	17.2	26.4	8.4	15.1
Fully formal	37.7	10.4	47.7	49.0
Mixed	33.4	12.7	49.2	51.7
Informal and legal	21.8	29.6	55.9	64.8
Informal and illegal	30.7	15.2	55.8	65.0

Source: Author's calculations based on data from Mexico's Economic Census.

The upper-right columns show entering high- and low-productivity firms as a share of all high- and low-productivity firms. Note first that in both cases the shares are over 50 percent, indicating that there was a lot of entry between 2008 and 2013.[6] That said, the more important result is that, contrary to expectations, entrants are a higher proportion of all low- than high-productivity firms: 64.1 versus 54.8 percent. This is consistent with Figure 5.2, which showed more mass in the left tail of the distribution of entrants compared to survivors. An alternative way of stating this result is to say that 27 percent of all entering firms are in the low-productivity segment of the 2013 TFPR distribution, compared to 23 percent in the high-productivity segment.

What are the allocative implications of entry? As can be seen in the upper-right columns, "productivity-reducing" entering firms absorbed 11.8 percent of the labor and 15.1 percent of the capital available in 2013; this compares with 14.1 and 8.4 percent, respectively, for "productivity-enhancing" entering firms. As with the exit process, on balance the entry process did not contribute to improving the allocation of capital and labor between 2008 and 2013.

---

[6] Altogether, 58 percent of all firms in 2013 entered after 2008, which is different from the 50 percent figure reported in Table 5.1. This difference is because, as noted before, this analysis leaves out firms with zero capital or value added, which implied dropping more survivors than entrants.

The lower rows of Table 5.6 disaggregate these trends by firm type. The lower left columns show that a higher proportion of formal (fully formal and mixed) than informal (legal and illegal) firms are highly productive. This is not surprising given the discussion in Chapter 4. Neither is the fact that informal and legal firms represent the highest share of low-productivity firms. These results mimic those presented in Table 5.4, with the difference that they refer to the 2013 TFPR distribution. The last point to note, in the lower-right columns, is that within low-productivity firms, informal entrants are significantly more important than formal entrants.

Table 5.7 explores the resource implications of the above results. The first column lists firm types; the second column lists high-productivity entering firms and their associated labor and capital; and the third columns lists low-productivity entering firms and their associated resources. To make numbers comparable, they are all expressed as shares of all firms, capital, and labor present in 2013.

There are two key results: first, even though formal firms are only 10.3 percent of all firms, they are 12.9 percent (= (0.76 + 1.01)/13.63) of all high-productivity entrants and only 3.8 percent (= 0.21 + 0.40)/15.97) of all low-productivity entrants. They also account for 46.6 percent of all labor and 56.3 percent of all capital in high-productivity entry, versus 21.1 percent and 41 percent, respectively, in low-productivity entry. This implies that informal firms account for most of the resources allocated to low-productivity entry.

The second key result is that within informal firms, those with non-salaried contracts account for the bulk of low-productivity entry: they constitute 70.7 percent of all firms, but 84.5 percent of all low-productivity entrants. Moreover, they account for 64 percent and 50 percent of the labor and capital, respectively, in low-productivity entry. As before, these firms are smaller

Table 5.7: Firms and Resources in High- and Low-Productivity Entering Firms, 2013
(Percent shares)

	All Firms	High-Productivity Entry			Low-Productivity Entry		
		Firms	Labor	Capital	Firms	Labor	Capital
Fully formal	4.2	0.76	3.25	2.58	0.21	0.96	2.14
Mixed	6.1	1.01	3.31	2.13	0.40	1.53	4.04
Informal and legal	70.7	8.62	4.25	2.18	13.5	7.53	7.56
Informal and illegal	18.9	3.24	3.27	1.47	1.86	1.75	1.32
Total	**100.0**	**13.63**	**14.08**	**8.36**	**15.97**	**11.77**	**15.06**

Source: Author's calculations based on data from Mexico's Economic Census.

than the rest, and the entry of each one individually would hardly matter for resource allocation. But because there are so many of them, together they contribute the most to the resources wasted through the entry process.

These results can be summarized thus: *Mexico's **E**(L,T,M) allows substantial resources to be channeled to low-productivity entering firms, particularly those with non-salaried contracts.*

It is useful to end this discussion underlining the implications of low-productivity entry for the allocation of investment. Of the total capital stock in 2013, 15 percent was accounted for by investments in low-productivity firms between 2008 and 2013, almost double the amount accounted for by investments in high-productivity firms (8.3 percent). This finding calls into question the usual association between more investment and increased productivity. Indeed, it is often stated that investments embed newer technologies (more sophisticated equipment and machines, and so on), and that therefore increasing investment will raise productivity. But as shown, in Mexico this is only partly so. Clearly, many bad investment projects were undertaken during this period, and this fact weakens the association between investment and productivity.

Digression: The Entry Process Ex-post

A shortcoming of the previous discussion is that it compares the productivity of entrants and survivors along the 2013 TFPR distribution only. One could reasonably argue that in the case of entry a more dynamic approach is needed, as entrants may initially have low-productivity but over time may acquire experience, improve their processes, learn, and eventually become high-productivity firms (and argue conversely that firms that enter with high productivity may then disappoint). Thus, to determine the extent of productivity-enhancing and productivity-reducing entry, one needs to observe entering firms in future years.

To properly assess this issue, one needs the 2018 census or, alternatively, one needs to identify entering firms in the 2008 census, which can only be done with a panel starting in the 2003 census (so it can be seen what firms were present in the 2008 census but not in the 2003 census). Neither of these possibilities is available. Nevertheless, to give more insights into the entry process, an ad-hoc combination of the information available in the 2008 and 2013 censuses is carried out, and some projections are then made to the 2018 census. More precisely, it is assumed that, for each productivity segment of the 2013 TFPR distribution, exit rates of entering firms will be the same as those observed for exiting firms in the corresponding segment of the 2008 productivity distribution (i.e., that future and past exit patterns are the same). Further, it is assumed that for entering firms in 2013 that survive to 2018, transition probabilities from one productivity segment of the TFPR distribution to another are the same as those observed for firms that survived from 2008 to 2013 (see the discussion below). Figure 5.3 maps these transitions, and includes the respective probabilities in parentheses next to each case (obtained from Tables 5.4, 5.5, and 5.6).

The results can be summarized as follows: considering all entering firms in the 2013 census, 47 percent will not survive to the 2018 census (with variations across productivity segments). In turn, once transits across productivity segments are considered, entering firms that survive would be distributed in the 2018 TFPR distribution as follows: 23.5 percent in the low-productivity segment, 50.1 percent in the medium segment, and 26.4 percent in the high one.

It should be emphasized that these results are hypothetical, as opposed to the ones presented earlier based on observed exit and entry behavior (and the ones presented below for transition patterns of surviving firms). With that caveat, two points need attention. First, ignoring exit, the probability that firms have high productivity five years after entry is larger than the probability at entry: 26 versus 23 percent. This is a welcome result, which follows from the fact that, on average, surviving firms move to the high-productivity segment of the TFPR distribution (see below). That said, the changes are relatively minor. The five-year perspective modifies the balance between productivity-enhancing and productivity-reducing entry, but not by much: there is still a lot of entry of low-productivity firms that, five years later, will remain low-productivity firms.

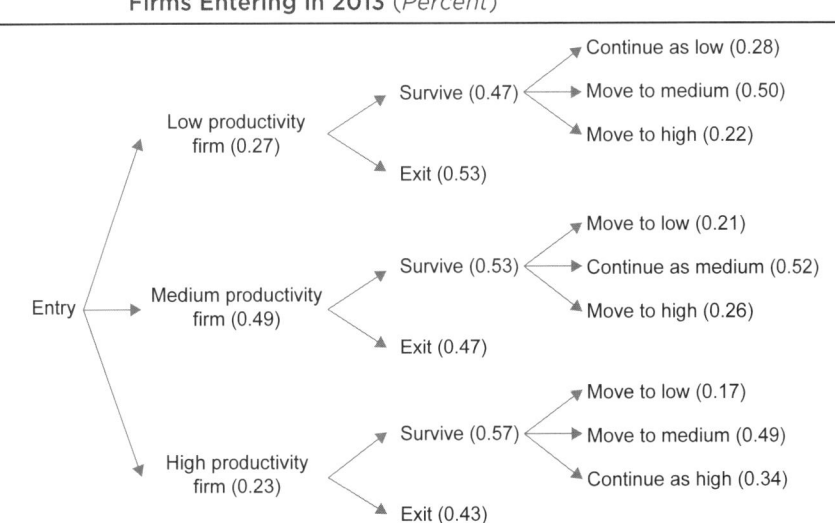

Figure 5.3: Hypothetical Survival and Transition Probabilities to 2018 of Firms Entering in 2013 *(Percent)*

Entry
- Low productivity firm (0.27)
  - Survive (0.47)
    - Continue as low (0.28)
    - Move to medium (0.50)
    - Move to high (0.22)
  - Exit (0.53)
- Medium productivity firm (0.49)
  - Survive (0.53)
    - Move to low (0.21)
    - Continue as medium (0.52)
    - Move to high (0.26)
  - Exit (0.47)
- High productivity firm (0.23)
  - Survive (0.57)
    - Move to low (0.17)
    - Move to medium (0.49)
    - Continue as high (0.34)
  - Exit (0.43)

Source: Author's illustration based on data from Mexico's Economic Census.

The second point, however, is that exit is very important, because it calls attention to the fact that almost half of all entrants will not survive five years. This consideration does change the balance between productivity-reducing and productivity-enhancing entry, and substantially so. Adding the probability of exit less than five years after entry with the probability of survival and transit to low productivity, the following result is obtained: given Mexico's $E(L,T,M)$, within a five-year period, 58 percent of all entrants will either die or survive as low-productivity firms.

The Change Process of Surviving Firms

The analysis of firm dynamics is completed by considering surviving firms. Their case is somewhat more complicated because we observe them twice and can therefore classify them by their location in the 2008 and 2013 TFPR distributions. Figure 5.4 plots both distributions. The 2013 distribution is less smooth but has more mass to the right of the mean, indicating that in 2013 more firms have higher than average productivity vis-à-vis 2008 (40 versus 36 percent). This provides preliminary evidence that the change process of surviving firms is operating in the right direction.

Figure 5.4: Revenue Total Factor Productivity Distributions of Surviving Firms, 2008 and 2013

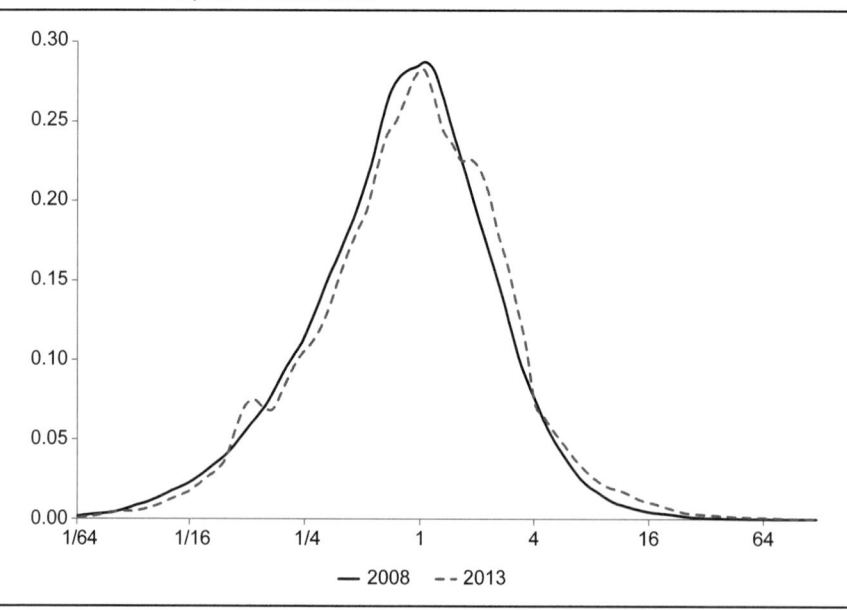

Source: Author's illustration based on data from Mexico's Economic Census.

Table 5.8: Share of Resources by Productivity Segment, Surviving Firms, 2008 and 2013

Productivity Segment		Percent Share of Firms	Percent Share of Labor		Percent Share of Capital		Firm Size (numbers of workers)	
2008	2013		2008	2013	2008	2013	2008	2013
Low	Low	6.3	4.9	4.6	6.3	6.7	3.5	3.1
Low	Medium	11.3	9.4	9.1	12.8	11.3	3.8	3.5
Low	High	4.9	4.0	3.7	4.0	2.2	3.7	3.2
Medium	Low	10.9	9.2	9.1	10.4	12.5	3.8	3.6
Medium	Medium	26.6	28.8	28.6	30.9	31.2	4.9	4.6
Medium	High	13.1	13.9	13.4	13.8	9.1	4.8	4.4
High	Low	4.5	3.8	4.0	2.8	4.7	3.8	3.8
High	Medium	13.2	14.6	15.6	10.9	15.0	5.0	5.1
High	High	9.2	11.3	11.8	7.9	7.2	5.6	5.5
Total		100.0	100.0	100.0	100.0	100.0		
Absolute values		1,392,720	6,318,532	5,969,475	1,354,696	1,577,458	4.5	4.3

Source: Author's calculations based on data from Mexico's Economic Census.

The resource allocation implications of this shift are quantified in Table 5.8. The first column classifies firms by their productivity status in both years. Since firms could change their relative productivity position between 2008 and 2013 (in both directions), there are nine possibilities: firms that in 2008 were in the low-productivity segment in the TFPR distribution and continued to be so in 2013; firms in the low-productivity segment in 2008 that shifted to the medium-productivity one in 2013; and so on. The second column records the share of firms in each possibility. The third and fourth columns report the share of labor and capital absorbed in each case in each year, and the fifth average firm size. To facilitate its reading the table is divided into three blocks, according to 2008 productivity segments.

Consider first the aggregate changes in capital and labor. The bottom row shows that total employment in surviving firms fell from 6.3 to 5.9 million workers, or 5.6 percent, while the capital stock increased by 16.4 percent (consistent with the prior observation that surviving firms became more capital-intensive); hence, their average size fell from 4.5 to 4.3 workers. That said, and again consistent with previous findings, firms that are in the high-productivity segment of the TFPR distribution in both years are the largest of all and, overall, firms located in the high- or medium-productivity segments in both years are larger than those located in the low- or medium-productivity segments.[7]

Focusing on changes in capital and labor allocations across TFPR distributions, it can be seen that firms that were in the high-productivity segment in 2013 absorbed a larger share of labor in that year than in 2008 (31.4 versus 29.7 percent). They also absorbed more capital (26.9 versus 21.6 percent). At the other end, firms in the low-productivity segment in 2013 absorbed less labor than in 2008 (17.4 versus 18.3 percent) and less capital (20.2 versus 23.1). In other words, between 2008 and 2013 the share of labor allocated to firms in the high-productivity segment of the 2013 TFPR distribution increased by 1.7 percentage points, and that of capital by 5.3 percentage points; and the share of labor allocated to firms in the low-productivity segment fell by 0.9 percentage points, while that of capital fell by 2.9 percentage points. Moreover, note that resource gains by firms in the high-productivity segment exceed resource losses by firms in the low-productivity one, implying that resources were also shifted from medium- to high-productivity firms. On balance, and as opposed to the case of exit and entry, the process of change within surviving firms contributed to shifting resources towards higher-productivity firms.

What are the characteristics of high- and low-productivity surviving firms? Table 5.9 classifies them by their size and type in 2008, and by their location in the productivity segment of the 2008 and 2013 TFPR distributions.[8] By construction, each column adds up to 100 percent, and thus describes how surviving firms of each type and size are distributed in the nine productivity segments.

The results are in line with the previous findings. The share of fully formal firms with consistently high productivity is more than double the share of informal and legal firms (17.6 versus 7.8 percent); and the share of fully formal firms with consistently low productivity is less than one-fourth (1.7 versus 8.1 percent) that of informal and legal firms. Mixed firms and informal and illegal firms are in between these extremes.

Since surviving firms may move across productivity segments, high- and medium-productivity combinations and low- and medium- productivity combinations are also considered. This analysis finds that 79.7 percent of all fully

---

[7] Consistently high-productivity firms were 25 percent larger than the average in 2008 and 28 percent larger in 2013. Consistently low-productivity firms were 22 percent smaller than the average in 2008 and 28 percent smaller in 2013.

[8] The classification could have been done as well by the type and size of surviving firms in 2013, but it is more illustrative to give a sense of firm characteristics at the start of the process of change.

Table 5.9: Surviving Firms by Type, Size, and Productivity Segment, 2008 and 2013 (*Percent shares*)

Productivity Segment 2008	2013	Formality Status in 2008 FF	M	IL	II	Size in 2008 (1–5)	(6–10)	(11–50)	(51+)
Low	Low	1.7	2.6	8.1	4.0	6.7	3.5	2.8	3.8
Low	Medium	4.2	7.1	13.4	8.7	11.7	8.7	6.4	8.2
Low	High	2.4	3.3	5.5	4.2	5.0	4.2	3.5	3.0
Medium	Low	7.4	8.2	11.7	10.4	11.3	8.3	7.4	8.6
Medium	Medium	27.2	28.5	25.0	29.5	26.4	28.4	27.1	30.3
Medium	High	15.2	16.4	11.6	15.3	12.8	15.6	15.9	13.1
High	Low	4.5	4.0	4.7	4.2	4.6	3.9	3.8	3.8
High	Medium	19.7	16.3	12.1	13.9	12.8	14.9	17.0	17.3
High	High	17.6	13.6	7.8	9.7	8.6	12.4	16.0	11.8
Total		100.0	100.0	100.0	100.0	100.0	100.0	100.0	100.0

Source: Author's calculations based on data from Mexico's Economic Census.
Note: FF = fully formal; M = mixed; IL = informal and legal; II = informal and illegal.

formal firms had consistently high or medium productivity, or moved between high and medium productivity levels (in either direction), in contrast to 56.5 percent of informal and legal firms; and that 40.5 percent of fully formal firms consistently had low or medium productivity, or moved between medium and low productivity, versus 58.2 percent of informal and legal firms. (As before, mixed and informal and illegal firms are in between those extremes.) Put differently, when formal firms survive, they are more likely to consistently have high productivity, or to move between high- and medium-productivity levels, particularly if they have only legal salaried contracts. When informal firms survive, they are more likely to consistently have low productivity, or move between low- and medium-productivity levels, particularly if they have non-salaried contracts.

Net Effects of Exit, Entry, and Survival on Resource Allocation and Productivity

So far, the processes of firm exit, entry, and change have been considered separately, but clearly all three occurred simultaneously. To see their combined effects, Figure 5.5 plots the TFPR distributions of all firms in 2008 and 2013. Even though these two distributions look similar, we now know that during this five-year period there was substantial change in the firms that populate

Figure 5.5: Revenue Total Factor Productivity Distributions, All Firms, 2008 and 2013

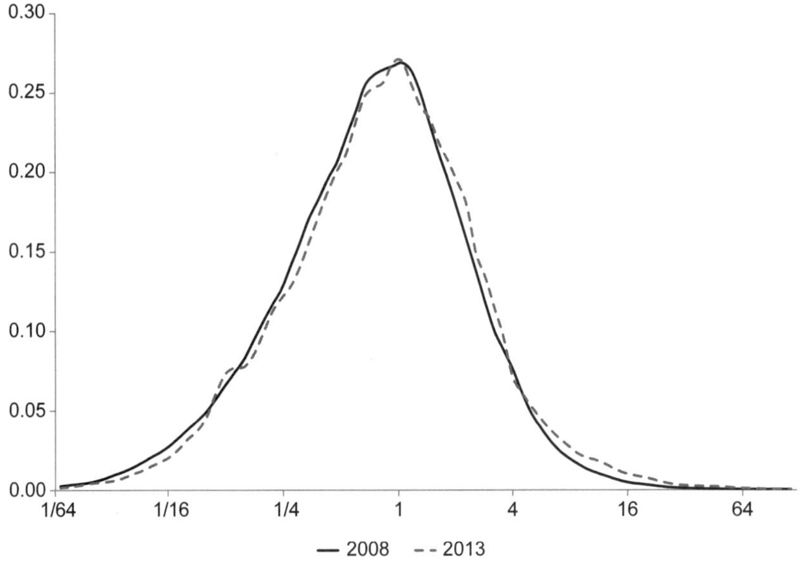

Source: Author's illustration based on data from Mexico's Economic Census.

them: 47 percent of the firms in the 2008 distribution are no longer present in the 2013 one; approximately 58 percent of the firms in the 2013 distribution were not present in the 2008 distribution; and many of the firms that are present in both distributions changed in size, type, and capital intensity.

The 2013 distribution has slightly less mass to the left of the mean: 60.1 percent of all firms versus 63.7 percent in the 2008 distribution. Further, the share of firms with one-fourth of mean TFPR was 20.4 percent in 2008 compared to 17.2 in 2013; on the other side, the share of firms with four times mean TFPR was 6.1 percent in 2013 versus 5.1 percent in 2008. These numbers, and visual inspection of Figure 5.5, would appear to be good news: when everything is said and done with firm exit, entry, and survival, there are more firms in 2013 with higher-than-average productivity than in 2008.

Critically, however, the fact that there are more firms with higher-than-average productivity does not immediately imply that these firms get more resources; large misallocation may offset that positive change, channeling excessive resources to lower-productivity firms. And, unfortunately, this was the case in Mexico. As Table 5.10 shows, the shares of capital and labor absorbed by high-productivity firms fell between 2013 and 2008, while the shares absorbed by low-productivity firms increased.

Table 5.10: Share of Resources by Productivity Segment, All Firms, 2008 and 2013
(Percent shares)

		Low	Medium	High
Labor	2008	19.7	51.2	29.1
	2013	19.9	52.5	27.5
Capital	2008	23.7	54.7	21.5
	2013	26.4	56.4	17.2

Source: Author's calculations based on data from Mexico's Economic Census.

This unfortunate outcome is the net result of three processes operating in opposite directions. On the negative side, an exit process that allows some low-productivity firms to survive and some high-productivity firms to die, together with an entry process that attracts too many low-productivity firms. On the positive side, a change process within surviving firms that channels more resources towards higher-productivity ones. Unfortunately, the positive impact on resource allocation obtained from the change process of surviving firms was dominated by the negative impact of entry and exit.

Table 5.1 helps explain why. Surviving firms absorbed only 47 percent of the increase in the capital stock between 2008 and 2013, and they reduced their use of labor by approximately 2.5 percent. Entering firms, on the other hand, absorbed 53 percent of the additional capital and all the increase in labor (plus the labor shed by surviving and exiting firms). Put differently, too many of the additional resources available between 2008 and 2013 were channeled to new firms and not enough to the growth of existing firms. This is a key finding: *given Mexico's E(L,T,M), it is easier for new firms to enter than for surviving firms to grow, even if the latter have high productivity.*

What would have happened if between 2008 and 2013 a larger share of the *same* capital investments and the *same* labor growth had been channeled to surviving firms, particularly those with high productivity, rather than to the entry of new firms? Why did high-productivity surviving firms, particularly formal ones, fail to grow more? Why was all employment growth and a large share of new investment dispersed among many small and very small entering firms, most of them informal low-productivity ones, and not concentrated in larger and higher-productivity entrants? And what if some of the low-productivity firms that survived had exited?

Chapters 7 and 8 try to answer some of these questions. At this point, however, the observation that needs to be emphasized is that if during this five-year period Mexico's *E(L,T,M)* had evolved differently, the *same* capital investments and the *same* labor force growth would have resulted in a size/type firm distribution in 2013 characterized by more and larger formal firms and by fewer informal firms, especially with non-salaried contracts. Of course, if Mexico's $E(L,T,M)$ had evolved differently, some high-productivity firms that died after 2008 would have survived to 2013, and some low-productivity firms that survived would have exited. Altogether, this would have yielded a TFPR distribution in 2013 with less misallocation and, in consequence, more output. In other words, *under a different $E(L,T,M)$, productivity growth between 2008 and 2013 would have been faster, and GDP growth higher.*

Extrapolation of Firm Dynamics between 1998 and 2013

The previous analysis was made possible by the panel structure of the 2008 and 2013 censuses and unfortunately cannot be carried out for the 1998–2013 period. That said, one can take advantage of the fact that the 2013 census records the age of all establishments to give some insights into firm dynamics over this longer time span.

Table 5.11 classifies firms in the 2013 census by age and type. For each firm type shares add to 100 percent and describe that type's age profile. Firms that are at most five years old must have entered after 2008, so they correspond to those classified as entering in the previous sections.[9] Firms six to 10 years old must have entered after 2003; in turn, those with 11 to 15 years must have entered after 1998; finally, those with 16 or more years must have entered before 1998.

Focusing first on all firm types, Table 5.11 confirms the information presented earlier in Table 5.1: nearly 50 percent of all firms in the 2013 census were not present in the 2008 census. More novel is the finding that only 19 percent of all firms in the 2013 census are 16 years old or older, implying that 81 percent of the firms in the 2013 census were not present in the 1998 census.

Focusing next on each firm type, note that the share of formal establishments (legal and mixed) 16 or more years old is higher than that of informal ones (legal and illegal). This longer survival pattern is consistent with the five-year patterns described earlier in Table 5.3. Because informal firms have higher entry and exit rates than formal ones, at any point in time they are younger. Put differently, although there is substantial churning of firms in the formal sector, such that over 50 percent of firms are at most a

---

[9] The numbers do not match exactly. Table 5.1 reports that 2,012,491 establishments entered after 2008 versus 2,054,971 in Table 5.11. However, the difference is very small (2 percent), probably due to misreporting of age or some borderline cases.

Table 5.11: Establishments in 2013 by Age and Type
(Number and percent shares)

	FF Number	FF Share	M Number	M Share	IL Number	IL Share	II Number	II Share	Total Number	Total Share
5 years or less	55,434	32.2	87,337	36.9	1,536,273	51.6	375,927	53.2	2,054,971	50.1
6–10 years	36,935	21.6	49,471	21.0	560,803	18.8	136,753	19.3	783,962	19.1
11–15 years	25,448	14.8	34,675	14.6	322,890	11.1	80,875	11.4	473,888	11.6
16+ years	53,868	31.1	64,930	27.4	553,646	18.5	113,835	16.1	786,279	19.1
Total	**171,685**	**100**	**236,413**	**100**	**2,983,612**	**100**	**707,390**	**100**	**4,099,100**	**100**

Source: Author's calculations based on data from Mexico's Economic Census.
Note: FF = fully formal; M = mixed; IL = informal and legal; II = informal and illegal.

Table 5.12: Share of Resources by Productivity Segment, 1998, 2003, 2008, and 2013
(Percent shares)

		Low	Medium	High
Labor	1998	18.5	51.2	30.3
	2003	19.4	52.7	27.9
	2008	19.7	51.2	29.1
	2013	19.9	52.7	27.4
Capital	1998	26.4	54.3	19.3
	2003	25.1	56.6	18.3
	2008	23.7	54.7	21.5
	2013	26.4	56.4	17.2

Source: Author's calculations based on data from Mexico's Economic Census.

decade old, churning is larger in the informal sector, where over 70 percent of firms are at most a decade old.

It is useful here to return to Figure 4.4 in Chapter 4, where the comparison of the 1998 and 2013 TFPR distributions revealed increasing dispersion in firm productivity. To relate this outcome to firm entry and exit over this longer time span, Table 5.12 compares the shares of capital and labor in the three segments of the 1998 and 2013 TFPR distributions. For convenience, it also includes the values for 2003 and 2008. Over this decade and a half, the share of labor allocated to firms in the low-productivity segment increased continuously. The share of capital in the low-productivity segment stayed constant but fell in the high-productivity segment. Altogether, over 1998–2013 more resources were allocated to low-productivity firms.[10]

---

[10] Table 4.7 in Chapter 4 identified high and low-productivity firms using four times and one-quarter times mean TFPR as thresholds, and revealed that with that criteria there very few high-productivity firms. And while their share increased between 1998 and 2013 (from 3.7 to 6 percent of all firms), the share of low-productivity firms increased as well (from 14 to 17.2 percent). Moreover, while high-productivity firms by the criteria of Table 4.7 attracted more resources, in 2013 their share was still very low (1.2 percent of capital and 5.6 percent of labor); low-productivity firms also attracted more resources, and their share in 2013 was significantly larger (11.6 percent of capital and labor). Put differently, while the number of "top-performing firms" increased, aggregate resource allocation patterns were dominated by the increase in "worst-performing firms." Table 5.12, using the 25th and 75th percentile as thresholds to separate low- from high-productivity firms, shows similar results, although less sharp because, by construction, the number of firms on each end is the same.

Firm dynamics are central to understand these findings. There was a huge amount of exit over this decade and a half: again, 81 percent of firms present in 2013 did not exist in 1998. Extrapolating from the 2008–2013 period analyzed before to this longer time span, many high-productivity firms must have exited, particularly with salaried contracts (Table 5.4). There was also a lot of entry. Extrapolating again, part of that entry must have been accounted for by low-productivity informal firms, particularly with non-salaried contracts. Of course, formal firms also entered with, on average, higher productivity. But the hypothesis that during this 15-year period entry was dominated by informal firms is consistent with the fact that between 1998 and 2013 these firms progressively absorbed a larger share of resources (see Table 3.7) and accounted for more than 50 percent of firms in an increasing number of six-digit sectors in manufacturing, commerce, and services (see Table 3.11). Some of the entrants eventually must have survived as high-productivity firms, but not many; the majority either exited before five years or survived as low-productivity firms (Table 5.7 and Figure 5.3).

During this 15-year period, even though the average size of formal firms increased, average firm size fell because the share of informal firms in all firms increased (see Table 3.7). Formal firms survived more than informal ones (Table 5.11). But on average there was little growth among surviving firms of any type, a critical issue since larger firms have higher productivity (Table 5.8). Extrapolating again from the behavior observed between 2008 and 2013, formal firms must have grown more than informal ones. This improved resource allocation, because among surviving firms, formal ones have consistently higher productivity than informal ones (Table 5.9). But surviving firms probably did not attract a lot of labor, as these firms grew more by capital deepening. Entry of new firms attracted more labor and about half of capital investments (Table 5.1).

The entry or growth of formal firms mostly explains the greater mass in the right tail of the 2013 TFPR distribution compared to the 1998 one, although some informal firms also contribute to it. At the same time, the entry and survival of mostly informal firms explains the greater mass in the left tail, although again some formal firms contribute to it. But the net effect of all these changes on resource allocation was unfavorable (Table 5.12). At the end of the day, misallocation was higher in 2013 than in 1998 (see Table 4.1), and so were productivity losses (Table 4.2).

In sum, although panel data are not available for the 1998–2013 period, the available evidence is consistent with the hypothesis that during this 15-year period the elements in Mexico's $E(L,T,M)$ that misallocate resources did so continuously in the direction of discouraging the survival and growth of higher-productivity, large and generally formal firms, and favoring the entry and survival of low-productivity and generally informal firms. *These elements in $E(L,T,M)$ dominated any other changes in policies, programs, and regulations put in place over the same 15-year period to increase efficiency and improve the allocation of resources.*

Moreover, there is evidence that these patterns, particularly the one associated with little firm growth, have been present in Mexico over longer time spans than the ones considered above, and that their impact on productivity is substantial. Hsieh and Klenow (2014) compare the dynamics of Mexican and United States manufacturing firms. They find that given a firm's size at birth, over a 40-year time span the average firm in Mexico that survives increases its size by a factor of 2, while a firm in the United States does so by a factor of 7. Hsieh and Klenow estimate that over time this difference in growth patterns lowers the productivity of Mexican manufacturing relative to that of the United States by about 25 percent.

Dysfunctional firm dynamics are at the heart of Mexico's productivity problem. Rather than having a Schumpeterian process of "creative destruction" by which low-productivity firms are replaced by high-productivity ones, and surviving high-productivity firms grow, between 1998 and 2013 Mexico experienced a more complex and contradictory phenomenon: in part Schumpeterian "creative destruction," but also in part something more akin to "destructive creation," as some low-productivity firms replaced high-productivity ones, and some low-productivity firms that should never have entered the market competed away resources and market share from high-productivity surviving firms that should have grown more.

Firm Dynamics and Job Changes

In any economy jobs are created and destroyed as firms exit, enter, grow, or contract (Davis, Haltiwanger, and Schuh 1997). Workers move out of low-productivity jobs and into high-productivity ones as the Schumpeterian process weans out low-productivity firms and fosters high-productivity ones. In these circumstances, firm-induced job changes contribute to increase productivity and, on balance, create better opportunities for workers. Better firms, better jobs.

But as just shown, this process works very imperfectly in Mexico. Because of dysfunctional firm dynamics, an important share of firm-induced job changes is not associated with better opportunities for workers. Workers move from one job to another without much gain in productivity. Firm churning, which could be a good thing, is not necessarily so. Some of it is in fact useless: entering firms are no better than the exiting firms that they replace.

The next chapter elaborates on the implications of large firm churning for workers' opportunities to acquire human capital from labor training and on-the-job learning. This section just takes advantage of the previous analysis to provide some stylized facts.

Table 5.13 displays the changes in employment derived from the 2008–2013 firm panel data. The first row lists the number of jobs lost because of firm exit, distributed by the location of exiting firms in the low-, medium-, and high-productivity segments of the 2008 TFPR distribution. The second row lists jobs created by firm entry, in this case by segments of the 2013 TFPR distribution. The third row lists the change in employment in surviving firms, obtained by subtracting workers in each segment of the 2013 TFPR distribution from workers in the corresponding segment of the 2008 TFPR distribution. Since employment in surviving firms fell, the row reports a loss of jobs.[11]

Four features are relevant. First, firm-induced job changes are very large. Altogether, the firms behind Table 5.13 employed 11.3 million workers in 2008 and 12.9 million in 2013. However, during the five-year period, 12.3 million workers changed jobs, an average of 2.5 million a year (a whopping 20 percent). Second, most job changes are associated with firm entry and exit. Of the 5.3 million jobs lost between 2008 and 2013, 93.4 percent were due to firm exit and only 6.6 percent to job shedding by surviving firms. And of the 12.9 million jobs available in 2013, 53.4 percent were associated with entering firms.

Third, exiting firms destroy more high- than low-productivity jobs: 1.41 million versus 1.07 million. Put differently, for every job lost by the exit of low-productivity firms, 1.3 jobs were lost by the exit of high-productivity ones. This highlights the costliness of dysfunctional exit to workers as measured by the loss of jobs in high-productivity firms. Fourth, entering firms create more jobs in high- than low-productivity firms: 1.8 million versus 1.5 million. This is good news, although it would be better news were it not for the fact that, as shown in Figure 5.3, only about 57 percent of entering high-productivity firms are expected to survive.

---

[11] The figures in Table 5.13 should not be interpreted as referring to turnover of individual workers. For instance, while we do know that 4.9 million jobs were lost because of firm exit between 2008 and 2013, we do not know what happened to the individual workers occupying those jobs. Perhaps a worker in one of the lost jobs left the labor force and never re-entered, another found a job in a high-productivity firm, while yet another one ended up employed in a firm that is not captured in the census data, or decided to become self-employed. To measure labor turnover over 2008–2013, a panel of workers for this five-year period is needed, which unfortunately is not available.

Table 5.13: Job Changes by Productivity Segment, 2008–2013
(Number of workers)

	Productivity			
	Low	Medium	High	Total
Jobs lost by firm exit	(−) 1,075,315	(−) 2,510,164	(−) 1,411,318	(−) 4,996,797
Jobs gained by firm entry	(+) 1,525,999	(+) 3,611,373	(+) 1,822,493	(+) 6,959,865
Jobs lost in surviving firms	(−) 97,016	(−) 99,900	(−) 152, 141	(−) 349,057
Net	(+) 353,668	(+) 1,001,309	(+) 259,034	(+) 1,614,011
Gross movements	2,698,330	6,221,437	3,385,952	12,305,719

Source: Author's calculations based on data from Mexico's Economic Census.

What are the net effects of these job changes? Following the previous discussion, one can distinguish between firm-induced productivity-enhancing and productivity-reducing job changes. The former are associated with workers who lose their job because low-productivity firms exit, and with workers who find a job because high-productivity firms expand or enter. The latter are associated with workers who lose their job because high-productivity firms exit, and with workers who find a job in low-productivity entering or surviving firms. Table 5.13 implies that these two types of job changes were almost the same: between 2008 and 2013 there were 2,994,824 productivity-enhancing job changes, and 3,089,458 productivity-reducing ones. This is a remarkable result: because of firms' decisions, workers were as likely to change jobs from high- to low-productivity firms as from low- to high-productivity ones. The other side of the coin of large firm churning is large job changes; if firm churning fails to reallocate resources towards high-productivity firms, as is the case in Mexico, many workers will change jobs, but few will end up employed in better firms.

Firm Dynamics beyond the Census Data

The previous analysis underestimates the extent of firm entry and exit in Mexico for two reasons. The first derives from the fact that the census only captures firms with fixed premises in localities of 2,500 inhabitants or more. Chapter 3 used the Employment Survey to infer that in 2013 there were approximately 2.6 million firms excluded from the census, employing 7.6 million workers in manufacturing, commerce, and services, in addition to the 4.1 million firms employing 17.4 million workers in the same sectors captured in the census.

Chapter 3 also reported that most of the excluded firms were informal and, on average, smaller than the ones captured in the census (see Table 3.9).

The fact that firms excluded from the census are mostly very small and informal suggests that their entry and exit rates are not very different from those of the very small informal firms captured in the census that, as shown in Table 5.3, are the highest of all. If this presumption is correct, the dysfunctional firm dynamics analyzed in this chapter have greater significance: in 2013, rather than operating over 4.1 million firms, dysfunctional firm dynamics operated over 6.7 million (=2.6+4.1). In parallel, firm-induced job changes, rather than operating over a universe of 17.4 million workers, operated over a universe of 25 million (=7.6+17.4).

The second reason why entry and exit are underestimated stems from the fact that the census captures information only every five years and ignores firms that were born and died in between, even if they carried out their activities in fixed premises in localities with 2,500 or more inhabitants. These firms never appear in the census, even though they qualify to be in it. However, they are part of the universe of firms in Mexico, absorb capital and labor, and have entry and exit rates that are unlikely to be different from those of the firms in fixed premises that are present when the census data are collected.

The upshot is that in all likelihood there is more firm churning in Mexico than can be documented, and, in parallel, more firm-induced job changes. And in all likelihood as well, most of the firm churning that cannot be documented is as useless from the point of view of productivity as that which can be documented. This is an important observation to keep in mind when the next chapter tries to assess the implications of firm-induced job changes for the acquisition of human capital while workers are in the labor force.

Firm Dynamics and the Allocation of Individuals across Occupations

Returning to Figure 2.1 in Chapter 2, a central outcome of the environment $E(L,T,M)$ is how it divides individuals between those who are workers, those who are entrepreneurs, and those who work on their own. If individuals with little entrepreneurial talent manage firms, it is unlikely that those firms will be very productive, even if they survive. On the other hand, individuals with a lot of entrepreneurial talent should ideally manage firms that survive, grow, and attract more workers.

This chapter provided empirical evidence to argue that Mexico's $E(L,T,M)$ results in insufficient firm growth, particularly of formal firms, and that high exit rates are accompanied by even higher entry rates, particularly of small informal firms. The result is that at any point in time there is a very large number of mostly small and informal low-productivity firms operating in the market (including those not captured in the census), and an equal number of individuals managing those firms. In terms of Figure 2.1, this implies that Mexico's ***E****(L,T,M)* does a poor job of dividing its individuals across occupations: if it did not misallocate so many resources towards the informal sector, fewer Mexicans would participate in economic activity as entrepreneurs, and more as workers; and there would be fewer but larger and more productive firms.

Put differently, a critical implication of Mexico's ***E****(L,T,M)* is that it obstructs the process of allocating individuals to the occupations where they have the highest potential. Because it takes the number of entrepreneurs and workers as given (see Figure 3.1), this dimension of misallocation is not captured in the Hsieh-Klenow model and is therefore missing in the productivity losses reported in Table 4.2. But it is a significant component of Mexico's misallocation problem.

Certainly, some individuals may want to try their luck as entrepreneurs and manage their own firm; ex-ante, individuals may not know, or may overestimate, their abilities as managers, and ex-post, there will always be some "productivity-reducing" entry. But in Mexico this phenomenon is exacerbated because, as shown earlier, entry is facilitated by the condition of informality, particularly under non-salaried labor relations. Under a different ***E****(L,T,M)*, entry would be costlier, and individuals with relatively less entrepreneurial talent would be deterred from it. In parallel, entry is incentivized because under Mexico's ***E****(L,T,M)* some high-productivity firms die and those that survive have difficulties growing, limiting the number of high-productivity jobs. Thus, individuals at the margin between being workers and being entrepreneurs opt for the latter. Entry is also incentivized because Mexico's ***E****(L,T,M)* allows many low-productivity entrants to survive. As seen, low-productivity entry, particularly of small informal firms, hardly translates into high-productivity survival. To the contrary, it mostly translates into exit or low-productivity survival with no growth. But because the elements in Mexico's ***E****(L,T,M)* that misallocate resources towards the informal sector persist, the phenomenon just described is repeated year after year: limited growth of, and therefore limited jobs in, high-productivity firms; individuals opting to be entrepreneurs managing very small firms or working as self-employed rather than as employees of a firm; entry, more capital, and labor into new firms rather than into the growth of existing firms; and ultimately exit or low-productivity survival. Along the way, there are large numbers of firm-induced job changes, but on average not better jobs. And on and on; *much movement, but little improvement.*

CHAPTER 6

The Misallocation of Human Capital

Chapters 4 and 5 discussed two dimensions of misallocation of Mexico's human resources. The first dimension referred to the distribution of individuals across occupations. The presence of numerous very small firms with extremely low productivity indicated that some of the individuals managing them could more productively participate in economic activity as workers; the same could be said about some self-employed individuals running their own one-person firm. The second dimension referred to the distribution of workers across firm sizes and types: too many workers with non-salaried or illegal salaried contracts, by and large in smaller sized firms; and not enough workers with legal salaried contracts, by and large in larger firms.

This chapter considers a third dimension: workers not matched with firms where their human capital is fully used. It documents that Mexico experienced large increases in schooling between 1996 and 2015 and that, contrary to what is at times asserted, the quality of schooling increased. Thus, there has been an unambiguous improvement in Mexico's human capital. This fact contrasts sharply with another fact noted in Chapter 1: productivity growth in the same period was, depending on the measure used, either close to zero or negative.

Taken together, these two facts highlight that there is no automatic connection between improving human capital and higher productivity—the former *may* improve the latter, but there is no guarantee. Whether it does or not depends critically on the policies and institutions that determine how the improved human capital is used. In Mexico's case, the evidence indicates that in the last two decades, the improvement in human capital did not raise productivity. Human capital improved, but because this occurred in a context of large and growing misallocation, its potential contribution to raising productivity was thwarted.

The chapter argues that human capital considerations cannot explain misallocation in Mexico. It then considers the other side of the coin and argues that the returns to education and the returns to experience are negatively affected by misallocation. More precisely, the chapter argues that Mexico's *E(L,T,M)* misallocates whatever human capital workers accumulated prior to their entry into the labor force, limits their opportunities to acquire more human capital while in the labor force, and reduces their incentives to invest in education prior to entry into the labor force.

Before beginning, it is central to state clearly that the argument here is not against the importance of education or the need for further educational advancement. Nor is the claim that the quality of education in Mexico is not in need of improvement. Certainly, Mexico must continue investing in education and forcefully pursue efforts to improve its quality. Clearly, all else being equal, a more educated and skilled labor force is a welcome development, for many reasons beyond growth and productivity. What is argued here is that the extent and patterns of resource misallocation documented in Chapter 4, and the dysfunctional firm dynamics discussed in Chapter 5, do not derive from a shortage of human capital, and that the often-made assertion that low-quality human capital is the main constraint to productivity growth in Mexico is not supported by the empirical evidence.

A Few Stylized Facts

Indicators of the Quantity of Schooling

Székely and Flores (2017) document a significant expansion of education over the last 25 years in Mexico. The coverage rate for primary education—the share of those attending school relative to the universe of potential attendees—was already at 97 percent in 1990 but increased to 98 percent by 2015. During the same period, the coverage rate for junior high school increased from 49 to 85 percent, and for senior high school and university from 23 to 65 percent and from 13 to 33 percent, respectively. More generally, Székely and Flores (2017) show that over the last two decades educational advancement in Mexico exceeded the average of Latin American countries. Similar findings are presented in Levy and Székely (2016).

The impact of this expansion on the schooling composition of the labor force is shown in Table 6.1, which was constructed by Levy and López-Calva (2016) using Employment Survey data. The salient feature is that between 1996 and 2015, the rates of growth of workers with completed senior high school or university education substantially exceeded the rate of growth of the whole labor force: 6.2 percent for senior high school and 4.4 percent for

Table 6.1: Educational Composition of the Labor Force, 1996–2015

| | Annual Growth Rate, 1996–2015 (Percent) || Composition (Percent shares) ||||
| | WAP | EAP | 1996 || 2015 ||
			WAP	EAP	WAP	EAP
Incomplete primary	−1.22	−1.68	23.80	20.99	11.59	9.26
Complete primary	0.85	0.81	24.60	23.05	17.77	16.34
Incomplete junior high	0.44	0.45	4.09	4.42	2.73	2.93
Complete junior high	5.03	5.03	15.51	16.62	24.80	26.24
Incomplete senior high	1.19	0.75	13.05	13.11	10.07	9.18
Complete senior high	6.18	6.16	6.46	6.95	14.40	15.24
University	4.67	4.39	12.47	14.85	18.62	20.79
All	2.20	2.31	100.0	100.0	100.0	100.0
Years of schooling			4.7	7.8	9.2	9.8

Source: Levy and López-Calva (2016).
Note: WAP: working-age population; EAP: economically active population.

university education, versus 2.3 percent growth of the labor force. As a result, the share of workers who at least completed senior high school rose from 21 to 36 percent. Correspondingly, the share of workers who at most completed primary education fell from 44 to 25 percent. By 2015, the labor force had on average almost 10 years of schooling, two more years than in 1996.

Indicators of the Quality of Schooling

There is no systematic data on the evolution of educational quality between 1996 and 2015. This section summarizes the evidence available for various subperiods from national and international sources. Table 6.2 presents data from Székely and Flores (2017) on three process indicators: the share of students who complete the educational cycle (terminal efficiency rate); the share who quit before completing the cycle (desertion rate); and the share whose age exceeds the average age for the corresponding grade level (over-age rate). All indicators show considerable improvement.

Although welcome, better process indicators by themselves do not provide direct evidence of improved educational outcomes. That said, all available indicators of educational outcomes also show improvement given their starting level. The discussion that follows is based on Székely and Flores (2017), first considering internationally comparable indicators and then national indicators.

Table 6.2: Process Indicators of Educational Quality, 1996 and 2015
(Percent)

	Primary		Junior High School		Senior High School	
	1996	2015	1996	2015	1996	2015
Terminal efficiency rate	84	99	76	87	54	66
Desertion rate	3	0	9	4	20	12
Over-age rate	13	7	16	10	14	10

Source: Székely and Flores (2017).

The Organization for Economic Cooperation and Development (OECD), through the Programme for International Student Assessment (PISA), administers a standardized test in mathematics, reading, and sciences to 15-year old students in various countries in the world. The first test was administered in 2000, with the participation of Chile, Brazil, Colombia, Costa Rica, Mexico, and Uruguay from Latin America. The last available test was administered in 2015. In both the 2000 and 2015 tests—widely used as a measure of educational quality in junior high school—all countries in Latin America, including Mexico, ranked significantly below participating countries from other regions.[1] That said, over the last 16 years Mexico's scores on all three tests increased, indicating that while the *level* of educational quality is low by PISA standards, the *trends* point in the right direction. Further, Mexico's improvement exceeds the average of Latin American countries. Between 2000 and 2015 Mexico's score in mathematics increased by 5.3 percent compared to 1.5 percent for Latin American countries on average; in reading, the improvement was 2.7 percent (versus 2.2 percent for the Latin American average) and in sciences, 1.7 percent (versus 1.3 percent).

The United Nations Educational, Scientific and Cultural Organization (UNESCO) applied standardized tests in language and mathematics to students in the third and sixth grades of primary school in Argentina, Brazil, Colombia, Honduras, Mexico, Paraguay, Peru, and the Dominican Republic. The first tests were administered in 1998 and the third and last in 2013. Between these two

---

[1] In 2015, the average score in the mathematics PISA exam for students in all 72 participating countries was 461.6, but only 408.0 for Mexican students. Mexico ranked 56th among all participating countries in mathematics, but fourth out of nine participating countries from Latin America and the Caribbean. Average scores for students from all participating countries were 461.5 in language and 466.2 in science, whereas these scores were 423.3 and 415.7, respectively, for Mexican students. Mexico ranked in 55th and 58th place in language and science, respectively, compared to all participating countries, and in sixth place in both subjects compared with other countries from Latin America and the Caribbean.

years, the share of students performing at the highest level in the language exam increased by 20 percentage points in Mexico, in contrast to 16 percentage points for the average of participating Latin American countries. In mathematics, the corresponding numbers were 1 percentage point for Mexico and -2 percentage points for the regional average.

Consider now national indicators. Mexico's Ministry of Public Education administered a test known as the Exámen Nacional de Logro Académico en Centros Escolares (Enlace) to students in primary and junior high school between 2006 and 2014, and to students in senior high school between 2008 and 2014. Tests measured performance in mathematics and language comprehension. Table 6.3 reports the share of students in each year, grade level, and subject matter that showed good or excellent performance. Except for language comprehension for senior high school students, all results show important improvements.

What about university education? Mexico's National Center for the Evaluation of Higher Education (Centro Nacional de Evaluación para la Educación Superior – Ceneval) administers a test to students who finish senior high school and continue on to university studies. In 2006, 32 percent of students tested showed satisfactory or excellent performance, compared to 55 percent in 2016.

There is little systematic data to assess the quality of students who finish university education. As a process indicator, one can point out that the share of colleges and universities that certify their programs with the Council for Certification of Higher Education (Consejo para la Acreditación de la Educación Superior – Copaes) increased from 15 to 65 percent between 2006 and 2016. As an outcome indicator, one can point out that in 2005 Ceneval started administering an exam (Exámen General de Egreso de la Licenciatura – Egel) to test the abilities of graduating college students. Although this exam is voluntary, the number of students taking it doubled between 2005 and

Table 6.3: Outcome Indicators of Educational Quality, Enlace, 2006–2014
(Percent shares with good or excellent performance)

	Primary School		Junior High School		Senior High School	
	2006	2014	2006	2014	2008	2014
Mathematics	17.6	48.8	4.2	21.9	15.6	39.3
Language comprehension	21.3	42.8	14.7	19.7	52.3	44.7

Source: Székely and Flores (2017).
Note: Enlace: Exámen Nacional de Logro Académico en Centros Escolares.

2016, and the share of students performing in the top 25th percentile of the grade distribution increased from 16 to 65 percent.[2]

In short, the available evidence shows that the quantity and quality of education in Mexico increased between 1996 and 2015. This is not to say that by international standards educational quality in Mexico does not lag other countries, particularly outside of Latin America. But it is to say that since quantity and quality have increased, *Mexico's human capital unambiguously improved in the last two decades.*

Human Capital, Misallocation, and Productivity

This section now turns to a brief discussion of the relation between human capital, growth, and productivity in a context of misallocation. It is useful to return to the relations introduced in Chapter 2 connecting existing resources **F[I.H,K]** with aggregate output **Q** and productivity **TFP** given the technology **T** and an environment **E(L,T,M)**. For convenience, they are reproduced here:

$$\{ \mathbf{E}(L,T,M), \mathbf{T}, \mathbf{F}[I.H,K] \} \longrightarrow \mathbf{Q} \tag{6.1}$$

$$\mathbf{TFP} = \mathbf{Q}/\mathbf{F}[I.H,K]. \tag{6.2}$$

As discussed in Chapter 2, the optimal environment **E*(L*,T*,M*)** yields maximum output **Q*** and maximum productivity **TFP***. When the environment is suboptimal, resources are misallocated, **Q** is below the maximum, and there are productivity losses, *PL*, measured by:

$$PL = (\mathbf{TFP^*} - \mathbf{TFP})/\mathbf{TFP^*}. \tag{6.3}$$

What happens when human capital is accumulated in a context of large and increasing misallocation? Figure 6.1 compares the allocation of individuals across occupations in two periods, t^0 and t^1. For simplicity, assume that the number of individuals is the same, but that in t^1 the human capital of at least some of them is higher so that $H^1 \geq H^0$. Assume as well that the technology **T** is the same, as is the stock of physical capital *K*. In each period, individuals divide across occupations given their human capital and the environment **E⁰(L,T,M)** and **E¹(L,T,M)**. Entrepreneurs and workers join to form firms (as in Figure 3.1), and the rest participate as self-employed.

---

[2] In parallel, Székely and Flores (2017) show that the share of students in science, technology, engineering, and mathematics also increased in the last two decades.

Many changes can occur between t^1 and t^0, because while human capital is accumulated the environment is also changing. Figure 6.1 shows fewer individuals participating as entrepreneurs or self-employed and more as workers in firms, although this need not be the case. Further, even if the aggregate division of individuals across occupations is constant, some may shift from entrepreneurs to workers if, say, their firms exit the market. Others may change from workers to entrepreneurs if, say, they saved and decided to start their own firm. Chapter 5 showed that there is large firm churning in Mexico, so clearly many possibilities are present.

Whatever the possibilities, given the change in human capital between t^0 and t^1, relations (6.1), (6.2), and (6.3) can be used to obtain the following pairs:

Observed and maximum output: $[Q^0, Q^{*0}; Q^1, Q^{*1}]$
Observed and maximum productivity: $[TFP^0, TFP^{*0}, TFP^1, TFP^{*1}]$ (6.4)
Observed productivity losses: $[PL^0, PL^1]$

Consider now three different propositions:

- **Proposition 1: Accumulating human capital increases output.** Put differently, if $H^1 > H^0$, then $Q^1 > Q^0$. Although the presumption from much of the literature on education and development is that this is true, note that because the proposition refers to observed and not to maximum output, it need not

Figure 6.1: Misallocation and Changes in Human Capital

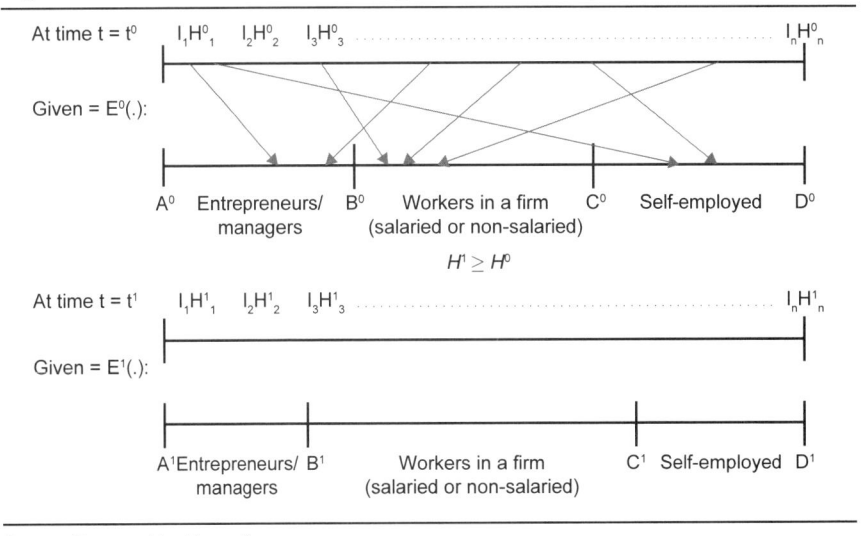

At time $t = t^0$: $I_1 H^0{}_1$, $I_2 H^0{}_2$, $I_3 H^0{}_3$ .... $I_n H^0{}_n$

Given = $E^0(.)$:

A^0 Entrepreneurs/managers | B^0 Workers in a firm (salaried or non-salaried) | C^0 Self-employed | D^0

$H^1 \geq H^0$

At time $t = t^1$: $I_1 H^1{}_1$, $I_2 H^1{}_2$, $I_3 H^1{}_3$ .... $I_n H^1{}_n$

Given = $E^1(.)$:

A^1 Entrepreneurs/managers | B^1 Workers in a firm (salaried or non-salaried) | C^1 Self-employed | D^1

Source: Prepared by the author.

always hold.[3] This depends on whether more educated individuals end up performing tasks where they produce more. In Figure 6.1, perhaps someone who, given ***E⁰(L,T,M)***, was a manager in *t⁰* and acquires more education and, given ***E¹(L,T,M)***, continues to be a manager in *t¹*, manages his or her firm better, and obtains more output. In this case, Proposition 1 is true. But as shown in Chapter 5, perhaps because of the change from ***E⁰(L,T,M)*** to ***E¹(L,T,M)*** that firm exits the market—even if it is a high-productivity one—and the individual managing it ends in self-employment in *t¹*, producing less output despite his or her higher education. In this case Proposition 1 is not true. Equally, perhaps a worker in a small low-productivity firm acquires more schooling between *t⁰* and *t¹*, but continues to be employed in that firm because the environment ***E¹(L,T,M)*** allows it to survive. In this case Proposition 1 is again not true. Thus, whether Proposition 1 holds is an empirical matter.

- **Proposition 2**: **Accumulating human capital increases productivity.** Put differently, if $H^1 > H^0$, then ***TFP¹*** > ***TFP⁰***. This proposition is less likely to hold than the first one. This is so because even if ***Q¹*** > ***Q⁰***, the additional output may not compensate for the fact that now the economy is also using more labor measured in efficiency units.[4] Again, Proposition 2 is an empirical matter.
- **Proposition 3**: **Accumulating human capital lowers misallocation.** Put differently, if $H^1 > H^0$, then $PL^1 < PL^0$. Clearly, this proposition is even less likely to hold than the first two. Even if ***Q¹*** > ***Q⁰***, and even if the gains in output are sufficiently large to compensate for the fact that the economy is using more resources, so that ***TFP¹*** > ***TFP⁰***, it does not necessarily follow that those additional resources are being put to their best possible use. A worker who acquires more education may perform more complex tasks in the same firm and increase the firm's output. But perhaps if that individual were employed in another higher-productivity firm, his or her additional education would add even more to the economy's output. However, as in Chapter 5, this does not occur because the environment ***E¹(L,T,M)*** allows the low-productivity firm to

---

[3] If Proposition 1 referred to potential output ***Q****, it would be true, to the extent that the economy now has more productive resources, which, by definition, are always put to their best use. The point here is that in economies with little misallocation, and where the difference between ***Q*** and ***Q**** is small, it is natural to presume that human capital will be allocated appropriately, and that therefore more of it will always result in more output. But the presumption can be quite misleading when the environment is far from the optimal one, as is the case in Mexico.

[4] If productivity is measured with respect to the number of individuals ignoring differences in abilities, i.e., if we use the measure ***TFP'*** = ***Q/F[l,K]*** instead of ***TFP*** = ***Q/F[l.H,K]***, then if ***Q¹*** > ***Q⁰*** it would also be the case that ***TFP'¹*** > ***TFP'⁰***. In other words, Propositions 1 and 2 are different only if labor is measured in efficiency units.

survive and forces the exit of the high-productivity firm. So, Proposition 3 is also an empirical matter.

The point of this discussion, aside from separating concepts that are at times conflated, is to highlight that the effects of accumulating human capital on growth, productivity, and misallocation depend on a country's environment ***E****(L,T,M)*. Although the presumption that increasing the education of individuals will produce more output is quite plausible (so much so that in many policy discussions it is considered a truism), it is still a presumption, not a logical necessity. The connection between more educated workers and higher productivity is not *automatic* because it is mediated by the environment, which may misallocate those more educated workers.

How does this discussion fit with the empirical evidence? Cross-country regressions show a positive association between schooling and GDP and are part of the evidence supporting Proposition 1 (Hanushek and Woessmann 2012; Hanushek 2013). But, critically, these regressions are averages over countries with different types of ***E****(L,T,M)*, and individual countries can deviate substantially from the average depending on their specific ***E****(L,T,M)*. The point is not that in general there is no positive relation between education and output; it is that in the last two decades in Mexico—where, as Chapter 4 showed, there was a large and growing gap between ***E****(L,T,M)* and ***E*****(L*,T*,M*)*—there was a substantial deviation from this relation.

On the other hand, note that even if the three propositions were empirically true, none supports the assertion that misallocation results from low human capital. Misallocation refers to the efficiency with which the *existing* resources of the economy, including its human capital, are used. In other words, it relates to a given level of *l.H*, whatever that level is. One cannot use the object being misallocated as the explanation for the misallocation of that object. Thus, as opposed to the first three propositions, the notion that misallocation results from "low" human capital is not an empirical matter; it is logically inconsistent.

The evidence for Mexico indicates that Proposition 3 does not hold. Figure 6.2 summarizes the information from Table 4.1 in Chapter 4 and Table 6.1. It plots average years of schooling of the economically active population on the left axis and the standard deviation of TFPR (taken here as an index of misallocation) on the right axis. The figure makes clear that *misallocation in Mexico has increased, despite the notable increases in the schooling of its workforce*.

Misallocation and the Level of Returns to Education

Having established that misallocation does not result from "low" human capital, on one hand, and that human capital has increased, on the other, we

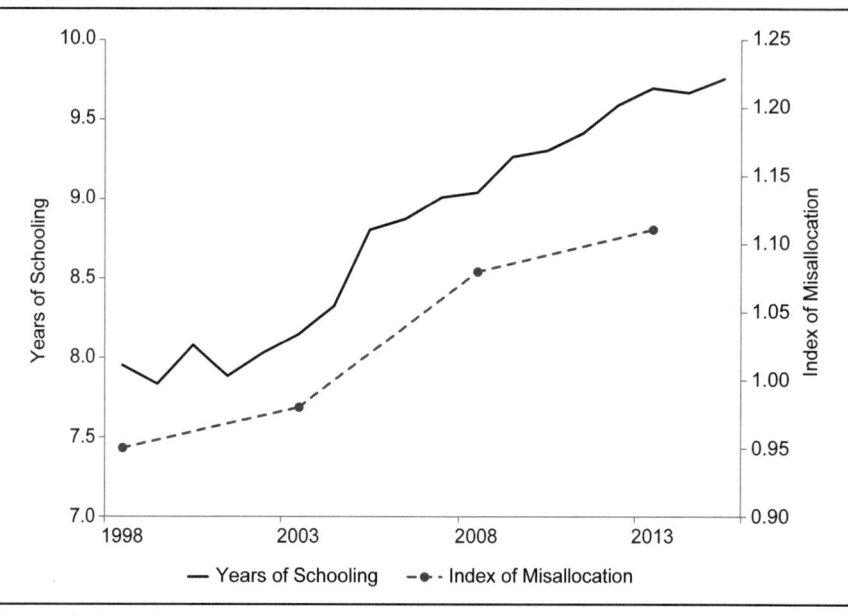

Figure 6.2: Misallocation and Years of Schooling, 1998–2013

Source: Author's illustration based on data in the main text.

now consider the opposite phenomena. Is misallocation impeding Mexico from taking full advantage of its investments in human capital? Are workers with more education finding jobs congruent with their abilities?

This and the next section draw from Levy and López-Calva (2016) to discuss the implications of misallocation for the match between firms' demand and workers' supply of labor of different educational levels. This section focuses on the static implications of a size and type distribution of firms strongly biased towards informality for the schooling compositions of the demand for labor and, consequently, for relative wages. The next section considers what happens when human capital is accumulated but misallocation increases at the same time.

Differences in the Schooling Composition of Firms' Demand for Labor

In Chapter 4, firms' production functions were given by relation (4.1), which, for convenience, is reproduced here:

$$Q_{is} = A_{is} K_{is}^{\alpha_s} L_{is}^{1-\alpha_s}. \tag{6.5}$$

To consider differences in workers' education it is useful to rewrite relation (6.5) as:

$$Q_{is} = A_{is}K_{is}^{\alpha_s}\left[L_{is}\left(L_{is}^1, L_{is}^2, \ldots, L_{is}^n\right)\right]^{1-\alpha_s}, \tag{6.6}$$

where *n* is the number of educational levels considered. In this richer context, given an environment **E**(L,T,M), differences in firms' A_{is} and in their mix of salaried/non-salaried and legal/illegal contracts have implications not only for the total number of workers demanded, but also for their schooling composition. Three examples are hopefully useful:

- Consider two firms with the same number of salaried workers producing jeans, hired legally in one case and illegally in the other (i.e., one firm is fully formal and the other informal and illegal). Assume that, given the tasks that need to be performed, for both firms it is indispensable that their workers have completed primary school. However, it stands to reason that the formal firm needs an accountant to pay taxes and make contributory social insurance payments, while the informal one does not. Further, since the formal firm is, as documented earlier, more capital-intensive, it also requires at least a few workers with a high school degree to operate more sophisticated machines.
- Assume there are 100 drivers and 100 trucks. Transportation services can be delivered through 100 self-employed individuals each operating their own truck, or through a formal firm hiring 100 drivers as salaried workers. In both cases, all drivers have completed junior high school, the educational level required to be a truck driver. In the second case, however, the firm needs an accountant, a worker with a senior high school degree to operate a geo-referenced system for logistics and dispatch, and a sales manager with a degree in business administration.
- Tortillas can be produced in very small firms deploying simple technologies where workers need only basic literacy and numeracy. Or they can be produced in very large formal firms that require engineers, lawyers, and financial managers.

These examples illustrate that the schooling composition of the demand for labor depends on the size and type distribution of firms. Firm size matters because larger firms tend to have more complex production technologies, more hierarchical organization within the firm, and more relations with other firms or the government, in turn requiring more lawyers, accountants, engineers, personnel managers, and financial analysts than smaller firms (see López and Torres-Coronado, 2017, and the references therein). Further, because larger firms invest more in research and development than smaller ones, they need more workers with degrees in chemistry, physics, biology, computer science, or mathematics. But firm type also matters because even if firms have the same size, formal ones need more-educated workers to perform functions associated with formality, or more complex tasks given the firms' higher capital intensity.

In Mexico, informal firms produce goods that are similar to those produced by formal ones, and they coexist in the same six-digit sectors. Indeed, recall from Table 3.11 in Chapter 3 that in 2013 informal firms accounted for more than half of all firms in 51 percent of the 279 six-digit sectors in manufacturing, in 81 percent of the 154 six-digit sectors in commerce, and in 88 percent of the 258 six-digit sectors in services. (Informal firms also coexist with formal firms in transportation, construction, mining and agriculture, but this was not documented here.) In parallel, recall from Table 3.5 in Chapter 3 that there are significant size differences between formal and informal firms: in 2013, fully formal firms had 22.1 workers and mixed ones 16.5 workers on average, whereas informal and illegal firms had 3.9 workers and informal and legal ones 2.3 workers on average.

The coexistence of formal and informal firms across many sectors of economic activity has substantive implications for the schooling composition of the demand for labor in Mexico. To the extent that, as Chapter 4 documented, the environment *E(L,T,M)* misallocates too many resources to informal firms, the relative demand for workers with more years of schooling is depressed. If there were fewer informal firms, and more formal ones, the demand for more educated workers would increase.

To assess the empirical relevance of this argument, one would ideally have information on workers' schooling levels for all firms captured in the census. Unfortunately, these data are not available. Nevertheless, it is possible to use Mexico's Employment Survey, which provides indirect but valuable information, as it records the formal or informal status of workers, their years of schooling and, critically, the size of the firm that employs them. This information allows for inferring the schooling composition of firms' labor demand given their size and formality status.[5]

Table 6.4 shows the distribution of workers by educational level and by firm type and size in the 2006 Employment Survey, chosen as an intermediate year between 1998 and 2013. The table excludes entrepreneurs and self-employed workers and restricts the analysis to workers in private firms. Each cell shows the share of workers of a given schooling level in the total number

---

[5] Because the Employment Survey is focused on the individual and not the firm, one cannot identify whether an informal worker is employed by a legal or illegal informal firm and, equally, whether a formal worker is employed by a fully formal firm or a mixed one. The assumption is that formal workers are hired by formal firms (without distinguishing between fully formal and mixed firms), and informal workers by informal firms (legal or illegal). Thus, in the analysis that follows, rather than considering four firm types, only two are considered.

Table 6.4: Distribution of Employees by Education and Firm Size and Type, 2006
(Percent shares)

Education Level of Workers	Informal Firms					Formal Firms				
	1–5	6–10	11–50	51+	Total	1–5	6–10	11–50	51+	Total
Incomplete primary	11.0	9.3	7.0	4.5	**9.6**	6.8	4.3	3.9	2.6	**3.3**
Complete primary	23.6	16.4	13.2	8.6	**19.8**	11.0	11.1	11.2	10.9	**11.0**
Incomplete junior high	6.0	6.0	6.1	3.1	**5.8**	2.4	3.2	2.9	2.6	**2.7**
Complete junior high	31.0	25.8	25.0	19.8	**28.4**	22.1	21.8	20.8	24.9	**23.3**
Incomplete senior high	11.6	12.6	13.0	14.3	**12.2**	19.1	18.6	16.1	17.1	**17.0**
Complete senior high	9.3	11.2	11.4	14.5	**10.3**	17.1	16.1	17.5	14.2	**15.5**
University	7.5	18.5	24.3	35.2	**13.9**	21.4	24.9	27.5	27.7	**27.1**
Total	**100**	**100**	**100**	**100**	**100**	**100**	**100**	**100**	**100**	**100**

Source: Levy and López-Calva (2016).

of workers in firms of that size and type. Thus, columns add to 100 percent and reflect the schooling composition of firms' workforces by size and type.

Two facts are worth highlighting. First, considering the totals for both firm types, formal ones are more intensive in educated workers: 42.6 percent of their workforce has completed senior high school or university, while 14.3 percent has at most completed primary school. This stands in contrast to 24.2 and 29.4 percent, respectively, for informal firms. Second, these patterns hold controlling for firm size. Thus, for instance, only 16.8 percent of the workforce in informal firms with up to five workers has completed senior high school or university studies, in contrast to 38.5 percent in formal firms of the same size. At the opposite end of the spectrum, 34.6 percent of the workforce in informal firms of that size has at most completed primary school versus almost half that, 17.8 percent, in formal ones.[6]

---

[6] The size distribution also matters, since larger firms (formal or informal) are more intensive in educated workers. Although not shown in Table 6.4, 63 percent of workers of all educational levels employed by informal firms work in firms that have up to five employees (versus 5.8 percent in formal firms), and only 8.4 percent work in firms with more than 50 workers (versus 57.4 in formal firms).

Misallocation and Wages across Educational Groups

What would be the schooling composition of the demand for labor if Mexico's *E(L,T,M)* did not misallocate so many resources towards informal firms? And what would be the wage structure across workers with different years of schooling? These are tough questions to answer, as they require knowing the size and type distribution of firms under a different *E(L,T,M)*. Levy and López-Calva (2016) provide a partial answer assuming that, in a context characterized by less misallocation, the schooling composition of the demand for labor of informal firms would mimic that of formal ones. More precisely, they estimate the wages of informal employees if, given their education, observable characteristics (age, gender, hours worked, location, and so on), and unobservable characteristics, they were distributed across firm sizes in the same proportions as formal employees with the same education. Their exercise exploits the panel structure of the Employment Survey and the fact that workers of all educational levels transit between formal and informal jobs and between firms of varying sizes, so that their wages are observed both when they are formally and informally employed.[7] Their procedure ensures that the difference in wages between the observed and the counterfactual is associated with the nature of the firm where workers are employed, and not their individual characteristics.

Figure 6.3 shows the impact of this change, contrasting workers employed by informal firms with completed primary and university education. The horizontal axis measures hourly wages in pesos and the vertical axis measures the frequency of observations; note that the scales on the horizontal axis differ. For those with completed primary education, the effect is minor: if employed by formal firms, their wages would on average be higher, but only by approximately 3 percent. But for those with university education, the effect is much larger: their wages, on average, would increase by 29 percent. More generally, for all educational levels the average difference is 17 percent. These results suggest that the effects of misallocation on relative wages in Mexico are substantial, *and that workers with more years of education are particularly affected by it.*

The scope of this exercise is limited because it assumes that under a different *E(L,T,M)* only the schooling composition of the demand for labor of informal firms would change. Of course, if Mexico's *E(L,T,M)* did not misallocate so many resources, other things would change as well: there would be more

---

[7] Campos-Vázquez (2013) notes that under-reporting of wages is relevant in Mexico and that it appears to have increased over time. Importantly, Levy and López-Calva (2016) correct for this problem using the so-called "hot deck" technique. This correction is also applied to all the wage comparisons made in the rest of this chapter.

Figure 6.3: Observed and Simulated Wage Distributions

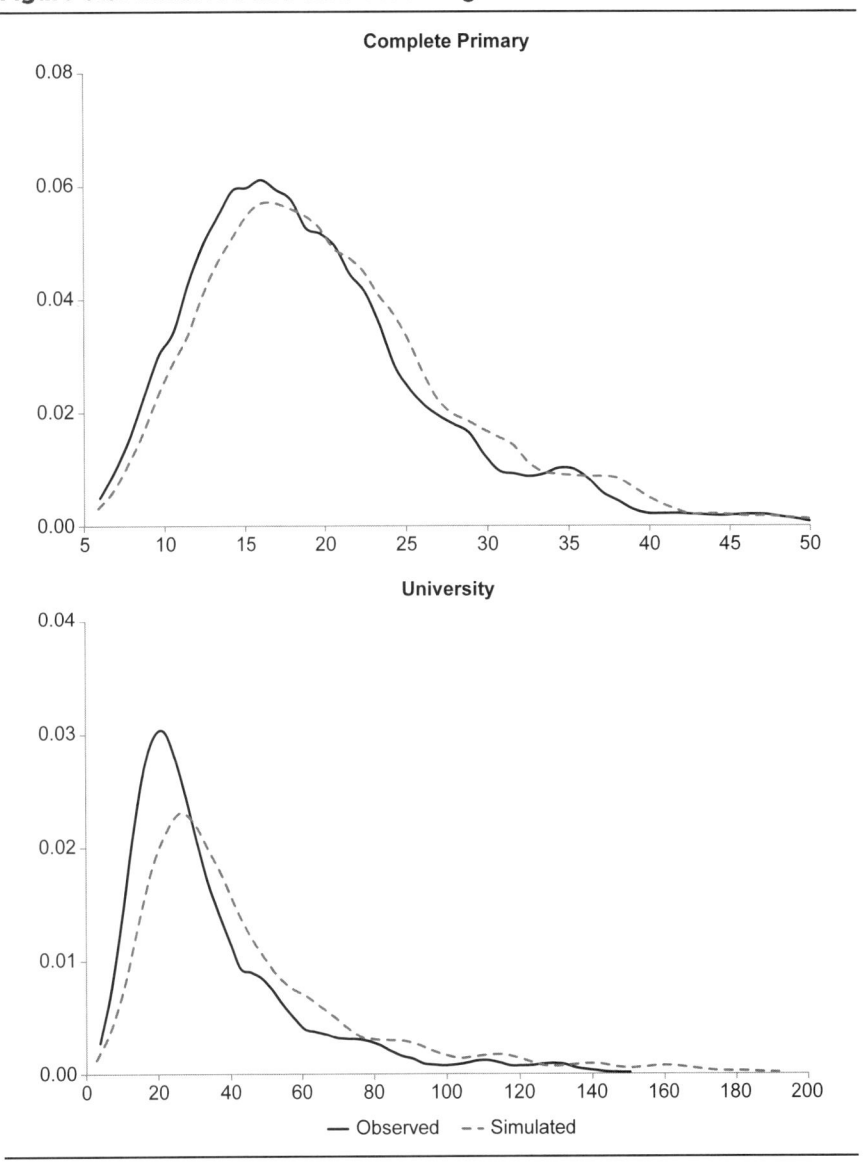

Complete Primary

University

— Observed   -- Simulated

Source: Levy and López-Calva (2016).

workers and fewer entrepreneurs, average firm size would be larger, entry and exit rates would favor more productive firms, and so on. These factors would further tilt the schooling composition of the demand for labor in the direction of more educated workers.

Thus, the exercise depicted in Figure 6.3 is best thought of as a lower bound on the impact of misallocation on relative wages. But the point to highlight is that, regardless of the precise quantitative estimates, an important dimension of misallocation in Mexico is that it produces a mismatch between firms' demands and workers' supply by educational level—a mismatch that is reflected in lower wages for more-educated workers relative to the wages of less-educated workers or, in other words, *in lower returns to education.*

This result is broader and holds in contexts other than the exercise performed by Levy and López-Calva (2016). For instance, López and Torres-Coronado (2017) develop a model where the environment ***E****(L,T,M)* discriminates against larger firms because they face higher taxes than smaller ones (a very relevant issue for Mexico, as discussed in Chapter 7). They show that this tax asymmetry distorts occupational choices and, as a result, employers are matched with less-talented employees in smaller firms and returns to skill are lower in the middle and top of the earnings distribution. Employers constrain the size of their firm to lower their tax burden but generate a talent mismatch that lowers the average returns to skills. The productivity costs are important: output losses are more than twice those estimated in studies that consider the impact of the tax distortion only on firm size and ignore its implications for skill misallocation. The fall in the average return to skills is close to 30 percent in their more conservative estimates.

At the end of the day, and regardless of the specificities of various models and numerical exercises, the issue is very simple: when because of ***E****(L,T,M)* there are too many low-productivity small firms with simple technologies, and too few larger and more productive firms with more complex processes, the demand for workers with more years of education is depressed, and so are their wages.

Misallocation and the Trends in the Returns to Education

Figure 6.4 shows the trends in the returns to education in Mexico between 1996 and 2015. For each year, returns are estimated with a Mincer-type regression with controls for age, experience, gender, location, and hours worked. Each year in the figure is the ordinary least square estimate of the mean wages of each educational level relative to the wages of workers with incomplete primary education. As can be seen, the trends are falling, particularly for workers with university and completed high school education.[8]

---

[8] Trends shown in Figure 6.4 are consistent with those found in the literature for Mexico for a similar period. See the references in Levy and López-Calva (2016).

Figure 6.4: Evolution of the Returns to Education, 1996–2015

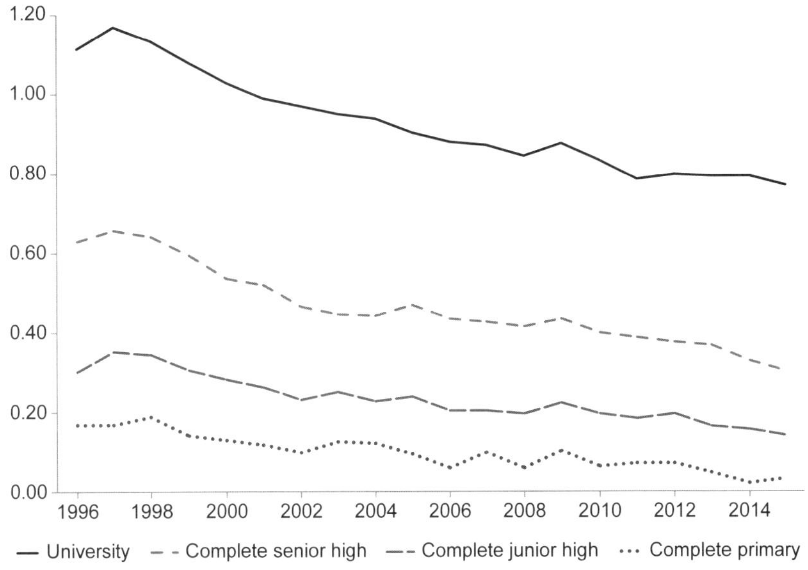

— University   – – Complete senior high   –·– Complete junior high   ··· Complete primary

Source: Levy and López-Calva (2016).

What explains these trends? If the level of misallocation in the economy were always the same, it would have a once-and-for-all impact on returns to education, but it would not affect trends in those returns. Consistent with the results of the previous section, reducing misallocation would shift the lines in Figure 6.4 upwards, but would not change their slope. Falling trends would result from other factors, notably the faster increase in the supply of workers with more years of education.[9]

And, surely, supply factors are an important part of the explanation behind Figure 6.4. However, in the case of Mexico another factor figures in: the fact that during the period considered misallocation increased. This implies that misallocation did not have a once-and-for-all effect on just the level of returns to education, but that it also affected the trends. This implies as well that the behavior depicted in Figure 6.4 reflects two factors that complement each other and operate in the same direction: the faster increase in the supply of workers with more schooling relative to those with less, and the bias in the schooling composition of the demand for labor resulting from increasing misallocation.

---

[9] This follows the standard analysis of the relative weight of supply and demand factors on returns to education; see Katz and Murphy (1992).

Levy and López-Calva (2016) simulate a counterfactual schooling composition of the demand for labor over the 1996–2015 period, assuming that in every year the composition in informal firms is the same as that observed in formal firms of the corresponding year. As discussed in the previous section, although incomplete, this is a simple way to capture firm behavior if Mexico's $E(L,T,M)$ did not misallocate so many resources towards informal firms. Their results show that in those scenarios, at the observed wages there would be excess demand for workers with more education and, more importantly, *that this excess demand would increase over time*.

Thus, given the observed growth in supplies of labor of each educational level, in the absence of misallocation the gap in wages between those with more and less education would have increased year after year to clear the market. In turn, this implies that, again, given supply, the trends in the returns to education would be different. And while it is not possible to determine exactly what those trends would have been, it is possible to at least say that they would have fallen more slowly.[10] Thus, part of the explanation for the observed downward path of the returns to education in Mexico is that during the period considered misallocation increased. In other words, if misallocation had been constant over the period, the returns to education would have fallen given the behavior of supply; but since misallocation was increasing, the fall was more pronounced.

While as noted the census does not have data on the educational composition of a firm's labor force, the changes in the composition of employment between 1998 and 2013 are consistent with the hypothesis of increasing misallocation. Table 6.5 shows the share of total employment by firm size and type in each year (shares add to 100 percent in each case, although this is not included in the table).

In a word, over this 15-year period the share of employment in very small and small firms increased by 3.6 percentage points, and the share of employment in informal firms increased by 17.5 percentage points. This occurred while the supply of workers with completed senior high school or university education was growing at more than twice the rate of other educational groups (see Table 6.1). In this context, it is difficult to argue that firms cannot grow larger, or change from informal to formal status, because there are not enough educated workers, when the wages of those who are supposedly in high demand are falling continuously relative to those who are supposedly less needed.

---

[10] The counterfactual trends depend on the assumptions made about the elasticity of substitution between workers of different schooling levels, which determines the magnitude of the wage adjustment necessary to eliminate the excess demand for more educated workers.

Table 6.5: Composition of Employment Captured in the Census, 1998 and 2013
(Percent shares)

	1998	2013
Size		
1–5 workers	36.5	39.7
6–10 workers	7.5	7.9
11–50 workers	15.9	15.3
51+ workers	40.1	37.1
Type		
Fully formal	20.6	21.8
Mixed	41.2	22.5
Informal and legal	26.0	39.7
Informal and illegal	12.2	16.0

Source: Author's calculations based on data from Mexico's Economic Census.

Falling Quality of Education?

An alternative explanation that is at times offered for the behavior depicted in Figure 6.4 is that the rapid expansion in the number of students who entered senior high schools and universities resulted in a deterioration in the quality of education. The argument is that new private or public senior high schools and universities that opened to accommodate the greater number of entrants are producing lower-quality graduates, because these schools are not as good as previously existing ones, or because the pool of junior high school students that they draw from is less prepared than the pool of students that the older more established schools and universities draw from. As a result, the mean wages of workers with senior high school and university education are falling not because of lagging demand, but due to the deteriorating quality of supply.

The evidence on the quality of education presented earlier does not support that hypothesis. This section provides additional evidence that falling quality is not the issue. This evidence is derived directly from what is observed in the market: the behavior of earnings. Note that under the alternative hypothesis, the quality of students graduating from older or preexisting universities and senior high schools should be at least the same over time; there is no reason to think that their quality has fallen. Average quality is pulled down because the left tail of the quality distribution grows larger with the entry of students into lower-quality institutions, not because the right tail is shifting to the left. Thus, earnings of the subset of senior high school and university students from the "best" schools—presumably those in the right tail of the wage distribution—should not be falling. On the contrary, the expectation is that they should be increasing, as firms compete for their talent in a market characterized by growing shortages of high-quality senior high school and university graduates.

Table 6.6 compares the right tail of the earnings distribution for workers with completed senior high school and university education between 1996 and 2015. Each column contains mean hourly earnings of various segments of the distribution measured in 2008 prices (making them directly comparable). The data refer to private sector workers in cities of 15,000 inhabitants or more, ages 18 to 65, and working 30 to 48 hours a week. To avoid potential biases from changes in gender composition, the numbers are reported separately for females and males.

Earnings at the top of the distribution have by and large remained constant. These data—which, again, reflect actual market outcomes—hardly suggest that over the last two decades there has been a growing shortage of workers with "high-quality" senior high school or university education.

In sum, the evidence from the Employment Survey is consistent with the hypothesis that earnings of workers with more years of schooling have fallen relative to those with less because, in a context of increasing misallocation, their demand has lagged their supply, not because their quality has decreased. *There is little empirical support for the proposition that firms in Mexico cannot become larger, survive longer, change from informal to formal status, or increase their productivity because they lack workers with sufficient human capital.*

Table 6.6: Right Tail of Earnings Distribution, 1996 and 2015
(Hourly wage in 2008 pesos)

	\multicolumn{10}{c	}{Mean Wages of:}
	Entire Distribution		Top 20 Percent		Top 10 Percent		Top 5 Percent		Top 1 Percent	
	1996	2015	1996	2015	1996	2015	1996	2015	1996	2015
Senior high school										
Female	22.1	23.1	46.0	45.3	55.4	57.1	65.6	70.0	84.6	90.6
Male	22.1	25.4	45.3	47.4	54.4	58.2	66.3	68.8	94.5	89.5
University										
Female	37.9	38.6	75.9	73.6	88.3	86.3	98.6	98.3	118.7	115.6
Male	43.1	43.3	86.2	81.8	98.6	95.4	109.0	105.3	120.5	113.5

Source: Author's calculations based on data from Mexico's Employment Survey.

None of this is to say that if managers acquired more education they could not manage their firms better and increase productivity. Cirera and Maloney (2017) provide evidence that investments in managers' education can facilitate technology adoption and increase firm productivity. (Although it is important to emphasize that the productivity gains are contingent on whether the environment $E(L,T,M)$ allows those firms to survive, or even provides them with the incentives to adopt modern technologies and increase output, as discussed in Chapter 7.) Nor is the aim here to suggest that in some circumstances there may not be shortages of a specialized labor skill. For instance, firms setting up in Mexico for the first time to produce parts for airplanes may find that there are not enough aeronautical engineers, because universities in Mexico have not in the past offered that specialization (since no firms were producing parts for airplanes). Although this specific shortage is gradually solved as this specialization is incorporated into the curriculum, it may transitorily affect a few firms (that in the meantime can hire foreign aeronautical engineers). But it is to say that Mexico is not suffering from a generalized shortage of skilled workers affecting firms across the whole spectrum of economic activity.

Misallocation and the Opportunities to Acquire Human Capital

So far, this chapter has considered the relation between misallocation and the human capital acquired by workers *prior* to their entry into the labor force. But misallocation also affects human capital accumulation *while* workers are in the labor force. Although their years of schooling when they start working are by and large given, workers can learn and acquire additional skills afterwards. The critical determinants are the nature of the firm with which they engage, and the years of schooling at the start of their working careers. Because more schooling enlarges the capability to learn over a lifetime, those who start with more years of schooling can accumulate more human capital during their working lives relative to those starting with fewer years. But that said, all can learn more.[11]

This section discusses the opportunities available to Mexican workers to acquire human capital after completing their schooling cycle, and to increase their earnings over time as a result of the learning and experience acquired while working. The discussion centers on the implications of the size and type distribution of firms and firm dynamics analyzed in Chapters

---

[11] IDB (2017, 228) notes that "The quantity, quality and trajectory of skills developed during a person's life depend crucially on two main things. First, it depends on his or her initial conditions: individual characteristics and the level of education attained prior to entry into the job market. Second, it depends on the quality of the firms available in the economy, the type of firm in which the person ends up working, and the type of job the person holds."

4 and 5 for skill acquisition through on-the-job learning and firm-sponsored investments in training. The section does not discuss opportunities associated with government-sponsored programs.

This issue is very relevant for Mexico. The schooling of its workforce has increased gradually as younger cohorts with more schooling have replaced retiring ones with less, but accumulating human capital through this route is inevitably slow. Past investments in education have raised average years of schooling by about one year per decade (Table 6.1). On the other hand, the evidence shows that, under the right conditions, workers can improve their skills and acquire new ones while at work. Workers living in the same place, and with the same age, gender, years of education, and other cognitive and noncognitive abilities can have different trajectories of skill acquisition and improvement, and therefore lifetime earnings.[12] For all workers who are, say, 25 years of age or older and who will not have the opportunity to return to school—that is, most workers currently in the labor force in Mexico—this issue is more important than improvements in the coverage and quality of schooling, which will benefit their sons and daughters, but not them.

Determinants of Human Capital Accumulation While at Work

Given workers' schooling, two related conditions determine human capital accumulation while in the labor force: the nature of firms and the extent of labor turnover. There is unfortunately insufficient data in the Economic Census to document firms' investments in worker training in Mexico. But the presumption is that, given the size and type distribution of firms, only a minority of workers benefit.[13] Alaimo et al. (2015) find that in Mexico 63 percent of workers will never receive any on-the-job training during their work life, and that those who do work mainly in formal firms. Small informal firms managed by individuals with little entrepreneurial talent are unlikely to invest in labor training. The same is likely when firms are illegal or when they carry out their activities in

---

[12] IDB (2017) uses panel data to compare the trajectories of Chilean workers over a seven-year period (from ages 25-35 to ages 32-42). As expected, workers with more schooling have higher wages than those with less schooling. That said, workers with more schooling increase their wage over the seven-year period by 27 percent if they work for a high-productivity firm versus 8 percent if they work for a low-productivity one. Workers with less schooling increase their wages by 16 percent if they work for a high-productivity firm, and by 8.3 percent if they work for a low-productivity one.

[13] The census gathers data on firms' expenses in labor training, but those data are unfortunately aggregated with expenses on scholarships, uniforms and other clothing used in work, and sports and recreational activities. Computation here of those expenses by size and type of firm found that they increase with firm size. But the information is too coarse to be used as a measure of firms' investments in labor training.

the street. Even when firms are formal, if they are very small there is little room for specialization. Moreover, if firms have short lives there is little time for their investments in labor training to bear fruit, or for on-the-job learning to occur.

Consider, next, labor turnover. Workers change jobs partly for personal reasons (moving from one city to another, changing work preferences, and so on), and partly for reasons derived from firm behavior, as firms exit, enter, or change size. To separate worker-induced turnover from firm-induced labor turnover, one needs a matched panel of firms and workers. These data are not available for Mexico. Nevertheless, some *indirect* evidence on the association between firm and labor turnover can be found by combining data from the Economic Census with data from the Employment Survey.

Table 5.13 in Chapter 5 showed that the other side of the coin of large firm churning in Mexico was large job changes. Although, as discussed there, job changes and labor turnover are not the same phenomenon, they are clearly related. Many workers in Mexico change jobs because the firm they work for exits the market, and many get jobs in new firms that, a few years after entry, will also exit the market.

To deepen that analysis, Table 6.7 presents data on the age distribution of firms and the length of tenure of workers in their current job. The data for firms

Table 6.7: Cumulative Age Distribution of Firms and Workers, 2013
(Percent shares)

Firm Age (years) Up to:	Firms Formal	Firms Informal	Firms All	Workers*
1	8	21	20	21
2	14	30	28	36
3	20	35	34	46
4	25	40	38	53
5	30	45	43	59
6	35	52	50	64
7	40	57	56	68
8	45	61	60	72
9	49	65	63	74
10	53	69	67	76
15	71	82	81	89
16 or more	100	100	100	100

Source: Author's calculations based on data from Mexico's Economic Census and Employment Survey.
*Share of workers with a given number of years in their current job.

comes from the 2013 census and thus refers only to firms in manufacturing, commerce, and services; for simplicity, firms are aggregated into formal and informal with the usual criteria. The data for workers come from the 2013 Employment Survey and refer to all activities (not only those in manufacturing, commerce, and services) and to all firms (not only those captured in the census). The Employment Survey data on length of job tenure implicitly reflect the behavior of a wider universe of firms, but also worker-induced job changes. Thus, the firm and worker data capture different behavior and are not directly comparable. That said, they suggest a close relation between firm churning and labor turnover.

Approximately 43 percent of firms are at most five years old, 34 percent at most three, and 20 percent one (although the differences between formal and informal firms are significant). In parallel, 59 percent of workers have been at their job for at most five years, 46 percent for at most three, and 21 percent for one. There is, of course, not an exact match because, as discussed, firm and worker data refer to distinct though related phenomenon. If firms excluded from the census were considered, the average age of firms would fall and the differences between firms' age and workers' tenure would narrow. Even without considering those firms, however, the data suggest a significant correlation between job tenure and firm age.[14]

Chapter 5 showed that firm-induced productivity-enhancing job changes were almost the same as productivity-reducing ones, and that most job changes were due to firm entry and exit and very few to firm growth (Table 5.13). This matters a lot from the point of view of skill acquisition and on-the-job learning. For workers, it implies that on average job changes are essentially useless. High rates of firm entry and exit imply that workers have short tenures in their jobs, little opportunities to learn, and insufficient time to benefit from firm-sponsored training programs. When high-productivity firms exit, high-productivity jobs are destroyed, and workers lose good opportunities. On the other hand, the survival of consistently low-productivity firms implies that the workers employed by them have reduced opportunities to acquire new skills.

---

[14] Another perspective is obtained from Hsieh and Klenow (2014), who compare the distribution of employment by firm age in manufacturing firms in Mexico with the United States. In Mexico, less than 5 percent of employment occurs in firms that are 40 years or older versus almost 30 percent in the United States. At the other end of the spectrum, in Mexico more than 30 percent of employment occurs in firms that are five years old or younger, versus less than 15 percent in the United States. While these data do not refer to workers' tenure, they are consistent with the argument that Mexican workers have substantially shorter spells of employment with a firm than workers in the United States because firms in Mexico are on average much younger.

Of course, the extent of useless firm churning is not independent of the size and type of firms. As shown in Chapter 5, useless churning is higher in smaller and informal firms than in larger and more formal ones. But because in Mexico a large share of employment occurs in the former set of firms, useless firm churning is quite relevant. *There are many "bad jobs" in Mexico—high turnover and little training or on-the-job learning—not because workers lack schooling or lack the capacity to learn, but because there are many "bad," firms—low-productivity, small, and short-lived.*

Returns to Experience and Cohort-Specific Earnings Paths

What are the implications for workers of the analysis so far? The standard procedure to measure the accumulation of human capital while in the labor force is to measure returns to experience. For a given educational level, wages of older workers should be higher than those of younger ones, reflecting learning and acquisition of abilities. Lagakos et al. (2018) compare the returns to experience across a large sample of developed and developing countries. Using comparable data, for each country they plot the returns to experience schedules (pairings of workers' earnings of a given educational level and their ages in a given year). They find that in all countries, as expected, the returns to experience schedules are steeper for workers with more education.

More relevant for our purposes here, they find that controlling for educational level, these schedules are on average twice as steep in developed countries compared to developing ones, a result they attribute to the more severe search frictions in developing countries that prevent workers from climbing up the job ladder. Their sample of countries includes Brazil, Chile, and Mexico from Latin America, and they find that for the same educational levels, the schedules for Mexico are flatter than those for Brazil or Chile (and, of course, developed countries). In other words, the returns to experience in Mexico are lower than in developed countries and in the other two Latin American countries considered.

Figure 6.5 provides further information for Mexico. The figure uses data from the Employment Surveys from 2005 to 2015, focusing on male workers with completed university education, employed in private firms in cities of 100,000 inhabitants or more, and working between 30 and 48 hours per week. The vertical axes in both panels measures earnings per hour in constant 2008 pesos.

The upper panel depicts the returns to experience schedules in three different years: 2005 (continuous line), 2010 (dashed line), and 2015 (dotted line). In all cases, earnings are averages over five-year age intervals: for workers between 25 and 29 years old, between 30 and 34, 35 to 39, and so on. While

Figure 6.5: Returns to Experience and Earnings Paths for Workers with University Education

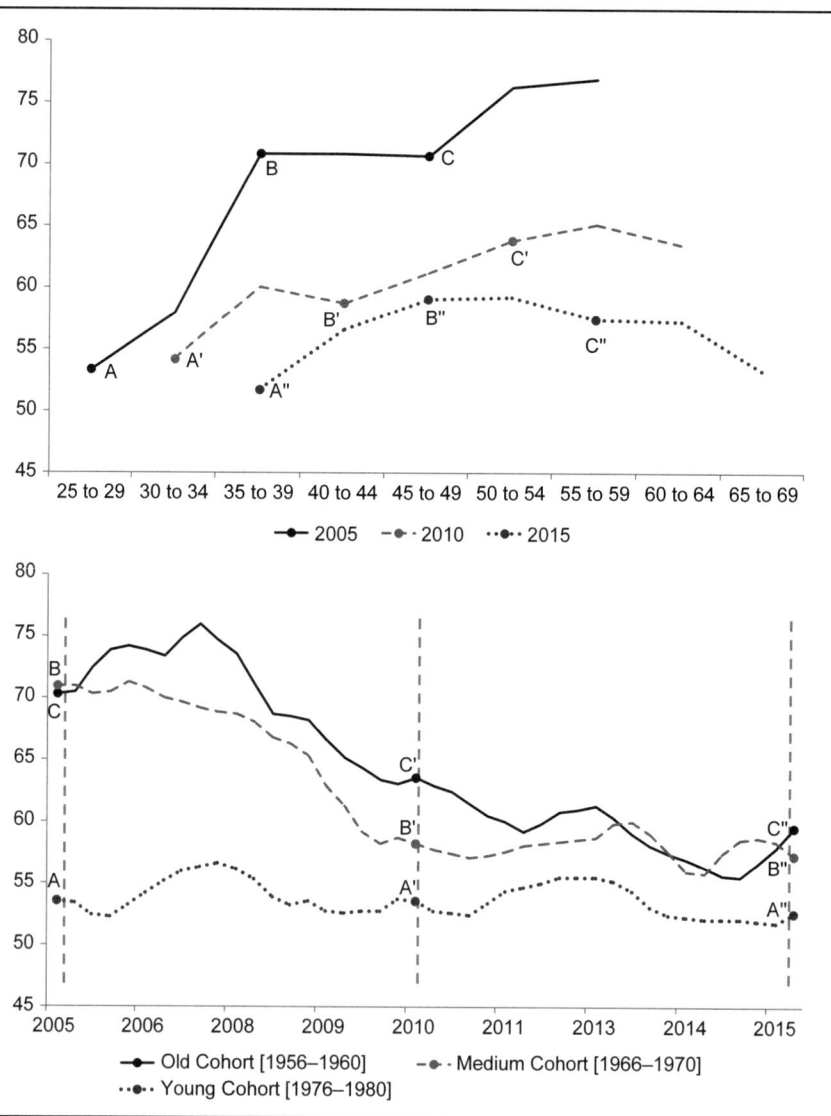

Source: Author's calculations based on data from Mexico's Employment Survey.

not a panel of individual workers, the three schedules refer to the same pool of workers: in 2005 they were in the 25-29 to 55-59 age range; five years later, in 2010, they were in the 30-34 to 60-64 range; and five years later, in 2015, they were in the 35-39 to 65-69 range. By focusing on the same pool, the figure avoids the potential selection bias from changing the mix of workers with different schooling quality, as some workers retired, and some new ones entered the labor force between 2005 and 2015. Because workers are randomly chosen in each year in the Employment Survey from the same pool, the three schedules in the upper panel refer to workers with on average the same educational quality.

Two observations are relevant in this panel: first, in line with the results of Lagakos et al. (2018), in each year returns to experience are increasing. Second, and more relevant to the discussion here, the returns to experience schedules shifted down between 2005 and 2015. Note that by construction these shifts cannot be attributed to changes in the mix of workers with different quality of schooling or related attributes. They must be due to other factors, principally among them, firm behavior.[15]

The lower panel of Figure 6.5 traces the implications of these shifts for specific cohorts of workers. The purpose here is to identify the path of earnings of a given cohort over this 10-year period. Thus, the horizontal axis refers to calendar years, as opposed to the upper panel, where it refers workers' age. Three different cohorts are followed:[16] an "old" cohort, made up of those born between 1956 and 1960 (continuous line); a "medium" cohort, born between 1966 and 1970 (dashed line); and a "young" cohort, born between 1976 and 1980 (dotted line).

What do the downward shifts in the returns to experience schedules mean for specific cohorts of workers? Consider the "young" cohort. In 2005, they are 25 to 29 years old. In the upper panel, this cohort is in point A, corresponding to the 2005 returns to experience schedule; they are the youngest workers, and the ones who earn the least. In the lower panel this cohort is also at point A, corresponding to 2005.

What happened to their earnings in 2010, five years later? If the returns to experience had been constant, they would have moved along the continuous line in the upper panel, earning the same as workers who were five years

---

[15] The downward shift between 2005 and 2010 could be attributed to the 2009 recession associated with that year's global financial crisis. But that cannot explain the downward shift between 2010 and 2015. After a sharp fall in 2009, GDP rebounded rapidly and was growing again by 2010.

[16] To maximize the number of observations, the average hourly wage is recorded for each cohort in 2008 prices for each quarter of the Employment Survey between 2005 and 2015. The series is smothered so that each quarterly observation is given by

$$\frac{1}{8}x_{t-2} + \frac{1}{4}x_{t-1} + \frac{1}{4}x_t + \frac{1}{4}x_{t+1} + \frac{1}{8}x_{t+2},$$

where *t* refers to a quarter.

older than them in 2005. But this did not happen. By 2010 the returns to experience schedule shifted down, and this cohort thus moved from point A to point A'. This is reflected in the lower panel as a movement from A in 2005 to A' in 2010. The cohort did earn more, but not as much as those workers could have earned if the returns to experience schedule had stayed constant.

What happened after another five years? The returns to experience schedule shifted down again (to the dotted line). In 2015, the "young" cohort is between 35 and 39 years old, and so it is at point A'' in the upper panel. Correspondingly, in 2015 that cohort is at point A'' in the lower panel. The upshot is that the earnings path of the "young" cohort was basically flat between 2005 and 2015—this despite being in the labor force for 10 years. This result is very important: in 2005 workers in this cohort had the reasonable expectation that 10 years later their earnings would be the same as those of workers who were then 10 years older than them. But this did not occur: 10 years later their earnings were basically the same. In other words, *for them the returns to their experience were zero*.

To follow workers of the "medium" cohort one moves along points B, B', and B'' in both panels of Figure 6.5, and to follow the "old" cohort one moves along points C, C', and C''. For these cohorts the results are even more disappointing, as their earnings are falling.

Figure 6.6 repeats the same exercise for workers who completed senior high school, with the same cohort groups and the same sample (male workers in cities of 100,000 inhabitants or more, working for private firms between 30 and 48 hours a week, and with earnings measured in constant prices of 2008). The returns to experience schedules are increasing but flatter than for those fowhor completed university, as expected. Moreover, returns begin to fall after 60 years of age. More importantly, as with workers who completed university education, the schedules shift down between 2005 and 2015. As a result, the earnings paths of these workers are qualitatively like the paths of those who completed their university education.

Two separate but related forces stand behind these results. First, as already noted, the returns to experience schedules in Mexico are flatter than in developed countries, and flatter than in Brazil and Chile. This indicates that Mexican workers acquire less human capital than workers in these countries while in the labor force. This result is consistent with the large job turnover, associated in turn with the large and mostly useless firm churning documented in Chapter 5.

The second force is that the schedules shifted down and that, as mentioned, this cannot be attributed to factors associated with the quality of workers. While macroeconomic factors might be part of the explanation of the shift between 2005 and 2010, this does not apply to the shift between 2010

The Misallocation of Human Capital **187**

Figure 6.6: Returns to Experience and Earnings Paths for Workers Who Completed Senior High School
(Hourly earnings in 2008 pesos)

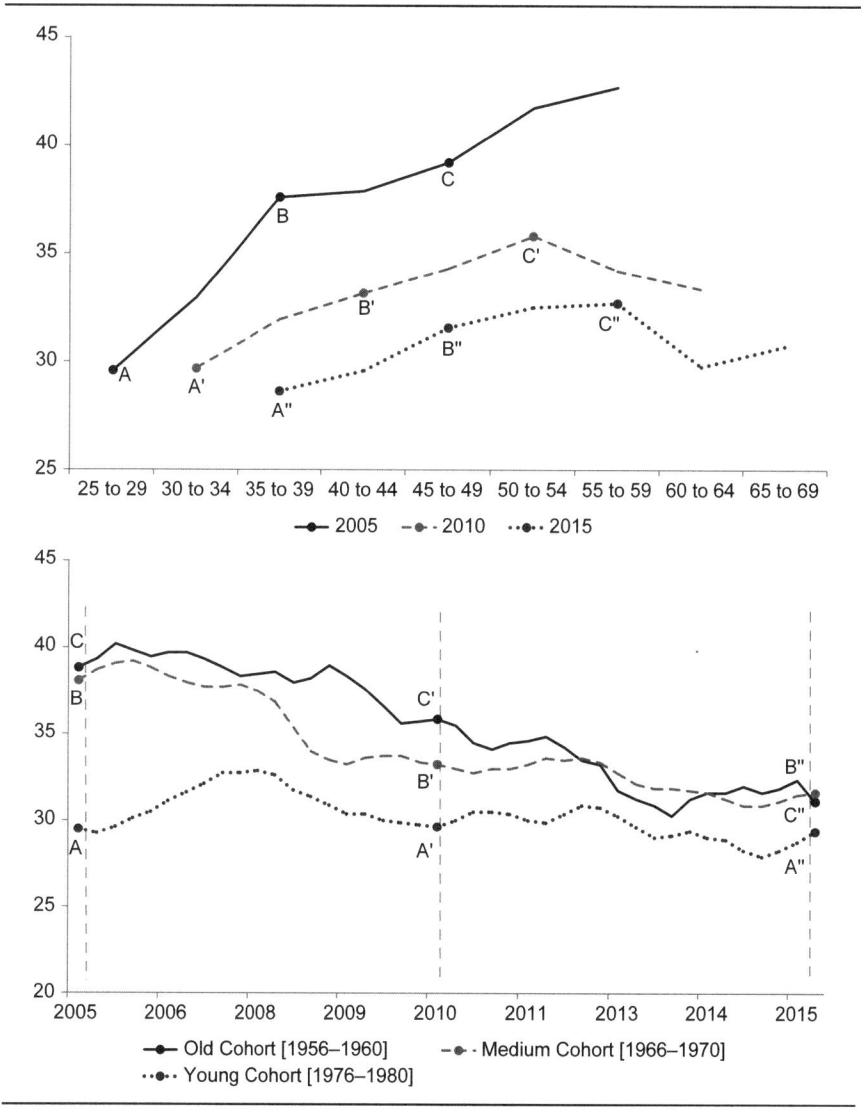

Source: Author's calculations based on data from Mexico's Employment Survey.

and 2015. These schedules shifted down principally for reasons attributable to firms, as average firm size fell and firm informality increased in a context of growing misallocation, as documented in Chapters 3 and 4.

Jointly, these two forces strongly suggest that an important by-product of the size and type distribution of firms and dysfunctional firm dynamics associated with Mexico's *E(L,T,M)* is to *limit workers' opportunities to acquire human capital while in the labor force, and in turn to limit their potential to increase their earnings over their lifetime.*

In closing this section, it should be highlighted that Figures 6.5 and 6.6 refer to averages of workers. Individual workers may experience increasing earnings during their lifetime, perhaps reflecting above-normal abilities or the fact that they were lucky enough to find a job in a high-productivity firm that survived during their lifetime and to benefit from training and on-the-job-learning. But few workers find jobs like that, because Mexico's *E(L,T,M)* discriminates against those firms.

Misallocation and the Incentives to Invest in Human Capital

There is a third channel by which Mexico's *E(L,T,M)* affects human capital: when workers realize that the benefits of acquiring education are lowered by misallocation, they invest less in education, and therefore they enter the labor force with fewer years of schooling. This has long-term implications for the stock of human capital available to the country.

Bobba, Flabbi, and Levy (2017) develop a model of firm-worker interactions in the context of Mexico's *E(L,T,M)* that focuses on the asymmetry in the scope and financing of social insurance, an issue further discussed in Chapter 7. When jobs are formal, the contributions for social insurance need to be internalized in the contract between the firm and the worker and are proportional to the workers' wage. Because workers undervalue the associated benefits, there is an implicit tax. And because part of the contributions is pooled to provide the same benefits to all, the tax is larger for higher-wage workers. On the other hand, when jobs are informal, the costs of social insurance are paid from an external source of revenue. And because benefits are distributed on a per capita basis, they are more valuable for lower-wage workers.

Congruent with the findings of Chapter 3, in the Bobba, Flabbi, and Levy framework firms can offer workers formal or informal jobs. Workers search for jobs from unemployment or from self-employment. When workers and firms agree on a contract (a match), they bargain over the wage, considering the match-specific productivity of the worker, the outside value to the worker of being unemployed or self-employed, and the costs and benefits of social insurance given the formality status of the job offered by the firm. The model reproduces two salient features of Mexico's labor market: the large overlap in the formal and informal wage distributions, and the large transition rates observed between formal and informal jobs.

For our purposes here, however, the most important feature of the Bobba, Flabbi, and Levy (2017) framework is that workers decide how much education to acquire *before* entering the labor force. This decision is based on the costs of postponing entry into the labor market and acquiring more education, versus the additional present discounted value of being in the labor force for the rest of their lives with more years of schooling. Clearly, if the market rewards workers who have more schooling, all else being equal, the incentives to acquire more education are higher, and young people will invest more in it. Conversely, if the differences in lifetime earnings between schooling levels are small, the incentives to invest in education will diminish and fewer young people will remain in school longer. The critical point is that the supply of workers of different educational levels is not exogenous, but rather depends on the parameters defining firm and worker interactions in the labor market. In other words, Mexico's *E(L,T,M)* affects not only the returns to education of workers currently in the labor force, and their ability to acquire human capital while in the labor force, but also the country's future stock of human capital as given by workers' decisions to invest in schooling prior to entering the labor force.

The critical point made by Bobba, Flabbi and Levy is that the dual nature of Mexico's social insurance system taxes high-productivity matches between firms and workers and subsidizes low-productivity ones. And because high-productivity matches are more likely for workers who have more years of schooling, the arrangement ends up taxing proportionately more workers with more years of schooling. In turn, because workers observe that the returns to schooling are lower, they invest less in education.

Bobba, Flabbi and Levy (2017) estimate their model using data from Mexico's Employment Survey, including the parameters capturing workers' valuation of formal and informal social insurance benefits. They then focus on the decision made by young people at a critical juncture: to abandon school after completing junior high school, or to continue studying and complete senior high school. The main result is that the dual social insurance system has a strong influence on a worker's schooling decisions. In the benchmark equilibrium, 60 percent of workers in the labor force complete junior high, and 40 percent complete senior high school. But when the system of implicit taxes and subsidies associated with the dual system is eliminated, the proportion of workers in the labor force who complete senior high school increases to 70 percent. This result suggests that the dual system is very costly in terms of workers' incentives to invest in education. Moreover, in the simulated equilibrium the value of total output increases by 17 percentage points. This increase reflects both an increase in the number of high-productivity matches between workers and firms (and lower self-employment), and the fact that a more educated labor force increases the underlying productivity of the economy.

As discussed in Chapter 7, a dual social insurance system is one of the elements of Mexico's *E(L,T,M)* responsible for misallocation, so these results are quite relevant to Mexico. But beyond the specifics of the framework used by Bobba, Flabbi and Levy (2017) and their numerical estimates, the main point is that the productivity costs of misallocation go beyond the static costs captured in Chapter 4 in the context of the Hsieh-Klenow (2009) model, focused as it was only on the distribution of workers of given educational levels across firms of differing sizes and types. *By lowering the returns to education, misallocation lowers the incentives to invest in it, and generates permanent costs to Mexico.*

CHAPTER 7

Policies, Institutions, and Misallocation

This chapter discusses the relation between misallocation and Mexico's policies and institutions. From the point of view of productivity and growth, this is the most critical issue. *What is it in Mexico's $E(L,T,M)$ that generates persistent misallocation and under-rewards everybody's efforts?*

In principle, the objective is to identify causality between individual policies and misallocation and obtain quantitative estimates of the relative importance of each. The discussion in this chapter makes clear that this can be accomplished only in part. On the one hand, misallocation in Mexico has various facets, and many policies affect it through multiple channels. On the other, there are insufficient data and there is an imperfect understanding about how the economy works. The issue is, simply put, too complex. That said, the chapter hopefully focuses on the subset of policies and institutions that are the main causes, although not the only ones, of misallocation in Mexico.

Core Stylized Facts

Chapters 3, 4, and 5 described a series of outcomes about firm and worker behavior. Before turning to identifying their determinants, it is useful to synthesize them in the following stylized facts:

- **Stylized Fact 1**: Mexico's $E(L,T,M)$ allocates too many resources to firms with non-salaried contracts relative to firms with salaried contracts and, within the latter, to those that violate applicable labor and social insurance regulations.

- **Stylized Fact 2**: Mexico's $E(L,T,M)$ induces the dispersion of production in smaller firms. A corollary of the excess of small firms is that too many individuals participate in economic activity as entrepreneurs or as self-employed, rather than as workers in firms.
- **Stylized Fact 3**: Mexico's $E(L,T,M)$ favors the entry of new firms and deters the growth of existing ones, even if incumbents have higher productivity; in parallel, it allows the survival of low-productivity firms, and the exit of high-productivity ones.
- **Stylized Fact 4**: Despite important reforms to various elements of Mexico's $E(L,T,M)$ over the last two decades, dysfunctional firm dynamics accentuated the outcomes described in stylized facts one and two.

In parallel, Chapter 6 established that these facts do *not* result from human capital considerations. (That said, it should be reiterated that this does not mean that improving Mexico's human capital is not important or desirable.)

These facts do not exhaust all facets of misallocation, but they capture the ones at the core of Mexico's productivity problem. This implies that not all policies that bear on misallocation need to be considered, but only those that are most relevant to these facts. Put differently, by concentrating on explaining these facts, the scope of the discussion is narrowed considerably; as a consequence, this chapter focuses on the subset of policies and institutions that bear directly on them. As shown below, this subset goes a long way towards explaining Mexico's productivity and growth problem.

The chapter faces two obstacles. The first is economists' partial and incomplete understanding of the connection between policies, on the one hand, and resource allocation and productivity outcomes, on the other. As noted in Chapter 2, we are far from having a full understanding of relations (2.3) and (2.6). Most analytical models focus on the impact of individual policies in $E(L,T,M)$ on misallocation. This is understandable, since their purpose is to identify and explore the transmission mechanisms of the policy under analysis in detail. A model where all policies are analyzed at the same time is not tractable; to gain insights, one must inevitably simplify. That said, for our purposes here this is an important limitation, since what we care about are the effects of various policies in $E(L,T,M)$, not the effects of any one policy on its own.

The second obstacle is that few studies on Mexico directly associate policies with productivity outcomes. Studies explore, for instance, such issues as how the entry of China into the World Trade Organization affected manufacturing employment; how changes in tax laws affected evasion and the legal/illegal composition of salaried employment; and how a social insurance program affected firm informality or the formal-informal composition of employment. These studies, summarized below, are of course very valuable, but their implications for productivity are established indirectly by inference, not by direct measurement.

Given these obstacles, the approach followed in this chapter is eclectic. It describes how individual policies affect occupational choices, the size and type distribution of firms, and the patterns of firm entry, exit, and growth. When possible, it refers to studies that make a direct connection between a policy and some measure of productivity. When this is not possible, it makes the connection indirectly, exploiting the patterns of correlation between firm sizes, types, and productivity obtained in Chapter 4 as well as the patterns between firm sizes, types, and entry, exit, and growth obtained in Chapter 5.

For instance, assume that we identify that a specific policy, call it X, increases the profitability of firms offering workers non-salaried contracts. From the point of view of productivity, that finding by itself is not truly useful. However, it becomes so when combined with the results of Chapter 4, because we know from that chapter that if resources could be reallocated to firms with salaried contracts, productivity would increase. In a rigorous sense, one cannot say that policy X "causes" low productivity because there is no direct evidence linking it with productivity. But one can say that policy X induces firms to engage in behavior that is associated with productivity losses.

In this vein, this chapter is built around the following question: what policies in the "world of entrepreneur-worker relations" (*L*), in the "world of taxation" (*T*), and in the "world of market conditions" (*M*) could induce firms and workers to behave in ways consistent with the first three stylized facts under consideration? To answer this question, we consider policies separately from *L*, from *T*, and from *M*, and then consider their joint effects. *Changes* in policies that stand behind stylized fact four are analyzed in Chapter 8.

One last observation: this and the next chapter present the author's views on the policies behind the outcomes summarized in the four stylized facts, and hopefully the reader will find them convincing. But even if the reader is not convinced, this would not invalidate those stylized facts. Rather, it would imply that an alternative explanation consistent with those facts needs to be offered.

Misallocation and the World of Entrepreneur-Worker Relations

This section begins by focusing on the role of *L* in $E(L,T,M)$. Of course, *L* is just a symbol representing an extremely complex yet central dimension of Mexico's social and economic landscape: the policies and institutions that regulate how entrepreneurs and workers form firms and jointly create value. Many policies are involved. This can be represented by $E[L(L_1, L_2,..., L_n), T, M]$. This section does not provide an analysis of all. Policies on minimum wages, profit-sharing, and unions, among others, are not discussed. Attention focuses only on those policies most relevant to the stylized facts of concern here: social insurance and dismissal regulations. Of course, these policies are motivated by the government's social objectives, but these objectives are not discussed here. The focus is only on their impact on misallocation.

We now describe a simple framework to analyze how entrepreneurs' and workers' contractual choices along with firm size are affected by the regulations of L. Let w_f be the wage paid to workers when formally employed (i.e., when entrepreneurs offer them a legal salaried contract), and w_i the remuneration paid when workers are informally employed (i.e., with an illegal salaried or a non-salaried contract). Let T_f and T_i be the costs of all nonmonetary benefits that formally and informally employed workers receive, respectively; β_f and β_i the share of those costs that workers consider to be valuable benefits in each case; and θ_f the share of T_f that is paid for by firms and workers, so that $(1 - \theta_f)T_f$ is the share paid from general government revenues; this in the understanding that T_i is fully paid from general government revenues (that is, $\theta_i = 0$). Finally, let $\lambda(.)$ be the probability that a firm hiring salaried workers illegally is detected by the authorities, and F the fine imposed on the firm for doing so. Table 7.1 compares the costs to firms and the benefits to workers of three contracting modalities.

Table 7.1: Costs to Firms and Benefits to Workers of Salaried and Non-Salaried Contracts

Type of Contract	Costs to Firms	Benefits to Workers	Implicit Tax (+) or Subsidy (−)
Legal salaried	$w_f + \theta_f T_f$	$w_f + \beta_f T_f$	$(\theta_f - \beta_f)T_f$
Illegal salaried	$w_i + \lambda(.)F$	$w_i + \beta_i T_i$	$\lambda(.)F - \beta_i T_i$
Non-salaried	w_i	$w_i + \beta_i T_i$	$-\beta_i T_i$

Source: Prepared by the author.

Brief Description of Policies and Institutions

Before exploring the relation between Table 7.1 and the stylized facts under analysis, it is helpful to relate it to Mexico's policies and institutions. One can begin with legal salaried contracts. There are many benefits to workers of being formally employed aside from the wage. Two are particularly relevant:

- Access to health insurance, day care services, recreational centers, and cultural and sports facilities provided by the Mexican Social Security Institute (Instituto Mexicano del Seguro Social – IMSS); access to housing loans offered by the country's housing agency for salaried workers (Instituto del Fondo Nacional para la Vivienda de los Trabajadores – Infonavit); and access to retirement, death, work accident, and disability pensions provided through individual savings accounts managed by private pension fund administrators (Administradoras de Fondos de Retiro – Afores) in the case of retirement pensions, and through risk-pooling arrangements managed by the IMSS for the rest.
- Regulations that give workers the right to severance payments when dismissed from their job, along with the right to be compensated or reinstated in their job if that dismissal is found to be "unjustified" by federal or state labor tribunals (Juntas de Conciliación y Arbitraje – JCAs).

The first set of benefits are associated with contributory social insurance and are financed through a flow payment proportional to workers' wages that, excluding the share $(1 - \theta_f)T_f$ paid by the government, must be internalized in the contract between firms and salaried workers.[1] The second is Mexico's substitute for unemployment insurance. Dismissal regulations have many effects on firms, but at this point, only the costs of severance pay incurred when firms dismiss workers are considered. Thus, we momentarily ignore the uncertainty associated with whether dismissals are justified, and whether workers are entitled to compensation or reinstatement. How this uncertainty affects firm behavior will be explored later.

Severance pay is a one-time lump sum payment, as opposed to flow payments into an unemployment insurance fund. However, the expected costs of this one-time outlay can be converted into a flow payment based on the probability that a firm will dismiss a worker, and on the worker's tenure when that event occurs (since payments are proportional to the duration of the relation between the firm and the worker). This expected payment must also be internalized in the contract between firms and workers.

The flow costs of these two benefits are represented by T_f in Table 7.1. But since in Mexico the government subsidizes contributory programs, workers and firms are only responsible for $\theta_f T_f$.

Various laws regulate benefits and obligations. But this is secondary because firms and workers in a salaried contract must comply with all of

---

[1] The incidence of $\theta_f T_f$ is ignored here. The key point is that it must be paid between the two parties. Antón, Hernández, and Levy (2012) estimate that approximately 64 percent is shifted back to workers in the form of a lower wage.

them at the same time; for practical purposes it is as if there were a single law. These laws bundle together all benefits and obligations: workers cannot choose to forego some benefits in exchange for a higher wage, and firms are obligated to pay for all benefits, including the contingent costs of firing.

Consider now the benefits that informally employed workers receive aside from their pay. These are associated with non-contributory social insurance programs, whose costs are represented by T_j in Table 7.1. There are three critical differences with T_f. The first is that programs are fully financed from general revenues and therefore their costs do not have to be internalized in the contracts between firms and workers. The second is that firms are not involved: they have no financial responsibilities, nor do they face any transaction costs from dealing with the IMSS or Infonavit, any contingent liabilities from firing costs, or any risks of being sued by workers in a JCA for "unjustified dismissal." The third is that benefits are unbundled: they are not bound together by any law.

Non-contributory social insurance benefits—which from the perspective of workers are an imperfect substitute for contributory ones—derive from a wide array of programs operated by federal and, more relevant in this case, state institutions (Antón 2016; Levy 2008). They basically consist of:

- Health services provided by state governments (but also, to a lesser extent, by the federal government and, paradoxically, the IMSS).
- Day care services provided by the federal government through the Social Development Ministry (Secretaría de Desarrollo Social – Sedesol) and by state and municipal governments through their social development agencies (Desarrollo Integral de la Familia – DIF).
- Subsidized housing loans offered through agencies associated with Sedesol.
- Retirement pensions provided by the federal and state governments.
- Life insurance (for women only) through Sedesol.

Contributory and non-contributory programs and regulations on dismissal are the core of Mexico's welfare state. Many institutions—federal, state, and municipal—are involved in delivering benefits, collecting contributions, and enforcing court rulings. When hiring salaried workers legally, firms interact with various authorities and pay the relevant contributions and transaction costs; when hiring them illegally, they face the risk of being fined. Rules faced by workers to access benefits are complex, and they include who qualifies for what pension, when entrepreneurs can be sued for unfair dismissal, who has a right to a housing loan, and so on. There is heterogeneity in effective access; sometimes it is rationed, sometimes not. The quality of health provision varies: services provided through the IMSS are, on average, better than those provided by non-contributory programs, but not everywhere. Courts adjudicating dismissal disputes can sometimes be expeditious and sometimes slow; in parallel, the amounts awarded for similar situations can vary considerably. *The key point is that the policies that determine who pays and who does not, when firms face responsibilities and when not, and who has a right to what, as well as the functioning of the institutions that enforce the rules and provide benefits, touch the daily lives of millions of workers and entrepreneurs in all sectors of the economy.*

We next use Table 7.1 to examine how these policies and institutions affect the behavior of entrepreneurs and workers.

The Implicit Tax on Salaried Contracts

Consider the first line of Table 7.1. If the value that workers attach to contributory programs and to the expected benefits from severance pay equaled the payments made by workers and firms, that is, if $\beta_f T_f = \theta_f T_f$, then salaried contracts would be neither implicitly taxed nor subsidized (beyond the explicit subsidies represented by $(1 - \theta_f)T_f$).

Levy (2008, 2009) documented that in Mexico this is not the case, and that the value that workers attach to contributory programs and to severance pay is less than what they and their firms pay for them, that is, that $\beta_f < \theta_f$. One reason for this is that benefits are bundled: workers are obligated to consume a fixed-proportion basket of present and future goods and services. But a more important reason is that, on the one hand, the institutions responsible for delivering benefits underperform and, on the other, some benefits may be inaccessible. In a nutshell:

- Because of underinvestment in facilities and issues of monopoly provision, the quality of health services provided by the IMSS is subpar.
- Access to day care centers is rationed (the probability that parents can get coverage for their child is about 25 percent).
- Not all workers want to own a house or need a housing loan.
- Almost 76 percent of workers saving in their individual account will *not* qualify for a retirement pension because they will not accumulate the required 25 years of contributions (CONSAR 2016). When they reach 65 years of age they will get back their savings (with interest) in a lump-sum payment but will bear the risks of longevity.
- Procedures at JCAs to claim compensation or reinstatement are lengthy and cumbersome. Many workers drop their claims without any compensation, and those who see them through only receive approximately 30

percent of established claims (Kaplan, Sadka, and Silva-Mendez 2008). Further, only 40 percent of plaintiffs who receive compensation eventually collect it from the firm (Kaplan and Sadka 2011). Almost no firms pay the judgments unless the worker initiates legal proceedings to seize its assets. Importantly, both the worker and the firm are estimated to incur substantial costs during the enforcement phase of the trial. In addition, firms face large uncertainty: 90 percent of all trials in JCAs derive from suits for "unfair" dismissal but, controlling for tenure, the difference between the lowest and the highest award is 5.5 times (IMCO 2014).

Workers valuation of T_f varies depending on personal circumstances: age, gender, marital status, location, risk aversion, migration plans, previous episodes of formal employment, and so on. In principle, therefore, there is a distribution of β_f, one for each worker. It is very difficult to recover this distribution from the available data, but econometric estimates suggest that its mean value is 0.55.[2] In parallel, based on the contributions mandated by law and actuarial calculations of the expected costs of severance pay, the mean value of $\theta_f T_f$ is approximately 33.2 percent of the average wage.[3]

The implication is that the interplay between the policies regulating benefits to salaried workers and the functioning of the institutions providing those benefits results in an implicit tax on salaried contracts of approximately 12 percent. Note that this is akin to a pure tax: something that must be paid for between workers and entrepreneurs when they agree on a salaried relation, with no benefit to either in return. Thus, the policies and institutions discussed punish firms and workers with salaried contracts, so, all else being equal, they will try to avoid these contracts whenever possible. This behavior is consistent with stylized fact one.

Imperfect Enforcement of the Implicit Tax on Salaried Contracts

Consider now the second line of Table 7.1 and, for the moment, ignore $\beta_i T_i$. Entrepreneurs and workers avoid a pure tax of $(\theta_f - \beta_f)T_f$ if they break the law but face a probability $\lambda(.)$ of paying a fine F if they do so. Since by law F is greater than $\theta_f T_f$, they will evade only if $\lambda(.)$ is sufficiently small. Importantly

---

[2] Bobba, Flabbi, and Levy (2017) estimate jointly the values of β_f and β_i using data from Mexico's Employment Survey, and obtain mean values of 0.55 and 0.90, respectively.

[3] Contributions for social insurance benefits are approximately 36 percent of the wage, of which 6 percentage points are paid by the government. In parallel, Heckman and Pages (2004) estimate that the implicit flow payments associated with Mexico's severance pay regulations are approximately 3.2 percent of the wage. The addition of the two is the number given in the text.

in this context, the IMSS and Infonavit are not only tasked with providing benefits but also with collecting contributions. In other words, these two institutions oversee enforcement, and their performance determines the shape of the function $\lambda(.)$.

Because there are fixed costs of collection, and because in the case of very small or small firms the market value of the assets impounded may be less than the sum of collection costs and contributions due, the IMSS and Infonavit pay substantially more attention to larger firms. As a result, the probabilities of detection $\lambda(.)$ are not the same for all firms, but rather increase with firm size. The presumption, therefore, is that smaller firms will break the law more than larger ones. This presumption was confirmed by Table 3.6 in Chapter 3, which showed that 86.9 percent of all informal and illegal firms have up to five workers, 8.9 percent have between six and 10, 4 percent have between 11 and 50, and only 0.2 percent have more than 51.

There is a very important implication of the imperfect enforcement of the tax on salaried contracts: it introduces an implicit tax on the growth of illegal and informal firms. This is because for these firms the expected average and marginal costs of hiring more workers increases, since the probability of being penalized is higher the bigger is the firm. This makes it difficult for these firms to grow and biases the size distribution of firms towards smallness, a result consistent with stylized facts two and three.

The Uncertainty Costs of Dismissal Regulations

Table 7.1 showed the costs of dismissal regulations as being equivalent to an expected flow payment for severance pay that firms and workers must internalize in a salaried contract, which in turn adds to the flow payments associated with contributory programs. If the expected costs of severance pay borne by firms equaled the expected benefits to workers, these regulations would not affect the costs of salaried contracts. In Mexico this is not the case, because as noted workers face uncertainty, delays, and transaction costs in collecting severance pay when fired. As a result, there is a wedge between firms' expected costs and workers' expected benefits, which adds to the implicit tax on salaried contracts associated with workers' undervaluation of social insurance benefits.

There is more. Dismissal regulations have other costs because they affect firm dynamics. Firms face uncertainty about future demand. If severance pay is high, productive firms are deterred from growing when they face a positive shock, because they do not know if the shock is transitory or permanent, and the costs of firing the additional workers if the shock turns out to be transitory can exceed the extra profits to be had by hiring them. In parallel, firms may not reduce their labor force when faced with a negative shock if they expect it to be transitory, but if the shock ends up being permanent, their workforce will be larger than needed and as a result their productivity will fall (Hopenhayn and Rogerson 1993).

The associated productivity costs can be large, depending on workers' tenure in the firm. Da-Rocha, Tavares, and Restuccia (2016) estimate that if severance pay is equal to one year of wages, total factor productivity will fall by 4.2 percent, and if severance pay is equivalent to five years of wages, total factor productivity will fall by 20.6 percent. In Mexico, severance pay is three months of wages regardless of tenure, plus two-thirds of the monthly wage for each year worked. In addition, for workers earning up to two minimum wages, severance also includes one-third of a monthly wage for each year worked, and one-third of two minimum wages for those earning more than that. Thus, for instance, severance pay for a worker earning two minimum wages with 10 years of tenure is equal to 13 months of wages, so it could be reducing total factor productivity by more than 4 percent.

But this is not all. In Mexico, these productivity costs are exacerbated because firms *cannot* legally dismiss workers when demand falls or when there is a labor-saving technical innovation. These are considered "unjust" causes for dismissal in Mexican legislation. Workers have the right to sue the firm for such dismissals and, if they win, the right to choose between being compensated or reinstated in their job. ("Just" causes are associated with flaws in workers' behavior.) Furthermore, if workers win and choose to be reinstated, firms must pay wages foregone during the period when the issue was being adjudicated by the JCA, and then of course continue to permanently pay wages for workers they no longer need. If workers win and choose compensation, firms face large uncertainty about the size of the award granted. In either case, firms must spend money on lawyers and fees (and so do workers).

Thus, severance pay captures only part of the effects of dismissal regulations. In addition, there are the effects associated with the possibility of not being able to fire the worker at all, at any cost (as if severance pay were infinite). These latter effects are more difficult to quantify because they affect behavior in more complex ways than just adding to the non-wage costs of labor T_f. Firms anticipate these contingencies and are deterred from hiring salaried workers to begin with, or from expanding their workforce when there are good opportunities. In parallel, firms may have to opt for bankruptcy to substantially reduce their workforce. Other firms, on the other hand, may consider it preferable to have non-salaried workers. Even if that contractual modality leads to some productivity losses, the gain in flexibility and the avoided contingent costs may make it profitable to use it. And then of course there is always the option of operating illegally.

This discussion implies that considering the costs of dismissal regulations as simply the flow equivalent of the contingent costs of severance pay leads to underestimating their costs, and perhaps significantly so. And while it is difficult to quantify the full costs of dismissal regulations, particularly their dynamic effects, they induce firms to behave in ways consistent with stylized facts one and three.

The Subsidy to Non-salaried and Illegal Salaried Contracts

Consider now the third line of Table 7.1. Entrepreneurs and workers can agree on contracts where pay is based on profit-sharing (as in most family firms), on sales, on numbers of units produced, and, indeed, on almost any arrangement other than a wage. When there are non-contributory benefits for non-salaried workers, however, these contracts are de facto subsidized: the value of the contract to the worker exceeds the costs to the firm.

How large is the subsidy? As opposed to T_f, there are no contribution rates specified in law that can be added up to obtain T_i. Rather, resources for these programs are specified annually in the federal and state budgets. Antón (2016) estimates that in 2013 they totaled 1.7 percent of GDP. He also estimates T_i assuming benefits are distributed pro-rata among all informally employed workers and finds it to be equivalent to 18 percent of mean earnings.[4] Given that $\beta_i = 0.9$, this implies a mean subsidy of 16.2 percent. This subsidy rate contrasts with the 12 percent pure tax rate implicit in salaried contracts. In parallel, the aggregate value of the subsidy, 1.7 percent of GDP, contrasts with the aggregate value of the subsidy to contributory programs, which was 0.5 of a percent of GDP in the same year.

It is useful here to recall from Chapter 2 that non-salaried contracts are more common among smaller firms. Because there are few workers in these firms, even if there are no relations of subordination, effort can be observed, shirking avoided more easily, and coordination of tasks facilitated. That is why informal and legal firms are mostly small (and not imperfect enforcement of social insurance contributions by the IMSS and Infonavit, which affects only firms hiring salaried workers). Indeed, it can be inferred from Table 3.6 in Chapter 3 that 97.8 percent of firms with non-salaried contracts have up to five workers, 1.3 percent have between six and 10, 0.7 of a percent between 11 and 50, and only 0.2 of a percent 51 or more. Thus, although in principle the subsidy to non-salaried contracts is neutral with respect to firm size, it

---

[4] But note that as a percentage of the wage, the subsidy is higher for lower-wage workers. For workers earning, say, the equivalent of one minimum wage, the subsidy is 37 percent; for those earning five times that amount, it is 7.4 percent.

will proportionately benefit smaller firms more. The behavior induced by this subsidy is consistent with stylized facts one and two.

Two more observations are important. First, in Mexico illegally hired salaried workers also benefit from non-contributory programs because these programs cover all informal workers. As a result, the programs de facto subsidize firms' illegal behavior. This can be seen in the second line of Table 7.1. Given fines F and probability of detection $\lambda(.)$, as T_j increases so does the value of an illegal salaried contract. Salaried workers can obtain social insurance benefits freely, but only if the firm hiring them breaks the law. And since it is more difficult for larger firms to behave illegally, this also biases the size distribution of firms towards smallness, consistent with stylized fact two.

The second observation is that firms with non-salaried workers do not face any costs from dismissals, either in terms of firing costs or any uncertainty from being sued for "unfair" dismissal. This is because the law in Mexico does not consider non-salaried workers to be subordinated employees of the firm. This factor will also induce behavior consistent with stylized fact one.[5]

The Costs of Labor under Contributory and Non-contributory Programs

Figure 7.1 captures the interplay between the pure tax on legal salaried contracts, the imperfect enforcement of that tax, and the subsidy to non-salaried and illegal salaried contracts. As it turns out, although the uncertainty costs associated with dismissal regulations are not captured, the figure sheds considerable light on the empirical results of Chapters 3, 4, and 5 and the stylized facts of concern in this chapter.

The figure is drawn from the perspective of a single firm and ignores any differences in a worker's individual characteristics; all workers are alike. The vertical axis measures the expected average cost of a worker, and the horizontal one the number of workers hired by the firm. The three vertical dotted lines at five, 10, and 50 workers separate firms by size, and are chosen to coincide with the size categories used in previous chapters. There are four blocks labelled I to IV. In each block is listed the number of firms, F, and the number of workers, L, in manufacturing, commerce, and services based on the 2013 census and on our estimates of firms excluded from the census in that

---

[5] That said, there may be some uncertainty in borderline cases between salaried and non-salaried labor. Workers can sue firms in a JCA even if they have a non-salaried contract alleging there was a relation of subordination with the firm prior to separation. This behavior is more likely with larger firms, and may yet be another factor deterring firm growth, although there is little evidence to assess this.

Figure 7.1: Expected Average Costs to Firms of Salaried and Non-Salaried Workers
(Index of average labor costs)

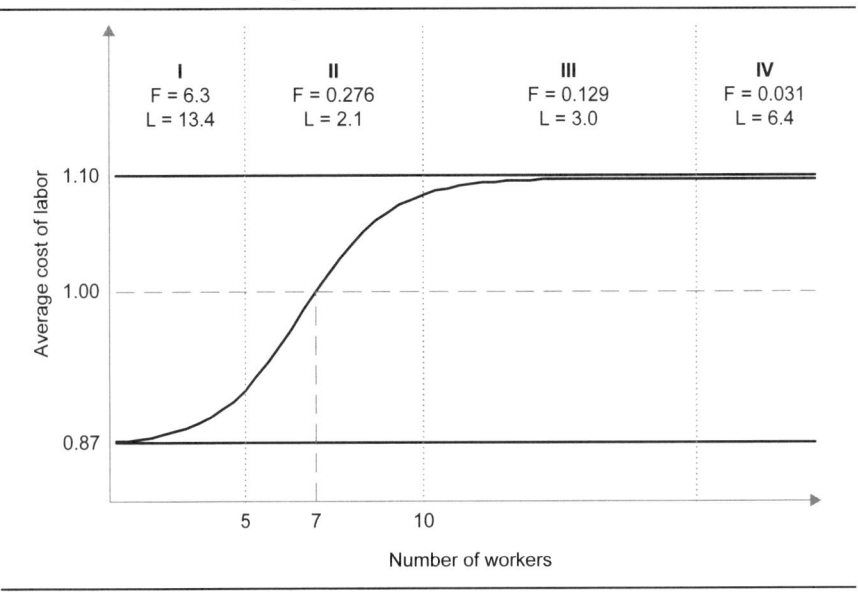

I	II	III	IV
F = 6.3	F = 0.276	F = 0.129	F = 0.031
L = 13.4	L = 2.1	L = 3.0	L = 6.4

Source: Prepared by the author based on data from Antón, Hernández, and Levy (2012).
Note: F: firms; L: workers.

year (see Table 1.1 in Chapter 1 and Table 3.9 in Chapter 3). Note that F and L are both measured in millions.

Two key points are made by Figure 7.1:

- There is a large agglomeration of firms and workers in block I: 93 percent of all firms and almost 54 percent of all workers.
- The expected average costs to a firm of hiring a worker depends on the size of the firm and on whether the worker is offered a salaried or non-salaried contract.

The three black solid lines capture the second point. The lower one shows the average cost of a worker under a non-salaried contract; it is flat because a firm can get as many workers as it needs under this contractual modality at the same costs of w_i (Table 7.1). The upper one shows the average cost of hiring a worker under a legal salaried contract, and it is also flat because a firm can hire as many of these workers as it needs at the same costs of $(w_f + \theta_f T_f)$. In turn, the solid line in the middle depicts the average cost of hiring a worker under an illegal salaried contract, and it is upward-sloping because as the firm hires more workers, the probability that it will be fined increases, and thus the expected average cost of hiring also increases. In addition, a horizontal dashed line in the middle captures a hypothetical scenario where the regulations on salaried and non-salaried contracts are the same and where, as a result, the average cost of workers under either modality is the same. For simplicity, this cost is set at unity.[6]

Figure 7.1 reveals that the asymmetries in the regulation of salaried and non-salaried labor in Mexico have substantive implications for firms' labor costs. First, note that if firms behave legally, the cost difference between a salaried and a non-salaried contract is on the order of 23 percent. This is a very large difference indeed that, all else being equal, would induce firms to hire only non-salaried workers. This, of course, is not possible, for the reasons explained in Chapter 2. Given the production technology, in many cases firms can only carry out their activities if workers have a salaried contract.

Of course, some firms break the law and hire salaried workers illegally. In 2013, considering only firms captured in the census, 707,660 firms did this. Figure 7.1 shows that given enforcement by the IMSS and Infonavit, the benefits of illegal behavior accrue mostly to very small and, to a lesser extent, small firms. Proportionately few firms with more than 10 workers break the law (as confirmed in Table 3.6 in Chapter 3). This is consistent with the fact that small illegal firms have difficulties growing (stylized fact three).

Figure 7.1 also helps explain the rankings of firm productivity documented in Chapter 4. Ignoring other determinants of firm behavior except labor costs, it suggests that to survive in the market, firms with legal salaried contracts must be more productive than those with illegal salaried contracts, which in turn must be more productive than firms with non-salaried contracts. This ordering matches the regression results in Table 4.4 in Chapter 4. As shown

---

[6] Figure 7.1, based on Antón, Hernández and Levy (2012), is generated by a model in which profit-maximizing firms and utility-maximizing workers jointly determine the legal-salaried, illegal-salaried, and non-salaried composition of employment, as well as the respective wages, in a context like the one laid out in Table 7.1. The probability of detection function $\lambda(.)$ is calibrated based on the size distribution of illegal and informal firms found in the census, and the values of T_f, T_j, β_f, θ_f, and β_j are as stated in the text. The model reproduces the employment composition observed in Mexico and associated macroeconomic aggregates. The average costs of labor in the absence of any social insurance programs (the horizontal dashed line in Figure 7.1) incorporate the endogenous adjustment of wages in response to setting $T_f = T_j = 0$. The average costs of labor with social insurance programs (the three solid lines) reflect the actual differences in the costs of hiring salaried or non-salaried workers. To ease comparisons, average costs in the $T_f = T_j = 0$ scenario are normalized at unity, and average costs under the observed values of T_f and T_j are expressed as a proportion of that. The model is, of course, a simplified picture of the labor costs faced by firms in Mexico. That said, it gives a sense of the orders of magnitude of the wedges created by the country's social insurance and dismissal regulations (or, more precisely given our treatment of dismissal regulations, a lower bound on the size of those wedges).

there, in each size category (blocks I–IV in Figure 7.1), fully formal firms are the most productive, and informal and legal firms the least productive, with informal and illegal firms in the middle. (Mixed firms are ignored here, as they are not easily depicted in Figure 7.1.)

In addition, Figure 7.1 sheds some light on firm dynamics:

- Consider an informal and legal firm with, say, five workers. Assume it wants to grow and needs more workers. For the reasons shown earlier, it is difficult for the firm to expand under non-salaried contractual relations. It could perhaps do so by adding, say, five more workers, but beyond that point this contractual arrangement would be increasingly dysfunctional and lead to shirking, coordination difficulties, interruptions in production given the absence of fixed working times, and so on. The firm would be better off with salaried contracts that allow it to dictate workers' time and place of work, coordinate their efforts, and so on. But changing the contractual structure of the firm would be very costly: if done legally, it would increase labor costs by about 23 percent and, equally important, the firm would now face contingent liabilities associated with dismissal regulations. The firm would also have greater difficulties adjusting its workforce when there are negative shocks. Changing from informal to formal status is not impossible, but Figure 7.1 indicates that this behavior will be strongly deterred by the policies analyzed here, particularly if the firm is small. This is consistent with the relatively few informal-to-formal transits found in Table 5.2 in Chapter 5, and it is also consistent with the third stylized fact.
- Consider now a firm with the same five workers but with legal salaried contracts. Assume it needs to reduce output because of a negative transitory shock. Given its formal status, it cannot lower wages, and it may not have sufficient resources to pay for the firing costs of laying some off. And even if the firm had access to credit to finance dismissals, it might be unwilling to face the risks of being sued in a JCA because, as noted, output adjustment is not a "justified" cause for dismissal. In this context, breaking the law may be a sensible adjustment strategy (particularly since the probability of detection is small), and so the firm may change to illegal and informal. Alternatively, it may change its contractual structure and become an informal and legal firm. This is part of the explanation of formal-to-informal transits shown in Table 5.2 in Chapter 5.

In parallel, it is clear from Figure 7.1 that low-productivity entry will be facilitated if the firm begins its operations with non-salaried contracts. The same is true of low-productivity survival, because the firm has a permanent labor cost advantage. Figure 7.1 also suggests that firms with legal salaried contracts may have to exit when there are negative shocks even if they have high productivity because they cannot reduce wages or their workforce. This is consistent with Figures 5.1 and 5.2 and the discussion thereof in Chapter 5, and it is also consistent with stylized fact three.

Finally, of special interest in Figure 7.1 is the horizontal dashed line that, as mentioned earlier, shows the average costs of labor in a counterfactual scenario where there are no differences in the regulation of salaried and non-salaried contracts. Note that this line crosses the upward-sloping line when firms have seven workers. This indicates that, after wages adjust to the equalization of regulations, the labor costs of all firms that under current policies are formal would be 10 percent lower, and the labor costs of firms that under current policies are illegal and informal and have seven or more workers would also be lower. In parallel, the labor costs of all firms with non-salaried workers would be 13 percent higher, and the labor costs of firms with illegal salaried contracts and less than seven workers would also be higher. Put differently, if the differences in the regulations applying to salaried and non-salaried contracts were eliminated, larger firms with salaried contracts (which from Chapter 4 we know are on average substantially more productive than the rest) would be able to attract more resources and capture larger market shares; and firms with non-salaried contracts would face higher labor costs, be less profitable, and attract fewer resources.

Misallocation and the World of Taxation

This section focuses on the role of T in $E(L,T,M)$. As with L in the previous section, T is a symbol, in this case representing the policies and institutions that regulate how firms and households are taxed in Mexico. Since many policies are involved, in principle we need to write $E[L, T(T_1, T_2,..., T_r), M]$. Taxes have revenue and distributional objectives, but these objectives are not discussed here. Nor is their impact on all dimensions of firm and worker behavior analyzed. The focus is only on those aspects that are relevant to the three stylized facts under consideration. We examine taxes on labor, firms, and consumption.

Taxation of Income from Labor

There is in principle no reason why taxation of workers' earnings should affect the size or type distribution of firms, but in Mexico it does. Three policies are relevant:

- A subsidy to salaried employment, applied on a declining scale to workers earning up to three minimum wages, established in the federal income tax law, labelled here as s_r.

- A state tax applied at a constant rate to salaried workers of any wage level, established in states' legislation, labelled here t_s.
- A personal income tax, established in the federal income tax law and applied on a progressive scale to salaried and non-salaried workers alike, and labelled here t_y.[7]

A word is in order on the institutions involved. All federal taxes in Mexico are in principle enforced by the tax administration service (Servicio de Administración Tributaria – SAT), but in some cases the SAT can delegate enforcement to state governments. In turn, each state has an agency in charge of collecting state taxes and delegated federal taxes. That said, it should be noted that Mexico's tax system is strongly centralized, and that over 90 percent of revenues are collected by the SAT.

The subsidy to employment s_f operates as a tax credit to firms hiring salaried workers; there are no outlays made from the federal budget. In parallel, firms hiring salaried workers are obligated to withhold their personal income taxes t_y (at times labelled payroll taxes). Of course, firms may fail to comply, in which case they face a probability $\lambda_y(.)$ of being detected by the SAT and paying a fine F_y. Non-salaried workers, on the other hand, are responsible for filing their income taxes directly to the SAT, and firms have no withholding responsibilities in this case. State governments play a secondary role in tax collections: t_s is also withheld by firms hiring salaried workers. Importantly, these governments do not tax the earnings of non-salaried workers.

Table 7.2 extends the framework of Table 7.1 to incorporate the effects of labor taxation on the costs and benefits of salaried and non-salaried contracts. As documented below, because the ability of the SAT to enforce the personal income tax on non-salaried workers is lower, in their case t_y is multiplied by a

Table 7.2: Taxation, Social Insurance, and Salaried and Non-Salaried Contracts

Type of Contract	Costs to Firms	Benefits to Worker	Implicit Tax (+) or Subsidy (−)
Legal salaried	$w_f + \theta_f T_f - s_f + t_s + t_y$	$w_f + \beta_f T_f$	$(\theta_f - \beta_f)T_f - s_f + t_s + t_y$
Illegal salaried	$w_i + \lambda(.)F + \lambda_y(.)F_y$	$w_i + \beta_i T_i$	$\lambda(.)F + \lambda_y(.)F_y - \beta_i T_i$
Non-salaried	w_i	$w_i + \beta_i T_i - \gamma t_y$	$-\beta_i T_i + \gamma t_y$

Source: Prepared by the author.

---

[7] Of course, t_y should be interpreted as a function and not as a scalar (similarly with s_f). However, the argument goes through with simplified notation.

factor $\gamma \leq 1$, capturing the fact that actual payments may be below statutory ones.[8] Very importantly, note that, as opposed to social insurance contributions, these taxes bring no direct benefits to workers. They are fully reflected in a wedge between what firms pay and what workers receive.

What is the impact of t_s, s_f, and t_y on the stylized facts of concern here? Consider first t_s. Although rates vary across states, most are in the 2 to 2½ percent range. In 2013, revenues from the state payroll tax were 0.39 percent of GDP, a relevant amount. More relevant is that since by design t_s only applies to salaried workers, it discourages firms and workers from establishing salaried contracts. This is consistent with stylized fact one.

What about s_f? As seen in Table 7.2, it operates in the opposite direction than the state payroll tax, and thus favors firms hiring salaried workers legally.[9] In 2013, this subsidy equaled 0.24 percent of GDP (SHCP 2013). In effect, ignoring distributional considerations, the subsidy serves to partly offset the impact of the state payroll tax. The net effect of s_f and t_s in that year was to tax salaried contracts by 0.15 of a percent of GDP, or to add around 1 percentage point to the implicit tax on legal salaried labor $(\theta_f - \beta_f)T_f$ associated with undervalued contributory programs. Incidence issues aside, this tax must be paid between workers and firms whenever they agree on a salaried contract.

Consider finally the personal income tax t_y. If the SAT's ability to enforce this tax on all workers were the same, that is, if $\lambda_y(.) = \gamma = 1$, it would be neutral from the perspective of a firm's size and contractual choices. But this is not the case. The SAT faces the same problems that the IMSS and Infonavit encounter collecting taxes from small firms. And for much the same reasons, the probability that firms are detected by the SAT breaking the law increases with firm size. In other words, the SAT's imperfect enforcement of firms' obligations to withhold payroll taxes from their salaried workers discriminates against larger firms. This is consistent with stylized fact two.

In addition, the SAT confronts a task that the IMSS, Infonavit, and state tax agencies do not face: collecting income taxes from non-salaried workers, including the self-employed. This is a more challenging task than collecting income taxes from salaried workers, as those taxes are withheld by firms. Many non-salaried workers have no fixed place of work, and even if they do their earnings are more difficult to measure than the easily observed wages

---

[8] This simplifies the notation: γ synthetizes the probability that an evading worker is identified, and the value of the fine imposed.

[9] The subsidy aims to promote formal employment among lower-wage workers. But this aim is more than offset because contribution rates for social insurance T_f are higher for lower-wage workers; and because subsidies from non-contributory programs T_i are higher for lower-wage workers. The net effect is towards more informal employment.

of salaried workers. The SAT's enforcement costs per peso of revenue are higher than for salaried workers and may in some cases exceed unity.

Unfortunately, published tax data are insufficient to accurately determine the values of γ and $\lambda_y(.)$ or to separate the share of personal income taxes evaded into that accounted for by non-salaried workers and that accounted for by salaried workers in firms evading federal payroll taxes. But at least for γ a sense of the orders of magnitude can be obtained by noting that in 2013 revenues from personal income taxes on salaried workers were 2.5 percent of GDP, compared to 0.1 of a percent from non-salaried workers (SAT 2017). This implies that, on a per capita basis, salaried workers paid 15,674 pesos compared to 1,511 pesos paid by non-salaried ones. On the other hand, the Employment Survey indicates that in 2013, average annual salaried and non-salaried earnings were 118,691 and 75,492 pesos, respectively. The average tax rate for salaried workers was thus 13 percent, while for non-salaried workers it was 2 percent. However, considering their earnings, and the progressivity of the tax schedule, non-salaried workers should have paid on average 7.5 percent of their earnings in income taxes, not 2 percent—that is, they should have paid 5,683 pesos, not 1,511 pesos. This implies that $\gamma = 0.26$. The difference of 5.5 percentage points between the average tax rate paid and the rate that should have been paid translates into foregone revenues of 0.4 of a percent of GDP, which is an approximate measure of the implicit subsidy to non-salaried contracts associated with the SAT's imperfect enforcement.

It is important to note that the intention here is not to measure evasion of the personal income tax. Other studies have done so more carefully.[10] Rather, the point is that, regardless of its exact value, the evidence indicates that γ is well below one. The implication is that the functioning of the SAT in enforcing the personal income tax de facto biases the decisions of workers and entrepreneurs towards non-salaried contractual relations (or towards salaried relations in very small firms that can get away with breaking the law). Importantly, the problem is not with the policy, but with its enforcement. If t_y were perfectly enforced, it would have no bearing on misallocation. This contrasts with social insurance and dismissal policies, and with the employment subsidy and state payroll tax, where, enforcement aside, the policies themselves discriminate between salaried and non-salaried relations. We return to this issue at the end of this chapter.

It is useful to relate this discussion to Figure 7.1. One can visualize the three lines describing the average costs of labor incorporating the effects

---

[10] Cantála, Sempere, and Sobarzo (2005) estimate that evasion of the personal income tax was 0.77 of a percent of GDP, higher than the back-of-the-envelope estimate presented here. That said, their estimate also includes evasion from illegally hired salaried workers and from other sources of income (such as rent from housing).

of t_s, s_f, and t_y. While the absence of detailed tax data impedes quantitative estimates, the difference in the average costs of legally hired salaried workers and non-salaried workers would widen. One would have to add 1 percentage point to the average costs of salaried contracts stemming from the state payroll tax (net of the federal employment subsidy); further, one would have to consider the effects of imperfect enforcement of the personal income tax, which considerably widens the difference in average costs. The gap between the two horizontal lines would increase beyond 23 percent. Although it is difficult to be precise, it would be closer to 30 percent. In parallel, the upward sloping line describing the expected average costs of labor when firms hire salaried workers but break the law would now reflect the interaction of $\lambda(.)$ and $\lambda_y(.)$, as firms adapt their behavior to the inspectors from the SAT, in addition to those from the IMSS and Infonavit.

The upshot is that the policies and institutions associated with labor taxation reinforce the effects that dismissal and social insurance policies and associated institutions have on the size and type distribution of firms: a bias towards firms with non-salaried contracts (which for reasons inherent to their own functioning tend to be small), and a bias towards firms with illegal salaried contracts (which for evasion considerations must remain small). The responses of firms and workers to these policies and institutions are consistent with stylized facts one, two, and three.

Taxation of Firms

A large literature focuses on how the corporate income tax affects firms' investments in machinery and equipment, research and innovation, labor training, and so on. All these dimensions of firm behavior matter for productivity. However, the focus here is only on those aspects relevant to the stylized facts under discussion.

Mexico's corporate income tax has large implications for the size distribution of firms and, indirectly, for the type distribution. In principle, all firms are subject to the same tax schedule under what is known as the general regime. However, the law contains a special regime for small firms known as the Repeco (Régimen de Pequeños Contribuyentes). The Repeco applies to firms with annual revenues of up to 2 million pesos in 2013 (approximately US$100,000). Rather than paying corporate income taxes at the general rate, firms instead pay 2 percent on the value of revenues.[11]

---

[11] The exact percentage is more complicated because some state governments allow firms to comply by paying a flat fee, and because fees vary across states. Zamudio, Barajas, and Brown (2011) provide a detailed description.

Table 7.3: Hypothetical Example of a Firm Taxed under the Repeco and General Regime
(Pesos)

			Repeco		General Regime	
Gross Sales	Labor and Materials	Before Tax Profits	Tax	After-Tax Profits	Tax	After-Tax Profits
1,000,000	700,000	300,000	20,000	280,000	90,000	210,000
2,000,000	1,400,000	600,000	40,000	**560,000**	180,000	420,000
2,100,000	1,470,000	630,000	N.A.	N.A.	189,000	**441,000**
2,680,000	1,876,000	804,000	N.A.	N.A.	241,200	562,800

Source: Prepared by the author.
N.A. = Not an available option.

Two features of the Repeco are relevant. First, firms must transit from the Repeco to the general regime if revenues increase beyond 2 million pesos. However, once in the general regime, firms cannot revert to the Repeco if revenues fall below that threshold. This creates an asymmetry in terms of how firms can adjust to positive and negative shocks (as exemplified below). The second feature is that while the Repeco is established under federal law, since 2003 the SAT has delegated enforcement and proceeds to state governments.[12]

The Repeco affects various margins of firm behavior.[13] Attention here is centered on the effect of the Repeco-general regime combination on firm growth and size. To undertake this analysis, it is best to assume initially that both regimes are perfectly enforced. Table 7.3 uses a simple numerical example to make the main points. Data from the Economic Census are then presented in Table 7.4.

Consider a firm with sales of 1 million pesos, and costs of materials and labor of 700,000 pesos. Before-tax profits are 300,000 pesos. Because sales are below the Repeco threshold, the firm pays 2 percent of sales in taxes, or 20,000 pesos, resulting in after-tax profits of 280,000 pesos. Note that under the general regime, where taxes are 30 percent of profits, the firm would

---

[12] In 2014, the federal income tax law replaced the Repeco with a new regime called the Régimen de Incorporación Fiscal (RIF). However, the analysis centers on the Repeco because this was the regime in place when the data for the Economic Census analyzed here were collected. The basic changes were that enforcement reverted to the SAT, and that instead of firms having to pay the 2 percent tax on revenues from the moment of registration, they could do so gradually over a 10-year period (in fact *lowering* their tax burden). All other features of the Repeco remained in the RIF.
[13] Kanbur and Keen (2014) provide an analysis of this type of size-dependent tax policy that is very relevant to this discussion. See also IDB (2010).

have paid 90,000 pesos in taxes and made 210,000 pesos in after-tax profits. Clearly, the Repeco is very attractive: after-tax profits are 33 percent higher.

Assume sales double. The firm still qualifies for the Repeco, and makes after-tax profits of 560,000 pesos (in bold), more than the 420,000 pesos it would have made under the general regime. Consider now that the firm could increase sales by an additional 5 percent, to 2.1 million pesos. The third line of Table 7.3 makes clear why the firm will not grow: if it did, it would no longer qualify for the Repeco. Since the firm would now be under the general regime, after-tax profits would fall to 441,000 pesos (in bold). *The firm is better off staying small.* This is consistent with stylized facts two and three.

In fact, the firm would consider growing only if, starting from 2 million pesos a year, sales increased by 34 percent, to 2.68 million pesos. Only then would after-tax profits in the general regime be higher than under the Repeco—and only by 0.5 of a percent, despite the large growth in sales. But even then, the firm may be unwilling to grow, unless it believes the increase in sales to be permanent. Recall that entry into the general regime is irreversible: if sales were to return to 2 million pesos (say, because of a fall in demand), the firm would have to pay 180,000 pesos in taxes under the general regime, rather than 40,000 pesos under the Repeco, for which it no longer qualifies.

This asymmetry in the Repeco is particularly onerous to small firms with legal salaried contracts, since they must also comply with dismissal regulations. If they grow and then contract because sales fall, their tax burden is permanently higher and must cover severance pay, all this while they experience a fall in sales and face the risks of being sued for "unfair dismissal." This helps explain why, as shown in Table 5.2 in Chapter 5, between 2008 and 2013 only 8.9 percent of fully formal firms with up to five workers (and only 11.1 percent of firms with six to 10 workers) grew and kept that status. It also helps explain why some of these firms may exit the market even if they have high productivity (see Table 5.5 in Chapter 5): it is difficult to transit through a negative shock when at the same time you also must face higher taxes and higher labor expenses.

Very importantly, notice that the Repeco-general regime combination allows small low-productivity firms to survive and punishes small high-productivity firms. A firm with sales of 1,999,999 pesos can be less productive than a firm with sales of 2,000,001 pesos, but more profitable. Indeed, the more productive firm with larger sales may not even survive in the market. Similarly, notice that the Repeco facilitates entry of small firms, since their tax burden is lower than if they enter with a larger size.

In sum, the Repeco-general regime policy creates four problems:

- It facilitates entry of small firms, since their tax burden is lower.

- It allows small low-productivity firms to survive because their tax burden is minimal, and may make it impossible for higher-productivity firms to compete with them if their revenues exceed the Repeco threshold.
- It introduces a discontinuity in firms' after-tax profit functions, making it profitable to grow only if there is a large and permanent jump in size.
- It impedes firms from taking advantage of transitory opportunities to expand—in fact, it punishes them if they do take advantage of such opportunities.

The behavior induced by this policy is not relevant to stylized fact one, since it applies equally to firms with salaried and non-salaried contracts. But it is clearly relevant to facts two and three.

How relevant are these issues? Table 7.4 classifies firms in the 2013 census by ranges of annual revenues and location in the low, medium, and high segment of their respective six-digit sector revenue total factor productivity (TFPR) distribution. Revenues are in millions of 2013 pesos, and a finer disaggregation is provided around the 2 million peso threshold. The upper block contains firms that could potentially qualify for the Repeco because their annual revenues are under 2 million pesos; the lower block refers to firms that must pay taxes under the general regime. The table also lists the share of labor and capital allocated to firms in each revenue range. Although the measure of revenues in the census may not match exactly with the legal definition used by state governments and the SAT to enforce the Repeco-general regime combination, it still provides very useful information.

Three results are noteworthy. First, 93.7 percent of all firms in manufacturing, commerce, and services captured in the census could qualify for the Repeco. Even ignoring firms excluded from the census, this leads to a very important observation: *for most firms in Mexico, the relevant corporate income tax regime is the Repeco, not the general regime.*

Second, firms that qualify for the Repeco attract substantial resources: 52 percent of all workers and 25 percent of the capital stock in census-captured firms (and more if firms excluded from the census are considered). Thus, *the performance of firms in the Repeco matters greatly for aggregate productivity.*

The third result is that annual revenues for most firms in the Repeco are substantially below the threshold dividing them from the general regime. Indeed, annual revenues for 95 percent of firms in the upper block in Table 7.4 are below 1 million pesos. This suggests that the threshold level is relatively high, and that few firms will be immediately affected by it. Instead, more firms will be affected by the large difference between the Repeco and the general regime tax rate.

Using the data behind Table 7.4, two simple exercises are now carried out that shed light on the effects of the Repeco on firm behavior. The first

Table 7.4: Firms by Ranges of Annual Revenues and Productivity Segment, 2013
(Number of firms and percent shares of capital and labor)

Revenue Range (millions of pesos)	Firm Productivity Segments — Low	Medium	High	Total	Share of Labor	Share of Capital
< 0.5	784,829	1,372,204	530,067	2,687,100	37.3	14.9
0.5–1.0	25,380	146,737	140,914	313,031	8.3	5.5
1.0–1.5	7,473	47,524	54,220	109,217	4.1	3.0
1.5–1.9	2,990	18,686	20,694	42,370	2.0	1.6
1.9–2.0	677	3,988	4,452	9,117	0.5	0.4
2.0–2.1	488	3,083	3,818	7,389	0.4	0.3
2.1–2.5	1,748	9,845	11,731	23,324	1.4	1.1
2.5–3.0	1,488	8,541	9,741	19,770	1.4	1.1
3.0–4.0	2,169	10,731	12,514	25,414	2.1	1.7
4.0–6.0	2,721	13,308	14,135	30,164	3.0	2.7
6.0–10.0	4,601	12,681	12,830	30,112	3.8	3.7
> 10.0	8,901	41,509	24,110	74,520	35.5	63.9
Total	**843,465**	**1,688,837**	**839,226**	**3,371,528**	**100.0**	**100.0**

Source: Author's calculations based on data from the Economic Census.

focuses on the discontinuity in firms' after-tax profit function around the threshold separating the Repeco from the general regime. To focus sharply on this discontinuity, only firms whose revenues are between 1.9 million and 2 million pesos are considered, that is, 5 percent or less below the threshold. These are labelled "close to but below threshold firms." As seen in Table 7.4, there are 9,117 firms in this range. Very importantly, only 7.4 percent of these firms are in the low-productivity segment of their TFPR distribution, and 48.8 percent are in the high-productivity segment. In other words, "close to but below the threshold firms" are substantially more productive than firms in general, and than other firms in the Repeco. In other words, these firms are very productive indeed.

What would be the change in these firms' after-tax profits if their revenues increased by 10, 20, or 30 percent? To keep the answer simple, assume that each firm's labor and intermediate costs as found in the 2013 census increase by the same amount (that is, no economies of scale), and drop all firms with negative before-tax profits (which leaves 7,755 firms). We next compute the percentage change in after-tax profits for each firm as their revenues increase and they transit from paying taxes of 2 percent of revenues under the Repeco to 30 percent of profits under the general regime.

The results of this exercise are depicted in Figure 7.2 and are very revealing indeed. *In all three cases, most firms are better off not growing.* Consider first an increase in revenues of 10 percent. In this case, as shown by point A, 6,878 out of the 7,755 firms would earn lower after-tax profits (below the horizontal line). In other words, 88 percent of firms experience lower after-tax profits if they grow. Note that the fall in profits can be quite large, close to 25 percent. If revenues increase by 20 percent, 80 percent of firms would experience lower after-tax profits (point B). And even if revenues increased by 30 percent, 54 percent of firms would still face lower after-tax profits (point C). This situation not only highlights the relevance of the Repeco-general regime policy, but also its costliness in terms of productivity, given that most firms deterred from growing are high-productivity firms.

The second exercise highlights another feature of the Repeco, namely that it allows many low-productivity firms to survive because their tax burden is minimal. This exercise considers all firms that qualify for the Repeco, not only those that are close to but below the threshold, and poses the following

Figure 7.2: Changes in After-Tax Profits for "Close to but Below the Threshold Firms"
(Percent change)

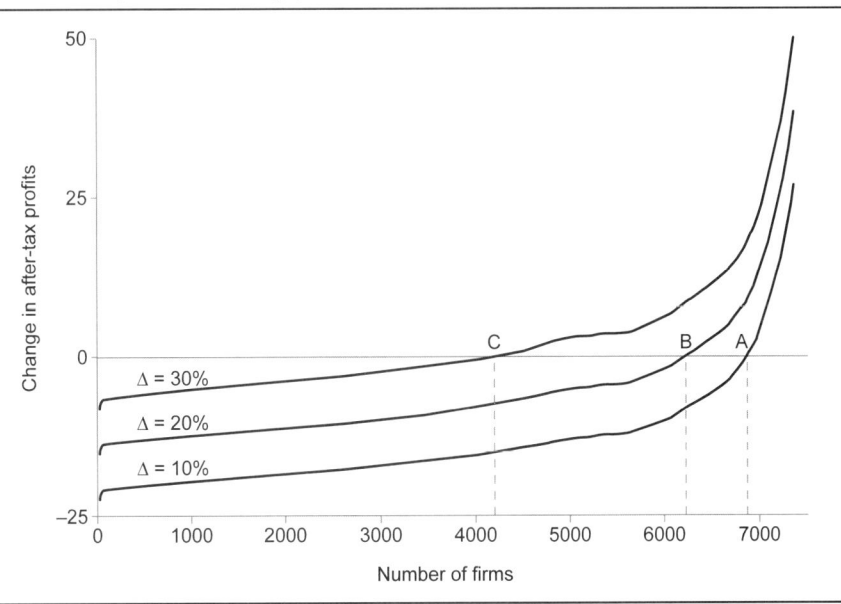

Source: Author's illustration based on data from Mexico's Economic Census.

question: What would happen to firms' after-tax profit margins (after-tax profits over labor and intermediate input costs) if there were no Repeco and firms had to pay taxes under the general regime? Figure 7.3 provides the answer by comparing three profit-margin distributions: the no-tax, the after-Repeco tax, and the after-general-regime-tax distributions. Profit margins are on the horizontal axis, while the vertical axis measures the frequency of observations.

Again, the results are very revealing. First, note that the no-tax and Repeco distributions are quite similar. Of course, the Repeco distribution is to the left, but the differences are very small. In other words, the Repeco tax rate makes almost no difference to a firm's profit margins. This confirms that, indeed, the Repeco tax burden is very low.

On the other hand, the contrast between the Repeco and general regime distributions is dramatic. Under the Repeco, 11 percent of firms have profit margins above 60 percent, while under the general regime only 1.4 percent do. At the other end of the spectrum, under the Repeco, 47.5 percent of firms have profit margins below 30 percent, while under the general regime 68 percent fall in this category.

Figure 7.3: Distribution of Profit Margins: No Tax, Repeco, and the General Regime

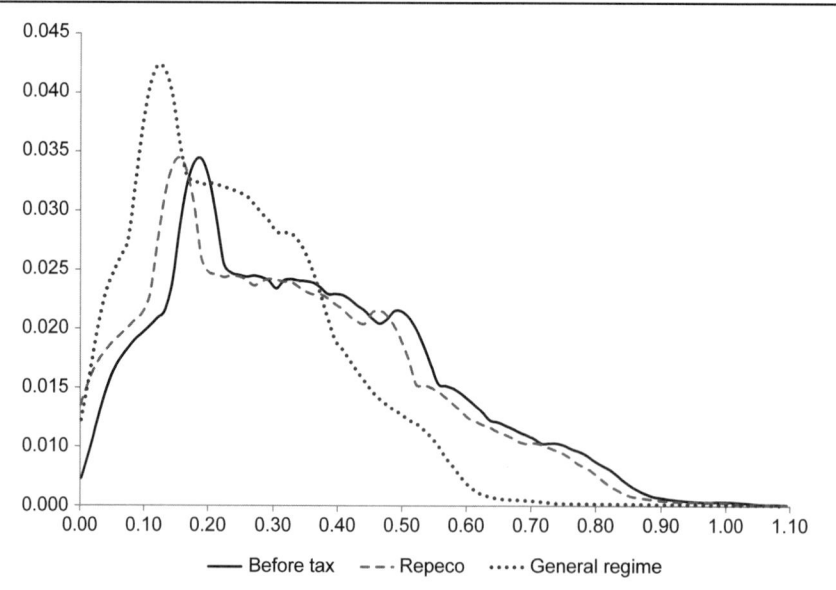

Source: Author's illustration based on data from Mexico's Economic Census.

How many firms in the Repeco would exit the market if they were taxed under the general regime? It is very difficult to answer this question because there is no information on the opportunity cost of capital for Repeco-qualifying firms. Many may be enjoying rents and would still survive even if they paid 30 percent of their profits in taxes. But many others would probably not, or at least not with the same size. While it is difficult to be precise, Figure 7.3 does show that firm survival is facilitated by the Repeco and, to the extent that low-productivity firms are over-represented among Repeco-qualifying firms, so is the survival of low-productivity firms. Moreover, because these firms absorb substantial resources (52 percent of labor and 25 percent of capital of census-captured firms), the Repeco evidently matters greatly for misallocation.

Figures 7.2 and 7.3 serve as the basis for another observation. Analysis of size-dependent tax regimes usually focuses on the agglomeration of firms just below the threshold (see, for example, Hsieh and Olken 2014). But this is only one of the many problems caused by these regimes and, in the case of Mexico, not necessarily the most relevant one. As just shown, the 2 million peso threshold is quite high, and few firms are close to it. It is true that these firms are among the most productive ones, such that impeding them from growing is quite costly to productivity. On the other hand, the ease of entry and survival of many low-productivity firms that are far from the threshold may be costlier, as it affects a much larger number of firms and a bigger share of resources.

The discussion so far has assumed that firms comply fully with the corporate income tax law. But this is not the case in Mexico. State governments face the same challenge that the IMSS, Infonavit, and SAT confront when dealing with small firms: enforcement costs are high. In fact, collecting one peso of revenue can exceed unity. (In parallel, these governments may find that a politically less costly route to obtain more resources is to lobby Congress or the federal government, or to contract debt.) Thus, while in 2013 there were 3.886 million firms registered in the Repeco, total revenues collected were 0.022 of a percent of GDP (SAT 2017). Note that revenues from Repeco are almost one-twentieth the revenues from the state payroll tax t_s (0.39 of a percent of GDP), which is much easier to collect because firms withhold this tax from salaried workers.

Altogether, Table 7.4 records 3.371 million firms with revenues of up to 2 million pesos in manufacturing, commerce, and services. In parallel, recall from Chapter 3 that in 2013 there were an additional 2.6 million firms in those same broadly defined sectors that were excluded from the census, almost all of them with up to five workers. There is no systematic data on their revenues, but a reasonable assumption is that they are equal to the average of firms of the same size captured in the census (215,000 pesos a year). This implies that all firms excluded from the census would qualify for the Repeco and, in turn, that there should be approximately 5.97 million firms (= 3.37 + 2.6) in that regime. This contrasts with the 3.88 million firms that, according to SAT, were registered for the Repeco (in *all* activities). While it is impossible to be precise, many firms simply do not register.

Zamudio, Barajas, and Brown (2011) estimate evasion of the Repeco between 2000 and 2010. They show that it is extremely high, and that it increased during this 11-year period. In 2000, firms only paid 10.3 percent of what they should have paid; in 2010, that figure was 3.8 percent. The figures from the SAT on total revenues from the Repeco are consistent with those findings: in 2000, they were 0.036 of a percent of GDP and in 2013, 0.022 of a percent (SAT 2017). Using the estimates of Zamudio, Barajas, and Brown, foregone revenues from evasion in 2013 were approximately 0.57 of a percent of GDP, which can be thought of as an implicit subsidy to very small and small firms derived from states' enforcement behavior.

Would productivity increase if the Repeco were better enforced? In principle, yes, as small firms, the majority of which are low-productivity ones, would be less profitable and would attract fewer resources. But the improvement would be minor. To understand why, note that in Figure 7.3 the no-tax profit-margin distribution is equivalent to the Repeco distribution with no enforcement at all. Because that distribution is very close to the Repeco distribution under perfect enforcement, the change in firm behavior induced by better enforcement would be secondary. This leads to a very important observation: *the problem with the Repeco is with the policy itself, not with the fact that its enforcement is lax.*

What about the general regime? The evidence also points to some evasion, although difficult to quantify (López 2016). Unfortunately, there are insufficient tax data to trace a function for the effective corporate tax rate faced by firms in a context of imperfect enforcement like the function presented in Figure 7.1 for the case of social insurance contributions. With this consideration in mind, Figure 7.4 traces the hypothetical behavior of the effective corporate tax rate resulting from the interplay of the federally established corporate income tax policy and the enforcement of that policy by the SAT and state governments.

The horizontal axis depicts firm size, in this case measured by sales or output rather than number of workers. The threshold level separating firms between the Repeco and the general regime is denoted by *R*. Under perfect enforcement, the corporate income tax policy—the combination of the Repeco and the general regime—is described by the step-shaped line, with the distance between the two horizontal lines capturing the jump in the tax

Figure 7.4: Hypothetical Shape of the Effective Corporate Tax Rate

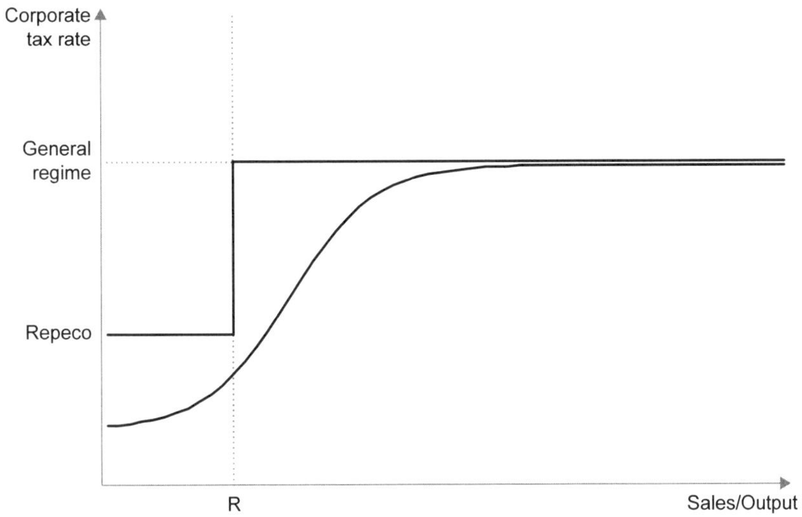

Source: Prepared by the author.

rate on profits implicit in the policy.[14] For the Repeco we only depict one tax rate, but it should be kept in mind that there are potentially as many rates as there are states in Mexico (32), depending on state government policies.

The upward sloping S-shaped line captures the de facto tax schedule that results from imperfect enforcement by the SAT (to the right of *R*) and by state governments (to the left of *R*). It begins below the Repeco rate because, as documented, firms in that regime under-declare sales. Further, firms may sell above *R* and remain under the Repeco, also under-declaring sales (Kanbur and Keen 2014). But after some hard-to-identify sales level, firms must be in the general regime, although there they can also evade some of the taxes due. However, this behavior is more difficult as sales increase, although the extent to which this is so depends very much on the slope of the S-shaped line.[15]

---

[14] The size of the gap is not given by the law but depends on firms' cost structures and profit margins. In the example in Table 7.3 the gap is 24 percentage points, given that the tax rate is 30 percent of profits under the general regime but only 6 percent of profits under the Repeco. But if the firm's labor and intermediate costs were different, the same Repeco rate of 2 percent of sales would differ expressed as a rate on profits.

[15] The figure implies full convergence to the statutory rate. A separate phenomenon is that very large firms can use aggressive tax strategies to minimize their tax burden, without necessarily engaging in illegal behavior. These strategies may allow some not-so-productive firms to achieve larger size than justified given their underlying productivity. This is another manifestation of misallocation caused by complex tax codes that open opportunities for elusion if not evasion; see López (2016).

Imperfect enforcement has two results. First, it smooths the discontinuity in the size of firms, as measured by their revenues, that would be observed if the Repeco-general regime combination were fully enforced. This is part of the explanation of why there are firms with all revenue levels in the data (in terms of Table 7.4, why there is no grouping of firms below 2 million pesos).[16] Second, more importantly, imperfect enforcement implies that the average tax rate is increasing (and the marginal rate more so), acting again as an implicit tax on firm growth. This is consistent with stylized fact three.

To the best of our knowledge, no studies have assessed the productivity costs of the Repeco-general regime combination. That said, two papers have modeled the effects of imperfect enforcement of corporate taxes on productivity even if not explicitly focused on the Repeco-general regime policy. Leal (2014) studies a situation where firms are taxed in proportion to output, with enforcement increasing with output levels. Although in his model the tax is not on profits, the behavior of the effective tax schedule is like the one depicted in Figure 7.4. He calibrates his model to replicate Mexico's size distribution and formal-informal composition of firms and finds that the productivity costs of such a schedule are very high: depending on assumptions about market structure, GDP is between 19 and 34 percent lower compared to the perfect enforcement scenario. Furthermore, and in line with the previous discussion, he finds that the schedule fosters the entry and survival of low-productivity firms. With a somewhat different model, López (2016) finds an even larger effect on output in a counterfactual exercise with full enforcement: an increase of 44 percent.

Two observations are relevant about these papers. First, because no distinction is made between the Repeco and the general regime, productivity losses derive only from imperfect enforcement. But as we have seen, even under perfect enforcement, the Repeco-general regime combination misallocates resources, an observation that highlights the importance of separating the effects of the policy from the effects of its imperfect enforcement. That said, second, these papers provide additional evidence that the productivity costs of a policy like the one depicted in Figure 7.4 are quantitatively very important.

Taxation of Consumption

Consumption in Mexico is taxed mainly through the value-added tax (VAT). This tax is administered by the SAT and is collected by the credit method:

---

[16] In addition, recall that there are many Repeco rates (potentially as many as 32), since states can change the policy from a 2 percent tax on sales to a flat rate. This also explains why in Table 7.4 there is no agglomeration of firms around 2 million pesos.

the tax applies to each sale, and firms can deduct the VAT paid on their intermediate inputs from the VAT due on sales.

In principle, the VAT should not bias the occupational decisions of individuals, the size of firms, or contractual relations between entrepreneurs and workers. But a combination of exemption regimes and imperfect enforcement make it relevant to the discussion here of misallocation. Although the general VAT rate is 16 percent, there are two special regimes:

- A set of goods and services exempt in the final stage of consumption, called the tax-exempt regime.
- A second set whose intermediate inputs are also exempt, called the zero-tax regime.

The distributional motivations for these regimes are not discussed here.[17] Nor are the administrative complexities and opportunities for corruption and arbitrage associated with them. As before, the focus here is just on the implications for productivity.

How does Mexico's VAT impact firm behavior? As in the analysis of the Repeco, it is simplest to first answer this question by means of a numerical example. Consider a firm that produces an internationally traded good that has a price exogenously set at 1,000 pesos. Assume first there is no VAT. The firm pays 600 pesos for materials and 200 pesos in wages. It sells its output for 1,000 pesos, so the profit margin, defined as profit over materials and wages, is 25 percent.

Table 7.5 captures the effect of the VAT. Consider first a uniform rate of 16 percent. If the firm is formal, it pays 96 pesos of VAT on its intermediate inputs and charges 160 pesos of VAT on sales, so output price is now 1,160 pesos. The firm receives a credit of 96 pesos for the VAT paid on inputs and makes a net VAT payment to the SAT of 64 pesos (= 160 – 96) pesos. As expected, the profit margin is not affected by the tax, and stays at 25 percent.

If, on the other hand, the firm is informal, it still pays 96 pesos of VAT on its intermediate inputs for which it gets no credit, since the firm charges no VAT on its sales. If the firm sells its product for 1,160 pesos (the price that the formal firm must charge), its profit margin is 33 percent; if it sells at 1,000 pesos (the lowest price it can charge), it is 13 percent. Depending on circumstances, the firm will sell at between 1,000 and 1,160 pesos. Whatever the price, it will take away market share from the formal firm and may have a higher profit margin.

---

[17] Various papers discuss the distributional effects of the VAT. See, for instance, Dávila and Levy (2003).

Table 7.5: Special Value-Added Tax Regimes: A Hypothetical Example
(Pesos)

	Uniform 16 Percent Rate		Zero-rate Regime		Exempt Regime	
	Formal	Informal	Formal	Informal	Formal	Informal
Materials	600	600	600	600	600	600
Wages	200	200	200	200	200	200
Price before VAT	1,000	1,000	1,000	1,000	1,000	1,000
VAT paid on inputs	96	96	0	0	96	96
VAT charged on sales	160	0	0	0	0	0
VAT paid to the SAT	64	0	0	0	−96	0
Final consumer price	1,160	1,000–1,160	1,000	1,000	1,000	1,000
Margins on sales (%)	25.0	13.0–33.0	25.0	25.0	25.0	13.0

Source: Prepared by the author.
Note: SAT: Servicio de Administración Tributaria; VAT: value-added tax.

Of course, not charging the VAT on sales is illegal from the point of view of the VAT law, and the firm will do so only if it believes that, given penalties, the probability of detection by the SAT is sufficiently small.[18] Because the SAT's enforcement increases with firm size, this will favor small firms in the usual way: expected profit margins fall as the firm grows.

If Mexico's VAT had a uniform regime, this would be the end of the analysis. The main point would be that the VAT is neutral vis-à-vis the salaried/non-salaried choices of firms and workers (so it has no bearing on stylized fact one), but that, as with the personal income tax, imperfect enforcement implicitly favors small firms and deters their growth (consistent with stylized facts two and three).

In Mexico, however, the uniform regime only applies to 58 percent of the consumption basket. As a result, the VAT has further implications on resource allocation. To see this, assume now that the product in question is subject to the zero-rate regime, so the VAT is not paid on either intermediate inputs or the final product. In Table 7.5 the formal firm buys its inputs for 600 pesos and sells its output for 1,000 pesos. There is no credit for the VAT paid on intermediates, no VAT charged on final sales, and no VAT paid to the SAT. The profit margin is, again, 25 percent.

---

[18] Note here that illegal behavior is with reference to the VAT, not with reference to social insurance regulations, as given by Definition 2 in Chapter 2. In principle, formal firms could also evade the VAT. However, to simplify matters in this discussion it is assumed that formal firms also comply with the VAT, while informal ones may not.

What if the firm is informal? The arithmetic is identical, but there is one crucial difference: the informal firm is no longer engaging in illegal behavior vis-à-vis the VAT law. This is excellent news for the firm: it can grow as much as it wants without worrying about SAT inspectors, as least with regard to this tax. And if the firm has non-salaried workers, it can also grow as much as it wants without worrying about the IMSS or Infonavit inspectors either, or about claims in the JCAs. In fact, it only needs to worry about the corporate income tax, as the firm does not have to withhold the personal income taxes of its workers, nor the state tax on salaried employment. And if the firm is in the Repeco, its taxes are minimal, as discussed earlier. All else being equal, the zero-rate regime facilitates the survival of informal firms, particularly if they have non-salaried contracts.

Consider finally the exempt regime, where only final sales are exempt from the VAT. The formal firm pays 96 pesos of VAT on its intermediates, then claims it back from the SAT (a devolution and not a credit, since there is no VAT on sales to credit against). Its profit margin is again 25 percent. The informal firm, on the other hand, cannot claim back the VAT paid on its inputs; its profit margin drops to 13 percent.

If this were the end of the story, it would be good news because it would mean that the exempt regime, as opposed to the zero-rate one, implicitly taxes informal firms. But, unfortunately, this is not the end of the story. Table 7.5 implicitly assumes that intermediate inputs are always supplied by a formal firm that charges 96 pesos of VAT on its sales. But the informal firm could reduce costs by buying its inputs from another informal firm, saving 96 pesos. If it did, its profitability would increase to 25 percent. The point here is that the chain structure of the VAT will induce informal firms to establish supply links with other informal firms, in turn creating markets for those firms.[19] To give an example, an informal firm supplying land transportation services will buy second-hand tires from an informal trader in truck parts, not from a formal tire producer; and it will have repairs done in an informal shop, rather than in the truck manufacturer dealer's shop. The informal firm's trucks may not run as well, but the 16 percent cost savings may justify it.

Put differently, purchasing inputs from informal firms may make perfect sense from the firm's point of view, but that behavior can be detrimental to productivity because firms' sourcing decisions are biased

---

[19] De Paula and Scheinkman (2010) provide econometric evidence of informal-to-informal supply chains in Brazil. Antón, Hernández, and Levy (2012) simulate these effects for Mexico. The issue is quite relevant for misallocation, because it affects the networks of production, and may prevent firms from using the intermediate inputs that maximize productivity; see Oberfield (2013).

by the peculiarities of the VAT. Of course, the relevance of this depends on the nature of the intermediate inputs. If some can be supplied only by formal firms, the implicit tax will be there (think of transportation services by air). But if some inputs can be substituted for by those that can be produced by informal firms, the implicit tax will be avoided, and supply chains distorted (as, say, if firms replace air transportation services with land transportation services).

What do the data say? The census has very little information on firms' tax payments, but it does record the VAT paid by firms on intermediate purchases and the VAT charged on final sales. This information is unfortunately insufficient for a proper analysis because devolutions by the SAT from the VAT paid on intermediate inputs when there is a net credit in favor of the firm are not recorded. With that caveat, it is illustrative to exploit the information that is available. In this vein, Table 7.6 records the share of firms in the 2013 census in each size and type category that did not pay the VAT on their intermediate inputs and did not charge the VAT on their sales.

Importantly, Table 7.6 includes firms in all three VAT regimes (uniform, zero-rate, and exempt), so the data reflect a mix of illegal and legal behavior. That said, the patterns are very much as expected: broadly, compliance increases with size, so as firms grow they pay more VAT on their inputs or charge VAT on their sales (or both).

On the other hand, the differences between formal and informal firms are noteworthy, particularly if the focus is on those that are very small or small. Between 48 and 58 percent of formal firms with up to five workers are outside the scope of the VAT. That range is 84 to 87 percent for informal firms of the same size. Importantly, this difference probably does not derive from the fact that informal firms are in the Repeco while formal ones are not. On the one hand, most firms with one to five workers, formal or informal, have sales below 2 million pesos and qualify to be in the Repeco. Further, even

Table 7.6: Share of Firms in Census that Do Not Pay or Charge the Value-Added Tax, 2013
(Percent)

	Fully Formal	Mixed	Informal and Legal	Informal and Illegal
1–5 workers	48.90	58.41	87.60	84.48
6–10 workers	36.09	48.80	54.66	78.43
11–50 workers	29.54	39.26	36.49	70.68
51+ workers	15.82	22.46	18.19	42.60

Source: Author's calculations based on data from Mexico's Economic Census.

firms in the Repeco should pay VAT on their intermediate inputs. More likely, the difference results from the fact that informal firms source their inputs from other informal firms, or from the fact that the zero-rate regime attracts more informal than formal firms. While more data are needed to research this issue further, a preliminary conclusion is that Table 7.6 is consistent with the behavior described in the discussion above.

How relevant are the exempt and zero-rate regimes to misallocation in Mexico? It is difficult to provide a quantitative answer. One would think that the effects are relevant because these regimes are large: in 2013, approximately 42 percent of total final consumption (the VAT base) was subject to them, 26 percent in the zero-rate regime and 16 percent in the exempt one. In that year, foregone VAT revenues from these regimes constituted 1.5 percent of GDP, a number that clearly affects firm behavior.[20] Another way to gauge the relevance of these regimes is to note that since consumption is approximately 58 percent of GDP, and since 42 percent of consumption is under these two special regimes, approximately 25 percent of GDP is affected by them.

Few studies have examined the impact on productivity of policies that transmit their impact through the input-output structure of the economy. Leal (2017) is an important exception. He provides quantitative estimates for Mexico showing that specific policies in sectors producing widely used intermediate inputs have high-productivity costs. He finds that removing these policies could increase aggregate output by up to 68 percent. While his analysis does not focus on the VAT special regimes, it is easy to see that the effects are similar, because these regimes are a special case of sector-specific policies.

The upshot is that the VAT uniform regime affects the size distribution of firms in much the same way that the personal income tax and the general regime of the corporate income tax do: SAT enforcement creates a bias against large firms. The behavior induced is consistent with stylized facts two and three. In addition, the special regimes add to misallocation. The zero-rate regime facilitates the growth of informal firms producing goods covered by that regime as, de facto, the VAT ceases to affect their behavior. Since there is nothing to evade, these firms can flourish. But because most of these firms have non-salaried contracts, this regime helps them proportionately more, consistent with stylized fact one. In turn, the exempt regime changes firms'

---

[20] Importantly, in 2013 Mexico had the lowest VAT/GDP ratio of all countries in Latin America with a ratio of 0.038 versus an average of 0.069 for Argentina, Bolivia, Chile, Colombia, Ecuador, Guatemala, Honduras, Nicaragua, Paraguay, Peru, Uruguay, and Venezuela. This difference derives mostly from the comparatively more extensive nature of Mexico's special regimes and the difficulties in enforcing them, and not as much from the level of the general rate (16 percent versus an average rate of 14.6 percent for the countries listed).

supply chain decisions in ways that may be detrimental to aggregate productivity. As informal-to-informal supply chains are fostered, more productive formal firms have smaller market shares and attract fewer resources.

Misallocation and the World of Market Conditions

This section considers the role of M in $E(L,T,M)$. As before, M symbolizes a large set of policies and institutions—in this case, all those not included in L and T, so it needs to be written as $E[L,T, (M_1, M_2, ...M_n)]$. Because M is so encompassing, even if attention focused on the subset of policies that bear on the stylized facts of concern here, the number would still be large. This section focuses only on two critical factors affecting firm behavior in Mexico: contract enforcement and access to credit.

Contract Enforcement

In his essay on trust, firm organization, and prosperity, Fukuyama (1995, 63) notes that:

> "Virtually all economic endeavors start out as a family business: that is businesses that are both owned and managed by families....Because their cohesion is based on the moral and emotional bonds of a preexisting social group, the family enterprise can thrive even in the absence of commercial law or stable structure of property rights....But family businesses are only the starting point for the development of economic organizations.... Beginning in the sixteenth century, England and Holland created legal arrangements permitting the vesting of ownership in larger groups, such as joint proprietorships, joint stock companies and limited liability partnerships....The contract and its associated system of obligations and penalties, enforced through a legal system, could fill the gap where the trust naturally found in families did not exist. Joint stock companies, in particular, allowed enterprises to grow in scale beyond the means of a single family by pooling the resources of a large number of investors."

Judicial institutions are central to the performance of markets. Firms need to know that if suppliers do not deliver the inputs purchased, or if clients fail to settle bills, they have recourse to the courts to claim damages. Similarly, commercial banks require the certainty that if debtors fail to service their loans, they can repossess their collateral. In turn, shareholders—particularly minority ones—need assurances that if they invest in firms, their wealth is protected. When contracts are properly and expeditiously enforced, firms can expand bringing in more shareholders, engaging with a broader set of clients and suppliers, widening their options to obtain credit, facing lower transaction costs, and worrying less about opportunistic behavior by others. Conversely, when contract enforcement is problematic, firm performance is negatively affected through three different channels:

- Difficulties with enlarging and diversifying their capital base by adding new shareholders
- Reduced access to credit as lenders underestimate the value of their assets as collateral
- Uncertainty in arm's-length relations with new or distant suppliers and clients.

In Mexico, very large firms, particularly foreign-owned ones, can benefit from provisions in the country's free trade agreements that provide protections to investors, including arbitration and dispute settlement mechanisms. These firms can also afford the services of specialized law offices, and by their very size tend to have more "voice," so to speak, in their dealings with the courts or the government. But most firms in Mexico are not in that situation. For small, medium-size, and even large firms, dealing with the courts, the public registries of properties, notaries, and specialized legal offices is costly and uncertain. These firms also have substantially less "voice" than very large firms, if any voice at all. For them, imperfect contract enforcement is a serious concern, and they adjust their behavior accordingly.

The evidence indicates that in Mexico the quality of contract enforcement varies widely across states. Moody's ratings agency constructed a state-level index of the enforceability of commercial contracts, using inputs from a Mexican law firm specialized in contract enforcement and from the School of Law of the Instituto Tecnológico Autónomo de México (Moody's 2011; see also Laeven and Woodruff 2007). The index is based on attributes of states' judges and magistrates such as impartiality, expertise in commercial law, and criteria for selection and promotion; duration and backlog of cases; the costs, ease of use, and completeness of property registries; and an evaluation of the support provided by the executive branch in each state to enforce verdicts (use of the police to seize assets, and so on). The index has a value of one when contract enforceability is highest and five when it is lowest. In 2011, out of 32 states (including the Federal District), four states had an index of five, another five an index of four, 11 an index of three, 10 an index of two, and two an index of one. More recently, the World Bank's Doing Business Report found that the quality of judicial processes varies considerably across states (World Bank 2016). To the extent that commercial laws and regulations are very similar, this suggests differences between the de jure and de facto legal context faced by firms across states—or, in somewhat starker language, that in Mexico the law is not the law everywhere.

Imperfect Contract Enforcement and Misallocation

Evidence of the impact of imperfect contract enforcement on firm behavior in Mexico is provided by Laeven and Woodruff (2007). They focus on the first channel listed above, considering that entrepreneurs face higher idiosyncratic risks if they invest an increasing share of their wealth in their own firm. If there is a negative shock—a market downturn, a lost suit followed by a high award from a labor tribunal in an "unjustified dismissal" dispute, a sudden stop in credit—such an entrepreneur might lose everything. The natural way to mitigate this risk but still expand the firm is to diversify ownership by taking on more equity partners. But when judicial quality is low this is deterred: on the one hand, protections for minority shareholders are insufficient and therefore they may not want to invest; on the other, the majority owner may fear opportunistic behavior by new shareholders.

Laeven and Woodruff emphasize that this deterrent to firm growth affects all firms, but proportionately more those not incorporated as a separate legal entity, that is, proprietorships where the assets of the firm are not separated from those of the owner. As shown in Table 3.8, this ownership structure is more prevalent among small informal and legal firms, many of which are very likely family firms in the sense that the owner and the workers are relatives.

Laeven and Woodruff use firm-level data from the 1998 census from all sectors (aggregated at the two-digit level), taking advantage of the state variation in the index of contract enforceability to measure the effects of imperfect enforcement. There are three findings. First, judicial quality is positively associated with firm size.[21] More precisely, a one standard deviation increase in judicial effectiveness increases firm size by one-sixth of a standard deviation. Second, these effects are stronger among firms that are proprietorships compared to those that are incorporated. And third, controlling for the use of inputs (intermediate inputs, capital, and labor), firms' sales are larger in states with better contract enforcement. Put differently, higher judicial quality improves productivity. These findings are consistent with stylized fact two.

---

[21] Giacomelli and Menon (2017) also present evidence that judicial quality increases firm size, in their case for Italy.

López-Martin (2017) focuses on the effects of imperfect enforcement on misallocation operating through the second channel: the undervaluation of a firm's assets as collateral for bank credit. His analysis captures how by reducing firms' access to credit, imperfect enforcement affects the occupational choices of individuals (as in Figure 2.1 in Chapter 2), and the size and type distribution of firms. In his framework, the division of individuals between those who are workers and those who are entrepreneurs, and in turn the division between formal and informal entrepreneurs, depends on the availability of credit as captured by the ability of firms to collateralize their assets, which is interpreted as a measure of the performance of the institutions enforcing contracts. Formal firms are assumed to be able to collateralize their assets more than informal ones. This is consistent with the fact that more formal firms are incorporated as legal entities, as shown in Table 3.8 in Chapter 3. In turn, a greater ability to collateralize assets is associated with lower contracting and collection costs and therefore more bank credit.

López-Martin shows that Mexico's weak contracting environment leads to a reduced supply of credit with significant productivity costs. Because more-productive formal firms fail to get enough credit, they are smaller than what they would otherwise be, and as a result there are more informal lower-productivity firms. Lower average firm productivity depresses wages, which in turn induces more individuals to run informal low-productivity firms rather than be workers in higher-productivity formal firms. These results are in line with the findings of Chapters 4 and 5. López-Martin carries out a series of counter-factual exercises showing that improving contract enforcement expands credit to formal firms, reduces the number of individuals running informal firms, and increases average firm size as more individuals work for firms. The gains in TFP from improving enforcement depend on parameter values but can be as high 13 percent. These findings are consistent with stylized facts two and three.

Further evidence of the impact of imperfect contract enforcement on misallocation is provided by Dougherty (2014). He also shows that, controlling for all other factors, imperfect enforcement results in lower firm size. His analysis uses data from the Economic Census but centers on manufacturing firms only. This is relevant because, as shown in Table 3.11 in Chapter 3, average firm size in this sector is substantially larger than in commerce or services (in 2013, 10.1 workers versus 3.1 and 3.8 workers per firm, respectively), so it can be speculated that his results would be stronger if data from commerce and services had been used as well. He then takes advantage of the state-level index of contract enforceability used by Laeven and Woodruff (2007), exploiting again its variation across states but also over time.

Dougherty finds that judicial quality has a strong and positive impact on firm size in Mexico: a one-step improvement in each state's index (from five to four, from four to three, and so on) translates into a 17 percent increase in average firm size in that state. More powerfully, he shows that if the index in all states moved to unity (that is, to the judicial quality of the best state), average firm size would increase by two-thirds, and TFP would increase by 8 percent, with the gains accruing proportionately more to those states with the lowest judicial quality.[22]

On the other hand, there are no studies on Mexico that focus directly on the third channel through which imperfect contract can hurt productivity: reducing a firm's abilities to establish relations with new or distant suppliers or clients. Firms may be reluctant to sell to new clients if, say, payments are in installments and those clients are not in the same location as the firm. This factor is more relevant for smaller firms, and may add to the bias in a firm's sourcing and selling decisions caused by the VAT exemption regimes discussed in the previous section. Jointly, imperfect enforcement and the VAT's special regimes restrict the size of the market faced by individual firms, contributing to the proliferation of small, mostly informal firms buying inputs from one another, and selling to clients in narrow geographical areas.

Imperfect contract enforcement may also be an obstacle to the separation of firm ownership from firm management, an issue of more relevance to medium-size and larger firms. Fukuyama (1995) provides an illuminating cross-country comparison showing that in countries with high social trust and strong legal systems, firms are run by professional managers as opposed to owners, who may not always have the required managerial talent.[23] Firms with bad management practices use their resources less efficiently (Bloom and Van Reenen 2007), innovate less, and are slower at adopting newer technologies (Cirera and Maloney 2017). This is an under-researched issue in Mexico, and more data would be welcome to gauge its importance to the country's productivity problem. Of course, the separation of ownership from control is affected as well by cultural norms. But, that said, it is easy to see that a context where courts are insufficiently trusted and contracts imperfectly enforced is not conducive to this type of separation.

Thus, this assessment of the impact of imperfect contract enforcement on misallocation and productivity is incomplete. And while further research

---

[22] Dougherty (2014) also finds, sadly, that the state-level crime rate is a determinant of firm size, and that states with higher crime rates have smaller firm sizes. Further evidence of the negative effects of crime on firms is provided by Rios (2016).

[23] This is yet another instance of the mismatch between individuals' talents and occupations discussed in Chapter 6. It is not that Mexico has an insufficient number of individuals with the appropriate skills to run firms efficiently, but rather that some of these individuals may not exercise such control due to a mix of cultural norms, insufficient trust, and imperfect contract enforcement.

could provide more evidence of the importance of contract enforcement, the available findings indicate not only that it is lowering firm size and impeding firm growth, consistent with stylized facts two and three, but that the effects are quantitatively important.

Contract enforcement in Mexico depends on the performance of multiple institutions, notably the courts. As a result, its quality is but one facet of the quality of the rule of law and is thus inextricably linked with the functioning of Mexico's judicial institutions. Discussing these institutions strays far from the purposes of this book. But the point that needs to be stressed here is that *the functioning of markets cannot be disassociated from the functioning of the institutions that determine the legal context in which these markets operate.*

Access to Credit

Assessing firms' access to credit in Mexico is difficult because data are scarce. Most data refer to lending by national commercial banks, leaving out credit from suppliers, family members, and international lenders, as well as bond issuance. And even the data from commercial banks cannot be disaggregated by firm size and contractual structure. There are also few data on firms' balance sheets, and it is not possible to systematically assess most firms' net worth.

That said, Table 7.7 presents the available data from the 2013 census. For each firm size and type, it records the share of firms with access to credit from commercial banks, and from nonbank sources such as savings cooperatives or suppliers, as well as the share without access from any of these sources. For each firm size and type, shares add to 100 percent.

Unfortunately, the census does not record whether firms without access to credit actually sought out such credit. Nor does it record the terms and

Table 7.7: Access to Credit by Size and Type of Firm, 2013
(Percent shares)

Firm Size	Fully Formal B	Fully Formal NB	Fully Formal N	Mixed B	Mixed NB	Mixed N	Informal and Legal B	Informal and Legal NB	Informal and Legal N	Informal and Illegal B	Informal and Illegal NB	Informal and Illegal N
1–5 workers	10.9	3.8	85.3	10.0	4.0	86.0	4.8	5.5	89.7	5.4	4.8	89.8
6–10 workers	23.1	4.5	72.4	16.6	4.2	79.2	29.4	3.8	66.8	9.3	4.4	86.3
11–50 workers	22.9	5.0	72.1	21.9	4.8	73.5	25.3	5.2	69.5	14.5	4.1	81.4
51+ workers	27.2	11.6	61.2	31.2	8.8	60.0	21.8	6.5	71.7	15.5	4.5	80.0

Source: Author's calculations based on data from Mexico's Economic Census.
Note: B: commercial banks; NB: savings cooperatives or suppliers; N : no access.

conditions for the subset of firms that obtained credit. In other words, the information presented in Table 7.7 is very crude. Moreover, it does not exhaust all sources of credit. Nevertheless, it is the only information available on credit that covers *all* firms in the census. (It is not possible to obtain comparable information for firms excluded from the census.)

Keeping in mind these limitations, three features merit attention. First, larger firms have more access to credit, with the differences vis-à-vis smaller firms explained mostly by commercial bank credit. In fact, access to nonbank sources of credit is similar across firm sizes (except for large formal firms). Second, not surprisingly, informal and illegal firms have less access to credit than the rest. However, third, *the most salient feature of Table 7.7 is that regardless of size or type, most firms have no access to credit.*

Haber (2009) provides abundant data to show that, by international standards, credit from commercial banks to firms in Mexico is very limited. More recently, López (2017) notes that Mexico's credit-to-GDP ratio is the same as that of the average country in sub-Saharan Africa. Figure 7.5 complements these sources with data from the Bank of International Settlements for a subset of countries on debt financing to households and nonfinancial corporations in 2013, defined as the sum of credit from commercial banks plus securities as a share of GDP (BIS 2017).

Figure 7.5 shows that debt financing for firms in Mexico is very limited. Indeed, except for Argentina, Mexico has the lowest level among all the large countries in Latin America and countries in the Organization for Economic Cooperation and Development (OECD). The gap with respect to OECD countries is notable, as firms in member countries of that organization get five times more credit as a share of GDP than firms in Mexico. But the comparison with Chile—the other Latin American country belonging to the OECD in addition to Mexico—is also very instructive: Chilean firms have four times more access to credit than Mexican firms.

Haber (2009) argues that there are two reasons for the very low levels of lending by commercial banks to firms in Mexico. First, a weak environment for enforcing contracts limits banks' ability to seize and repossess firms' assets. This is consistent with the evidence presented above and is therefore no longer discussed here. Second is concentration in the banking sector, which allows banks to be profitable by restricting credit volumes and charging high fees and commissions.

Multiple studies coincide with Haber's view on the high level of concentration in the banking sector. Guerrero, Villalpando, and Benitez (2009) show that the high profitability of Mexican commercial banks is associated with rent extraction, not efficiency (see also Castellanos, del Ángel, and Garza-García 2015). Studies using price-cost margins as measures of market power find

Figure 7.5: Total Debt Financing to Households and Firms, 2013
(Percent of GDP)

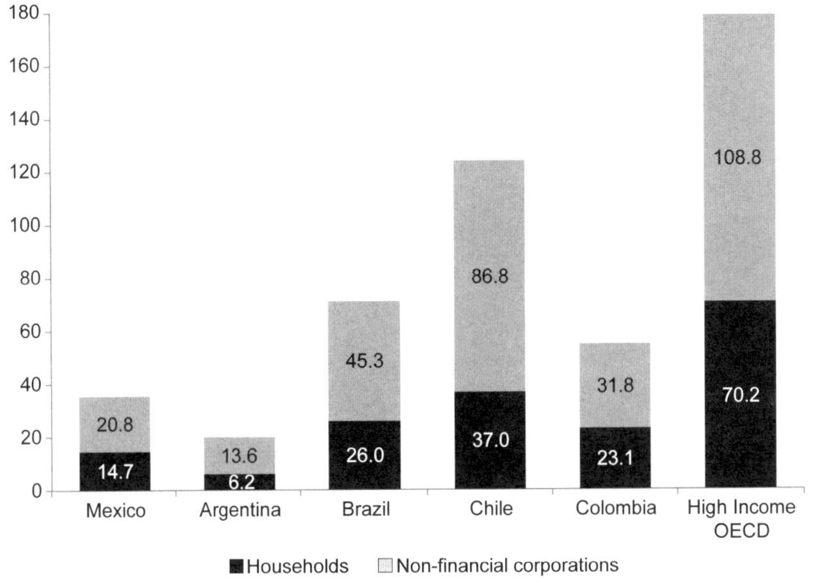

	Mexico	Argentina	Brazil	Chile	Colombia	High Income OECD
Households	14.7	6.2	26.0	37.0	23.1	70.2
Non-financial corporations	20.8	13.6	45.3	86.8	31.8	108.8

Source: Bank for International Settlements (2017).
Note: OECD: Organization for Economic Cooperation and Development. High-income OECD: Austria, Australia, Belgium, Canada, Switzerland, Czech Republic, Germany Denmark, Spain, Finland, France, United Kingdom, Greece, Hungary, Ireland, Israel, Italy, Japan, Korea, Luxembourg, Netherlands, Norway, New Zealand, Poland, Portugal, and Sweden.

that bank competition in Mexico is below that in Argentina, Brazil, Colombia, and Peru. In fact, by this measure Mexico is in the tail of the world distribution, with one of the least competitive banking sectors (World Bank 2017). Similarly, a recent report by the Inter-American Development Bank provides measures of bank-level market power for various Latin American countries and finds that Mexico is the least competitive (IDB 2018). Moreover, this report finds that the exercise of market power by banks results in higher financing costs to firms, particularly smaller ones.

Evidence of Credit Misallocation

The allocation of credit across firms of various productivity levels is key for growth everywhere but takes on greater importance in a context of credit scarcity, as in Mexico. If there is little credit in general, it should at least be directed to firms with the highest productivity. Commercial banks, however, are interested in lending to firms that are privately profitable or have high net worth—whether or not those firms are also the ones with the highest productivity is not their concern.

If credit is misallocated, high-productivity firms may be impeded from growing as much as they should, since their investments are restricted to those that can be financed by their own cash flow. Worse, some may have to exit because they cannot finance a transitory negative shock. In parallel, low-productivity firms can survive because they are privately profitable and can obtain commercial bank credit or have access to government-subsidized credit programs. The mechanisms by which credit misallocation affects productivity depend on circumstances, but most models show that the associated productivity losses can be significant (Banerjee and Dufflo 2005; Hopenhayn 2014).

Given Mexico's ***E**(L,T,M)*, do firms with higher productivity get more credit relative to those with lower productivity? To answer this question, data are needed on volumes of credit to individual firms linked to measures of firms' productivity. As mentioned, the census unfortunately records only access to credit, not volume. Nevertheless, to shed some light on this question one can take advantage of firms' classifications by productivity level used in Chapter 4. As before, firms are separated by their location in the high- and low-productivity segment of the corresponding six-digit sector TFPR distribution (above the 75th percentile, and below the 25th percentile), and firms in those segments are correlated with the data from Table 7.7 on firms' access to credit. This is clearly not fully satisfactory, as this dichotomous variable (access/no access) is insufficient to make assessments about the allocation of the volume of credit. That said, it is the only option with the data available.

With these limitations in mind, Table 7.8 shows the share of all high- and low-productivity firms by size and type with access to commercial bank credit, as well as the absolute number of firms in each case. The focus is on this type of credit because it is the most important to firms (Table 7.7), and because it is intermediated at arm's-length through the financial sector (as opposed to suppliers' credit, which reflects bilateral agreements between firms). For each firm size and type, the upper line reflects shares, and the lower line reflects the absolute number of firms.

The results are very telling. With one exception (informal and legal firms with 6 to 10 workers), the share of low-productivity firms with access to credit is higher than the share of high-productivity ones. This result is indicative of misallocation of credit and is not surprising: given Mexico's ***E**(L,T,M)*, there is no assurance of a high correlation between firms' TFPR (the attribute that matters for productivity), and firms' profitability or high net worth (the attributes that commercial banks care about).

Table 7.8: Access to Commercial Bank Credit by High- and Low-Productivity Firms, 2013
(Percent shares and number of firms)

	Fully Formal		Mixed		Informal and Legal		Informal and Illegal	
Firm Size	HP	LP	HP	LP	HP	LP	HP	LP
1–5 workers	12.6%	14.4%	10.9%	13.7%	4.8%	5.0%	5.2%	6.8%
	3,250	881	4,337	2,269	21,410	32,429	8,511	5,712
6–10 workers	20.3%	53.9%	17.4%	21.8%	14.8%	9.1%	9.2%	11.2%
	2,454	2,445	2,612	1,025	653	666	1,666	840
11–50 workers	23.2%	32.8%	23.6%	27.4%	21.5%	22.6%	13.0%	27.4%
	3,159	1,106	2,801	1,121	614	830	1,006	947
51+ workers	33.6%	41.9%	33.2%	42.6%	22.2%	33.2%	16.7%	25.6%
	852	369	632	406	216	528	68	45

Source: Author's calculations based on data from Mexico's Economic Census.
Note: HP : high-productivity; LP : low-productivity.

That said, it is important to consider that the proportions of low- and high-productivity firms differ among types. As shown in Chapter 4, fully formal firms are on average the most productive. As a result, they are overrepresented among high-productivity firms. This implies that considering the number rather than the share of firms, more high- than low-productivity fully formal firms receive credit. As usual, informal and legal firms are at the opposite end of the spectrum: the number of low-productivity firms receiving credit in this group is larger than the number of high-productivity ones.

What is the upshot of Table 7.8? All in all, considering all types and sizes, 51,619 low-productivity firms had access to commercial bank credit, 6.4 percent of the total number of firms with this productivity level. In contrast, 54,241 high-productivity firms had such access, or 7.1 percent. In other words, given Mexico's $E(L,T,M)$, the probability that a low-productivity firm had access to commercial bank credit was not that different from that of a high-productivity one. These results are consistent with the findings of Chapters 4 and 5 and illustrate a very important point: *commercial bank credit is misallocated in an environment where firms' after-tax profitability is strongly distorted by labor, social insurance, and tax regulations, and where the value of their assets as collateral is affected by imperfect contract enforcement.*

Because there are no data on loan volumes, terms, and conditions, Table 7.8 is only suggestive of credit misallocation, no more. It may be that low-productivity firms have access to more-expensive credit, or face more credit rationing, than high-productivity ones. Unfortunately, the census provides no further information, and there are no other data sources that cover the universe of firms.[24]

García-Verdú and Ramos-Francia (2017) provide alternative evidence that commercial bank credit in Mexico is not necessarily channeled to the more productive firms. They use data from the National Banking Commission, which for our purposes are much better than the data used in Table 7.8, since the commission's data refer to volumes of credit and not only access to it. The trade-off is that these data cover a smaller set of mostly formal firms, making it difficult to assess credit misallocation across firm types and size. Given that limitation, García-Verdú and Ramos-Francia explore whether credit growth is explained by growth in a firm's labor productivity, output, costs (as captured by wages), or market concentration. Their results are very important because they show that even among this subset of firms, there is a bias in the growth of commercial bank credit towards sectors characterized by high market concentration, not towards those with high (labor) productivity. García-Verdú and Ramos-Francia argue that this behavior is explained partly by banks participating in the monopoly rents generated by firms in sectors with high market concentration, and partly because lending to a few large firms lowers banks' contracting and monitoring costs. The authors also present evidence suggesting the presence of counterproductive dynamics between concentration growth and firm credit growth: higher concentration leads to higher lending, which in turn leads to higher concentration.

Urrutia, Meza, and Pratap (2015) provide further evidence that in Mexico the allocation of credit negatively affects productivity. In their framework, credit constraints limit firms' access to working capital for intermediate inputs, creating wedges between the marginal revenue product of those inputs and their market prices. In other words, intermediate inputs are worth more to firms than what they cost. Firms would like to purchase more inputs and expand output, but they cannot do so because credit is insufficient. As credit constraints become more binding, these wedges grow, and so does misallocation and associated productivity losses. (These wedges are like the ones discussed in Chapter 4 in the context of the Hsieh-Klenow model with reference to capital and labor but extended to include intermediate inputs.)

To test the significance of this channel, Urrutia, Meza, and Pratap (2015) merge data from 82 four-digit manufacturing sectors with credit data at the same sector level, exploiting differences among sectors. Rather than focusing

---

[24] The World Bank Enterprise Surveys, although focused on a much smaller set of firms, provide an international perspective on access to credit by productivity level. In 2010, only 29 percent of the most productive small firms in Mexico in this survey had access to credit, compared to 74 percent of such firms in Chile, 59 percent in Brazil, and 52 percent in Peru. Almost identical results obtain with medium-size and large firms.

on the level of the distortions created by the wedges (as in Chapter 4), they focus on their evolution over time. They find that between 2003 and 2012, restrictions to firms' access to working capital closely track the behavior of TFP, and that relaxing those restrictions could have a significant effect on TFP growth. In a parallel paper (Urrutia, Meza, and Pratap 2017), the authors use the same database and extend their analysis of constraints to bank credit to study its impact on capital accumulation, finding that heterogeneity in these constraints matters greatly for firms' investment decisions.

Finally, López (2017) calibrates a model of credit constraints to the universe of firms in the 2013 census, assuming each firm can borrow only in proportion to its wealth, as defined by its capital stock. Credit is misallocated because the most productive firms are not necessarily those with higher net worth. He shows that this misallocation reduces aggregate TFP by about 10 percent. Interestingly, he finds that if the credit-to-GDP ratio in Mexico were to equal Chile's ratio, TFP could increase by about 9 percent.

What are the implications of these results for the three stylized facts discussed in this chapter? Monopolistic behavior by banks results in low levels of credit to firms regardless of size or type. In parallel, because under large misallocation the more productive firms are not necessarily the most profitable ones, or the ones with the highest net worth, the reduced supply of credit is not necessarily channeled to the more productive firms. These two factors make it difficult for productive firms to grow, consistent with stylized fact two. They also make it difficult for them to weather negative transitory shocks, and some might have to exit the market, consistent with stylized fact three. On the other hand, so long as firms have assets that commercial banks consider as valuable collateral, there is in principle no reason why they would discriminate between those with salaried and non-salaried contracts, and thus there is no direct bearing on stylized fact one.

This discussion concludes by highlighting the distinction between the aggregate supply of credit, which is restricted by commercial banks' uncompetitive behavior, and the misallocation of whatever credit is available given the impact of $E(L,T,M)$ on firm performance. To reiterate, commercial banks lend to firms that have high net worth or are privately profitable, a group that in a context of large misallocation does not necessarily coincide with those firms that are productive. As discussed in this chapter, there are unfortunately plenty of elements in Mexico's $E(L,T,M)$ aside from bank behavior that reduce the profitability or growth potential of productive firms, and that allow unproductive ones to survive and at times thrive. In this context, simply expanding credit because, say, competition laws are better enforced in the banking sector, or because development banks augment their operation, may not necessarily improve resource allocation and raise productivity.

The experience of Spain is an important eye-opener. Gopinath et al. (2017) analyze the impact of credit expansion on TFP in that country. They show that credit became cheaper between 1999 and 2012 partly because of the convergence process associated with the euro. Using the Hsieh-Klenow (2009) model presented in Chapter 4, they provide evidence of misallocation and show that the credit expansion benefited manufacturing firms with higher net worth but not necessarily with higher productivity. As a result, they document that during this period more credit actually increased the misallocation of capital and widened the gap between the observed and efficient level of TFP.

Mutatis mutandis, an analogous situation could occur in Mexico. If credit is expanded because there is more competition among commercial banks, or because development banks are more active, but the other elements of *L, T,* and *M* in *E(L,T,M)* discussed earlier are left untouched, some firms will grow, but not necessarily the more productive ones. In other words, expanding credit under large misallocation can be a double-edged sword. As things stand in Mexico, expanding credit to firms with non-salaried contracts of any size, or to small firms benefiting from the Repeco regime (regardless of the types of contracts that they offer to their workers), may actually *hurt* productivity. In the end, credit cannot bypass the deep problems caused by malfunctioning tax, labor, social insurance, and contract enforcement regimes. Chapter 9 will return to this observation.

The Joint Effects of *E(L,T,M)* on Misallocation

The previous sections analyzed the effects on misallocation of individual policies in *E(L,T,M)* separately. Entrepreneurs and workers, however, face all policies at the same time and make their decisions in reaction to all of them, not in reaction to any single one. Ideally, one would like to have a ranking of the relative importance of each. But it is very difficult to do so because, as noted earlier, there are insufficient data, and even if the data were there, the analytical tools available would preclude devising such a ranking. Nevertheless, while quantitative rankings cannot be produced, it is still illustrative to consider the effects of all policies at the same time. This is the purpose of this section.

Table 7.9 summarizes the effects of the policies and institutions discussed so far. The table makes clear that the incentives associated with *E(L, T, M)* are not only very complex, but that they operate through different channels and at times in contradictory directions.

Separating the Effects of Policies and Institutions on Firm Size and Type

Inspection of Table 7.9 allows for two observations. First, on balance incentives are strongly biased against salaried relations between entrepreneurs

Table 7.9: Summary of Impacts of $E(L, T, M)$ on Misallocation

Policy/Institution	Observations/Impact
Contributory Social Insurance	
Benefits paid by firms and workers with a contribution proportional to workers' wages	Policy applies only to salaried workers
Low-quality services by the IMSS and Infonavit; many workers will not qualify for pensions or health benefits after retirement	Implicit tax on salaried contracts of 12 percent despite 0.5 of a percent of GDP in government subsidies
Imperfect enforcement by the IMSS and Infonavit	Tax discriminates against medium-size and large firms with salaried workers
Regulations on Dismissal and Reinstatement	
Firms face contingent firing costs and risks of suits from "unjustified dismissals"	Policy applies only to salaried workers
Imperfect adjudication by JCAs; workers and firms bear high legal fees; firms face large uncertainty; workers face delays and difficulties collecting awards	Implicit tax on salaried contracts augmented beyond 12 percent; costly adjustment to negative shocks
Non-contributory Social Insurance	
Workers receive free benefits regardless of their earnings; firms not involved	Policy applies to non-salaried workers and, de facto, to illegally hired salaried workers
Benefits fully paid by government equivalent to 1.7 percent of GDP	Implicit subsidy to non-salaried and illegal salaried contracts of 16 percent of earnings
Labor Taxation	
State payroll taxes of 2 to 3 percent of wages, collecting 0.39 of a percent of GDP	Policy applies only to salaried workers
Federal employment subsidy of 0.24 of a percent of GDP	Policy applies to salaried workers with up to three minimum wages
Federal income taxes withheld by firms for salaried workers (payroll taxes) but filed directly by non-salaried ones	Policy applies to all workers
Imperfect enforcement of federal income tax by the SAT; large evasion by non-salaried workers who pay about one-fourth of what should be paid	Taxes on salaried workers of 2.5 percent of GDP, and only 0.1 of a percent on non-salaried (implicit subsidy of 0.4 of a percent of GDP)
Firm Taxation	
Approximately 93 percent of firms in census qualify for the Repeco, absorbing 52 percent of all labor and 25 percent of all capital	Discriminates by firm size, favoring small firms; growth of high-productivity firms penalized; survival of low-productivity firms facilitated
Imperfect enforcement of the Repeco by state governments	Implicit subsidy to small firms of 0.5 of a percent of GDP relative to the already very low statutory Repeco rate
Imperfect enforcement of general regime by the SAT	Average and marginal tax rates increasing with size

(continued on next page)

Table 7.9: Summary of Impacts of *E(L, T, M)* on Misallocation *(continued)*

Policy/Institution	Observations/Impact
Consumption Taxation	
42 percent of tax base in special regimes	Policy discriminates by sectors
Approximately 25 percent of GDP subject to exemption regimes results in 1.5 percent of GDP in foregone revenues	Informal firm survival facilitated; informal-to-informal supply chains fostered
Enforcement of Contracts	
Large variation in contract enforceability across states; most states have very imperfect enforcement	Smaller firm size, as diversified ownership structure is penalized; client base reduced
Uncertain property rights, costly seizure of collateral	Lower value of firms' assets as collateral; credit to firms reduced
Insufficient Competition	
Concentration in banking and sectors less exposed to international trade	Lowest bank credit to firms of any OECD country; most firms with no access to commercial bank lending; credit biased towards large firms in concentrated sectors

Source: Prepared by the author.
Note: JCAs: Juntas de Conciliación y Arbitraje; IMSS: Instituto Mexicano del Seguro Social; Infonavit: Instituto del Fondo Nacional para la Vivienda de los Trabajadores; OECD: Organization for Economic Cooperation and Development; Repeco: Régimen de Pequeños Contribuyentes; SAT: Servicio de Administración Tributaria.

and workers. Although not all effects can be quantified, salaried relations involve:

- An implicit tax of 12 percent of wages on salaried employment, after considering subsidies of 0.74 of a percent of GDP from the employment subsidy in the income tax law and subsidies to contributory social insurance. In addition, salaried workers pay 2.5 percent of GDP in federal payroll taxes, and 0.39 of a percent of GDP in state payroll taxes.
- An implicit subsidy of 16 percent of earnings on non-salaried employment given subsidies of 1.7 percent of GDP to non-contributory social insurance programs, and an implicit subsidy of 0.4 of a percent from imperfect enforcement of the personal income tax on non-salaried workers.
- Uncertainty, possible litigation, and potentially large outlays from regulations on dismissal that apply only when workers have salaried contracts.

Second, on balance incentives are biased towards small firms and against firm growth. Although again not all effects can be quantified, those that can include the following:

- Lower statutory corporate tax rates for firms if they qualify for the Repeco, the impossibility of returning to the Repeco if they grow but then need to adjust downwards, and an implicit subsidy to small firms of 0.5 of a percent of GDP from imperfect enforcement of the Repeco relative to the very low statutory rate.
- Effective average and marginal tax rates on firms with salaried contracts that increase with size given imperfect enforcement by the IMSS and Infonavit of contributions for social insurance.
- Higher contingent labor liabilities if firms grow and hire salaried workers.
- Effective average and marginal tax rates on all firms that increase with firm size given imperfect enforcement by the SAT of the general regime of the corporate income tax and the VAT.
- Large variations in contract enforceability across states that reduce firm size.
- Scarce credit from commercial banks, particularly for smaller firms.

From the point of view of productivity, these two biases are not equally important. Tables 4.4 and 4.5 in Chapter 4 showed that while productivity differences between larger and smaller firms were relevant, differences across firm types were substantially more so. To recall an important conclusion from that chapter: firm type is more important than firm size. As a result, the policies and associated institutions shown in Table 7.9 that discriminate by firm type matter more than those that discriminate by firm size.

Separating the Effects of Policies from the Effects of Their Imperfect Enforcement

Inspection of Table 7.9 also shows that the forces biasing the size and type distribution of firms are sometimes due to the policy itself, and sometimes to the way it is enforced. Separating them is critical because many policies expressly discriminate between firms depending on their size, type, or sector. Indeed, surprisingly, from Table 7.9 it can be inferred that of all policies considered, the only one that is neutral from the point of view of firm size, type, or sector is the federal personal income tax. Quite a few policies discriminate by firm type, including social insurance, dismissal regulations, the state payroll tax, and the federal subsidy to salaried employment. Some policies discriminate by firm size, saliently the Repeco-general regime combination of the corporate income tax. And some policies discriminate by sectors, notably the special regimes of the VAT.

It is difficult to overestimate the importance of this distinction for Mexico. Misallocation of resources is not only a result of the fact that some laws are imperfectly enforced, and that some institutions underperform. Even if the

IMSS, Infonavit, and the JCAs all delivered top-quality services and were fully trusted, even if the first two institutions together with the SAT and state governments enforced all taxes and contributions perfectly, even if all states enforced contracts efficiently, and even if banks allocated credit based only on firms' productivity regardless of size or type, resources would *still* be misallocated towards firms with non-salaried contracts. This is because their workers would continue to be subsidized by non-contributory programs, and because firms with salaried contracts would still be taxed by state authorities and face greater contingent liabilities and larger difficulties adjusting to negative shocks as a result of dismissal regulations. Moreover, resources would *still* be misallocated towards small firms (with salaried or non-salaried contracts) because the Repeco-general regime corporate income tax policy, even if perfectly enforced, favors them.

Of course, the fact that institutions delivering services or enforcing taxes, contributions, and contracts underperform matters greatly. In response to their underperformance, firms stay small, engage in illegal behavior, switch their contracts to non-salaried ones (when they can), restrict the number of shareholders, and rely on credit from suppliers or relatives. For their part, workers are more willing to accept illegal salaried or non-salaried contracts, or to work on their own. All this magnifies misallocation. But the critical point is that even if institutions delivering services and enforcing taxes, contributions and contracts functioned perfectly, resources would still be misallocated towards small firms and towards firms with non-salaried contracts.

In other words, misallocation is inherent in the *design* of some policies in Mexico, particularly those associated with taxation, social insurance, and dismissal regulations. In this sense, its roots go beyond imperfectly functioning institutions. Indeed, from the point of view of misallocation, it is necessary to answer two separate questions:

- Why do so many firms have non-salaried contracts with their workers?
- Why are so many firms small?

The answer to the first question cannot be imperfect enforcement of taxes or contributions. It can only be that, enforcement aside, some policies expressly discriminate against firms with salaried contracts. The answer to the second question is partly technology (because, as discussed in Chapter 2, firms with non-salaried contracts tend to be small), partly policies (the Repeco favors small firms even if there is no evasion) and, yes, partly imperfect enforcement of other taxes and contributions.

Aside from enhancing our understanding of the forces driving misallocation in Mexico, the observation that it would persist even if taxes and contributions were perfectly enforced is critical for policy. It argues forcefully against an across-the-board prescription of enhancing enforcement as the route to reduce misallocation, while keeping policies constant. Ignoring enforcement costs, better enforcement of policies that are inherently neutral across firm types would certainly contribute to reducing misallocation—this would be the case, for instance, with the personal income tax, or with the enforcement of commercial and credit contracts. Better enforcement of policies that discriminate by firm size would also reduce misallocation—this would be the case, for instance, of the Repeco, although, as noted, the gains would be minor. But better enforcement of policies that inherently discriminate between firm types could in fact increase misallocation. Thus, for instance, better enforcement by the IMSS and Infonavit may reduce the number of firms with illegal salaried contracts and increase those with non-salaried ones. The same would be true if state governments better enforced the state payroll tax on salaried employment.

Misallocation in Mexico Has Many Causes

The outcomes analyzed in Chapters 3, 4, 5 and 6 derive from a broader set of policies than those listed in Table 7.9. But even ignoring those policies, the ones listed in that table are sufficient to make the following point: *misallocation in Mexico results from the interaction of many policies and institutions at the same time; there is no single cause.*

Ideally, one would like to identify and quantify how each policy affects firm behavior. Which policy is responsible for biasing the type distribution of firms? The implicit tax from contributory programs, the implicit subsidy from non-contributory ones, dismissal regulations, the state payroll tax on salaried employment, or asymmetry in the enforcement of the personal income tax? The same question can be asked in the case of size. Do firms stay small because of imperfect contract enforcement, because of the Repeco, because of uncompetitive behavior by commercial banks, because they cannot bear the risks of dismissal regulations associated with hiring more workers, or because they have salaried workers but are evading? And in the latter case, are they evading social insurance contributions, taxes, or both?

The available models do not provide answers to these questions because they mostly analyze one policy at a time.[25] Moreover, it is likely that the

---

[25] However, some models consider the interaction of two policies. As noted earlier, López-Martin (2017) finds that improving contract enforcement increases TFP, as formal firms have more access to credit. He then introduces a size-dependent tax (like the Repeco-general regime) and finds that the same improvement in contract enforcement produces a smaller gain in TFP. In other words, the gains from changing one policy depend on how it interacts with other policies.

relevance of each policy depends on circumstances. For firms close to the border of the Repeco-general regime threshold, access to credit is probably secondary because even if they had such access they would be unwilling to grow.[26] For firms above that threshold, such access may be vital. For firms located in places where the IMSS offers abundant health and day care facilities, the implicit tax from contributory programs is less relevant than for those located in places where facilities are scarce. For firms with relatively more lower-wage workers, the implicit subsidy from non-contributory programs is more relevant than for those firms whose workforce earns higher wages. Firms that sell to the government probably comply more with taxes and do not stay small to evade, but perhaps to avoid the contingent costs of dismissal regulations. And so on.

It is useful to relate this discussion to the analysis in Chapter 4. There, the Hsieh-Klenow (2009) model was used as a vehicle to measure the dispersion in the marginal revenue products of capital and labor across firms in a sector, introducing firm-specific wedges $\tau_{Q_{is}}$ and $\tau_{L_{is}}$ as summary measures of all the policies affecting firm behavior (see relation 4.3 in Chapter 4). Ideally, one would like to measure how each policy in Table 7.9 contributes to these firm-specific wedges. In other words, one would like to map policies into wedges. The fact that with the available models this cannot be done highlights the urgency of developing more sophisticated models that can analyze many policies at the same time. It also highlights the need for more data, particularly on taxes and credit.

Nevertheless, the fact that one cannot quantify the relative contribution of individual policies to the wedges causing misallocation should not detract from the more important fact that misallocation has systematic patterns, and that it is possible to identify policies that induce behaviors consistent with those patterns. It is true that one cannot quantify their relative importance with precision (although we do know that policies affecting the type distribution of firms matter more than those biasing the size distribution). This shortcoming, however, should not detract from a central conclusion of the analysis, which is that it is indeed possible to identify the main culprits of misallocation in Mexico. *Many policies need to change to increase productivity in Mexico, but the core ones are those summarized in Table 7.9.*

---

[26] For these firms programs to foster technology adoption or improve managerial practices may also be unattractive, as ‚growing or acquiring greater market share would lower their after-tax profits.

CHAPTER 8

Why Did Misallocation Increase between 1998 and 2013?

Mexico carried out many reforms to increase efficiency during the two decades studied in this book. However, as Chapters 4 and 5 documented, misallocation increased. Dysfunctional firm dynamics implied that by the end of the period more resources were allocated to firms with non-salaried contracts relative to those with salaried contracts, while average firm size fell and illegal behavior increased. This phenomenon—summarized in stylized fact four in Chapter 7—is puzzling indeed, because the natural expectation of the reforms to increase efficiency is that misallocation would have fallen. What explains stylized fact four?

This chapter does *not* discuss the efficiency-enhancing reforms. Rather, it focuses attention on policy changes that contributed to increasing misallocation and that, somewhat surprisingly, were strong enough to more than offset the effects of efficiency-increasing reforms. The policy changes considered here may be motivated by social objectives such as expanding the coverage of social insurance, by fiscal objectives such as increasing revenues, or by yet other considerations such as promoting small firms. But as before, these objectives are not discussed; the focus is only on their impact on resource allocation.

The analysis here is not exhaustive, and it is not always possible to provide systematic empirical evidence; moreover, in some cases the discussion is only suggestive. Further research may suggest other policy changes not discussed here that are also negatively affecting resource allocation. As a result, although the chapter sheds considerable light on the issue, it does not provide a full explanation for the increase in misallocation.[1] That said, the expectation is that it calls attention to some policy changes that are worrisome and costly from the point of view of productivity. Following the structure of Chapter 7, this chapter separately considers changes in *L, T,* and *M* in *E(L,T,M)* that are inducing workers and entrepreneurs to behave in ways consistent with stylized fact four, and then discusses their joint effects.

Changes in the World of Entrepreneur-Worker Relations

Increasing Implicit Taxes from Contributory Social Insurance Programs

In July 1997, a new social insurance law came into effect in Mexico with large implications for the value that workers attach to the benefits of contributory programs (β_f in Table 7.1 in Chapter 7) and, therefore, for the magnitude of the implicit tax associated with them. This section considers some implications for pension and health programs.

Beginning with pensions, the new law changed the retirement pension regime from a pay-as-you-go defined benefit to a defined-contribution one managed through individual saving accounts. The reform affected only workers entering the labor force for the first time after 1997; workers who had contributed to the old regime retained their right to retire under it.

The pay-as-you-go regime was actuarially unbalanced, since the contribution rate was lower than the future value of the pension. In other words, workers retiring under that regime are heavily subsidized by the federal government; indeed, approximately 75 percent of the pension is a subsidy.[2] Under the new regime, workers must accumulate at least 24 years to qualify for a pension, as opposed to 10 under the previous one, and they receive a pension proportional to their contributions, in principle without any subsidy.

---

[1] Methodologically, the issue in this chapter is more complex than the one tackled in the previous one. If, as seen in Chapter 7, one cannot provide a quantitative ranking of the relative importance of policies in *E(L,T,M)* causing misallocation, it is less likely that one can provide a ranking of the contribution of *changes* in *E(L,T,M)* to *changes* in misallocation.

[2] Berstein et al. (2018) point out that the old regime was one of the most generous in Latin America and the Caribbean. They estimate that the interest rate at which workers' contributions should have been capitalized to finance the pension benefit was 8.7 percent. Assuming an interest rate of 3.5 percent, this implies a subsidy of around US$138,000 per worker. Aside from being fiscally unsustainable, the old regime was regressive, and these features were very much the motivation for the change, along with the desire to increase national savings. A full assessment of the reform must therefore consider these features, which are ignored here because the focus is only on its impact on firms' and workers' incentives.

The new regime did introduce a minimum pension guarantee, which may eventually imply a government subsidy if workers' savings in their individual accounts cannot finance a pension of at least one minimum wage. But as noted in Chapter 7, and critically in this context, three out of four workers contributing in the new regime will not accumulate the required 24 years. Because of this, public subsidies resulting from this guarantee, and therefore public subsidies for pensions under the new regime, will be very small indeed. In contrast, it is estimated that seven out of 10 workers in the old regime will accumulate the required 10 years to qualify for a pension, and thus benefit from a large subsidy. In sum, longer contribution requirements and substantially lower subsidies (if any) imply that for workers under the new regime pensions are less valuable than pensions for workers who retained the right to a pay-as-you-go pension.[3]

The upward sloping line in Figure 8.1 shows the share of workers entering the labor force for the first time after 1997 (on the right axis). The data are obtained from the Employment Survey. The figure assumes workers begin their careers when they are 20 years old and retire at 65, and excludes public sector workers (who have their own pension regime). These workers cannot benefit from a highly subsidized pay-as-you-go pension. As can be seen, their share has been steadily increasing since 1997, and by 2015 they represented more than half of the labor force.

What is the implication of the change in the composition of the labor force between those who entered before and after 1997? At any point in time, workers' valuation of the retirement pension component of contributory programs is a weighted average of each cohort's valuation, where the weights are the share of each cohort in the labor force. Since the share of cohorts without a right to a highly subsidized old-regime pension has been increasing, workers' average valuation of retirement pensions should be moving in the opposite direction. This implies that β_f should be falling and, in turn, that the implicit tax on legal salaried contracts is increasing (see Table 7.1 in Chapter 7).[4] This induces behavior consistent with stylized fact four.

---

[3] As part of the reform, the government absorbed responsibility for all pay-as-you-go pensions. But these fiscally costly outlays only benefit retirees who entered the labor force before 1997, and it is critical to distinguish those outlays (0.87 of a percent of GDP) from the outlays made to subsidize contributory programs of workers currently in the workforce (given by $(1 - \theta_r T_r)$), which are smaller (0.5 of a percent of GDP in 2013), and distributed over a much larger group of people (3.4 million retirees versus 16.5 million active workers).

[4] Another factor lowering workers' valuation of pensions under the new regime derives from the high fees charged by the private retirement fund administrators (Administradoras de Fondos de Retiro – Afores) for managing their funds, at least in the initial years after the reform; see Levy (2009).

Figure 8.1: Workers and Retirees, 1996-2015
(Workers per retiree; and percent share of workers entering workforce after 1997)

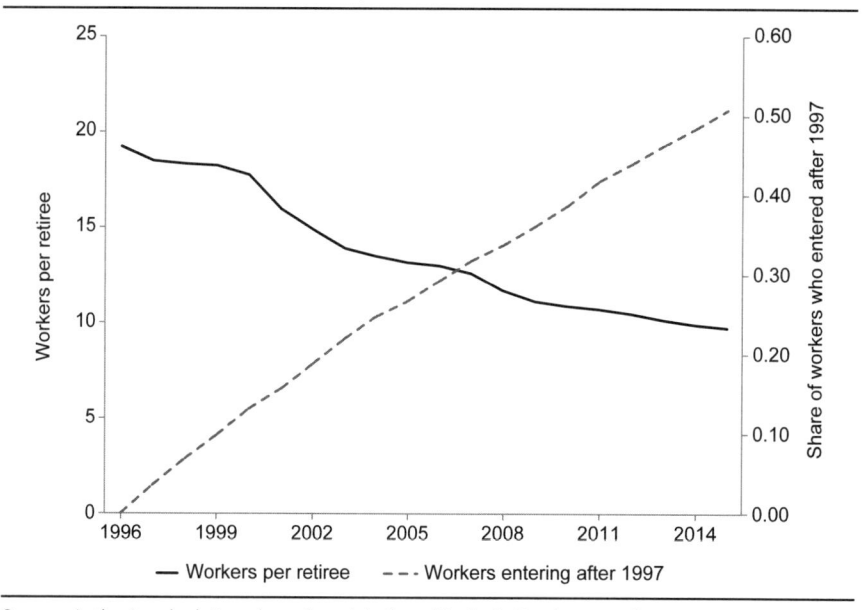

———— Workers per retiree   ---- Workers entering after 1997

Source: Author's calculations based on data from Mexico's Employment Survey.

What about health? Under the new law, workers' contributions for health insurance are used to finance services for themselves and for retirees *who qualify for a retirement pension*. If all workers currently contributing were to qualify for a pension, this would not imply any intergenerational subsidies; when they retire, new cohorts of workers would contribute to their health benefits. But as noted before, many workers currently contributing to health insurance, particularly those who obtained their first formal job after 1997, will not qualify for a pension. These workers will not receive health benefits from the Mexican Social Security Institute (Instituto Mexicano del Seguro Social – IMSS) when they retire even though a part of their current contributions is being used to pay for the health benefits of those who are already retired.

The left axis of Figure 8.1 shows that the number of workers per retiree fell in the last two decades, implying that an increasing share of health contributions are channeled to provide services to retirees, not to active workers. Thus, the value of the health component of contributory programs, particularly for those who got their first formal job after 1997, must be progressively falling. The result is again to gradually lower β_f and increase the implicit tax on legal salaried contracts, inducing behavior consistent with stylized fact four.

Larger Subsidies for Non-contributory Social Insurance Programs

Figure 8.2 shows that between 1996 and 2015, resources for these programs increased four-fold, from 0.4 to 1.6 of a percent of GDP. Resources for health programs have increased continuously since 1996.[5] In parallel, after 2006 resources for retirement pension programs increased noticeably, as various states started their own programs, and the scope of the federal program was progressively enhanced.[6] The net effect of these trends was to increase the per worker subsidy to non-salaried and illegal salaried contracts (T_i in

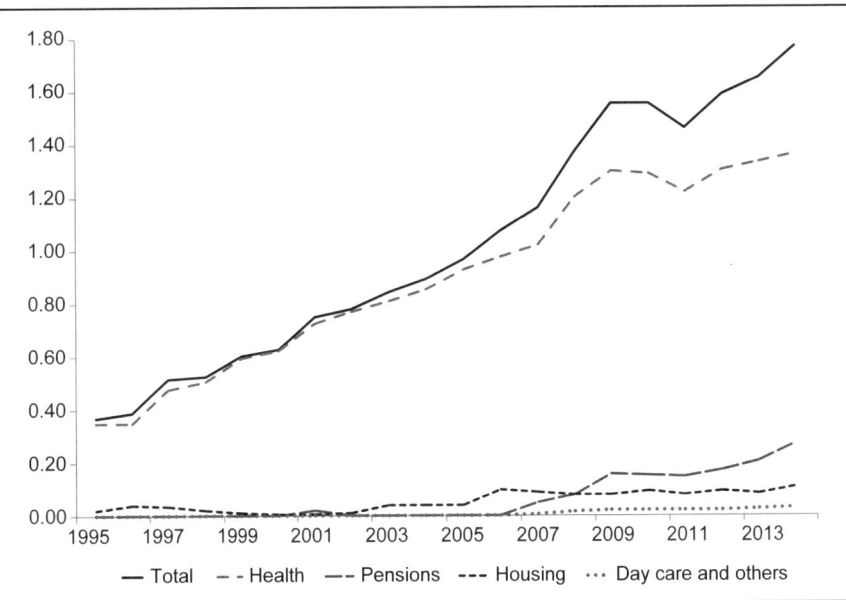

Figure 8.2: Resources for Non-Contributory Programs, 1996–2015
(Percent of GDP)

Source: Antón (2016).

---

[5] There have been non-contributory health programs in Mexico for many decades, under various names. Initially they were all operated and funded by the federal government, but some programs were decentralized to state governments in the late 1980s. Additional federal resources for health were decentralized in 1998 as part of a larger policy to transfer resources to subnational governments. In 2003, a new federally funded but state-run non-contributory program was introduced—commonly referred to as Seguro Popular—that further increased resources for health with the aim of attaining universal health insurance.

[6] The first such program started in Mexico City in 2002. A federal program was launched in 2007 initially aimed at persons aged 70 and older living in small rural communities. Over time the coverage of this latter program expanded and the age to qualify was lowered. It currently

Table 7.1 7) from 3 percent of average informal earnings in 1996 to 16.5 percent in 2015 (Antón 2016).

As opposed to the case of contributory programs, many studies have analyzed the impact of non-contributory programs on various dimensions of behavior. For instance, non-contributory pension programs may be reducing household labor supply and savings (Alonso, Amuedo-Dorantes, and Juárez 2016), or reducing gifts from younger family members to the elderly receiving these pensions (Amuedo-Dorantes and Juárez 2013). The interest here, however, is in their impact on misallocation. As it turns out, most studies focusing on this dimension are related to health.

Bosch, Cobacho, and Pagés (2014) carry out a meta-analysis of numerous studies identifying the effects of Seguro Popular on the formal-informal composition of employment. These studies take advantage of the program's gradual rollout, comparing regions of Mexico where it started earlier with those where it started later. Considering all studies, the authors find that over the period 2003–2010 the program reduced formal employment by between 0.4 and 1 percentage point of the labor force, which is equivalent to between 160,000 and 400,000 workers. Since during the period when the program was rolled out about 2 million formal jobs were created, the program reduced formal employment creation by between 8 and 20 percent, with the effect stronger among smaller firms and less-skilled workers. This is a very relevant number indeed, and its relevance is augmented by noting that in 2010 Seguro Popular represented only 25 percent of the budget of non-contributory health programs (Antón 2016). Considering all non-contributory health programs, the negative effects on formal employment creation must be larger. The behavior induced by the growth in non-contributory health programs is consistent with stylized fact four.

Bosch and Campos-Vásquez (2014) consider the impact of Seguro Popular on firm behavior. Using a similar methodological approach, they show that the program reduced the number of very small, small, and medium-sized firms (less than 50 workers) registered with the IMSS by 4.6 percent and the number of formal workers by 4 percent, indicating an increase in firms' illegal behavior. This is consistent with the analysis of Table 7.1 in Chapter 7, and with the increase in the number of illegal and informal firms documented in Table 3.7 in Chapter 3. It is also consistent with stylized fact four.

---

covers all adults over 65 years of age regardless of where they live *so long as they do not have a contributory pension*. In parallel, various states started programs of their own (implying some individuals can get two pensions). In 2015, 18 out of 32 states operated a program, with different benefits and rules.

Finally, Juárez (2008) studied the effects of a non-contributory health program in Mexico City, comparing the evolution of female employment there with that of Guadalajara and Monterrey (Mexico's second and third-largest cities), where the program was not put in place. Her results indicate a reduction in the probability that females would hold formal jobs in Mexico City. Again, these results are consistent with stylized fact four.

Combined Effects of Social Insurance Programs

In sum, there is unambiguous evidence that the expansion of non-contributory programs has increased informal employment and firms' illegal behavior over the last two decades, and that the effects are substantial. On the other hand, there are no studies that provide empirical evidence to show that the implicit tax on salaried employment derived from contributory programs has increased in the same period. Thus, although based on the discussion above the direction of change induced by changes in contributory programs is consistent with stylized fact four, the empirical relevance of those changes has yet to be determined.

That said, what matters are the combined effects of changes to contributory and non-contributory programs. To the best of our knowledge, there are no studies that consider these effects. But since an increasing tax on legal salaried contracts and an increasing subsidy to non-salaried and illegal salaried contracts both operate in the direction of increasing misallocation, one can say that the lower bound on the effects of changes to these programs are given by the effects of changes to non-contributory programs. While it would be desirable to have more empirical evidence on the impact of changes to contributory programs, at this stage the available evidence is enough to establish the following conclusion: *changes to social insurance policies over the last two decades have induced behavior consistent with stylized fact four.*

Changes in the World of Taxation

Taxation of Income from Labor

Figure 8.3 compares the tax burden of the federal personal income tax on salaried and non-salaried workers between 1996 and 2015. Earnings before taxes are shown on the horizontal axis and are expressed in monthly 2015 pesos. Taxes paid on those earnings are shown on the vertical axis and are computed applying the tax code in place in each year assuming perfect enforcement. The changes in taxes paid shown in the figure reflect changes in statutory rates between these two years; changes in the real value of the wage

Figure 8.3: Earnings and Taxes, 1996 versus 2015
(In 2015 pesos)

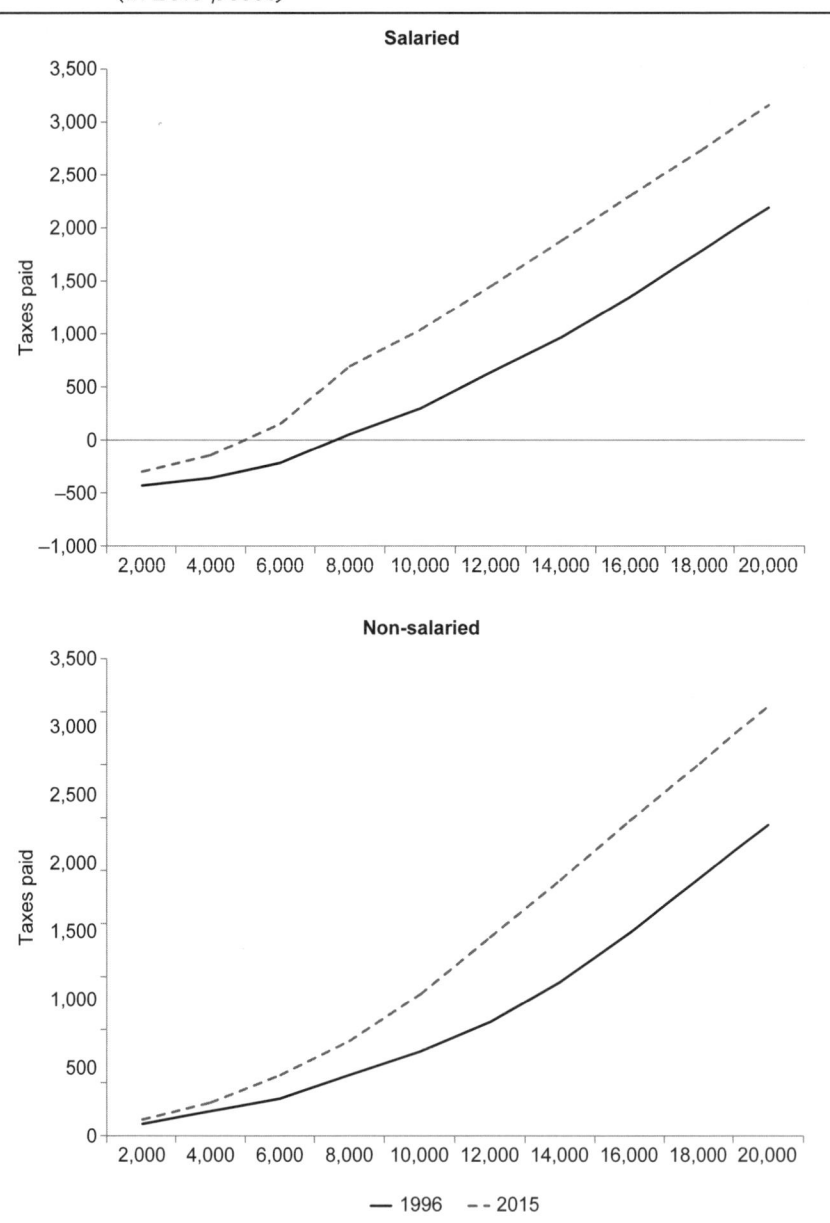

Salaried

Non-salaried

— 1996   -- 2015

Source: Author's calculations based on Mexico's income tax law.

subsidy for salaried workers (s_f in Table 7.2 in Chapter 7); changes in the real value of the income thresholds used to apply the progressivity of the tax, as nominal earnings increased but the nominal value of the thresholds did not, particularly since 2008 (so-called "inflation creep"); changes in deductions for social insurance contributions; and changes in deductions for social benefits.[7]

The upper panel refers to salaried workers and shows that lower-wage workers pay negative taxes, reflecting the wage subsidy. The lower panel refers to non-salaried workers, and because there are no subsidies in this case, taxes paid are always positive. Both panels make clear that there has been an unambiguous increase in the personal income taxes paid by workers across the range of the earnings distribution.

Figure 8.4 summarizes the implications of these changes. The rectangles compare the percentage reduction in salaried and non-salaried workers' after-tax real earnings between 1996 and 2015 for each level of earnings resulting

Figure 8.4: Changes in Taxation and Reduction in Workers' Real Income between 1996 and 2015
(Percent reduction)

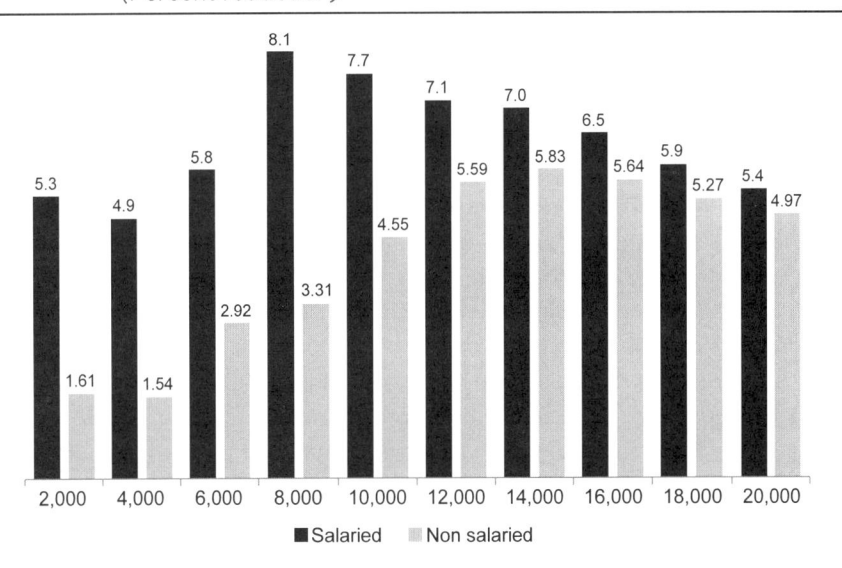

Earnings	Salaried	Non salaried
2,000	5.3	1.61
4,000	4.9	1.54
6,000	5.8	2.92
8,000	8.1	3.31
10,000	7.7	4.55
12,000	7.1	5.59
14,000	7.0	5.83
16,000	6.5	5.64
18,000	5.9	5.27
20,000	5.4	4.97

Source: Author's calculations based on Mexico's income tax law.

---

[7] Social benefits (*prestaciones sociales* in Spanish) need to be distinguished from social insurance benefits (*seguro social* in Spanish). Some social benefits are mandated by law (a 13th month of salary a year and payments for vacations), and some reflect contractual agreements between firms and workers that vary across firms (such as allowances for transportation, clothing, and the like).

from the shift in the tax schedules shown in Figure 8.3, with earnings measured again in monthly 2015 pesos. There are two salient features. First, the tax-induced reduction in earnings was higher for salaried workers compared to non-salaried ones. Second, this effect is more pronounced in the lower half of the earnings distribution.

Figure 8.4 assumes that the incidence of higher taxes was fully borne by workers. In the case of salaried workers, however, part of the incidence probably fell on firms. But as noted in Chapter 7, incidence considerations are second-order for our purposes here. What matters is that legal salaried contracts between firms and workers must internalize a higher tax in 2015 than in 1996; the wedge between what firms pay and what salaried workers receive has unambiguously widened, clearly discouraging salaried employment.

How relevant is this issue? One way to answer this question is to consider the changes in revenues stemming from the changes to the tax code, as well as from any changes in enforcement. As it turns out, they are very large indeed. In a nutshell, excluding taxes on Mexicans working abroad, revenues from this tax more than doubled between 1996 and 2015, from 1.6 percent to 3.3 percent of GDP.

The tax data only allow for separating revenues from this tax between salaried and non-salaried workers from 2005 onward. In 2005, total revenues were 2 percent of GDP, of which 1.9 percentage points were collected from salaried workers and 0.1 of a percentage point from non-salaried ones. In 2015, total revenues were 3.3 percent of GDP, of which 3.2 percentage points were collected from salaried workers and 0.1 of a percentage point from non-salaried ones (SAT 2017). In other words, at the margin, *practically the totality of the increase in revenues from personal income taxes over the period was collected from salaried workers*. If one assumes that the same shares were observed in the previous decade, the result is that between 1996 and 2015 income taxes on salaried workers increased by 1.7 percentage points of GDP. In other words, due to changes in the tax code and in the enforcement efforts of the tax administration service (Servicio de Administración Tributaria – SAT) over the period under consideration, firms and workers had to gradually internalize an *additional* 1.7 percentage points of GDP if they associated under a legal salaried contract.

But that is not all. In parallel, the state payroll tax on salaried employment also increased (t_s in Table 7.2). It was not possible to obtain the rate applied by each state in 1996 and compare it with the 2015 rate, but some of the largest states in Mexico raised the rate from 2 to 3 percent of the wage bill.[8] That said, it was possible to obtain data on the revenues collected from

---

[8] Six states (Mexico, Nuevo Leon, Puebla, Quintana Roo, Tabasco, and Veracruz) plus the Federal District had a rate of 2 percent in 1996 and a rate of 3 percent in 2015.

all states, although only from 2000 to 2015. During this period, revenues increased from 0.17 to 0.41 of a percent of GDP, a net increase of 0.24 of a percent of GDP (SAT 2017). Since by design this tax only applies to salaried workers, this implies that the *combined* federal (1.7 percent) and state (0.24 of a percent) increase in taxes on salaried labor over the period was quite substantial, approximately 1.94 percent of GDP.

The natural reaction of firms and workers to this tax increase is to switch from salaried to non-salaried contracts, to the extent that firms' production technologies and business strategies allow. Another natural reaction is, of course, to change to using illegal salaried contracts, although for the reasons discussed in Chapter 7 this option is open mostly to smaller firms. In any event, both reactions are consistent with the trends described in Chapter 3 and, more importantly here, stylized fact four.

One final observation: the changes just noted imply that by 2015 Mexico had the highest burden of taxes on salaried labor in Latin America, even excluding the state payroll tax (Barreix et al. 2017). Considering federal and state taxes, Mexico's tax burden on salaried employment in 2015 was 3.6 percent of GDP.

Taxation of Firms

Evasion of the corporate income tax by firms in the Régimen de Pequeños Contribuyentes (Repeco) increased between 2000, when firms paid 10.3 percent of what they should have paid, and 2010, when firms paid 3.8 percent (Zamudio, Barajas, and Brown 2011). Accordingly, revenues from Repeco fell from 0.036 of a percent of GDP in 2000 to 0.022 of a percent in 2013 (SAT 2017). Since the statutory rate did not change, this reflects a weakening of states' enforcement efforts, at the margin increasing the profitability of small firms that qualify for this regime. This is consistent with stylized fact four.

Changes in the World of Market Conditions

Contract Enforcement

There is little systematic data to assess changes in the performance of institutions charged with enforcing contracts in Mexico. Some evidence suggests weaker performance, particularly at the state level. Dougherty (2014) notes a deterioration in the index of contract enforceability in two-thirds of all states between 2001 and 2011. This is consistent with the more recent findings of the World Bank's 2016 *Doing Business Report*. A weakening of contract enforcement would strengthen the forces inducing firms to stay small, consistent with stylized fact four.

International Competition

China's entry in 2000 into the World Trade Organization (WTO) represented an important negative shock to firms in Mexico, as they faced greater competition both within Mexico and in the United States, by far Mexico's main export destination.

Blyde et al. (2017) explore the effects of China on the level and composition of manufacturing employment in Mexico.[9] They show that aggregate manufacturing employment fell by approximately 7 percent and that its composition changed, increasing the proportion of informal employees. Artuc, Lederman, and Rojas (2015) also explore the impact of Chinese competition in Mexico, finding as well a negative, although somewhat smaller, impact on aggregate manufacturing employment of approximately 5 percent, and a similar change in composition towards more informal employment. To the extent that increased informality is positively correlated with increased misallocation, these findings suggest that the China shock contributed to stylized fact four.

Two observations are relevant in this context. First, Blyde et al. show that most of the effect of increased Chinese competition was felt between 1998 and 2003, and that by 2013 it had largely dissipated. Second, while the size of the effect is relevant, it is small relative to the size of employment in manufacturing, and smaller relative to all employment.

These observations contrast with the fact that the trends towards increased misallocation and more informality in manufacturing continued after the effects of the China shock had dissipated, and that these trends were observed as well in commerce and services, activities that were not directly exposed to Chinese competition (see Table 3.11 and the discussion therein in Chapter 3). This suggests that while China's entry into the WTO increased informality, because the effect was transitory, relatively small, and confined to manufacturing, it most likely played a secondary role in explaining the sustained economy-wide increase in misallocation.

The Joint Effects of Changes in $E(L,T,M)$ on Misallocation

Table 8.1 complements Table 7.9 in Chapter 7 and summarizes the findings of the previous sections, identifying the main changes in policies behind stylized

---

[9] Blyde at al. (2017) use the same census data and firm classification used in this book. The advantage here is that the 1998 census provides information before the China shock, while the 2003, 2008, and 2013 censuses provide information three, eight, and 13 years after that shock. Their methodology exploits the fact that the degree of Chinese import competition varies across regions of Mexico and captures the effect of both greater Chinese competition with Mexican exports to the United States, and the effect of increased exports from China to Mexico.

Table 8.1: Summary of Impact of Changes in $E(L,T,M)$ between 1996 and 2015

Policy/Institution	Observations/Impacts
Contributory Social Insurance	
Lower subsidies and longer contribution requirements for retirement pensions as the regime changed from defined-benefit to defined-contribution	As new cohorts enter the labor force, there is a gradual decline in the valuation of retirement pensions and higher implicit taxes on salaried contracts
Access to health benefits for retired workers tied to access to the pension; most workers in new regime will not qualify for a pension	Most workers in new regime will not have access to health services when they retire, lowering the valuation of benefits and increasing the implicit tax on salaried contracts
Non-contributory Social Insurance	
Increase in resources for pension, health, and other programs from 0.4 of a percent of GDP in 1996 to 1.7 percent in 2015	Subsidy to non-salaried and illegal salaried contracts increased from 3 to 16.5 percent of workers' earnings over same period
Labor Taxation	
Increases in personal income taxes from 1.6 to 3.3 percent of GDP from 1996 to 2015, practically all concentrated on salaried workers	Higher taxes on salaried contracts
Increases in state payroll taxes on salaried labor from 0.17 to 0.41 of a percent of GDP from 2000 to 2015	Higher taxes on salaried contracts
Firm Taxation	
Increased evasion of Repeco, as revenues fell from 0.036 of a percent GDP in 2000 to 0.022 of a percent in 2015	Increased profitability of small firms
Contract Enforcement	
Falling state indices of contract enforceability in two-thirds of states between 2001 and 2011	Increased bias towards smaller firm size
International Competition	
China's entry into the World Trade Organization in 2000	Fall in manufacturing employment of 5 to 7 percent and change towards more informal labor

Source: Prepared by the author.

fact four. Together, these two tables go a long way in explaining why misallocation in Mexico is so large, and why it has increased.

Figure 8.5 complements Table 8.1, showing some of the trends that can be quantified as a share of GDP. Because of the differences in magnitude, resources for non-contributory programs and revenues from the federal

Figure 8.5: Tax Revenues and Expenditures in Non-contributory Programs, 1996–2015
(Percent of GDP)

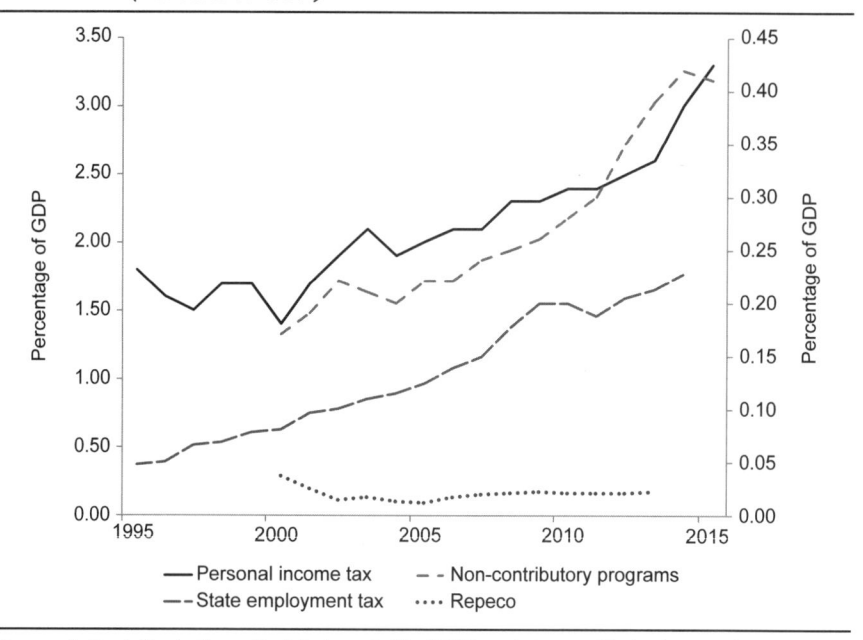

[Line chart showing Personal income tax, Non-contributory programs, State employment tax, and Repeco as percentages of GDP from 1995 to 2015. Personal income tax and Non-contributory programs use the left axis (0.00–3.50); State employment tax and Repeco use the right axis (0.00–0.45).]

— Personal income tax   – – Non-contributory programs
– – State employment tax   ···· Repeco

Source: Author's illustration with data from Antón (2016) and state and federal tax registries.
Note: Resources for non-contributory programs and revenues from the federal income tax on salaried workers are on the left axis; revenues from the state payroll tax and the Régimen de Pequeños Contribuyentes (Repeco) are on the right axis.

income tax on salaried workers are on the left axis, while revenues from the state payroll tax and the Repeco are on the right axis, in both cases measured as a share of GDP. Summing the increase in resources for non-contributory programs (1.3 percentage points of GDP), plus the increase in federal income taxes on salaried workers (1.7 percentage points) plus the increase on state taxes on salaried labor (0.24 of a percentage point) shows that *between 1996 and 2015 there was a shift in resources of 3.24 percentage points of GDP in the direction of taxing salaried and subsidizing non-salaried labor. The direct effect of this shift was to induce firms and workers to opt for non-salaried or illegal salaried contracts—that is, to increase firm informality.*

Because of these changes, by 2015 the combined federal and state burden on salaried labor from payroll taxes equaled 3.6 percent of GDP; in parallel, in that year subsidies to non-salaried labor through non-contributory programs were 1.7 percent of GDP, for a combined tax-cum-subsidy of 5.3 percent of GDP. This contrasts with subsidies to contributory social insurance

Figure 8.6: Simplified View of the Policy Environment, 1996–2015

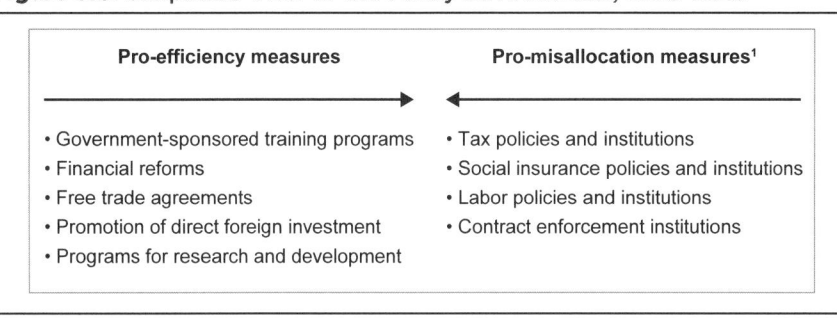

Pro-efficiency measures	Pro-misallocation measures[1]
• Government-sponsored training programs • Financial reforms • Free trade agreements • Promotion of direct foreign investment • Programs for research and development	• Tax policies and institutions • Social insurance policies and institutions • Labor policies and institutions • Contract enforcement institutions

Source: Prepared by the author.
[1] See Tables 7.9 and 8.1 for more detail.

programs of 0.5 of a percent of GDP, and a burden on non-salaried contracts from the federal personal income tax of 0.1 of a percent of GDP.

The effects of these changes need to be complemented with others that cannot be quantified and depicted in Figure 8.5, but that nonetheless work in the same direction: a gradual deterioration in the quality of contract enforceability in some states, and probably a gradual decline in workers' valuation of contributory health and retirement pension programs as the cohort-composition of the labor force changed. In parallel, firms and workers faced transitory shocks such as the entry of China into the WTO.

This summary makes it evident that over the two decades the incentives towards non-salaried contracts and illegal salaried contracts were very strong indeed in Mexico. Of course, during the period under study firms and workers also experienced the benefits of many policy reforms to increase efficiency (which, as mentioned at the beginning of this chapter, are not discussed here). Thus, over the last two decades firms and workers were reacting to a complex and contradictory set of incentives.

Figure 8.6 is a simplified representation of this process. The left column lists policies to improve the allocation of resources and increase productivity. The list is far from exhaustive; it is just meant to be indicative of policies expressly focused on improving efficiency. The right column lists policies that, regardless of their intentions or motivations, de facto operated in the opposite direction.

Unfortunately for Mexico, the evidence indicates that between 1996 and 2015 the forces pushing in the direction of increased misallocation dominated, as evidenced by the trends in resource allocation documented in Tables 3.5, 3.7, and 3.11 in Chapter 3; by the growing dispersion of measures of firms' revenue total factor productivity (TFPR) documented in Table 4.1 in Chapter 4; and by the increase in the number of self-employed workers or workers employed in firms excluded from the census.

The increase in misallocation observed in Mexico in the period considered is clearly disappointing. But it is not an accident, or the result of a random process. It is the rational response of individuals to the contradictory and complex incentives they face. Many individuals opted to be self-employed or to be entrepreneurs and run very small firms because, despite the effects of the policies listed in the left column of Figure 8.6, the policies listed in the right column made it profitable to do so. Similarly, despite the left column, many low-productivity firms survived or entered the marketplace because of policies in the right column, and for the same reasons many high-productivity firms did not grow as much as they could have given their underlying potential, or even exited the market when they should have stayed. And yet again because of policies in the right column, the investments made in workers' education failed to translate into higher earnings.

From the point of view of productivity, policies listed in the right column of Figure 8.6 acted as Penelope in Homer's Odyssey, unknitting during the night the efforts made during the day by policies in the left column. *At the end of the day, total factor productivity stagnated.*

CHAPTER 9

Conclusions

Why Has Prosperity Eluded Mexico?

Most answers to this question start from the premise that for the period considered in this book, prosperity has not eluded Mexico because the country lacked proper macroeconomic management or failed to integrate into the world economy. This is consistent with the facts discussed in Chapter 1. Rather, most answers focus on the fact that total factor productivity (TFP) stagnated, consistent in turn with the growth accounting decompositions summarized in that chapter. Thus, the question posed above can be reformulated as follows: Why is it that in a context of macroeconomic stability and an open trade and investment regime, productivity has failed to grow?

One answer emphasizes the relation between investment and productivity, under the assumption that firms' investments automatically translate into new capital goods embodying better technologies and more complex processes that make workers more productive. In this view, productivity growth is driven by the investment rate, and insufficient investment is central to explaining the country's stagnant productivity. This view may be relevant to other countries but is inconsistent with two facts about Mexico discussed in Chapters 4 and 5: first, that during the period analyzed the investment rate increased gradually but TFP stagnated, and second, that many investments were made in low-productivity firms, while higher-productivity firms failed to attract more capital. This indicates that in Mexico's case, the problem is that some investments are partly wasted in firms that should not survive in the market—or, worse still, grow—while investments in more productive firms fail to take place. As discussed at various points, more investment would probably raise the growth rate. But why, as things stand, would it increase productivity if it has not done so before?

Another answer focuses on human capital. The view here is that insufficient investments in education or low-quality schooling imply that Mexico's labor force lacks the skills and abilities required by modern technologies. Again, this view might be relevant to other countries, but it is inconsistent with three facts documented in Chapter 6. First, there have been large increases in the schooling of the population. Second, the evidence points to increasing educational quality. And third, there is no empirical evidence of excess demand for high-quality workers with more schooling. In fact, the evidence points in the opposite direction. Of course, more human capital would raise the growth rate. But why, if current conditions continue, should the impact of more human capital on productivity in the future be different than in the past?

Yet a third answer highlights uncompetitive behavior in key sectors of the economy such as telecommunications or energy. Without denying that this behavior is a source of misallocation, the problem with this view is that it fails to explain why it would affect firms depending on the contractual composition of their labor force. Uncompetitive behavior by firms supplying key intermediate inputs lowers the profitability of all firms, formal and informal, large and small. But it cannot induce the productivity rankings documented in Chapter 4, nor the increase in misallocation documented in Chapter 3. Furthermore, if the rents extracted by uncompetitive practices in energy or telecommunications were a significant component of firms' costs, firm entry and survival would be substantially more selective than what was documented in Chapter 5, as only higher-productivity firms could pay those rents. Undoubtedly, more competition in energy and telecommunications is beneficial for many reasons. But why would it correct the biases in the size and type distribution of firms and the dysfunctional firm dynamics that lie at the root of Mexico's productivity problem?

A similar observation applies to a fourth answer: that productivity growth has been absent because of insufficient investments in infrastructure. Once again, without denying that more infrastructure is welcome, this view is problematic because it fails to explain why insufficient infrastructure tilts the size and type distribution of firms in the direction documented in Chapter 3, produces the productivity rankings documented in Chapter 4, or induces the dysfunctional firm dynamics documented in Chapter 5. All firms should be affected similarly by insufficient infrastructure. Indeed, why is the formal-informal composition of firms in Mexico City—the largest urban conglomerate in the country and presumably the one with the best infrastructure—no different than in the rest of the country?

Finally, a fifth answer stresses that malfunctioning institutions account for stagnant productivity. Cast at such a general level, this view is not so much right or wrong as it is uninformative of the specific institutions that hurt productivity and the mechanisms by which they do so. Not all institutions in Mexico that bear on economic activity malfunction. Take, for instance, the central bank, an important institution to say the least, but one that can hardly be held responsible for the size and type distribution of firms and the large self-employment described in Chapter 3, or the patterns of firm entry, survival, and exit described in Chapter 5. The subset of institutions that is hurting productivity in Mexico is not doing so randomly—those institutions are inducing specific patterns of resource allocation and firm dynamics that need to be explained.

The answer offered in this book can be captured in a nutshell: *productivity growth stagnated because of large and persistent misallocation*. This answer coincides with the view that Mexico's macroeconomic management has, overall, been sound, and that on balance the country has gained from integrating into the world economy. These are not the reasons why Mexico has underperformed. It also coincides with the view that malfunctioning institutions are a serious impediment to productivity growth. But the book advanced beyond that general statement to identify the specific institutions involved and the mechanisms through which they negatively affect the behavior of workers and entrepreneurs. In parallel, however, the book argued that even if all institutions worked perfectly, there are policies that bias the size and contractual composition of firms in ways that are detrimental to productivity. It is not all about malfunctioning institutions; some policies are deeply problematic.

To buttress the answer offered, this book documented that by international standards misallocation in Mexico is large, and that it increased in the last two decades despite a higher investment rate and a more educated workforce. It also documented that misallocation has specific patterns associated with, first, the contractual structure of firms and, second, their size. The book then provided evidence to show that these patterns affect the process of firm entry, exit, and survival. It further argued that the patterns in the size and type distribution of firms associated with misallocation were partly responsible for the falling returns to education in the period considered. In turn, the book contended that the observed static and dynamic patterns of misallocation were the rational response of workers and entrepreneurs to the country's social and economic environment—symbolized by *E(L,T,M)*—and did not result from insufficient entrepreneurship, lack of risk-taking, unwillingness to work, or deficient skills and abilities.

At the end of the day, Mexico cannot prosper when significant amounts of investments are channeled to low-productivity projects; when many individuals are engaged in activities for which they have little if any comparative advantage; when there is a weak connection between firm productivity and firm survival and entry; when incentives are stacked against the growth of productive firms; when large firm churning and labor turnover is mostly useless; when production is scattered over a plethora of self-employed individuals or small units, and economies of scale and scope are under-exploited; when illegal behavior is implicitly subsidized; when entrepreneurs and banks are uncertain whether the law will be applied expeditiously and fairly if contracts are breached; when investments in education are underutilized; and when workers have few opportunities to learn on the job or receive training from the firms that hire them.

Many factors in Mexico's $E(L,T,M)$ explain these outcomes. The discussion in Chapters 7 and 8 identified the most important ones and traced the mechanisms by which they affected the behavior of workers and entrepreneurs. Although the analysis in these chapters was not exhaustive, the claim is that the factors discussed in them are the most relevant. This is so because these factors—summarized in Tables 7.9 and 8.1—are consistent with the occupational choices, patterns of misallocation and firm dynamics, increases in misallocation, and falling returns to education and to experience documented in Chapters 3 to 6. *The various pieces of the puzzle make up a coherent whole.*

The book's findings were made possible by using information from Mexico's Economic Census and Employment Surveys. Of course, using these data does not imply that the results are right, and there may yet be other explanations of why productivity growth stagnated in Mexico. But hopefully those explanations will also be based on these rich and informative data sets. It would be a pity if the debate on Mexico's growth underperformance ignored them.

Understanding the technical reasons responsible for under-rewarding everybody's efforts, as this book has strived to do, is essential for crafting the way forward. But it is still insufficient because the obvious next question is: *Why does the policymaking process result in institutions and policies that are so punishing to productivity?* Tables 7.9 and 8.1 are the product of a complex interaction between beliefs originating in the country's history, societal understandings and discourse, and political equilibriums between the government and various groups. Beliefs, understandings, and interests shape the space and determine the constraints under which the government sets policies and carries out core functions like collecting revenues, enforcing contracts, and pursuing social objectives. In other words, Tables 7.9 and 8.1 are not an accident; they have their *raison d'être*. Analyzing these reasons exceeds the limits of this book, but a few remarks may complement the analysis of the two previous chapters and shed some light on the way forward.

History and Deeply-Held Beliefs

The first revolution of the 20th century took place in Mexico. A central feature of the constitution that emanated from it was a strong mandate to promote social welfare through various means, such as land redistribution, universal and free basic education, and, critically to our purposes here, detailed provisions on workers' rights. These provisions reflected an ideal, but also embodied beliefs about the efficacy of the specific policies deployed to reach that ideal.[1]

One belief was that obligating firms to pay for the social insurance of their workers was an effective policy to redistribute income in their favor, while protecting them from illness, disability, and other risks. As a by-product of this belief, Mexico's social insurance system was born truncated, completely dependent on the salaried status of workers. This was not the intention. In fact, the expectation was that social insurance would eventually cover the whole labor force. In his inaugural address on December 1, 1940, President Avila Camacho stated that: "We should all pursue the goal, to which I shall devote my full energies, that soon social security laws protect *all* Mexicans [author's emphasis] in times of adversity, when children are orphaned, when women are widowed, in sickness, unemployment and old-age, to replace the hardships that we have all experienced as a result of the poverty of the Nation."

Another belief was that severely restricting firms' abilities to dismiss workers was an effective policy to bring about job stability and ensure workers' permanent access to social insurance and other work-related benefits. In his proposal to Congress to reform Mexico's Labor Law, President López Mateos argued that economic reasons were not justified causes for dismissal: "The stability of workers in their jobs…goes together with the idea of social insurance.…It would be paradoxical if through social insurance workers enjoyed security when they are no longer working, but not while they give their physical energy and intellectual ability to somebody else. The compensation received by workers when they are unjustly dismissed does not compensate for all the damage suffered by them."[2]

These beliefs were reflected in various laws, which in turn created key institutions such as the labor tribunals (Juntas de Conciliación y Arbitraje – JCAs), the social security institute (Instituto Mexicano del Seguro Social – IMSS), and the housing institute (Instituto del Fondo Nacional para la Vivienda de los Trabajadores – Infonavit).[3] And yet another belief, implicit in this case, was that these policies and associated institutions would not deter the expansion

---

[1] The constitution was promulgated in 1917, and its Article 123—the key provision related to labor—in part reflected grievances and abuses suffered by Mexican workers prior to the revolution. In part, however, it also reflected the ideological debates waged worldwide at that time regarding the need for public interventions to protect workers and, equally if not more importantly, the specific policies used to pursue this objective.

[2] Seventh "Whereas" of the prelude (*Exposición de Motivos*) to the reform of the Federal Labor Law, December 27, 1961. The author thanks Angel Calderón for bringing this text to his attention.

[3] These institutions would, literally, protect individuals from birth to death. Infants would be born in IMSS hospitals and cared for in IMSS day care centers. Families would live in IMSS-provided housing (a responsibility later strengthened with the creation of Infonavit) and, in addition to

of salaried employment. But beliefs and intentions notwithstanding, in the end wage-based contributory programs can only apply to workers employed by firms that pay wages; and dismissal regulations can only apply to subordinated workers who can be dismissed by the firms that employ them. *Paradoxically, a system conceived for social inclusion ended up excluding more than half of the labor force.*

Yet, leaving non-salaried workers without coverage was incompatible with the social ideals of the constitution, and the aspiration to a more encompassing social contract. Given the constitutionally driven association of social insurance with salaried labor, however, to expand coverage policy-makers had no choice but to create non-contributory programs.[4] And while rarely stated, an accompanying belief was that these programs would not interfere with firms' and workers' contractual choices, nor therefore with the country's growth potential.

The point that needs to be highlighted here is that the problems with the regulations of L in $E(L,T,M)$ discussed in Tables 7.9 and 8.1 do not stem from the objective of protecting workers against the loss of employment and providing them with health, pension, and other benefits, or from the objective of redistributing income in their favor. They stem from the beliefs that these objectives could be reached through a specific combination of policies: strict restrictions on dismissal and contributory programs, inevitably complemented with non-contributory ones. In other words, the issue is not with the end, but with the beliefs in the means to achieve that end.

These beliefs have persisted, even though a century after the constitution came into effect more than half of workers in Mexico are excluded from the coverage of dismissal regulations and contributory programs; even though all empirical studies show that the incidence of social insurance contributions

---

receiving health services from the IMSS, exercise in IMSS sports facilities, take holidays at IMSS vacation centers, purchase food and other household supplies in IMSS stores, and attend IMSS theatres. During retirement workers would receive a pension from the IMSS. Finally, the IMSS would provide funerary services. In parallel, the JCAs would ensure job stability, since access to all these benefits depended on workers' salaried status. In other words, these institutions were expected to be the cornerstone of Mexico's welfare state and key components of its social contract.

[4] Kaplan and Levy (2104) review the origins of social insurance in Latin America and argue that, mutatis mutandis, a comparable situation can be observed in other countries of the region. They make an illustrative contrast with basic education, where the commitment to universal and free coverage is not associated with workers' status in the labor market, and where therefore the salaried/non-salaried and formal/informal distinctions are irrelevant. As in Mexico, less than half of the region's labor force is covered by contributory social insurance, but coverage of basic education is practically universal. The difference is not in the objective of universal coverage, but in the beliefs in the policies that can effectively achieve those objectives.

is mostly borne by workers (Antón, Hernández, and Levy 2012); even though workers' transits between formal and informal status imply that the effectiveness of social insurance is low (Levy 2008); and even though the inefficiencies created by dismissal regulations and the segmentation of social insurance contribute to the large misallocation that limits workers' opportunities to get better jobs and earn higher wages over their lifetime.

Social Advancement, Inequality, and Political Discourse

Since the 1980s, Mexico's constitutional commitment to improved living standards and more equality has been undermined by low growth. Society's aspirations for advancement have not been fully realized. After the 1994–1995 crisis, there was growing impatience that macroeconomic stability was not reflected in higher earnings. The resulting frustration, underpinned by the country's large inequalities, generated political demands for policies to compensate, at least in part, for the stagnant earnings associated with low growth.

In this context, social policy was called on to do the job that economic policy was unable to do. As part of this process, a redistributive political discourse developed in which policies perceived to be regressive were by and large ruled out, and policies perceived to be redistributive or directed towards social aims were adopted, in both cases regardless of whether they helped or hurt productivity. Also as part of the process, intertemporal trade-offs were strongly tilted in the direction of current consumption. This discourse was understandable, but this did not imply that the adopted policies would attain their stated objectives, much less reduce misallocation and increase growth, closing an unfortunate circle.

Two elements of this redistributive political discourse stand behind Tables 7.9 and 8.1. The first indicates that small firms play an important social role and that public policy should support them. At times this is justified on the basis that these firms are responsible for most job creation, although at times vaguer considerations are invoked.[5] Whatever the motivation, supporting these firms enters political discourse and becomes the policy objective. Never mind that from the point of view of productivity this is the wrong objective. As documented in Chapter 4, medium-size and larger (mostly formal) firms are substantially more productive than smaller (mostly informal) ones. To

---

[5] Language is illustrative of the view that small firms are special. On occasions they are called "social enterprises" (*empresas sociales*), even though they are employing workers and producing goods for the market like any other firm.

raise productivity the former should attract more resources and the latter less. However, as documented in Chapter 7, medium-size and large firms are discriminated against by Mexico's $E(L,T,M)$ and face greater difficulties attracting more resources.

Without denying the relevance of administrative considerations motivating the dual Repeco-general corporate tax regime discussed in Chapter 7, this dual regime also reflects a political discourse that emphasizes the need to support small firms for "social" reasons, along with the view that special tax regimes are effective policies to do so. And without denying the relevance of political groups that de facto administer property rights in the main avenues and streets of Mexico's cities and extract rents from small firms carrying out their activities there, the governmental tolerance and forbearance shown towards the millions of self-employed individuals and small firms on those avenues and streets stealing electricity from the grid, evading taxes and fees, and violating zoning and safety regulations also stems from the view that these firms are special and need help (and, in any event, the thinking goes, where else would these workers find a job?).

The issue transcends tolerance for activity on the streets. Small firms, regardless of whether they carry out their activities in the streets or in fixed premises, are also aided through subsidized credits and other government programs specially designed for them, in addition to the policies listed in Tables 7.9 and 8.1. The fact that many of these firms trap workers in mostly informal low-productivity jobs, reduce the demand for workers with more years of education, take market share from productive firms limiting the number of productive jobs, and hurt productivity and growth, becomes secondary to a political discourse stating that social welfare is enhanced by promoting small mostly informal firms (accompanied by the discourse, *comme il faut*, that these manifestations of economic activity are transitory and will fade away as economic growth accelerates).

The second element of political discourse indicates that exemptions to the value-added tax (VAT) are an effective way to raise the welfare of low-income households. The fact that given Mexico's large income inequality most of the revenue foregone from these exemptions is captured by higher-income households, that these exemptions contribute to foster informality and misallocation, and that there are better mechanisms to transfer income to low-income households is secondary to a political discourse that considers that exemptions to the VAT should be part of the country's social policy.

In turn, a byproduct of these elements of political discourse is to significantly constrain policymakers' options in the design of tax policy. Revenues from the VAT are substantially below their potential given the exemption regimes and the difficulties of enforcement associated with them; revenue from the corporate income tax is also depressed given that most firms qualify for the Repeco. In parallel, limited coverage of contributory social insurance programs reduces revenues from wage-based contributions and increases spending on non-contributory programs. In this context, the pressures to collect revenues from payroll taxes, including state-level ones, are high indeed. Put differently, high payroll taxes partly reflect the constrained choices of policymakers in a context where political discourse limits the revenue potential of other taxes.[6]

While evidently many other considerations affect the design of Mexico's tax system, the point here is that the policies and institutions behind T in $E(L,T,M)$ discussed in Tables 7.9 and 8.1 partly derive from political discourse about the efficacy of exemptions to the VAT as redistributive instruments, and of special tax regimes for small firms as tools to increase social welfare.

The net result is an environment $E(L,T,M)$ where the high-productivity segment of the economy is heavily taxed, and the low-productivity segment strongly subsidized. This is not, of course, what policy aimed at doing.[7] In principle policy should aim to tax high-income individuals (regardless of whether they are workers or entrepreneurs) and subsidize low-income ones. But this tax-cum-subsidy combination is what policy ended up doing—the almost unavoidable result of expanding social insurance, creating jobs, and pursuing redistribution in the very constrained policy context resulting from deeply held beliefs about L and political discourse about T.

The Role of Interest Groups

Tables 7.9 and 8.1 also reflect particular interests in at least two ways. First, quite obviously, are the interests of the small subset of large public sector unions that are partly responsible for the low quality of public services, and of the very small subset of private firms in oligopolistic markets that extract rents and are partly responsible for the misallocation of firm credit (see the essays in Levy and Walton 2009). Second are the interests—less visible but potentially more important—of groups standing in the way of effective rule of law.

---

[6] In the case of state payroll taxes, they also reflect a context in which state governments can, so to speak, piggyback on federal payroll taxes at little political and administrative cost, rather than raise revenues from other sources that are more visible and politically costly (like taxes on automobiles or surcharges on federal fuel taxes).

[7] A central result of optimal tax design is that tax systems should maintain full production efficiency even in second-best environments (Diamond and Mirrlees 1971).

Certainly, imperfect contract enforcement does not result from the lack of public funds to operate property registries, pay for the salaries of judges and magistrates, construct buildings where trials can be held, and hire police to enforce rulings. Nor is it a result of shortcomings in the abilities of Mexican lawyers. Imperfect enforcement is a byproduct of a weak rule of law, a situation that allows the exercise of discretionary power by public officials to favor themselves and a tiny number of very large firms and influential individuals, and that facilitates influence-peddling, impunity, and corruption.

As opposed to the case of L and T, imperfect contract enforcement does not reflect deeply held beliefs or political discourse. In this case the issue is different. The centrality of the rule of law to societal well-being is broadly recognized and paid lip service by all. The issue is that powerful groups—politicians, firms, unions—obstruct and undermine the effective operation of the institutions in charge of enforcing contracts and applying competition laws. The elements of M in $E(L,T,M)$ discussed in Tables 7.9 and 8.1 reflect the functioning of a society in which a few powerful groups benefit from rent extraction and influence-peddling. It is not that these groups are intent on interfering in all commercial or credit contracts or in all competition disputes. It is that it is not possible to have judicial institutions that work well except when some powerful group needs them not to work well. Thus, perhaps unintentionally but not for that less effectively, these powerful groups increase misallocation.[8]

In sum, Tables 7.9 and 8.1 result from the interplay between beliefs, political discourse, and interests—an interplay that constrains policymakers' choices with regards to policies to create jobs, collect taxes, redistribute income, and provide social insurance, and that in turn traps Mexico in a low-productivity low-growth equilibrium. And while the remarks in this section are schematic and incomplete, they hopefully make the point that *it is impossible to understand why prosperity has eluded Mexico without considering the belief systems, political processes, and interest groups behind large and persistent misallocation.*

Recent Policy Reforms

During 2014 and 2015, Mexico carried out significant policy reforms. The authority of the Federal Competition Commission—Mexico's anti-trust

---

[8] In a historical essay examining long-term growth in Europe, Mokyr (2017, 18) observes that "An economy that grows as a result of favorable institutions requires a world of well-delineated and respected property rights, enforceable contracts, law and order, a low level of opportunism and rent-seeking, a high degree of inclusion in political decision making and the benefits of growth, and a political organization in which power and wealth are as separate as humanly possible." That is a very relevant observation when thinking about Mexico.

agency—was enhanced. The same occurred with Mexico's specialized body to regulate telecommunications, the Instituto Federal de Telecomunicaciones (Ifetel). More significantly given the country's history, the monopoly position of state-owned enterprises in energy was ended and the sector was opened to domestic and foreign private investment. In parallel, a reform was launched to increase the quality of basic education through improved mechanisms for teacher selection and promotion.

These are profound and welcome changes. As noted in Chapter 1, reforms in energy and telecommunications will increase consumers' welfare, and likely raise the investment rate and thus the rate of GDP growth.

The effects of these reforms are evidently not reflected in the census data used here that cover only through 2013. Looking forward, it is difficult to judge what will be their impact on aggregate productivity. Entry of new competitors in energy and telecommunications will most likely increase the productivity of resources in those sectors. But these sectors absorb a relatively small share of aggregate resources. Entrants would need to have significantly higher productivity relative to incumbents to have a noticeable impact on aggregate productivity. On the other hand, because energy is a widely used intermediate input, the gains from a more certain and competitive supply can result in larger gains in aggregate productivity than the direct gains from the increased productivity of resources in that sector. To a lesser extent, the same could be true of telecommunications.

The reform enhancing the authority and autonomy of the Federal Competition Commission could potentially be beneficial to productivity, although of course this depends on the effectiveness of the commission's efforts. As Chapter 7 discussed, market concentration in banking and non-banking sectors is one of the reasons behind the low level of credit to firms and its misallocation towards larger but not necessarily more productive ones.

Assessing the effects of these reforms is beyond the scope of this book, but a point to make is that they mostly focus on a subset of policies and institutions in the "world of market conditions"—M in $E(L, T, M)$. By and large, they have little or no impact on the policies in L and T that, as discussed, are central to misallocation in Mexico. Nor do they address the issues of contract enforceability in M that also contribute to misallocation.

This point is key. If the analysis in this book is broadly correct, the Mexican economy in the years ahead will be subject to the same contradictory forces shown in Figure 8.6. Some elements of the "world of market conditions"—M in $E(L,T,M)$—will push in the direction of better resource allocation, partly as a result of recent reforms. And some other elements, notably those associated with the "world of entrepreneur-worker relations" L and the "world of taxation" T, but also some from the "world of market conditions" M, will continue to pull, as they have done over the past two decades, in the direction of increased misallocation.

A critical question in this context is whether more competition in product markets can reduce misallocation while the tax, labor, and social insurance policies described above persist, along with the deficiencies in contract enforcement. In other words, can changes to policies governing product markets substitute for changes to policies governing contracts between parties, taxation, and relations between entrepreneurs and workers?

It is difficult to provide a definitive answer to these questions, but it is unlikely that the answer is positive. On the one hand, more abundant credit when labor, social insurance, and tax regulations are far from optimal may in fact increase misallocation, as the discussion in Chapter 7 pointed out. On the other, the biases towards non-salaried contracts and small size that are at the core of misallocation in Mexico are unlikely to be corrected simply by more competitive product markets. Smaller firms will continue to have advantages from the design of the tax system, and firms will continue to have preferences for non-salaried contracts because of the asymmetries in tax, labor, and social insurance regulations, as analyzed in Chapter 7.

But that is not all. In the years ahead, Mexico will experience population aging and pressures to expand the scope of pension, health, and other social benefits. Under the current social insurance architecture, this will likely translate into more resources for non-contributory programs, strengthening in turn the forces towards firm informality and more misallocation. The other side of this process will be the need to increase the tax burden. But under the current tax architecture, additional revenues will most likely derive from a combination of enhanced enforcement and increased tax rates on formal firms and workers, leading again to more misallocation. In other words, the forces pushing towards more taxes on formality and more subsidies to informality are deeply embedded in the current architecture of L and T in $E(L,T,M)$, and are unlikely to be overcome by more competition in product markets, as welcome as that competition would be.

The reform to improve the quality of basic education needs separate mention. As pointed out in Chapter 6, improving Mexico's human capital is very welcome for many reasons, and therefore so is the reform. However, its potentially positive effects on productivity will be felt many years in the future when youngsters receiving a better education today because of the reform enter the labor force and gradually replace workers currently in the labor force (who will not directly benefit from the reform). In any event, actual outcomes will depend on the degree of misallocation in the future, given that the connection between increased human capital and higher productivity is not automatic.

Rethinking Policy Priorities

Priorities for Growth

Discussions on productivity and growth in Mexico often result in a long list of measures: better infrastructure; more and higher-quality education; entrepreneurship programs to foster technology adoption; resources for research and development; public-private partnerships to resolve coordination failures or exploit complementarities between firms; institutions to protect intellectual property rights; venture funds to facilitates firms' access to capital; trade agreements to increase competition and expand markets; government-sponsored training programs for workers; sector-specific interventions to remove bottlenecks; firm credit from development banks; direct foreign investment in technologically advanced areas; and so on.

In the future, some of these measures may be the most relevant ones to raise productivity and accelerate growth in Mexico. But the discussion in Chapters 7 and 8 points out that they are not focused on the roots of the country's *current* productivity problem. It is not that these measures are flawed and should not be pursued; it is that so long as the issues identified in Tables 7.9 and 8.1 persist, the efforts invested in such measures will be underrewarded. In a different context they could all be more valuable.

In the end, aggregate productivity is the outcome of the decisions of millions of individuals responding to a complex set of incentives and constraints. The measures listed above remove constraints and tilt incentives in the direction of better resource allocation. *But they fight against a powerful undertow of incentives and constraints that are continuously pulling in the opposite direction, and that affect all individuals participating in all areas of economic activity.* Judged by the empirical evidence presented in Chapters 3 to 6, in the last two decades the latter set of incentives and constraints, summarized in Tables 7.9 and 8.1, had the upper hand. While a subset of productive firms expanded and attracted some resources, a substantially larger subset of unproductive firms ended up absorbing more resources, and aggregate productivity stagnated.

Looking forward, it is essential to rethink priorities. Without denying the usefulness of the measures listed, nor suggesting that they be abandoned, or ruling out that in the future some should occupy center-stage, *at present* the most effective route to raise productivity and accelerate growth in Mexico is to reform the main policies and institutions that stand behind misallocation. Governments cannot do everything at the same time, at least not with the same efficacy. Political capital and administrative capabilities are scarce resources that should be directed to the undertakings that yield the highest rewards. Fiscal resources are equally scarce, as is societal attention.

In this context, there needs to be a policy shift to give the highest priority to substantively redesigning Mexico's tax-cum-social-insurance-cum-labor-protection system, and to strengthening the country's judicial institutions, with the twin objectives of improving social protection and aligning workers' and firms' incentives in the direction of higher productivity. In essence, this shift consists of four tasks:

- De-linking social insurance from the salaried/non-salaried status of workers. Risks common to all types of employment (illness, death, disability, and longevity) should be financed from the same source of revenue, and services should be provided to all workers with equal scope and quality. Risks specific to salaried employment—like work accidents in the factory or dismissal by a boss—should be financed by a source of revenue associated with salaried contracts.
- Replacing severance pay regulations with proper unemployment insurance, ideally associated with labor training schemes, allowing firms to dismiss workers in response to negative output shocks or labor-saving technical change. Critically, unemployed workers should also be protected by social insurance, breaking the association between job stability and access to social insurance, and protecting workers against risks at all times.
- Eliminating all exemptions to the VAT, compensating low-income households for the real income loss, reducing payroll taxes (including state-level ones), and reconsidering the dual corporate tax regime, with the objective of balancing the tax rate across firms of different sizes.
- Increasing the autonomy of judicial institutions in charge of contract enforcement while increasing transparency and accountability, simplifying the adjudication process and strengthening arbitration, and modernizing public property registries.

Considered *in toto*, the first three tasks represent a significant shift in tax, labor, and social insurance policies. These tasks are technically complex and generate intense ideological debates. On the other hand, the fourth task is in principle not subject to much ideological debate, but presents a serious political challenge: stronger, more transparent, and more accountable judicial institutions would serve to combat the influence-peddling and corruption that are often part of the modus operandi of politics in Mexico. Undoubtedly, these four tasks are extremely difficult. But, that recognized, *at present they are at the core of Mexico's growth agenda.*

From the point of view of productivity, the objectives are to narrow as much as possible the differences between the costs of salaried and non-salaried labor to firms, replacing wage-based contributions for social insurance with other sources of revenue; to minimize the incentives to evade labor and social insurance regulations and stop subsidizing the hiring of salaried workers illegally; to eliminate the implicit subsidizes to small, unproductive firms and the barriers to firm growth associated with the current dual corporate tax regime; to eliminate the deterrent to hiring salaried workers associated with dismissal regulations, giving firms flexibility to adjust their labor force and certainty about their labor costs; and to give firms and banks certainty that the law will be enforced expeditiously when contracts are breached.

From the social point of view, the objectives are to improve benefits to workers by offering them the same coverage against common risks regardless of whether they are salaried, non-salaried, or transitorily unemployed; to ensure that this coverage is a social right all the time and not, as currently, only when workers are salaried; to replace the uncertainty, delays, high legal costs, and at times corruption associated with severance pay with the certainty and timeliness of unemployment insurance; and to give workers better opportunities to augment their human capital and increase their earnings through their life cycle.

This is not a book about policy reform, and many specifics would need to be discussed if these tasks were to be tackled. These tasks should be thought of as the broad strokes of where policy needs to go, not as rigid prescriptions. There is no perfect model of tax, labor protection, and social insurance provision, and there are always difficult trade-offs. There are many views as to how publicly funded health services should be provided, how the pension system should be set up, what combination of taxes should replace revenues from wage-based social insurance contributions, how unemployment insurance should be structured, what the right level of corporate and payroll taxes should be, and so on.[9] There are also many views about the reforms required to improve the functioning of institutions in charge of contract enforcement. Moreover, not everything can be done at the same time, and some reforms have longer gestation periods than others. Sequencing clearly matters.

---

[9] Antón, Hernández, and Levy (2012) present quantitative estimates of the proposal made in Levy (2008) to eliminate exemptions to the VAT and use the proceeds to compensate the poor and fund universal social benefits. Bobba, Flabbi, and Levy (2017) also make quantitative estimates of the fiscal costs of unifying the health component of social insurance. Of course, these proposals can be improved upon and need to be complemented with others for taxes and unemployment insurance.

It is tempting to delve into a technical discussion of these proposals. But while this discussion is clearly very important, it is not at present the main issue. What is critical at this juncture is to arrive at a collective understanding that Mexico's tax-cum-social-insurance-cum-labor-protection system is the main obstacle to faster growth and improved worker welfare, and that it is urgent to search for a better alternative.

Developing such an understanding would provoke a much-needed discussion about the scope of social insurance. Should it continue to include housing? What about sports, cultural facilities, and vacation centers? Such an understanding would also provoke much-needed discussion about the generosity of social insurance benefits. Should pensions be X or Y? Should health services cover W or Z? And it would provoke discussion about the role that institutions like the IMSS and Infonavit should play, and about the alternatives to unemployment insurance (a centralized fund or individual accounts?).

In addition, such an understanding would encourage equally needed discussions about the objectives of programs to support small firms—that is, whether their purpose should be to create any jobs or productive jobs, or to promote smallness for its own sake—as well as about the objectives of exemptions to consumption taxes (to transfer income to all or only to the poor?). In parallel, that understanding would promote an examination of the balance between taxes on income, consumption, and other sources of revenues. Critically, there should also be a discussion of the extent to which tax, labor, and social insurance policies fit together in a coherent incentive structure, something that at present they evidently fail to do. These issues, together with the options to improve the functioning of institutions in charge of enforcing contracts, are the ones that need to be at the core of the debates to accelerate growth in Mexico.

Ideally, these discussions would result in a vision of the tax-cum-social-insurance-cum-labor- protection system that the country should aim to have. This vision would provide clear direction for policy—a compass, so to speak, for what would inevitably be a long and complex reform process. This compass would help Mexico break out of the cycle of isolated and often inconsistent reforms that has characterized the country in the past. It would also help prevent the country from pursuing reforms that for other countries may have the highest priority, but at present for Mexico do not. Finally, such a compass would prevent Mexico from diverting attention, political capital, and fiscal resources to promoting policies that happen to be the latest fad in international forums or academic circles. *To put it bluntly: Mexico's tax-cum-social-insurance-cum-labor-protection system is broken, and the country needs to fix it to accelerate growth. Until this is done, other measures will help, but their impact will be second-order.*

Priorities for Social Policy

Discussions on social welfare, poverty, and inequality in Mexico also result in a long list of measures: tax exemptions for consumption goods, subsidies to contributory social insurance programs, extension of health insurance and day care services to informal workers through non-contributory programs, pensions for the elderly who lack them, special tax regimes for "social enterprises," micro-credits for self-employed individuals or very small firms, conditional cash transfer programs, food distribution programs, a basic guaranteed income for all, higher minimum wages, and so on.

While the motivation for these measures is understandable, particularly given Mexico's context of high inequality and slow growth, some will make it more difficult to reach the desired aims. In the end, improved living standards are the outcome of a two-pronged process: on the one hand, a growing economy, where increasingly educated workers find opportunities in better firms, and where productive entrepreneurs flourish; and on the other, effective social programs to protect all against risks and to redistribute to those in need.

Unfortunately, at times discussions of policies to increase social welfare ignore the fact that some of these policies cause misallocation. As Chapter 7 showed, policies that segment social insurance into contributory and non-contributory programs, and policies on dismissal, are partly responsible for the scarcity of jobs in productive firms with opportunities for increasing earnings.

But there is another side to this coin. Independent of their impact on misallocation, these policies are ineffective judged from the perspective of their *own* objectives. The scope of contributory and non-contributory programs differs. But in large measure because of the large firm churning documented in Chapter 5, individual workers transit between formal and informal jobs, and thus between being covered by contributory and non-contributory programs, a context in which neither pension nor health programs work well. In parallel, because dismissal regulations limit salaried employment, they cover less than half of the labor force, and those covered receive tardy and uncertain benefits when dismissed. Mexican workers thus lose doubly: they are not well protected by current social insurance and labor regulations, and they face few opportunities for career advancement partly because of the misallocation induced by these regulations.

Social policy should not proceed under the assumption that the level of self-employment, the number, type, and size of firms in Mexico, and the quality of jobs that they offer to workers are independent of how social insurance programs and labor regulations are structured. Nor should social policies be oblivious to the sources of revenues used to finance them.

As things stand today, what Mexican workers need most are productive firms that can offer them stable jobs where they can take advantage of the education that they have invested in, and where they can learn on the job and increase their earnings over their lifetime. Social programs cannot substitute for good firms that can provide workers with those jobs. Workers would be better off if instead of the current combination of policies, they were all covered by a single system of social insurance and had access to unemployment insurance, there were more good jobs, and the revenues foregone from special regimes for small firms and exemptions to the VAT were used instead to lower federal and state payroll taxes, and to compensate poor households with direct income transfers.

In other words, the policy shift sketched above to accelerate growth is by and large the policy shift that would improve workers' welfare. This does not imply, of course, reducing social spending or limiting the aims of social policy. On the contrary, *the policy shift proposed would result in more social spending, better protection against risks, and more redistribution.* But it does imply the urgency of realizing that, as things stand in Mexico today, reducing misallocation is indispensable to achieve the objectives of social policy, and should thus be an explicit aim of such policy.

This is the context in which recent proposals to raise minimum wages or introduce a basic universal income should be assessed. In other countries these proposals could well be appropriate, indeed desirable. But *in Mexico's current context*, while understandable, they are questionable. Is increasing the cost of salaried workers desirable given that firms employing non-salaried workers are the most unproductive of all? On the other hand, given the transfers already in place, wouldn't the additional fiscal resources required for a universal basic income be better spent fixing $E(L,T,M)$? Wouldn't workers be better off if they all had the same social benefits including unemployment insurance, and if they had better chances of obtaining higher-paying jobs, rather than receiving another transfer but continuing with a status quo that under-rewards their own efforts? More generally, one can question whether the country should pursue redistribution through policies that, no matter how appealing, fail to address the reasons behind its slow-growing economy, and that in fact could exacerbate those reasons, hurting all along the way. One can question as well whether, at least from a fiscal point of view, this is a sustainable strategy over the medium term. And one can question, finally, whether lasting prosperity can be built ignoring the factors behind stagnant productivity.

These remarks are critical for poverty alleviation. More than two decades ago Mexico pioneered an incentive-based program to invest in the human capital of the poor through monetary transfers (Levy 2006). Multiple impact evaluations show that this program—initially known as Progresa, then as Oportunidades, and now as Prospera—has had a positive effect on nutrition, schooling, and health indicators (see Parker and Todd 2017 for a review). But for the reasons discussed in this book, these investments are *not* translating into higher earnings. Poor workers need better jobs, but Mexico's **E**(L,T,M) thwarts them from getting them, more in fact than it thwarts the efforts by higher-income workers (Levy 2008). Given the current level of Prospera's transfers, reducing misallocation to raise productivity and accelerate growth is the best route to help them. They are not finding productive jobs because of the problems with **E**(L,T,M) documented in Chapters 7 and 8, not because of shortcomings in Prospera.[10] Trying to bypass these problems by augmenting Prospera's transfers, or by complementing these transfers with food distribution programs or other mechanisms to transfer income, will increase poor households' consumption, but it will not break the intergenerational transmission of poverty. In other words, under the current system, healthier and more educated workers will not earn more through their own efforts than their elder peers earned. The policy shift proposed is thus also a shift in Mexico's poverty alleviation policy: improve Prospera and fix **E**(L,T,M).

Is Formalization a Policy Priority?

"Formalization" programs are often proposed, although their aims are not always clear. Two objectives need to be distinguished in examining them: expanding the coverage of social insurance and increasing productivity. Chapter 8 documented that in the last two decades Mexico extended the coverage of social insurance by expanding non-contributory programs (see Figure 8.2 and the discussion therein). Since these programs subsidize firms with non-salaried and illegal salaried contracts, these are really "informalization programs."

On the other hand, from the point of view of productivity, eliminating self-employment and firms with non-salaried contracts is not the right objective, which is what formalization would imply under the current legal and institutional arrangements. The objective should be to equalize revenue productivity of resources across all firms, regardless of their size or contractual structure. Of course, this will never be fully realized, but policy can reduce the variance of the revenue productivity distribution and equalize the mean revenue productivity of firms with salaried and non-salaried contracts.

---

[10] This is not to say that the program cannot be improved. There is ample room to improve targeting, increase the quality of services, and strengthen the program's impact on human capital formation by adding a component focused on early child development (or linking Prospera to a parallel program with that aim).

Chapter 2 argued that from the point of view of productivity the labels "formal" and "informal" are unnecessary. In parallel, Chapter 4 documented that given Mexico's $E(L,T,M)$, too many resources were allocated to firms with non-salaried and illegal salaried contracts, and too few resources to firms with legal salaried contracts. Reluctantly but in deference to conventional usage, the former firms were labelled informal and the latter formal. But the risk in using those labels is that policy may confuse changing $E(L,T,M)$ with changing the labels that are applied to firms while leaving $E(L,T,M)$ basically intact.

Formalization programs are clearly welcome if they tackle the issues in Tables 7.9 and 8.1. But if all they do is provide transitory incentives for informal firms to register somewhere (the municipality, the tax authorities) and be counted as formal firms, then they could potentially be quite misleading. Formality measured by these metrics would increase, and the assumption would be that productivity would increase as well. But that assumption would be flawed, because the underlying misallocation in the economy would not change, as $E(L,T,M)$ would not have changed in any meaningful way.

In short, "formalizing" the economy is not the policy priority in Mexico; the priority is to change $E(L,T,M)$ along the lines of the policy shift sketched above. If this policy shift were undertaken, the coverage of social insurance would extend to all, and aggregate productivity would be higher because the differences in firms' revenue productivity would narrow. As a byproduct of this shift, self-employment and the share of capital and labor in firms with non-salaried contracts would decrease, and the share in firms with salaried contracts would increase. But some firms would still be informal in the sense of offering their workers non-salaried contracts. And fortunately so, because as Chapter 2 indicated, there are efficiency reasons for some workers to work on their own and for some firms to offer their workers non-salaried contracts. Critically, however, from the point of view of the coverage of social insurance, and from the point of view of productivity, it would not matter how many workers are employed in those firms, or how much investment occurs in them. Nor would it matter what the size distribution of firms is or what the number of self-employed individuals is. Indeed, if Mexico's $E(L,T,M)$ were reformed along the lines suggested, the labels formal and informal would be unnecessary and uninformative, a relic of the past.

A Program for Prosperity

A Program for Growth with Additions for Social Inclusion

The lost decade of the 1980s was extremely costly to Mexico. After it, the country embarked on a program to promote growth whose essential elements were macroeconomic stability, an open trade regime, investments in human capital, promotion of domestic competition, and sector-specific reforms to increase efficiency.

Despite a setback in 1994–1995, this program has brought very significant benefits to Mexicans. They enjoy macroeconomic certainty, low inflation, and access to international markets, which without a doubt are first-order achievements. Firms face lower risks and can hedge some of them in active foreign exchange markets, and they also benefit from a more diverse and competitive supply of intermediate inputs and a growing supply of educated workers. Many firms compete successfully in the world and have turned Mexico into Latin America's export manufacturing powerhouse. Large investments in education have significantly raised the schooling of the population. Households can obtain long-term mortgages in pesos at fixed nominal rates, and credit for automobiles or home appliances. Households also enjoy a much greater variety of options for consumer goods, a result in part of trade liberalization and in part of newer and larger firms entering the services and commerce sectors. Increasingly educated citizens have more access to higher-quality telecommunications services. Transport infrastructure has expanded, and economic activity is more diversified regionally than in the past. Some cities, particularly in the northern half of the country, have grown noticeably and reaped efficiency gains from agglomeration, while others have also developed clusters of innovation and research.

In parallel, and this is the key expression here, the country deepened existing programs and launched new ones to increase social inclusion. Aside from large investments in education and human capital formation, new poverty programs were implemented. Health, pension, housing, day care, and other programs focused on informal workers were created or expanded, while policies and programs for formal workers were maintained. These efforts increased the coverage of education, improved access to health services, and reduced income poverty.

This program for growth, along with its additions for social inclusion, also provided a narrative for the country; a where to and a why. This narrative could be summarized as follows: "The combination of macroeconomic stability, an open trade regime, investments in human capital, and sector-specific reforms to increase efficiency, coupled with numerous and increasingly generous social programs, will result in better jobs, higher wages, and more opportunities for all—growth with social inclusion."

However, almost a quarter of a century later, it is not possible to assert that this program delivered the growth and prosperity expected from it. This does not mean that it should all be abandoned—far from it. Most of its components were right on mark and need to be consistently pursued. But it does mean that this program had an Achilles' heel: large and persistent misallocation.

Although this is a subjective interpretation, the thinking was that economic reforms—particularly the combination of macroeconomic stability, an open regime, product market competition, and investments in human capital—would be sufficiently powerful to increase the rate of GDP growth and, along with it, real wages. Informality would gradually decline as growth accelerated. Productive and formal firms would grow, and unproductive informal ones would progressively fade away. In parallel, increasingly educated workers would get better jobs. The implicit assumption was that this process would happen regardless of the combination of tax, social, and labor policies deployed to increase social inclusion, and regardless of shortcomings in the functioning of the associated institutions. At the very least, the assumption was that the deficiencies of those policies and the shortcomings of those institutions could be overcome by the pro-growth forces unleashed by macroeconomic, trade, and sector-specific reforms—*as if economic activity in the country could be de-linked from the broader social and legal context in which this activity was taking place.*

With the benefit of hindsight, one can see that this program for growth with, *in parallel*, additions for social inclusion, was internally inconsistent. The policies deployed to pursue social inclusion deterred growth as they taxed the high-productivity segment of the economy and subsidized the low-productivity one. This tax-cum-subsidy combination, compounded by a context of a weak rule of law, resulted in a poor distribution of the country's talents across occupations and firms, in too many low-productivity firms, and in dysfunctional firm dynamics. The productivity gains required for rapid GDP growth were absent, and so were the gains in real wages, despite large increases in the education of the labor force.

Perhaps the most revealing aspect of this process was that, at the end of the day, flawed microeconomic incentives dominated the efforts devoted to macroeconomic management, sound as those efforts were, and dominated the efforts to invest in human capital as well. Mexico's growth performance over the last two decades is a sobering example that, at least in some cases, "free trade and sound money" coupled with more human capital may not be enough. A country's social and judicial institutions—particularly those associated with contract enforcement, taxation, social insurance, and labor protection, also need to be sound if socially inclusive growth is going to transit from political rhetoric into measured outcomes.

A Program for Prosperity

So, what is next? Mexico is far from a consensus that misallocation is the reason why everybody's efforts have been under-rewarded, and that the policies and institutions identified in Tables 7.9 and 8.1 need to be reformed as the core component of a program to accelerate growth and create a more prosperous country. This book is an attempt to contribute to such a consensus.

Of course, even if a consensus could be built that the themes discussed here point in the right direction, this would not be enough. The specifics of the policy shift sketched above need to be discussed. And while this discussion is critical, it should not cloud the broader perspective motivating the need for a policy shift—it would be easy but unfortunate to get bogged down by the details. Much would be lost if an overall perspective of the problem was buried by a narrow debate on some of the details—say, whether raising this or that tax would increase revenues by a quarter or a half point of GDP, or whether the contribution rate for unemployment insurance should be 3 rather than 3½ percent of the wage. In the end, something substantial must be behind the stylized facts described in Chapters 3 to 6, and therefore something substantial needs to change to modify them. Tinkering at the edges will not do.

To convince society that a policy shift is indispensable to achieve prosperity, a debate is needed as to whether current policies and institutions are conducive to the social ideals embedded in Mexico's constitution. Critically, however, the debate is about the means, not the ends. And in this difference, Mexico has a phenomenal source of strength. As opposed to some other countries, there is no questioning that in addition to providing security and defending property rights, a fundamental task of the Mexican state is to combat poverty, increase welfare, and pursue social justice. There is no thought that in this very unequal country the government should sit by while the market does its job. The debate is not about whether workers should be protected from the loss of employment, whether everybody should have access to publicly funded health care, whether the tax system should be used to redistribute income, or whether the government should help the poor. Fortunately for Mexico, *the debate is about how*.

This book argues that current tax, social insurance, and labor protection policies are flawed, that they are the main reason why growth is slow, and that a policy shift is necessary. But this shift needs to be accompanied by a narrative, to use this expression again, as to what is next in Mexico's quest for prosperity, and why. The beliefs about policies standing in the way of Mexico's prosperity are either embedded in Mexico's constitution, or have been part and parcel of political discourse for many years. Mexican society will not give up on those beliefs unless better ones are on offer. Societies have interests, but also passions. Thus, to gather the political support necessary for a policy shift, it is indispensable to construct a new narrative: a vision and an explanation that this shift will indeed result in the *productive and inclusive* society that Mexicans aspire to live in.

Discussing the specifics of the policy shift proposed and constructing the accompanying narrative exceeds the limits of this book, focused as it is only on trying to understand why prosperity has eluded Mexico. Yet, an implication of the analysis here is worth repeating because it may provide a valuable starting point for these tasks: the core reforms needed to increase growth and productivity—more efficient taxation, an improved social insurance and labor protection system, and better judicial institutions—imply a better distribution of the benefits of growth; *this provides the material basis of a program for prosperity.*

Prosperity does not occur in a vacuum; it takes place under specific circumstances in a time and a place. In Mexico today, it may well be the case that prosperity can occur only if it is shared through inclusive policies and institutions. Shared prosperity is within reach, but to get there, some deeply held beliefs and some often-repeated assertions in Mexico's political discourse will have to change. Some views on the relations between social and economic policy will also have to modified. And some entrenched interests will have to be faced. A formidable ideological and political challenge, no doubt, but potentially a wonderful opportunity as well.

Appendix

Chapter 3 noted that the 2008 and 2013 censuses allow for identifying how many establishments belong to the same firm. The calculations carried out at the firm level are presented here. The criteria used to aggregate establishments into firms, and to classify those firms at the six-digit level, were the following:

- For each establishment in a firm, the largest is determined by the number of workers. If this criterion is not definitive, the largest establishment is determined by capital and then by value added. In turn, the six-digit sector of that establishment is taken as that of the firm.
- Employment, capital, value added, and other variables of all establishments are added to give the values for the firm.
- For each firm, the legality and formality indices are calculated using the criteria given in Chapter 3.

The results of this exercise are shown in Tables A.1 and A.2. Table A.1 provides information on the average size of firms and establishments in the 2008 and 2013 censuses, as well as their number by size and type. Table A.2 compares the share of capital, K, and labor, L, allocated to firms and establishments, in both cases by size and type.

The specification for the regressions carried out in Chapter 4 follow. For Tables 4.3 and 4.4 in Chapter 4 the basic form is:

$$\ln\left(TFPR_{si}/\overline{TFPR_s}\right) = \beta_0 + \beta_1 Z_{1i} + \beta_2 Z_{2i} + \beta_3 Z_{3i} + \theta_s + \theta_a + \theta_r + e_i,$$

where $\overline{TFPR_s}$ is the mean of TFPR in sector s, Z_{1i} is a dummy for mixed establishments, Z_{2i} is a dummy for informal and legal establishments, Z_{3i} is a

Table A.1: Size and Type Distribution of Firms and Establishments, 2008 and 2013

	2008		2013	
	Establishment	Firm	Establishment	Firm
Average Size (number of workers)				
All	4.50	4.62	4.24	4.37
Fully formal	27.85	34.42	22.15	27.15
Mixed	16.26	21.13	16.53	19.52
Informal and legal	2.47	2.24	2.31	2.25
Informal and illegal	4.02	4.08	3.93	4.02
Size				
1–5 workers	3,243,275	3,202,049	3,754,013	3,704,962
6–10 workers	207,798	187,390	186,471	158,363
11–50 workers	124,591	102,955	127,986	97,575
51+ workers	27,854	18,968	30,630	19,227
Total	3,603,518	3,511,362	4,099,100	3,980,127
Type				
Fully formal	108,000	84,870	171,685	138,376
Mixed	240,912	219,426	236,413	217,492
Informal and legal	2,438,610	2,398,217	2,983,612	2,926,472
Informal and illegal	815,996	808,849	707,390	697,787
Total	3,603,518	3,511,362	4,099,100	3,980,127

Source: Author's calculations based on data from Mexico's Economic Census.

dummy for informal and illegal establishments, and $\theta_{s,a,r}$ are fixed effects for firm size, age, and region (state).

The same specification is used for TFPQ. When, as in Table 4.4 in Chapter 4, regressions are carried out separately for each firm size, fixed effects for size are excluded.

The specification for the regression in Table 4.5 in Chapter 4 is:

$$\ln(TFPR_{si}/\overline{TFPR_s}) = \beta_0 + \sum_{m=1}^{4}\sum_{n=1}^{4} \beta_{mn} Z_{mni} + \theta_a + \theta_r + e_i,$$

where m is {1 = fully formal, 2 = informal and legal, 3 = mixed, 4 = informal and illegal}; and n is {1 = [1–5 workers], 2 = [6–10 workers], 3 = [11–50 workers], and 4 = [51+ workers]}

The excluded category is informal and legal (1–5 workers).

Table A.2: Allocation of Resources, Firms versus Establishments, 2013

Part 1: Firms

Number of Workers	Fully Formal L	Fully Formal K	Mixed L	Mixed K	Informal and Legal L	Informal and Legal K	Informal and Illegal L	Informal and Illegal K	Total L	Total K
1–5	1.2	1.2	2.4	2.0	26.5	8.3	8.9	4.4	39.0	15.9
6–10	1.3	1.1	1.9	1.5	1.1	0.6	2.9	1.7	7.2	4.9
11–50	4.5	5.6	4.3	3.7	1.4	2.2	2.7	1.3	12.9	12.8
51+	14.6	24.3	15.8	21.8	8.9	18.2	1.6	2.1	40.9	66.4
Total	21.6	32.2	24.4	29.0	37.9	29.3	16.1	9.5	100.0	100.0

Part 2: Establishments

Number of Workers	Fully Formal L	Fully Formal K	Mixed L	Mixed K	Informal and Legal L	Informal and Legal K	Informal and Illegal L	Informal and Illegal K	Total L	Total K
1–5	1.4	2.0	2.5	2.3	26.8	9.9	9.0	4.6	39.7	18.7
6–10	1.6	2.1	2.0	1.7	1.6	1.5	2.7	1.4	7.9	6.7
11–50	5.2	5.4	4.6	3.8	2.5	4.2	3.0	1.9	15.3	15.3
51+	13.6	20.6	13.3	19.4	8.8	17.9	1.3	1.4	37.1	59.3
Total	21.9	30.1	22.5	27.2	39.7	33.4	16.0	9.2	100.0	100.0

Source: Author's calculations based on data from Mexico's Economic Census.
Note: K: capital ; L: labor.

Table A.3: Dispersion of Revenue Total Factor Productivity, Firms versus Establishments, 2008 and 2013

	2008		2013	
	Establishment	Firm	Establishment	Firm
All sectors				
Standard deviation	1.08	1.09	1.11	1.12
25th–75th percentile	1.39	1.44	1.39	1.46
10th–90th percentile	2.73	2.79	2.82	2.85
Manufacturing				
Standard deviation	0.96	0.93	1.05	1.06
25th–75th percentile	1.24	1.23	1.23	1.35
10th–90th percentile	2.41	2.36	2.73	2.70
Commerce				
Standard deviation	1.15	1.20	1.14	1.17
25th–75th percentile	1.50	1.62	1.43	1.50
10th–90th percentile	2.93	3.07	2.86	2.98
Services				
Standard deviation	1.04	1.04	1.05	1.06
25th–75th percentile	1.36	1.36	1.38	1.42
10th–90th percentile	2.66	2.66	2.67	2.71

Source: Author's calculations based on data from Mexico's Economic Census.

Table A.4: Correlation of TFPQ and TFPR, Firms versus Establishments, 2013

	Firm		Establishments	
	TFPQ	TFPR	TFPQ	TFPR
Mixed	−0.220 [0.0035]	−0.100 [0.0022]	−0.186 [0.0033]	−0.177 [0.002]
Informal legal	−1.424 [0.0035]	−0.545 [0.0022]	−1.557 [0.0031]	−0.633 [0.0019]
Informal illegal	−0.409 [0.0035]	−0.105 [0.0023]	−0.705 [0.0035]	−0.184 [0.0021]
Size dummies	Yes	Yes	Yes	Yes
Age controls	Yes	Yes	Yes	Yes
State dummies	Yes	Yes	Yes	Yes
Observations	3,273,007	3,273,007	3,371,272	3,371,272
R-squared	0.340	0.059	0.388	0.072

Source: Author's calculations based on data from Mexico's Economic Census.
Note: TFPR: revenue total factor productivity; TFPQ: physical total factor productivity.

Table A.5: Interaction between Establishment Size and Type, Revenue Total Factor Productivity, 2013

	Coefficient	Standard Error
Fully formal (51+ workers)	0.800	0.003
Informal and illegal (51+ workers)	0.646	0.006
Fully formal (11–50 workers)	0.606	0.003
Informal and illegal (6–10 workers)	0.576	0.004
Mixed (6–10 workers)	0.544	0.004
Fully formal (1–5 workers)	0.517	0.004
Mixed (51+ workers)	0.498	0.003
Fully formal (6–10 workers)	0.477	0.004
Mixed (11–50 workers)	0.467	0.003
Informal and illegal (11–50 workers)	0.405	0.003
Informal and illegal (1–5 workers)	0.381	0.002
Mixed (1–5 workers)	0.365	0.003
Informal and legal (6–10 workers)	0.007	0.005
Informal and legal (1–5 workers)	Excluded	
Informal and legal (51+ workers)	−0.039	0.003
Informal and legal (11–50 workers)	−0.096	0.003
Observations	3,371,272	
R2	0.075	
Age controls	Yes	
State dummies	Yes	

Source: Author's calculations based on data from Mexico's Economic Census.
Note: All coefficients are significant at the 99 percent level except for the one for informal and legal (6–10 workers).

References

Alaimo, V., M. Bosch, D. Kaplan, C. Pagés, and L. Ripani. 2015. *Jobs for Growth*. Washington, DC: Inter-American Development Bank.

Alonso, J., C. Amuedo-Dorantes, and L. Juárez. 2016. "The Effect of Non-contributory Pensions on Saving in Mexico." IDB Working Paper 95976. Inter-American Development Bank, Washington, DC.

Amuedo-Dorantes, C., and L. Juárez. 2013. "Old-Age Government Transfers and the Crowding Out of Private Gifts: The 70 and Above Program for the Rural Elderly in Mexico." CReAM Discussion Paper No. 1327, Centre for Research and Analysis of Migration, Department of Economics, University College London.

Antón, A. 2016. "Cálculo del Gasto Público en Programas No-Contributivos en México." Centro de Investigación y Docencia Económica, México. Unpublished.

Antón, A., F. Hernández, and S. Levy. 2012. *The End of Informality in Mexico? Fiscal Reform for Universal Social Insurance.* Washington, DC: Inter-American Development Bank.

Artuc, E., D. Lederman, and D. Rojas. 2015. "The Rise of China and Labor Market Adjustments in Latin America." Research Policy Working Paper No. 7155. World Bank, Washington, DC.

Banerjee, A, and E. Dufflo. 2005. "Growth Theory Through the Lens of Economic Development." In *Handbook of Development Economics*, Volume 1, edited by H. Chenery and T.N. Srinivasan. Amsterdam: North-Holland.

Bank for International Settlements (BIS). 2017. "Long Series on Credit to Private Non-Financial Entities." Available at: http://www.bis.org/statistics/credtopriv.htm.

Barreix, A., L. Corrales, S. Díaz, and C. Garcimartin 2017. "Actualización de la Presión Fiscal Equivalente en América Latina y el Caribe." IDB Discussion Paper No. 548. Inter-American Development Bank, Washington, DC.

Barro, R., and J.W. Lee. 2013. "A New Data Set of Educational Attainment in the World, 1950–2010." *Journal of Development Economics* 104: 184–98.

Berstein, S., M. Bosch, M. Garcia Huitron, M.L. Oliver, and A. Altamirano. 2018. "Diseñando las Pensiones del Futuro en América Latina y el Caribe." IDB Monograph. Inter-American Development Bank, Washington, DC.

Bloom, N., and J. Van Reenen. 2007. "Measuring and Explaining Management Practices across Firms and Countries." *Quarterly Journal of Economics* 122(4): 1351–408.

Blyde, J., M. Busso, V. Faggioni, and D. Romero. 2017. "The Impact of Chinese Competition on Mexican Labor Outcomes." Inter-American Development Bank, Washington, DC. Unpublished.

Bobba, M., L. Flabbi, and S. Levy. 2017. "Labor Market Search, Informality and Schooling Investments." IZA Discussion Paper No. 11170. Institute of labor Economics, Bonn, Germany.

Bosch, M., and R. Campos-Vázquez. 2014. "The Trade-offs of Welfare Policies in Labor Markets with Informal Jobs: The Case of the 'Seguro Popular' Program in Mexico." *American Economic Journal: Economic Policy* 6(4): 71–99.

Bosch, M., M.B. Cobacho, and C. Pagés. 2014. "Effects of Non-Contributory Systems of Informality: Taking Stock of Eight Years of Implementation of Mexico's Seguro Popular." In *Social Insurance, Informality and Labor Markets*, edited by M. Frolich, D. Kaplan, C. Pagés, J. Rigolini, and D. Robalino. Oxford, UK: Oxford University Press.

Busso, M., M.V. Fazio, and S. Levy. 2012. "(In)Formal and (Un)Productive: The Productivity Costs of Excessive Informality in Mexico." IDB Working Paper No. 341. Inter-American Development Bank, Washington, DC.

Busso, M., L. Madrigal, and C. Pagés. 2013. "Productivity and Resource Misallocation in Latin America." *B.E. Journal of Macroeconomics* 13(1): 1–30.

Campos-Vázquez, R. 2013. "Efectos de los Ingresos no Reportados en el Nivel y Tendencia de la Pobreza Laboral en México." Centro de Estudios Económicos Documento de Discusión IV-2013, El Colegio de México.

Cantála, D., J. Sempere, and H. Sobarzo. 2005. "Evasión del Impuesto Sobre la Renta de Personas Físicas." Centro de Estudios Económicos, El Colegio de México.

Castellanos, S., G. Del Ángel, and J. Garza-García. 2015. *Competition and Efficiency in the Mexican Banking Industry: Theory and Empirical Evidence.* Palgrave-McMillan.

Cirera, X., and W. Maloney. 2017. *The Innovation Paradox: Developing-Country Capabilities and the Unrealized Promise of Technological Catch-Up.* Washington, DC: World Bank.

Comisión Nacional del Sistema del Ahorro para el Retiro, Secretaría de Hacienda y Crédito Público (CONSAR). 2016. "¿Cuántos y Quiénes Alcanzarán Pensión?" CONSAR, Mexico City.

Da-Rocha, J., M. Tavares, and D. Restuccia. 2016. "Firing Costs, Misallocation and Aggregate Productivity." NBER Working Paper No. 23008. National Bureau of Economic Research, Cambridge, MA.

Dávila, E., and S. Levy. 2003. "Taxing for Equity: A Proposal to Reform Mexico's Value Added Tax." In *Latin American Economic Reform, The Second Stage.* Edited by J.A. González, V. Corbo, A. Krueger, and A. Tornell. Chicago: University of Chicago Press.

Davis, S., J. Haltiwanger, and S. Schuh. 1997. *Job Creation and Destruction.* Massachusetts Institute of Technology Press.

De Paula, A., and J. Scheinkman. 2010. "Value Added Taxes, Chain Effects and Informality." *American Economic Journal: Macroeconomics* 2(4): 195–221.

De Soto, H. 1989. *The Other Path: The Invisible Revolution in the Third World.* New York: Harper and Row.

Diamond, P., and J. Mirrlees. 1971. "Optimal Taxation and Public Production. I: Production Efficiency." *American Economic Review* 61(1): 8–27.

Doubova, S., V. Borja-Aburto, G. Guerra-y-Guerra, N. Salgado, and M.A. González. 2018. "Loss of Job-Related Right to Healthcare is Associated with Reduced Quality and Clinical Outcomes of Diabetic Patients in Mexico." *International Journal for Quality in Health Care.*

Dougherty, S. 2014. "Legal Reform, Contract Enforcement and Firm Size in Mexico." *Review of International Economics* 22(4): 825–44.

Economic Commission on Latin American and the Caribbean (ECLAC). 2016. *Productividad y Brechas Estructurales en México.* Mexico City: ECLAC.

Fernández-Arias, E. 2017a. "Productivity and Factor Accumulation in Latin America and the Caribbean: A Data Base." IDB Research Department Paper. Inter-American Development Bank, Washington, DC.

Fernández-Arias, E. 2017b. "Productivity and Factor Accumulation in Latin America and the Caribbean: Database Description." IDB Research Department Paper. Inter-American Development Bank, Washington, D.C.

Fukuyama, F. 1995. *Trust: The Social Virtues and the Creation of Prosperity.* New York: Simon and Schuster.

García-Verdú, S., and M. Ramos-Francia. 2017. "Bank Credit Allocation and Sectorial Concentration in Mexico: Some Empirical Evidence." Departamento de Investigación, Documento de Investigación No. 2017-14, Banco de México.

Giacomelli, S., and C. Menon. 2017. "Does Weak Contract Enforcement Affect Firm Size? Evidence from the Neighbor's Court." *Journal of Economic Geography* 17(6): 1251-282.

Gopinath, G., S. Kalemli-Ozcan, L. Karabarbounis, and C. Villegas-Sanchez 2017. "Capital Allocation and Productivity in South Europe." *Quarterly Journal of Economics*.

Guerrero, I., L.F. López-Calva, and M. Walton. 2009 "The Inequality Trap and Its Links to Low Growth in Mexico." In *No Growth without Equity? Inequality, Interests and Competition in Mexico*, edited by S. Levy and M. Walton. New York: Palgrave MacMillan for the World Bank.

Guerrero, I., R. Villalpando, and M. Benitez. 2009. "Profitability, Concentration and Efficiency in the Mexican Banking System." *El Trimestre Económico* 76.

Guha-Khosnobis, B., R. Kanbur, and E. Ostrom. 2006. *Linking the Formal and Informal Economy: Concepts and Policies*. Oxford, UK: Oxford University Press.

Haber, S. 2009. "Why Banks Do Not Lend: The Mexican Financial System." In *No Growth without Equity? Inequality, Interests and Competition in Mexico*, edited by S. Levy and M. Walton. New York: Palgrave MacMillan for the World Bank.

Hanushek, E. 2013. "Economic Growth in Developing Countries: The Role of Human Capital." *Economics of Education Review* 37(c): 204-12.

Hanushek, E., and L. Woessmann. 2012. "Schooling, Educational Achievement, and the Latin American Growth Puzzle." *Journal of Development Economics* 99(2): 497-512.

Heckman, J., and C. Pages. 2004. *Law and Employment: Lessons from Latin America and the Caribbean*. Chicago: University of Chicago Press for the National Bureau of Economic Research.

Hopenhayn, H. 2014. "Firms, Misallocation and Aggregate Productivity: A Review." *Annual Review of Economics* 6(1): 735-70.

Hopenhayn, H., and R. Rogerson. 1993. "Job Turnover and Policy Evaluation: A General Equilibrium Analysis." *Journal of Political Economy* 101(5): 915-38.

Hsieh, C., and P. Klenow. 2009. "Misallocation and Manufacturing TFP in China and India." *Quarterly Journal of Economics* 124(4): 1403-448.

Hsieh, C., and P. Klenow. 2014. "The Life-Cycle of Plants in India and Mexico." *Quarterly Journal of Economics* 129(3): 1035-084.

Hsieh, C., and B. Olken. 2014. "The Missing "Missing Middle."" *Journal of Economic Perspectives* 28(3): 89-108.

Inter-American Development Bank (IDB). 2010. *Development in the Americas Report: The Age of Productivity: Transforming Economies from the Bottom Up*. Washington, DC: IDB.

Inter-American Development Bank (IDB). 2015. *Development in the Americas Report: Re-Thinking Productive Development: Policies and Institutions for Economic Transformation.* Washington, DC: IDB.

Inter-American Development Bank (IDB). 2017. *Development in the Americas Report: Learning Better: Public Policy for Skills Development.* Washington, DC: IDB.

Inter-American Development Bank (IDB). 2018. "Bank Competition and Firm Finance in Latin America: Evidence from Bank and Loan-Level Data." IDB Monograph. IDB, Washington, DC.

Instituto Mexicano de la Competitividad (IMCO). 2014. *Por una Mejor Justicia Laboral.* Mexico City: IMCO.

Juárez, L. 2008. "Are Informal Workers Compensated for the Lack of Fringe Benefits? Free Health Care as an Instrument for Formality." Working Paper No. 0804. Centro de Investigación Económica, Instituto Tecnológico Autónomo de México.

Kanbur, R. 2009. "Conceptualizing Informality: Regulation and Enforcement: The V.V. Giri Memorial Lecture." *Indian Journal of Labour Economics*, 52(1): 33–42.

Kanbur, R., and M. Keen. 2014. "Thresholds, Informality and Partitions of Compliance." Working Paper No. 2014-11. School of Applied Economics and Management, Cornell University.

Kaplan, D., and S. Levy. 2014. "The Evolution of Social Security Systems in Latin America." In *Social Insurance, Informality and Labor Markets*, edited by M. Frolich, D. Kaplan, C. Pagés, J. Rigolini and D. Robalino. Oxford, UK: Oxford University Press.

Kaplan, D., and J. Sadka. 2011. "The Plaintiff's Role in Enforcing a Court Ruling: Evidence from a Labor Court in Mexico." IDB Working Paper No. 264. Inter-American Development Bank, Washington, DC.

Kaplan, D., J. Sadka, and J.L. Silva-Mendez. 2008. "Litigation and Settlement: New Evidence from Labor Courts in Mexico." *Journal of Empirical Legal Studies* 5(2): 309–50.

Katz, L., and K. Murphy. 1992. "Changes in Relative Wages, 1963–1987: Supply and Demand Factors." *Quarterly Journal of Economics* 107(1): 35–78.

Kehoe, T.J., and F. Meza. 2012. "Catch-Up Growth Followed by Stagnation: Mexico, 1950–2010." Federal Reserve Bank of Minneapolis Working Paper No. 693.

Laeven, L., and C. Woodruff. 2007. "The Quality of the Legal System, Firm Ownership and Firm Size." *Review of Economics and Statistics* 89(4): 601–14.

Lagakos, D., B. Moll, T. Porzio, N. Qian, and T. Schoellman. 2018. "Life-Cycle Wage Growth Across Countries." *Journal of Political Economy* 126(2): 797–849.

La Porta, R., and A. Shleifer. 2008, "The Unofficial Economy and Economic Development." NBER Working Paper No. 14520. National Bureau of Economic Research, Cambridge, MA.

Leal, J. 2014. "Tax Collection, the Informal Sector and Productivity." *Review of Economic Dynamics* 17(2): 262–86.

Leal, J. 2017. "Key Sectors in Economic Development: A Perspective from Input-Output Linkages and Cross-Sector Misallocation." Departamento de Investigación, Banco de México.

Levy, S. 2006. *Progress Against Poverty: Sustaining Mexico's Progresa-Oportunidades Program.* Washington, DC: Brookings Institution Press.

Levy, S. 2008. *Good Intentions, Bad Outcomes: Social Policy, Informality and Economic Growth in Mexico.* Washington, DC: Brookings Institution Press.

Levy, S. 2009. "Social Security Reform in Mexico: For Whom?" In *No Growth without Equity? Inequality, Interests and Competition in Mexico*, edited by S. Levy and M. Walton. New York: Palgrave MacMillan for the World Bank.

Levy, S., and L.F. López-Calva. 2016. "Labor Earnings, Misallocation and the Returns to Schooling in Mexico." IDB Working Paper 671. Inter-American Development Bank, Washington, DC; forthcoming, *World Bank Economic Review.*

Levy, S., and M. Székely 2016. "¿Más Escolaridad, Menos Informalidad? Un Análisis de Cohortes para México y América Latina." *El Trimestre Económico* 83(4): 499–548.

Levy, S., and M. Walton. 2009. *No Growth without Equity? Inequality, Interests and Competition in Mexico.* New York: Palgrave MacMillan for the World Bank.

López, J.J. 2016. "A Quantitative Theory of Tax Evasion and Informality." University of Memphis. Unpublished.

López, J.J. 2017. "Financial Frictions and Productivity: Evidence from Mexico." *The Quarterly Review of Economics and Finance* 66(C): 294–301.

López, J.J., and J. Torres-Coronado. 2017. "Size-Dependent Policies, the Allocation of Talent, and the Return to Skill." Department of Economics, University of Memphis.

López-Martin, B. 2017. "Informal Sector Misallocation." Departamento de Investigación, Banco de México, México.

Mokyr, J. 2017. *A Culture of Growth, The Origins of the Modern Economy.* Princeton, NJ: Princeton University Press, Princeton, NJ.

Moody's. 2011. "Indicadores de Ejecutabilidad Contractual." Moody's Investor Services with Instituto Tecnológico Autónomo de México and Gaxiola, Moraila and Associates, Mexico City.

Oberfield, E. 2013. "Business Networks, Production Chains and Productivity: A Theory of Input-Output Architecture." Department of Economics Working Paper, Princeton University.

Organization for Economic Cooperation and Development (OECD). 2017. "Employment and Labour Market Statistics." Available at: http://dx.doi.org/10.1787/data00306-en.

Parker, S., and P. Todd. 2017. "Conditional Cash Transfers: The Case of Progresa/Oportunidades." *Journal of Economic Literature* 55(3): 866–915.

Rios, V. 2016. "The Impact of Crime and Violence in Economic Sector Diversity." Wilson Center, Washington, DC. Unpublished.

Secretaría de Hacienda y Crédito Público (SHCP). 2013. "Presupuesto de Gastos Fiscales 2013." Available at: http://www.shcp.gob.mx/INGRESOS/Ingresos_pres_gasto/presupuesto_gastos_fiscales_2013.pdf

Servicio de Administración Tributaria (SAT). 2017. "Datos Abiertos del SAT." Available at: http://www.sat.gob.mx/cifras_sat/Paginas/datos/vinculo.

Syverson, C. 2004. "Product Substitutability and Productivity Dispersion." *Review of Economics and Statistics* 86(2): 534–50.

Székely, M., and I. Flores. 2017. "Educación y Desarrollo en México: Una Historia de Baja Capacidad de Aprovechamiento de Capital Humano." Inter-American Development Bank, Washington, DC. Unpublished.

Urrutia, C., F. Meza, and S. Pratap. 2015. "Credit, Sectoral Misallocation and Productivity Growth: A Disaggregated Analysis." Instituto Tecnológico Autónomo de México. Unpublished.

Urrutia, C., F. Meza, and S. Pratap. 2017. "Credit Conditions, Dynamic Distortions, and Capital Accumulation in Mexican Manufacturings." Instituto Tecnológico Autónomo de México. Unpublished.

World Bank. 2016. *Doing Business in Mexico: Midiendo la Calidad y la Eficiencia de la Regulación*, Washington, DC: World Bank.

World Bank. 2017. *Global Financial Development Report 2017/2018: Bankers without Borders*. Washington, DC: World Bank.

Zamudio, A., S. Barajas, and A. Brown. 2011. "Estudio de Evasión Fiscal en el Régimen de Pequeños Contribuyentes." Instituto Tecnológico y de Estudios Superiores de Monterrey, Ciudad de México.

Index

A

Alaimo, V., 180
Alonso, J., 250
Amuedo-Dorantes, C., 250
Antón, Arturo, 196, 201, 250, 267
Argentina, 1n2, 5n3, 109, 162, 225n20, 232–233
Artuc, E., 256

B

Banerjee, A., 234
Bank of International Settlements, 232
Barreix, A., 255
Barro, R., 6n4
Belize, 1n2, 5n3
Berstein, S., 246n2
Bloom, N., 230
Blyde, J., 256
Bobba, Matteo, 188–190, 198n2, 275n10
Bolivia, 1n2, 109, 225n20
Bosch, Mariano, 250
Brazil, 1n2, 5n3, 35, 162, 183, 186, 223n19, 236n24
Busso, Matias, 109, 114

C

Campos-Vásquez, R., 172n7, 250
Canada, 4–5
Cantála, D., 209n10
Castellanos, S., 232
causation, 74–75
census data, 18–20
  firms and, 156–157
  firms excluded from, 20–21
  productivity and, 125–126
Chile, 1n2, 35, 42, 109, 162, 180n12, 183, 186, 225n20, 232, 236n24, 237
China, 46
Cirera, X., 179, 230
Colombia, 1n2, 5n3, 109, 162, 225n20, 233
contracts
  contract enforcement, 226–231, 255
  non-salaried/illegal salaried, 201–202
  salaried, 197–199
Costa Rica, 1n2, 5n3, 162
credit
  access to, 12, 41–43, 231–233
  development banks and, 47, 75, 134n4, 237–238, 273

firms and, 47, 68, 94, 134n4, 205
Hsieh-Klenow model and, 103–105, 107
interest groups and, 269–270
misallocation and, 233–238, 242–244, 269–270
policy and, 268, 273, 277, 281
ratio to GDP, 42
reforms and, 271–272
shortages, 42
taxes and, 207, 220–224
world of market conditions and, 41–43, 226–229
see also microcredit programs

D

Da-Rocha, J., 200
Dávila, E., 221n17
Davis, S., 154
De Paula, A., 223n19
De Soto, H., 118n10
development banks
  credit and, 47, 75, 134n4, 237–238, 273
  see also Inter-American Development Bank (IDB)
Diamond, P., 269n8
digression, 142–144
Dominican Republic, 1n2, 162
Doubova, S., 51n14
Dougherty, S., 229, 230n22, 255

E

economic census
  establishment sample, 78–79
  overview, 77–78
  scope of, 78–79
Ecuador, 1n2, 225n20
efficiency, increase in, 5
El Salvador, 1n2, 5n3, 109
Emerging Market Bond Indices, 3
entrepreneurship
entrepreneur-worker relations, 13
firms and, 32–33
productivity and, 73–74
entry process, 139–142
exit process, 134–138

F

Fernández-Arias, E., 6n4
firms, 134–147
  dynamics, 27–30
    allocation of individuals across occupations, 157–158
    beyond census data, 156–157
    definitions and stylized facts, 128–130
    misallocation and, 127–128
    patterns of entry and exit, 133
    surviving firms, 130–133
  dynamics and job changes, 154–156
  employment beyond the census, 90–92
  entrepreneurship and, 32–33, 73–74
  establishments *vs.*, 81–83
  exclusion from census data, 20–21
  extrapolation of firm dynamics (1998-2003), 150–154
  four types, 15–16
  human capital and, 31–32
  incorporation, 89–90
  net effects of exit, entry, and survival, 147–150
  overview, 10–12
  presence of informal firms, 92–95
  productivity distribution and resource allocation
    change process of surviving firms, 144–147
    digression, 142–144
    entry process, 139–142
    exit process, 134–138
  resource allocation, 86–89

across sectors, 95–97
size and type distribution, 83–85
type *vs.* size, 24–25
foreign trade regime, 4
formality/informality
  causation and, 74–75
  firms and, 19–20, 83–84, 89, 92–97, 130, 158, 168, 170, 187–188
  growth and, 30–31, 282
  legality and, 19, 43, 45, 68–71, 74, 117–118, 285
  misallocation and, 66–68, 88, 112, 114, 256, 258
  overview, 14–17
  policy and, 272
  productivity and, 32, 55, 71–73, 192, 280
  salary and, 258, 268
formalization, 29, 131–133, 279–280
Fukuyama, F., 57n2, 226, 230

G

García-Verdú, S., 236
Garza-García, J., 232
Giacomelli, S., 228n21
Gopinath, G., 238
growth
  formality/informality and, 30–31, 282
  future prospects for, 52–53
  investment rate and, 48–49
  overview, 49–50
  productivity and, 47–48
  relation to social policy, 50–52
Guatemala, 1n2, 5n3, 225n20
Guerrero, I., 10n6, 232
Guha-Khsnobis, B., 66

H

Haber, S., 232
Hanushek, E., 167

health care, 37–38, 43, 46, 50–51, 58n3, 59n4, 75, 77, 90–91, 194, 196–197, 246–251, 259, 266
  see also social insurance programs
Heckman, J., 198n3
Honduras, 1n2, 162, 225n20
Hopenhayn, H., 200, 234
Hsieh-Klenow model, 100–107
  credit and, 103–105, 107
Hsieh, Chang-Tai, 30, 100–107, 118n10, 127, 129n1, 154, 158, 182n14, 190, 217
human capital
  determinants of accumulation, 180–183
  firms and, 31–32
  misallocation
    incentives to invest in human capital, 188–190
    level of returns to education, 167–174
    opportunities to acquire human capital, 179–188
    productivity, 159–160, 164–167
    quality of education, 177–179
    trends in returns to education, 174–179
    wages across educational groups, 172–174
  overview, 4–5
  returns to experience, 183–188
  role played by, 33–35
  schooling
    quality, 161–164
    quantity, 160–161

I

Inter-American Development Bank (IDB), 110n6, 179n11, 180n12233
  see also development banks
International Monetary Fund, 4
International Student Assessment (PISA), 162

investment
  growth and, 48–49
  incentives to invest in human capital, 188–190
  investment rate, 5, 48–49

J

Juárez, L., 250–251

K

Kanbur, Ravi, 66, 211n13, 219
Kaplan, David, 197–198, 266n4
Katz, L., 175n9
Kehoe, T. J., 7n4

L

La Porta, R., 74n11
labor, salaried and non-salaried, 58–59
Laeven, L., 227–229
Lagakos, D., 183, 185
Leal, J., 220, 225
Levy, Santiago, 4, 8, 58–59, 68n11, 114, 160, 168, 172, 174, 176, 188–190, 195n1
López Mateos, Adolfo, 265
López-Calva, L. F., 160, 168, 172, 174, 176
López-Martin, B., 229, 243n25
López, J. J., 42, 169, 218, 220, 232, 237

M

macroeconomic management, 3–4
market conditions, 14
microcredit programs, 75
  see also credit
misallocation
  credit and, 233–238, 242–244, 269–270
  formality and informality, 66–68
  formality/informality and, 66–68, 88, 112, 114, 256, 258
  increases between 1998 and 2013, 44–46
  joint effects of E(L,T,M) changes on, 256–260
  low productivity and, 64–66
  within manufacturing, commerce, and services, 119–121
  overview, 6–7
  patterns of, 22–24
  policies and institutions behind, 36–37
  policy reforms and, 9–10
  relation to social policy, 50–52
  social and political impact on, 8–9
  world of entrepreneur-worker relations and, 37–39
  world of market conditions and, 41–43
  world of taxation and, 39–41
Mokyr, J., 270n9

N

Nicaragua, 1n2, 225n20
North American Free Trade Agreement (NAFTA), 5, 46, 119

O

Oberfield, E., 223n19

P

Panama, 1n2
Paraguay, 1n2, 5n3, 162, 225n20
Parker, S., 279
policy and institutions
  costs of labor, 202–206
  described, 194–197
  dismissal regulations, 199–201

effects of imperfect enforcement, 241–243
firm size and type, 238–241
misallocation, 9–10, 36–37, 191–193
  causes, 243–244
  joint effects of E(L,T,M) on, 238–244
non-salaried/illegal salaried contracts, 201–202
reforms, 9–10, 271–273
rethinking priorities
  formalization, 279–280
  growth, 273–277
  social policy, 277–279
salaried contracts, 197–199
world of market conditions, 233–238
  access to credit, 231–233
  contract enforcement, 226–228
  credit misallocation, 233–238
  imperfect contract enforcement, 228–231
world of taxation
  of consumption, 220–226
  of firms, 210–220
  of income from labor, 206–210
policy design *vs.* institutional functioning, 43–44
productivity
  beyond census data, 125–126
  causation and, 74–75
  correlations between firm size, type, and, 111–118
  determinants of occupational outcomes, 59–62
  distributions, 26–27, 121–125
  formal-informal, 121–123
  formality, informality, and, 71–73
  gains from eliminating misallocation, 111
  informality, illegality, and types of firms, 68–71
  misallocation and low productivity, 64–66
  observed productivity, 62–63
  overview, 6
  potential productivity, 63–64
  resource allocation and, 123–125
  technology, entrepreneur-worker contracts, and firm size, 73–74
prosperity
  growth and social inclusion, 280–282
  programs for, 282–284

R

Ramos Francia, M., 236
reforms
  contributory social insurance and, 45
  credit and, 271–272
  efficiency and, 5–6, 52–53
  investment and, 49
  Labor Law, 265
  misallocation and, 9–10, 36, 45–47, 245–246
  policy and, 9–10, 50–51, 259, 271–273
  productivity and, 47
  sector-specific, 2
Repeco, 40–41, 43, 45, 210–225, 238, 241–244, 255, 258, 268–269
resources and environment, 55–57
Rios, V., 103n2, 230n22

S

schooling
  quality, 161–164
  quantity, 160–161
Schumpeterian process of "creative destruction," 7, 27, 30, 48, 127, 154
social insurance programs
  combined effects, 251
  contributory, 246–248

non-contributory, 249–251
see also health care
subsidies
    credit and, 234
    Hsieh-Klenow Model and, 103–104
    misallocation and, 8–9, 45–46, 51, 243–244
    policy and, 2, 43, 56, 74–75, 241–242
    productivity and, 59n4, 134n4
    Repeco and, 218
    salaried/non-salaried contracts and, 118, 197, 201–202, 253, 258
    social insurance programs and, 67, 189, 195–196, 249–251
    taxation and, 206–210, 240–241, 246–248
    world of entrepreneur-worker relations and, 37–41
Syverson, M., 109

T

taxation, 13–14
Total Factor Productivity (TFP), 100–102, 104–106, 108–120
Total Revenue Productivity (TPFR), 108–111

U

United States, 4–5, 22, 30, 35, 46, 109–111, 154, 182n14, 256
Urrutia, C., 236–237
Uruguay, 1n2, 5n3, 109, 162, 225n20

W

World Bank, 1n2, 5n3, 227–228, 236n24, 255
world of entrepreneur-worker relations
    overview, 13
    social insurance programs
        combined effects, 251
        contributory, 246–248
        non-contributory, 249–251
world of market conditions
    access to credit, 231–233
    contract enforcement, 226–228, 255
    credit misallocation, 233–238
    imperfect contract enforcement, 228–231
    international competition, 256
    overview, 14
world of taxation
    of consumption, 220–226
    of firms, 210–220, 255
    of income from labor, 206–210, 251–255
    overview, 13–14
World Trade Organization (WTO), 4, 46, 256, 259

Z

Zamudio, A., 210n11, 218, 255